EQUALIBERTY

A JOHN HOPE FRANKLIN CENTER BOOK

ÉTIENNE
EQUALIBERTY
BALIBAR

POLITICAL ESSAYS TRANSLATED BY JAMES INGRAM

Duke University Press   Durham and London   2014

La Proposition de l'Égaliberté by Étienne Balibar,
© 2010 Presses Universitaires de France.
English translation by James Ingram
© 2014 Duke University Press.
Designed by Courtney Leigh Baker
Typeset in Minion by Westchester Book Group

Library of Congress Cataloging-in-Publication Data
Balibar, Etienne.
[Proposition de l'égaliberté. English]
Equaliberty : political essays / Étienne Balibar ;
translated by James Ingram.
pages cm
"A John Hope Franklin Center book."
Includes bibliographical references and index.
ISBN 978-0-8223-5550-2 (cloth : alk. paper)
ISBN 978-0-8223-5564-9 (pbk. : alk. paper)
1. Citizenship. 2. Democracy. 3. Political science—
Philosophy. I. Balibar, Etienne, 1942– Proposition
de l'égaliberté. Translation of: II. Title.
JF801.B3613 2013
320.01—dc23
2013025529

CONTENTS

The present collection brings together three series of texts that extend over a period of twenty years and are thus coextensive with the larger part of my recent work in political philosophy. Some of them have already appeared in other frameworks; others have remained unpublished in this form until now. In organizing them in a rational fashion, I have sought to present them not, to be sure, as parts of a system, but nonetheless as correlative dimensions of a problematic centered on what I call in the introductory essay the antinomies of citizenship.[1]

The first series of essays outlines the general idea of a dialectic of insurrection and constitution that I presented in 1989 (at the Conférences du Perroquet) in "The Proposition of Equaliberty," the complete version of which is produced here. It was subsequently extended by "New Reflections on Equaliberty" (presentations from 2002–2003 in England and Mexico), in which I compared the idea of a democratic power associated with the invention of rights with the institution of social rights within the framework of the national-social state, the crisis of which we are experiencing today, and discussed its tendency to reduce anthropological differences to sociological categories. Owing to the place the examination of Robert Castel's theses on social property occupies in this discussion, and also to the importance I place on the analysis of the category of property in a general sense as a constitutional mediation of equaliberty, competing with community, I have inserted between these two moments a genealogical investigation of the reversals of possessive individualism, presented in 1999 at the conclusion of a Cerisy colloquium on property.[2]

The second series brings together some critical analyses devoted directly or indirectly to the works of contemporary theorists whose writings have been particularly useful for me: Hannah Arendt, Nicos Poulantzas, Ernesto Laclau, Roberto Esposito, and Jacques Rancière. The list is by no means exhaustive; it would be easy to show that there are more absences than presences, partly made up for by references I give elsewhere. For me the point is, above all, to emphasize, in the form of confrontations or re-readings, the essentially contested (as W. B. Gallie would say) character of the concepts of political philosophy I use (sovereignty, emancipation, community, and others), and to extend certain explications in a dialogical form when circumstances of commemoration or study have given me the opportunity.[3]

The third series of texts collects interventions and analyses provoked by contemporary episodes of sometimes violent conflict where what is at stake is the form of citizenship, within republican institutions or at their frontiers—in particular, conflicts in France in the last years that have highlighted the intensity of the postcolonial dimensions of politics (around secularism, nationality, and security).[4] I have entitled them "For a Democracy without Exclusion" as a way of indicating their general stakes: what I call elsewhere, following others (Boaventura de Souza Santos), the democratization of democracy—in my view the only thinkable alternative to the "de-democratization" (Wendy Brown) of contemporary societies. And I conclude them with a proposal for "co-citizenship" in the world of migrations and diasporas in which we now live, which is like the institutional pendant to the insurrectional proposition of equaliberty, and tries to work out its realization in a particular, but strategic, domain.

By way of conclusion I reproduce a meditation on "Resistance, Insurrection, Insubordination," written for the Festival d'Avignon in 2007. I hope that it will not seem exaggeratedly emotional or subjective. It is also an occasion to insist finally on the critical dimension of politics as I defend it, not only in theory but in practice, and thus on what distinguishes citizenship conceived as a guaranteed status from citizenship as the exercise of constituent power.

References to the initial publications and subsequent modifications to the texts are given in the notes. My thanks go first to Jacques Bidet, Gérard Duménil, Emmanuel Renault, and Jacques Texier, who welcomed the original edition of this work, which corresponds exactly, in my view, to what can be understood by a "current confrontation" with the heritage of Marx and Marxism, into their collection ["Actuel Marx—Confrontations," with Editions de Seuil]. They also go to the colleagues, friends, institutions, and journals who have solicited and previously published the essays collected in this book. To Mehdi Dadsetan, whose irreplaceable assistance has been coupled with a sympathy that is precious to me. And in particular to Yves Duroux, who encouraged me to attempt this synthesis, helped me get rid of what was useless or redundant, and—as always, since we were students together—benefited me by his judgments and his ideas with an unparalleled generosity.

THE ANTINOMY OF CITIZENSHIP

When I initially proposed this topic, I made a strange but perhaps significant mistake.[1] Outlining a discussion of the antinomies of citizenship, I left out the word "democracy." The reader could conclude that in my view the notion of citizenship is what counts, and that "democracy" represents only a qualification to which we can retrospectively attribute more or less importance in its definition. Such hierarchical—or, as Rawls would say, "lexicographical"—considerations are by no means secondary. They go to the heart of debates that oppose a republican (or neo-republican) conception of politics to a (liberal or social) democratic conception of politics, and in a sense the very understanding of political philosophy, and therefore of its critique, depends on it, as Jacques Rancière and Miguel Abensour, each in his own fashion, have recently underlined.[2] Not only do I not want to subordinate the consideration of democracy to that of citizenship. I maintain that democracy—better still, the "democratic paradox," according to Chantal Mouffe's felicitous formulation—represents the decisive aspect of the problem around which political philosophy gravitates, precisely because it makes the institution of citizenship problematic.[3] Citizenship has known different historical figures, and there can be no question of reducing some to others, even if we could ask what is transmitted under the name and by means of these "translations."[4] Between them there is always an analogy, connected to its antinomical relation to democracy as a dynamic of the transformation of politics. When I qualify this constitutive relation of citizenship as antinomical, which at the same time puts it in crisis, I refer to a philosophical tradition that has insisted on two ideas in particular: a permanent tension between the positive and the negative, between processes of construction and destruction; and the coexistence of the impossibility of resolving the problem (or resolving it definitively) and the impossibility of making it disappear. My working hypothesis will be precisely that at the heart of the institution of citizenship contradiction is ceaselessly born and reborn in relation to democracy. In other words, I will seek to characterize the moments of a dialectic that includes both historical movements and relations of force, as complex as they are, and the conditions for articulating theory with practice.

This is to say that I see nothing natural in the association of citizenship and democracy. And yet I want to extend a theme that runs, with inflections, through a complex tradition from Aristotle to Spinoza to Marx, and makes democracy the "natural regime" or "most natural form" of citizenship.[5] My feeling is that it is necessary to interpret this against the letter by adopting precisely the perspective of dialectical contradiction: it is the antinomy lodged at the heart of the relations between citizenship and democracy that constitutes, through a succession of figures, the engine of the transformations of the political institution. This is why the name "democratic citizenship" cannot conceal an insistent problem, the object of conflicts and antithetical definitions, an enigma without a definitive solution (even if periodically, in the context of a decisive invention, someone declares that this solution has finally been found), a "lost treasure" to be rediscovered or rewon.[6] I do not conceal from myself the fact that such formulations imply a certain conception of political philosophy, the presuppositions of and objections against which must be examined at length.[7] I prefer not to launch directly into such a discussion. It is not that I consider it to be purely speculative; to the contrary, I am persuaded that it has practical implications. But I want to allow them to emerge on the basis of another hypothesis: that there are situations and moments in which the antinomy becomes particularly visible because of the double impossibility of rejecting all figures of citizenship and perpetuating them in a particular constitution, which goes to the roots of the crisis of "really existing" democracy and opens onto the exhaustion of the signification of the very word "democracy," the dominant uses of which now seem either obsolete or perverse.

It seems that we find ourselves in a situation of this kind, which profoundly affects, by reason of the very interdependence of which I am speaking, the definitions and qualifications that had for a very long time seemed indisputable (such as those of national citizenship or social citizenship). But, beyond that, it also affects the category of citizenship itself, whose power of transformation, whose capacity to historically reinvent itself, suddenly seems to be shattered. It is on the basis of this question, full of uncertainty, that I will examine a bit further Wendy Brown's proposed interpretation of the paradigm of neoliberal governance, which she sees as a process of the "de-democratization of democracy" and asks whether it is irreversible. For my part, I see it as an expression of the destructive aspect inherent in the antinomies of citizenship, and consequently an indication of a challenge faced by any attempt to rethink collective political capacity in the contemporary period.

I propose to address three aspects of this dialectic. The first concerns what I will call the trace of equaliberty in the history of modern citizenship, defined as national citizenship (or citizenship in a nation-state). I identify this trace as a differential of insurrection and constitution. The second aspect lies, in my view, in the internal contradiction of social citizenship as it was constituted—essentially in Europe—within the framework of the national-social state (an expression which, on materialist grounds, I prefer to *l'État-Providence*, "welfare state," or *Sozialstaat*, used in various European countries). This means that this figure of citizenship historically represents democratic progress, even if with certain limits, which for their part paradoxically prohibit further progression, although it is inherent in the idea of progress. The third aspect concerns, as a result, what we are accustomed to regarding as the neoliberal response to the crisis of the national-social state (or, if you prefer, the contribution of neoliberalism to the onset of this crisis), namely, the unlimited promotion of individualism and utilitarianism. To what extent can we say that this contains a mortal threat to democracy? To what extent can we imagine that it contains, at least negatively, the bases of a new configuration of citizenship beyond its traditional institutions (especially representative democracy, for which neoliberalism tends to substitute diverse forms of "governance" and "mass communications")? On this basis, I will attempt to outline a problematic of bearers or actors that I virtually associate with the idea of a democratization of democracy. I will take the opportunity to explain why I prefer the terminology of a (hybrid, collective, transitory) political actor to that of a subject of politics, which does not mean that I reject questions related to the process of subjectivation and the alternatives often discussed today in terms of "politics" and "post-politics" on the basis of a reflection of the contemporary history of subjectivity.

LET US BEGIN WITH the trace of equaliberty. I have previously had occasion, when introducing this portmanteau word to which I have stubbornly clung, to sketch its genealogy back to the Roman formulas *aequa libertas* and *aequum ius*, which Cicero in particular used to indicate the essence of the regime he called *res publica*.[8] I proposed that we regard as crucial the moment of revolution that inaugurates political modernity, making "equal right" the concept of a new kind of universality. It would be essentially contructed as a double unity of opposites: a unity (even an identity of *goal*) of *man* and *citizen*, which from then on would appear as correlative despite all the practical restrictions on the distribution of rights and powers; and a unity (even an identity of *reference*) of the concepts of *freedom* and *equality*, perceived as two faces of a single "constituent power," despite the constant tendency of bourgeois political ideologies (what we could generically call "liberalism") to give the former an epistemological and even ontological priority by making it the "natural right" par excellence (to which the inverse socialist tendency to privilege equality responds).[9] What particularly interests me is the element of conflict that results from this unity of opposites. It allows us to understand why claims for increased powers for the people or emancipation from domination that result in new rights inevitably take a revolutionary form. In simultaneously demanding equality and freedom, one reiterates the enunciation that is at the origin of modern universal citizenship. It is this combination of conflict and institution that I call the trace of equaliberty.

No doubt, it is when political power is conquered in a way that is itself revolutionary, implying a change of regime (for example the classic passage from a monarchy to a republic) or the pulling down of a dominant class, which is forced to renounce its privileges, that this reiteration finds its privileged symbolic representation. But the *petitio juris*, the emancipation movement connected to a rights claim, always has an "insurrectional" meaning that can be manifested in an infinity of ways, through popular movements, democratic campaigns, or the formation of more or less durable parties. It includes a relation of forces that is violent or nonviolent according to the conditions, the use or rejection of existing juridical forms and political institutions. One need only think here of the diversity of national histories in Europe when it comes to the conquest of civil, political, and social rights, even if these histories are not really mutually independent, or of the multiplicity of forms decolonization has taken, or of the sequence of episodes of civil war and civil rights movements over more than a century leading to the emancipation of African Americans, and so on. Despite the diversity of this phenomenology, we see that conflict is always determining in the last instance, because equaliberty is not an originary disposition, and because the dominant never give up their privileges or their power voluntarily (even if sometimes, under the pressure of events, they are caught up in the drunkenness of fraternity, as in the symbolic example of the night of August 4—but did it happen as it has been heroized in republican imagery?).[10] It always therefore takes struggle, and moreover the *legitimacy* of struggle, what Rancière calls the "part of those who have no part," which confers a universal signification on the demand of those who had been kept outside the common good or the general will to be counted.[11] What we see emerge here is the essential incompletion of the "people" as a political body, a process of universalization by way of conflict and the negation of exclusion concerning dignity, property, security, and basic rights in general. The insurrectional moment characterized in this way thus looks at once to the past and to the future: to the past because it returns to the popular foundation of every constitution that does not take its legitimacy from tradition, revelation, or mere bureaucratic efficiency, however determinative these forms of legitimation are in the construction of states; and to the future because, faced with the limitation and denials that affect the realization of democracy in historical constitutions, the return to insurrection (and the return *of* insurrection, which had been warded off for a longer or shorter time) represents a permanent possibility.[12] Whether this possibility is realized or not is, to be sure, another problem that cannot be deduced a priori.

Let us specify the status and implications of this dialectic of insurrection and constitution, of which I have given a very general, in a sense ideal-typical, definition. First of all, we must admit that, if the political community is based on the articulation of citizenship with different insurrectional modalities of emancipation or the conquest of rights, it inevitably takes a paradoxical form: exclusive of any consensus, it can neither be realized as a homogenous unity of its members nor represented as an achieved totality. But neither can it be dissolved into the individualist aggregate of subjects who would be the "invisible hand" of utility and the interdependence of needs, or, conversely, a "war of all against all"—that is to say, a generalized antagonism of interests that, as such, would be the "common." In a sense, therefore, the citizens (or co-citizens) of equaliberty are neither friends nor enemies. Here we come very close to what Chantal Mouffe has proposed calling the "democratic paradox," but we are also on the threshold of the ceaselessly renewed forms in which an institution of citizenship that has remained essentially antinomical can be manifest in history as the changing norms, spaces or territories, historical narratives, and ideological formations associated with its recognition by subjects who see in it their political horizon and conditions of existence.[13]

Why is this essentially unstable, problematic, contingent character of the community of citizens not more apparent, or why is it not manifest more often? Why, when it is manifest, is it readily called a collapse of citizenship? No doubt this is due especially to the fact that in the modern period the notions of citizenship and nationality have been practically identical in what we can regard as the founding equation of the modern republican state—all the more indisputable and (apparently) indestructible as the state constantly reinforces itself, and as its mythical, imaginary, and cultural forms proliferate.[14] And yet the historical cycle of the sovereignty of the nation-state may come to an end, as seems to be the case today, so that the character of this equation, which is also contingent, becomes visible (again)—in other words, the fact that it is a historically determined equation, essentially fragile, relative to certain local and temporal conditions, and exposed to decomposition or mutation.[15] This is also the moment when it becomes visible (again) that the national interest or the national identity do not as such, absolutely, contribute to the unity of the community of citizens.

But our reflections cannot end there. For however effective the nation form (and its double, national identity) has been in modern history, it is only one of the possible historical forms of a community of citizens—one that, moreover, never absorbed all its functions or neutralized all its contradictions. What is important to me above all, beyond this reference to the vicissitudes of citizenship as nationality, is to make it understood that citizenship in general, as a political "idea," implies, to be sure, a reference to community (since the model of a citizenship without institutions, the idea of citizenship without community, is practically a contradiction in terms).[16] Yet it cannot have its essence in the consensus of its members— whence the strategic function fulfilled in history by terms like *res publica* (which the Romans considered equivalent to the Greek *politeia*), but also their profoundly equivocal nature.[17] Citizens as such are always con-citizens or co-citizens, mutually conferring on one another the rights they enjoy; the dimension of reciprocity is constitutive.[18] How, then, could they exist outside a community, be it territorial or not, imagined as a fact of nature or as a cultural heritage, defined as a product of history or a construction of the will? Aristotle had already proposed a fundamental justification for this that is foundational for political philosophy: what connects citizens to one another is a rule of the reciprocity of rights and duties. It would be better to say that it is the fact that the reciprocity of rights and duties implies both a limitation on the power of the governors and an acceptance of the law by the governed.[19] The magistrates are thus responsible to their principals, and the simple citizens obey the law they helped elaborate, be it directly or through representatives. But this inscription of citizenship within the horizon of community is by no means a synonym for consensus or homogeneity—to the contrary, since the rights it guarantees have been won, that is to say, imposed despite the resistance of those who hold privileges, of "special interests," and of powers that express social domination. They have been (and will have to be again) invented (as Claude Lefort says), and their content, like that of the corresponding duties and responsibilities, is defined on the basis of this conflictual relation.[20]

With this we come to an essential characteristic of citizenship, which is also one of the reasons I present its history as a dialectical movement. It is clearly very difficult to define the idea of a community that has neither dissolved nor reunified in purely juridical or constitutional terms, but it is not impossible to conceive of it as a historical process governed by a principle of reproduction, interruption, and permanent transformation. This is in fact the only way to understand the discontinuous temporality and historicity of citizenship as a political institution. Not only does it have to be traversed by crises and periodic tensions; it is intrinsically fragile or vulnerable. This is why, in the course of its two thousand year history (in the West), it has been destroyed many times and reconstituted in a new institutional framework, from the city-state to the nation-state, and perhaps will be beyond the nation-state if certain postnational federations and quasi-federations become realities. But as a constitution of citizenship, it is threatened and destabilized, even delegitimized (as Max Weber already saw) by the very power that makes up its constituent power (or of which it is the constituted form): the insurrectional power of universalistic political movements that aim to win rights that do not yet exist or expand those that do by realizing equaliberty. This is why I spoke at the beginning of a differential of insurrection and constitution that no purely formal or juridical representation can encapsulate, which is in fact an essential characteristic of the concept of politics once we transpose it onto the terrain of history and practice. If we proceeded in this way, we would be obliged to imagine that the democratic inventions, the conquest of rights, the redefinition of the reciprocity between rights and duties according to broader and more concrete conceptions, proceed from an eternal idea, always already given, of citizenship. And at the same time we would be obliged to replace the idea of the invention with that of the preservation of democracy. But a democracy whose function is to preserve a certain definition of citizenship is doutless also for this very reason incapable of resisting its own de-democratization. To the extent that politics has to do with transforming existing realities, adapting them to changing environments, formulating alternatives within ongoing historical and sociological evolutions, such a concept would not be political but antipolitical.

This is why we now have the task of showing, against any prescriptive or deductive definition of politics, that citizenship has never stopped oscillating between destruction and reconstruction on the basis of its own historical institutions. The insurrectional moment associated with the principle of equaliberty is not only founding; it is also the enemy of institutional stability. And if we admit that it represents, through its more or less complete realizations, the universal within the political field, we must surely then admit that there exists in history nothing but such an appropriation of the universal, or an installation in the reign of the universal, in the way that the classical philosophers thought that the advent of the

Rights of Man and Citizen could represent a point of no return, the moment when man, as a power of citizenship, became in reality the bearer of the universal he was already destined to be. Let us borrow here an expression from Gilles Deleuze: the historical modality of the existence of the political universal is that of an "absent people," the provisional figures of which arise precisely from its own absence, or from its own repression.[21]

I think that if we combine the idea of this differential of insurrection and constitution with the representation of a community without unity, in a process of reproduction and transformation, the dialectic at which we arrive does not remain purely speculative. The conflicts it implies can be very violent. And above all they affect the state as well as, against it or within it, emancipatory movements themselves. This is why we can no longer remain with the idea of institution, which is still very general, that I have employed so far: it still eludes what is perhaps the principal contradiction.

I HAVE NOT YET referred to the state, not so as to reject the consideration of specifically state institutions, but in an effort to indicate precisely what the identification of political institutions with a state construction adds to the antinomies of citizenship. Should we think that the subjection of politics to the existence and power of a state apparatus only ever intensifies them? Or should we admit that it displaces them onto an entirely different terrain, where the dialectic of rights and duties, command and obedience, no longer presents itself in the same terms, so that the categories of political philosophy inherited from antiquity only serve to mask and dress up, aesthetically or ideologically, a fiction of politics?

It is not unhelpful to recall here that the notion of constitution has undergone profound evolutions in the course of its historical development, connected to the growing importance of the state and its hold on society, before and after the generalization of the capitalist mode of production to which it directly contributed.[22] Ancient constitutions were centered around the distribution of rights among categories of the population, rules of exclusion and inclusion, ways of choosing magistrates and their responsibilities, definitions of powers and counterpowers (like the famous Tribunal of the Plebes of the Roman constitution, in which Machiavelli thought he saw an image of republican politics as civil conflict).[23] They were thus essentially *material* constitutions, producing an equilibrium of power, lacking the neutrality conferred by juridical form (or ignoring its signification).[24] To the contrary, modern constitutions are formal constitutions, drawn up in the language of law, which corresponds—as legal positivism saw very clearly—to the autonomization of the state and its monopoly on representing the community, allowing it to exist at once as an idea and in practice (in the daily business of acts of legislation and constraint) beyond its divisions and its incompletion.[25] Modern constitutionalism thus combines the performative declaration of the universality of rights (and judicial guarantees against their violation) with a new principle of the separation of the governors from the governed, which (in her commentary on Weber's thesis affirming the tendential predominance of bureaucratic legitimacy over the other forms in the modern period) Catherine Colliot-Thélène has provocatively called the principle of the "ignorance of the people." We could also say, on an institutional level, the "incompetence in principle" of the people, of which the capacity of representation is the contradictory product.[26]

Here we see how acute the contradictions between participation and representation, representation and subordination, had to be within modern citizenship, and why the differential of insurrection and constitution was displaced especially onto the operation of the educational system. Without ignoring its glaring imperfections, many people, myself included, regard the development of a public educational system as a fundamental democratic achievement and a preliminary condition for the democratization of citizenship. But we also know that here democracy and meritocracy (what Aristotle called *timocracy*) are in an extraordinarily tense relation. The bourgeois state, which combines political representation with mass education (that is, national education, whatever its legal modalities), virtually opens up participation in political debate to the common man or "whatever citizen," and thus the contestation of its own monopoly on power. To the extent that it is effective in reducing inequalities (which varies greatly, as we know), it contributes to the inclusion of social groups that have never had access to the public sphere, thereby establishing a "right to have rights" (according to the famous Arendtian expression, which is not a bad way of renaming what I called the insurrectional moment of citizenship).[27] But the meritocratic principle that governs these education systems (and is as one with the academic form itself: What would a nonmeritocratic system of general education be?

Academic utopianism has always chased after this enigmatic goal) is also in itself a principle for selecting elites and excluding the masses from the possibility of effectively controlling administrative procedures and participating in public affairs, in any case on equal footing with magistrates recruited (and reproduced) on the basis of knowledge or competence. By creating a hierarchy of knowledge that is also a hierarchy of power, if necessary redoubled by other oligarchic mechanisms, it legitimately excludes the possibility of the collectivity governing itself. It engages in a "retreat forward," where representation ceaselessly celebrates its marriage with elitism and demagoguery.[28]

In recalling by this means some of the mechanisms that confer a class character on the constitution of citizenship in the contemporary world, I do not want only to indicate the existence of a gulf between democratic principles and oligarchic reality, but also to raise the question—no doubt highly embarrassing for many emancipatory activists—of how it affects insurrectional movements themselves. It is perhaps not necessary to justify at length the idea that class struggles have played (and play) an essentially democratic role in the history of modern citizenship. This is due, to be sure, to the fact that the organized struggles of the working class (through all the specters of its reformist and revolutionary tendencies) have brought about bourgeois society's recognition and definition of certain social rights that the development of industrial capitalism made both more urgent and more difficult to impose, thus contributing to the birth of social citizenship, to which I will return in a moment. But it is also due to a direct relation to what I am calling here the trace of equaliberty, to the fact that they realized in their own way an articulation of individual engagement and a collective movement that is the very heart of the idea of insurrection. It is a typical aspect of modern citizenship, indissociable from its universalistic reference, that the rights of the citizen are borne by the individual subject but won by social movements or collective campaigns that are able to invent, in each circumstance, appropriate forms and languages of solidarity. Reciprocally, it is essentially in the forms and institutions of solidarity and in collective action to win or extend rights that "subjectivation" autonomizes individuals, conferring on them their own power to act. The dominant ideology does not want to know anything about it, or presents it in inverted form, by suggesting that collective political activity is alienating, not to say enslaving or totalitarian, by nature. While resisting this prejudice, we can nurse the illusion neither that organized class struggles are immunized by nature against internal authoritarianism that leads them to become a "counterstate," and thus counterpower and counterviolence, nor that they represent an unlimited or unconditional principle of universality.[29] That for the most part the European workers' movement and its class organizations remained blind to the problems of colonial oppression, domestic oppression, and the domination of cultural minorities (when it was not directly racist, nationalist, and sexist), despite many efforts and acute internal conflicts that formed a sort of "insurrection within the insurrection," owes nothing to chance. It has to be explained not by such and such a material condition, such and such a "corruption" or "degeneration," but by the fact that resistance and protest against determinate forms of domination and oppression always rests on the emergence and construction of countercommunities that have their own principles of exclusion and hierarchy.[30] This whole history, which is often dramatic, draws our attention to the finitude of insurrectional moments, in other words to the fact that there are no such things as "absolutely universal" emancipatory universalities, which escape the limits of their objects. The contradictions of the politics of emancipation are thus transposed and reflected within the most democratic constitutions of citizenship, thereby contributing, at least passively, as we shall see, to the possibility of their de-democratization.

I NOW WANT TO try to connect the next two points, which I announced form a progression comparable to a "negation of the negation," and which I will examine on the basis of problems in the current conjuncture (at least as we can perceive it in a determinate place).[31] Let us begin with the relation between social citizenship and the transformations of the representative function of the state, and thus of the modes of organization of the political itself. This question is fascinating in its complexity; this is why it is at the root of a debate whose end is nowhere in sight.[32] It bears in particular on the interpretation of the transformations of the class composition of developed capitalist societies where social rights have been expanded in the course of the twentieth century, and on their more or less reversible political repercussions. It is not easy to say whether the notion of social citizenship definitely belongs to the past, and to what extent the crisis into which the development of liberal globalization has plunged has already destroyed the ability of social systems to resist the development of what Robert Castel has called negative forms of individuality, or negative individualism.[33] Here we must say again to what extent the descriptions and evaluations to which we proceed depend on the "cosmopolitan" place from which they are enunciated. Can social citizenship, developed in the twentieth century, above all in western Europe (and to a lesser extent in the United States, the dominant capitalist society during this period), be regarded as a potentially reversible innovation or invention belonging to the history of citizenship in general?[34] This question will remain open here, since the answer would depend on an analysis of the structures of dependence in relation to imperialism that exceed the possibilities of this essay and the competence of its author. I nevertheless presume that there is in the trajectory of social citizenship, owing to the way it crystallizes a political tendency inscribed in the very form of the class struggle between capital and labor and attaches it to the history of the renewals of citizenship, an irreducible question whose significance is general. The current crisis sharpens this question, and thus leads us to investigate its roots in order to imagine its possible evolutions.

Three points seem to me to call for discussion here. The first concerns the emergence of social citizenship insofar as it is distinguished from a simple recognition of social rights, or confers on it a universalistic dimension that bears the trace of equaliberty. The second concerns the modality in which, by incorporating a state form (that of the national-social state), the struggles that accompany claims for these rights are simultaneously politicized and displaced, or inscribed in a topography and an economy of displacements of class antagonism that authorize regulation and eventually engender a crisis of politics. The third concerns the complexity of the historical relations then forged between the idea of socialism (in a general sense) and democracy, whose stakes are above all the representation of "progress" as a political project and the value of public action as a way of instituting the collective. Let me summarily examine these three points.

SOCIAL CITIZENSHIP

In my view, the most important thing about the way social citizenship is constituted is the fact that, at the end of vehement discussions whose terms go back to controversies during the Industrial Revolution, discussions over the articulation of philanthropy or charity with bourgeois strategies to discipline the workforce, that citizenship was not conceived as a simple mechanism of protection or insurance against the most dramatic forms of poverty (or the effects of the exclusion of the poor from the possibility of reaching a "decent" family life according to bourgeois norms), but as a mechanism of universal solidarity.[35] This mechanism indeed involved virtually all citizens and covered the whole of society, which is to say that the rich and the poor had an equal right to it. Rather than say that the poor were now treated like the rich, it would be better to say that the rich were, symbolically, treated like the poor by universalizing the anthropological category of work as the specific characteristic of the human. Most social rights then guaranteed or conferred by the state were in effect conditioned by the more or less stable engagement of "active" individuals (or "heads of households") in a profession that gave them a status recognized by the whole of society (Hegel would say a *Stand* or "estate"). This point is fundamental for explaining why I speak of social citizenship, including a democratic component, and not simply of social democracy.[36] Let us note in passing that one of the most acute problems posed by this extension of citizenship was associated with an anthropological revolution concerning the equality of the sexes, taking into account the fact that most women were still socialized at this moment as wives of active workers, and thus subjectivated as such. Access to professional activity became by the same stroke one of the great roads to women's emancipation.[37] It is important to note as well the at least indirect connection, economic as well as ideological, that associates social protection and the prevention of insecurity (which Marx made one of the central characteristics of the proletarian condition) to a whole program of progressively reducing inequalities.[38] This connection was so powerful that, until the emergence of neoliberalism, no party could abandon it, at least verbally. The program included the development of equality of opportunity, or an increase of individual social mobility by generalizing the access of future citizens to the educational system (in other words, theoretically dismantling or delegitimizing the cultural monopoly of the bourgeoisie, which guaranteed its exclusive access to capacities and, moreover, properties) and the institution of progressive taxation, on income from work as well as from capital, which classical capitalism had totally ignored and which, as we know, is increasingly eroded in practice today.[39] These correlations ensured that the new political system that tended to be put in place (in strict relation with social democratic programs, even if the decisions were made by managers of the right) was not reduced to a list of social rights and still less to a paternalistic system of social protection granted from the top to vulnerable individuals perceived as the passive beneficiaries of social aid (even if liberal ideologues presented it this way in order to conclude that it was necessary to constantly supervise "abuses" of social security and "economically" manage its allocation). The whole question today is what remains of this universalism when its principle is not only denounced by the theorists of liberalism, but undermined by the two related phenomena: a relativization of the political borders within which it was tending to be instituted (in certain countries of the North), and a destabilization of the relation between work and individuality (or, if you like, of the anthropological category of "activity").

MATERIAL CONSTITUTION

The institutions of social citizenship make the ensemble of social rights they legitimate as basic rights a fluctuating reality, more fragile than other democratic achievements, dependent on a relation of historical forces and subject to advances and retreats on the basis of a structural asymmetry between the power of capital and labor, which there has never really been a question of bringing to an end. We see here that in none of the states of western Europe has the full system of social rights ever been written into the formal constitution by social democratic parties as a "basic norm" of the legal system, according to Hans Kelsen and his disciples.[40] This is why it is appropriate again to appeal to a notion of "material constitution" applied to citizenship, on which the balance of power it institutes between social classes is indirectly sanctioned by the law (or more generally by a norm) on different levels, but essentially represents a contingent correlation of rights and struggles, and thus of social movements that are themselves more or less institutionalized. In my view, there is, no doubt, a considerable kernel of truth in the idea largely shared by Marxists that the Keynesian (or, in other variants, Fordist) compromise consisted in exchanging the recognition of social rights and the institutional representation of the workers' movement in regulatory authorities for the moderation of wage demands and the working class's giving up the prospect of overthrowing capitalism (and thus in a sense the end of the proletariat in a "subjective" sense, as bearers for Marx of the revolutionary idea and project).[41] The consequence of this historical bargain was also a relative neutralization of the violence of social conflict, which was constantly sought; but this was only one side of the coin. We see today, in hindsight and in light of the contrast provided by a new cycle of proletarianization (designated by Castel, Negri, and others as the emergence of a "precariat"), in which the disequilibrium of social forces on a global level combines with the ossification of social citizenship, that the struggles never simply disappeared.[42] But it is certain that their violence has tended to be displaced onto other terrain, preventing a direct confrontation between classes: that of colonization and postcolonial confrontations (but also, quite simply, that of war between nations), and that of "anomie" in the Durkheimian sense, that is, "irrational" individual or collective violence correlative to the imposition of a whole micropolitical system of moral norms and behavioral rationality. Here we can see the essential form taken by the category of "duty" when individual rights are no longer simply civil and civic but also social, all the while remaining attached to the individual, or rather to individualization.[43]

But, more generally still, we must register the functioning of social citizenship under the sign of the displacement of antagonism, the operator (and, for a time, beneficiary) of which was the national-social state. The characteristic phenomenon of the self-limitation of the violence of struggles (which we can see as an effect of civility) is explained by the relative effectiveness of a model of political organization that combines parliamentary and extraparliamentary action.[44] But this in turn can only be understood within the framework of a double displacement, inscribed in the conditions of possibility of the political system:

- A displacement of definitions of fundamental rights in the sphere of work strictly speaking, or, in Marxist terms, from production to the reproduction of the workforce (that is, forms and conditions of individual and familial existence). The latter can in effect be an object of normalization; the former can be only with great difficulty, in an always precarious relation of forces.[45]
- A displacement of social antagonism onto the level of international relations, between state systems. The division of the Cold War world into two camps acted in an ambiguous way. On the one hand, it gave the struggle for social rights the support of a

real or imaginary danger, a Soviet-type revolution in the West, whose actors would be the workers (and to a lesser extent peasants, white-collar workers, and intellectuals ideologically won over to Communism), leading the political representatives of national capitalism to seek a compromise with the organized working class and, more generally, to develop their own model of social progress.[46] On the other hand, it allowed for the introduction of an ideological division within the workers' movement that took up and encompassed other cleavages (secular versus Christian unionism and so on). With the end of the Cold War and globalization, fear is displaced anew, and in a certain way it switches sides: it is no longer capitalists who fear revolution, but workers who fear competition from immigrants. Thus the relation of forces that underlay the exterior of the constitution of the national-social state is destabilized the moment the limits of its universalism also appear from within.

SOCIALISM AND DEMOCRACY

This schematic survey of the problems we can attach to the category of social citizenship thus leads us to the characteristic tension of conflict and institution: it is indeed what expresses the persistence of a political dimension, the continuation of the dialectic of insurrection and constitution by other means. In my view, it is completely insufficient (whatever the undeniable reality of the social and moral preoccupations of the bourgeoisie) to represent the rise of social citizenship as the bourgeois state's unilateral concession to the need to compensate for the pathological effects of the Industrial Revolution and unlimited capitalist exploitation, or else as a logical consequence of capitalism's need to regulate the free play of the market, which threatened to destroy the whole of the workforce on which the production of surplus value depends.[47] No doubt these two factors were at work, but a third element was also required to bring about their combination. I am thinking of the element that was socialism, in all its variety of currents, formulations, and organizations.[48] Elsewhere I had occasion to argue that the state that more or less completely instituted social citizenship should be defined as both a national and a social state. By this we should understand that its program of social reforms was by definition conceived and enacted within national borders, under cover of national sovereignty (which means that it could not exist without a sufficient degree of autonomy and economic independence), but reciprocally that the nation-state could not survive (overcome its own internal and external contradictions) without universalizing social rights. This was, to be sure, especially the case in moments of acute crisis, when the political as such vacillated, as under the conditions of total war in the twentieth century.[49] Long demanded by the workers' movement, the proclamation of social rights as fundamental rights only occurred after two world wars in which workers died by the millions fighting each other.

This is how I explain the bond that formed between two attributes of the state (the national and the social), and led each to become the presupposition of the other. But it took another step. The socialist element of modern politics incarnated, in part and for a certain time, the insurrectional side of citizenship; it was thus also the bearer of a tendency toward radical democracy. Finding itself integrated into the horizon of nationalism, it did not simply confuse itself with it, except when conjunctures of acute social and moral crisis gave rise to totalitarian discourse and politics. I believe that it was this distance or difference, maintained within the national-social state, that allowed the socialism born in the nineteenth century to contribute—for a time—to the formation of a public and political sphere, a sphere relatively autonomous from the state and its parliamentary institutions as well as from civil society and its commercial and contractual operations. Socialism, in this sense, was the common envelope for a whole series of progressive contradictions. It never attained its ultimate objectives; it remained a project or program of reforms, contested both internally and externally. But as a "horizon of expectation" internalized by the masses, it never stopped reigniting the conflict within the institution articulated by capital and labor, private property and solidarity, commercial and state rationality, and thereby helped make the public sphere a political sphere as well. It did so within certain limits, however, since, as I have said, social citizenship had to be articulated with the reproduction of capitalist relations and political struggles inscribed within the framework of a relative neutralization of antagonism— which is to say that the state equipped itself with apparatuses for reproducing political consensus, and thus prevented its adversaries from making themselves its enemies. This also means that society as a whole had to be reconfigured as a process of the generalized normalization of conduct.

But by the same stroke the system tended to freeze the relation of social forces and to establish a compromise that would in the end seem untenable to the dominant as well as to the dominated.

I think that we must depart from this point to understand what I earlier called the antinomy of progress, for which the history of social citizenship furnishes an almost perfect illustration. Indeed, it was only the prospect of unlimited progress, that is, the idealized collective desire to effectively arrive at equality of opportunity for everyone in society, that could maintain the pressure that tended to curtail privileges and hold perennial forms of domination in check, enlarging the space of freedom for the masses. The limits of progress are no less inscribed in the material constitution, where the national and the social, the accumulation of capital and the generalization of social rights, collective action and majoritarian ethical conformism, are combined. Democratic victories within the framework of the national-social state have thus been very real; they made up so many progressive moments of its construction (sometimes in quasi-insurrectional form, as with the Popular Front). But each time they were outlived by a reaffirmation of structural limits in the form of creeping counterreforms or more violent reactions.

This is decisive for our analysis of the crisis that is now affecting the very notion of social citizenship and the dismantling of the welfare state—namely, the main cause of this crisis that affects job security as well as universal medical coverage, the democratization of access to higher education and the domestic or professional liberation of women, and finally the representative principle. Is it simply the result of an assault launched by capitalism from the outside, relying on the exigencies of an increasingly transnationalized economy, where financial logic prevails over industrial logic? Or is it also the aggravation of social citizenship's internal contradictions, and the fact that it has reached its own historical limits? The prospect of a continuous progress of basic rights, especially when it comes to the articulation of individual autonomy and solidarity—in short, everything that, returning to the spirit of the famous formula of his *Presuppositions of Socialism* [1899]: "The goal is nothing, the movement is everything," we could collect under the name "Bernstein's theorem"—would collide not only with the interests of dominant social groups and the system of exploitation they counteract, but with its own immanent contradiction.[50] The socialism of the nineteenth and twentieth centuries is the prisoner of a fusion of progressivism and statism. It is caught in the aporia of conflictual democracy: it is indissociable from the permanence of conflict, but also from the institutionalization of its forces, organizations, and discourse as components of a public sphere that is identified with the national community. The result is completely paradoxical with respect to the Marxian topography of politics (but also prone to outflank its liberal critics): the politicization of social questions does not abolish the dualism of "politics" and "the police" (Rancière), but reinforces it. A consequence of this was that the extension of the domains of political invention and intervention, which announces the possibility of a democratization of democracy, did not occur so much around work, to which rights remain symbolically attached, as reproduction: the family, culture, public services. It is on this side that neoliberalism has carried out its offensive, having broken worker resistance in places of production by a combination of new technologies, the reorganization of the system of professions, and circulating the workforce beyond borders.

We see that this, I hope, more dialectical hypothesis by no means abolishes the consideration of social antagonisms, but it rules out the idea of a conspiracy of capitalists. It is also more political in the sense that it proposes schemas of intelligibility that speak not only of structures, but of actions (be it in Weber's sense or in Foucault's): the popular classes of the North, who have benefited from important social gains (as salaried classes) and now find themselves largely deprived of their security and their prospects for betterment, do not figure in this history as simple victims. They were and are always to a certain extent actors, whose ability to influence their own history depends on internal conditions and external movements, especially the way they represent themselves in the system in which they act, and the collectives that practically give them the power to act. This hypothesis seems to me the right one, and I would like to use it to discuss some aspects of what we now call neoliberalism. I will do so on the basis of an interpretation proposed by Wendy Brown in her essay "Neoliberalism and the End of Democracy" (2003), which has been highly influential in ongoing debates within critical circles.

BROWN'S HYPOTHESIS IS WELL known: there is an essential difference between classical liberalism and neoliberalism that has to do with the relative autonomy of the economic and political spheres, which was insurmountable for classical liberalism, since it was based on the exteriority of the state to the economy, but is now clearly obsolete. As a result, it becomes possible to combine market deregulation with constant interventions by the state and other agencies into the field of civil society and even into the intimate sphere of subjects, which tends to create out of nothing a new citizen, exclusively governed by the logic of economic calculation. Brown then proposes a picture of combinations of libertarian discourses, programs of moralization, and the subjection of private life to a religious stranglehold, applied in an increasingly brutal way during the Reagan and Thatcher revolutions of the 1980s. This part of the analysis seems absolutely convincing to me. It could be supplemented by other contributions to the critique of the neoliberal paradigm.[51] They all rest on the study of the way criteria of individual or collective profitability, of cost-benefit maximization, are generalized to private and even public activities, which, on the classical capitalist model and especially within what I have called the national-social state, were supposed to fall outside economic calculation (or, according to Marxist terminology, the domain of the "law of value")—for example, education, scientific research, the quality of public services or administration, the general level of public health and security, and the judiciary (the list could be extended).[52] I completely agree with this description, and propose to discuss the philosophical thesis that accompanies it: neoliberalism is not just an ideology; it is the mutation of the very nature of political activity, borne by actors situated in all regions and locations in society. But it is a highly paradoxical form of political activity, since not only does it tend to neutralize as completely as possible the element of conflict essential to its classical figure (for example, in Machiavelli), to say nothing of the idea of a constituent insurrection, without which I suggested there could never be collective rights claims; further, it seeks to deprive conflict of any significance in advance, and to create the conditions for a society in which individual and group actions (including violent ones) refer only to a single criterion: economic utility. It is therefore in fact not a matter of politics but of antipolitics, of the preventive neutralization or abolition of sociopolitical antagonism. To give an account of it, Brown proposes to generalize the category of governmentality, as elaborated by Foucault in his genealogy of power in the modern period, and take it to its extreme consequences.[53]

Let me recall that we must understand governmentality in its Foucauldian sense: it is a whole ensemble of practices by means of which the "spontaneous" behavior of individuals can be modified, which amounts to exercising a power on their own power of resistance and action, be it through disciplinary (and thus inevitably constraining as well as productive) methods, or by diffusing models of ethical (and thus cultural) conduct. Why suggest that, in this regard, neoliberalism poses a challenge to traditional definitions of politics, relating to class politics as well as to the forms of liberalism on which critiques of domination or arbitrary power in the democratic tradition are based, for which Brown employs the term "de-democratization," and which constitutes a mortal threat to the classical republican idea of active citizenship? Because apparently neoliberalism is not content to plead for a retreat of the political, but has undertaken to redefine it on its subjective side (motivations for engagement) as well as its objective side (institutional instruments). Because the conditions of possibility of collective political experience, or the economic constraints on a rising number of individuals of all social classes, and the systems of value or conceptions of good and bad according to which they judge their own actions (and thus, in the last analysis, the model they have for deciding whether their lives are valuable or worth living) are affected simultaneously, Brown can speak of a "new rationality" in the philosophical sense of the term. Here I would like to indicate, even if very briefly, the problems that in my view are implied by such a generalization.

In the first place, it seems that we must linger on the crisis diagnosis concerning traditional liberal or authoritarian political systems. The description I have just evoked implies regarding this crisis not as a mere episode of malaise or tension in a cyclical process, of which there have been many before, but as a profound mutation, an irreversible fact after which it will no longer be possible to return to old modalities of action. Even if we agree on this point, there are at least two ways of interpreting the figures of subjectivity that follow from it. On a first hypothesis (which seems to me, for example, to dominate the recent analyses of Immanuel Wallerstein as well as Robert Castel, the one on the basis of a global systemic perspective, the other on the basis of a more localized historical sociology), it would essentially be a matter of a negative symptom that corresponds to the decomposition of traditional structures of domination and resistance (even if the tradition in question here is in fact a recent formation, that is, a product of the modernization of industrial societies).[54] By itself this decomposition does not lead to any form of life in society that would be tenable; it leads to a highly unstable situation (which could be described as "anomic" or described in terms of a "state of exception") in which the most contradictory developments become possible in an unpredictable way. Brown herself, in accord with the Foucauldian idea of the productivity or positivity of power, inclines toward another interpretation: it is not so much a dissolution as an invention, another historical solution to the problems of adapting individuals to capitalism, or adjusting individual behavior to the policies of capital. Here the hypothesis I just developed, that a crisis of social citizenship as a model (unequally developed) for the configuration of the political would not proceed solely from the "revenge of the capitalists" or the deteriorating relation of forces between socialism and its adversaries but from the development of its internal contradictions, assumes its full significance. But we must be aware of what will be the result at the end of the day: this hypothesis leads us to conceive of the possibility of political regimes that are not only weakly democratic (or democratic within the limits compatible with reproducing structures of inequality) or antidemocratic (on the model of dictatorships, authoritarian regimes, or historical fascism), but in reality *ademocratic*, in the sense that the values inherent in rights claims (which I have collected under the name "equaliberty") no longer play any role in their operation and development (even as forces of resistance or contestation).[55] Is this why the discourse on democratic values and the spread (or even export) of democracy has become so pervasive? Rendered official and banal, it no longer has any discriminating function in the language of power in the contemporary period and forms an integral part of the decomposition of citizenship. If such a change is really under way, affecting the very modality of change, it would be appropriate to speak of entering into "posthistory," and at the same time into "postpolitics," to take much more seriously the visions of an "end of history" popularized by ideologues like Fukuyama at the moment of the fall of the Soviet system in Europe, which were based, on the contrary, on the idea of a triumph of liberalism in its classic form.[56]

But I am not convinced that the matter can be limited to this diagnosis. I ask myself what in Brown's proposed interpretation of the phenomenon of de-democratization reflects a particularity of American society and history that is not immediately generalizable. I would tend to connect this to the fact that the United States, for geopolitical (its hegemony within the capitalist world during the second half of the twentieth century) as well as cultural (going back to the origins of its frontier ideology, and thus to its character as an individualistic colonial society) reasons, is precisely not—despite the depth of the egalitarian tendencies emphasized by Tocqueville—typical of the formation of social citizenship and the national-social state. The principle of the universality of social rights, in particular, was never fully recognized there. Conversely, its oscillations between phases of state regulation and deregulation have been exceptionally brutal.[57] It would be presumptuous to reproach Brown for not having taken into account in advance what the so-called global financial crisis is now in the process of demonstrating, namely, the existence of sources of instability and radical contradictions at the heart of the Reagan-Thatcher neoliberal model (adopted more or less completely by the "Third Way" politicians who succeeded them); and perhaps in reality it is not a model for stabilizing capitalism so much as a model of permanent crisis (or crisis as normal regime), which tends to lead us to side with the other interpretation (that of a symptom of dissolution). Her essay, let me recall, dates from 2003 in its original form. It would be all the more interesting to see how she would account for the strictly North American aspects of capitalism that the crisis has brought to the foreground (for example, the constitution of a society based entirely on debt) as well as the political responses to its early developments.[58] Obviously nothing has been univocally decided from this perspective. But this leads me to examine another inherent difficulty of critiques of neoliberal innovation as the rise of antipolitics, insofar as they confer on the idea of de-democratization a truly apocalyptic dimension.

What strikes me here, at a distance of a century and a half, are the analogies and perceptible differences between Brown's theses and what we could call "Marx's nightmare." Recall that Marx outlined a notion of the "real subsumption" of the workforce under capitalist relations in a chapter that in the end was not incorporated into the first volume of *Capital* at the moment of its publication (1867).[59] Why did Marx decide to exclude this analysis when it bore the ultimate consequences of a dialectic that played a central role in his own analysis of capital as a social relation? No doubt for reasons that were as much political as scientific. Its implications would have been disastrous for the idea of a proletarian politics: in the absence of any prospect of revolutionary organization or even working-class collective consciousness, he would have had to go back to the alternative of a disappearance of politics or a messianic solution arising from the very destruction of the conditions of politics, from which he had continuously distanced himself since his youthful propositions on the decomposition of bourgeois civil society.[60] The "real subsumption" Marx envisaged in the unpublished chapter signifies that capitalism is not only a system for "consuming the workforce," the objective of which is to maximize productivity by developing various methods for exploiting the workers or extracting surplus value, but becomes a system for producing and reproducing the workforce as a commodity, which tends to conform to its qualities, in order to render it utilizable and manageable within a determinate system of production, that is, which imposes its exigencies a priori by conditioning individuals' capacities, needs, and desires.[61] Here Marx's vision is apocalyptic indeed. He sees the extinction of politics, a constitutive dimension of past history, produced as the result of a pure economic logic pushed to its extreme. In the same way, the Foucault-inspired discourse of de-democratization sees in it the result of a certain logic of power and the invention of a new cultural rationality. Obviously both visions are haunted (who would not be?) by the question of how modern societies produce "voluntary servitude" in their own way: not, as in de La Boétie's classic account, as an imaginary effect of the fascination engendered by a sovereign figure (the One or the monarch), but as the combined effect of anonymous modern technologies, multiple mass practices, micropowers, and the daily behaviors of the dominant as well as the dominated within a certain normality—whence the short-circuit that is then established between analyses of the everyday and analyses of the exception (or the state of exception). I know very well that Brown is extremely prudent about offering predictions. Others are less prudent, and we see in contemporary critical theory a general return to apocalyptic themes, inspired by a certain Marxist tradition or by completely different references, from the idea that history has now passed into the reign of the ontological "simulacrum" or the virtual to the idea that politics, transformed into biopolitics, has acquired a self-destructive dimension that makes "bare life" the horizon of all subjection to power.[62]

But the question of contemporary processes of de-democratization calls on other discussions that seem to me central in view of the decomposition of the national-social state, whether one regards it as a cause or as a situation of creeping crisis that other forces have turned to their advantage. No one will contest, it seems to me, that there has been an intrinsic connection between this reversal of democratic claims and the intensification of procedures of control—of life, geographical mobility, opinions, social behavior—calling on increasingly sophisticated technologies, on a territorial or communicational, national or transnational basis. Deleuze could speak of this as the emergence of a "society of control."[63] Think of the techniques of marking and filing, denounced in particular by Agamben, that are now being extended into a sort of generalized census, in real time, of Internet users.[64] But think, above all, of methods of psychological and behavioral classification applied to the observation of children with a view to their future "dangerousness," the generalization of which throughout schools has been proposed in France (not without giving rise to debate), or of new forms of psychiatric diagnosis being established at the expense of clinics. They are more destructive from the point of view of an attack on the "property in one's person" that constitutes (even ideally) the foundation of the subjectivity of the classic citizen. And, above all, let us not forget that there is a positive counterpart to the development of these procedures of control that is in a sense no less incompatible with the political form of citizenship: the development of a new ethic of self-care, whereby individuals must moralize their own conduct by submitting themselves to the criterion of utility maximization or the productivity of their individuality.[65] The recognition of the dark face of this ethic goes along with what Robert Castel in particular has described as negative individualism, which he associates with the dismantling and ruin of institutions of social security and forms of solidarity or socialization that enable the affiliation of individuals, over several generations, into a community of citizens (coinciding in practice, as we have seen, with the national community in which both conflicts of interest, especially institutionalized class conflicts, and processes of socialization, education, and medical supervision guaranteed by formally egalitarian public services, occur). The disaffiliated or disincorporated individual—for example, a young proletarian who has neither a job nor the prospect of stable work, whether or not he is from an immigrant background—is a subject constantly addressed by contradictory injunctions: he has to behave as an "entrepreneur of himself," following the new code of neoliberal values by exhibiting an autonomy for which all the conditions of possibility (which are necessarily collective, social) have been taken away or rendered inaccessible.[66] This leads to despair, but also occasionally to the extreme violence directed against themselves as well as others: the very violence of devaluation.[67] But it also leads to a search for compensatory communities, often founded on an imaginary of collective omnipotence (or, as Derrida and Roberto Esposito would say, "auto-immunity"). Such communities are as negative and impossible as the "negative individualities" or "impossible individualities" produced by the dismantling of social citizenship, or toward which statist communities are tending.[68] They can be ideally constructed on a local basis, in the form of ethnocultural or microterritorial gangs.[69] Or else they can be projected into global space by communications networks that control them as much as they use them by globalizing a (postcolonial) religious or racial imaginary.

Thus also equally arises the now unavoidable question of the forms and functions of populism in the contemporary political space. It seems to me that Ernesto Laclau is right to insist that populism in general not be stigmatized or amalgamated to fascism, not only because, under this typically "projective" name, it is generally the participation of the masses in politics that is the object of a veritable prohibition (here we see the full antidemocratic fear of the masses), but because in a sense we have to admit that there would no more be a "people" in politics without populism than a nation without nationalism or a common without communism. In each case, it is the ambivalence that surrounds these names of collective action—these metonyms of the ideological "we"—that is the problem.[70] Certain forms of populism, despite their equivocal nature or perhaps because of it, appear as conditions for a generalization of political discourse that exceeds (or integrates) the particularity of the claims of different social groups, different emancipatory movements denouncing a heterogeneous multiplicity of forms of domination. Laclau's thesis is that, supporting a reformulation of what Gramsci called hegemony, this is the very essence of democratic politics. If he is right on this point, we must admit that the specter of populism always already haunted the dialectic of insurrection and constitution that I spoke of at the beginning—for better and for worse. This is very possible.[71]

But I also ask myself the opposite question, for which I have no preestablished answer, or in any case no universally valid answer beyond conjunctural considerations: under what conditions does a populist modality of identification with the absent community, or the imaginary community, become (and remain) the framework of mobilization for democratic objectives? What distinguishes equality (or equaliberty), even if it is utopian, from a logic of equivalence between the discourse or images different groups use to identify with the same "bloc in power"? When must we say, conversely, that populism as a fiction of community is simply the screen on which the compensations or imaginary vengeance called for by improverishment or desocialization are projected, the production of "negative individuals," the stigmatization and exclusion of the bearers of alterity or foreignness? Or are the two sides of this alternative really never separate, so that collective political capacity can never be practically dissociated from them by deploying at once a capacity for mobilization and a capacity for civilization by means of a determinate imaginary?[72]

It could not really be a question, it seems to me, of separating such a discussion about the violent tensions and ambiguous effects of the conjunction of affiliation and disaffiliation, communitarian (especially national) incorporation and internal exclusion, negative and positive individualism, from that about the crisis of representation in contemporary political systems. There, quite obviously, is another aspect of the transformations of the political that we can ascribe to neoliberalism. Thousands of pages have been published concerning what has perhaps become the privileged platitude of contemporary political science.[73] All this is not negligible, far from it, from the point of view of a critique of politics in the age of the "end of politics." For it would be much too hasty and reductive, as in a certain Marxist (or Rousseauian) vulgate, to confuse the question of representation in general with that of parliamentarism, which represents only one of its aspects and possible historical forms. It was as a guarantor of pluralist political systems, which were abolished by the totalitarianisms of the left and right in the name of the organic unity of their respective "peoples" (or what they regarded as the "people of the people," a race or a class), that parliamentary representation was presented by liberal political science as the touchstone of democracy.[74] And it is as a mechanism for expropriating citizens' direct political capacity (their general competence, their right to speak, their capacity to decide) that it was criticized as such by communism or anarchism. But the crisis of parliamentarism is nothing new, and some of its symptoms (especially the corruption of the people's representatives, who find themselves in a strategic position between their constituencies, economic interest groups, administration, and those who hold state power, and precisely the so-called populist, antiparliamentary reactions they engender) are as old as its constitution.[75] Much more interesting for reflecting on the antinomies of citizenship would be a discussion of the crisis of representation as such, beyond the parliamentary mechanism, as the capacity to delegate power to representatives at each level of the institutions where there are demands for a public function (what the ancients called a "magistracy" or "public office") and to supervise the results of this delegation, for this capacity is part of the fundamental rights of free and equal citizens. In other words, it is necessary to return from a democratic perspective, from below, to the fundamental question that Hobbes, at the dawn of modern political philosophy, posed from above, from the perspective of a complete identification of the public sphere (the commonwealth) and sovereign power: the question of a collective procedure for acquiring power in the form of its transfer or communication.[76] This amounts to rediscovering the dialectic of the "constituting power" and the "constituted power," of insurrection and constitution—this time beyond the state or by taking away its political monopoly rather than founding it. We cannot set any a priori limit or internal border on this dialectic. Let us not forget that in the republican tradition (which is not at all, strictly speaking, French) a teacher or a judge, whether or not he was a public official, was a representative of the people as well as a deputy, as long as the modalities of his selection and the effects of his action could be subject to democratic scrutiny (which, it must be recognized, differ enormously). The crisis of the political institution designated by the general term "de-democratization" does not reside just in the devaluation of this or that form of representation; it resides in the disqualification of the principle of representation itself. For, on one side, we imagine that it has become useless, "irrational," due to the emergence of forms of governance that allow social programs and procedures for reducing social conflict to be calculated and optimized as a function of their utility; while, on the other, we proclaim more than ever that representation is an impractical, dangerous political form when the responsibility of the "citizen-subject" is defined, above all, in terms of normality or deviance in relation to a social norm that is to be controlled, not expressed or made to be expressed, by giving him a vote (which means that the "hatred of representation" is also a form of the "hatred of democracy").[77]

It is at this point, of course, that we must pose the question of alternatives—and, consequently, of hopes. Both rest entirely on the existence of forms of resistance, solidarity, collective invention and individual revolt that the expansion of the methods of neoliberal governance itself tends to produce. Taken together, in their heterogeneity, these elements outline or will outline the contours of an insurrectional politics, and thus allow us to imagine the constitution of new modalities of citizenship, combining spontaneity and institution, participation and representation, in unprecedented ways.[78] Above all, they will have to take into account the fact that with the crisis of social citizenship, followed by the extension of the "society of control" and more generally by phenomena of de-democratization in the framework of forms of neoliberal rationality and governmentality, the imaginary linearity of the progress of citizenship (or its democratization) has been shattered. Not only has the calling into question of existing social rights practically restricted the content and value of the political rights won in the course of modernity; it has radically thrown into question the achievement of civil rights or rights of the person, which seemed irreversible. It is in all these dimensions at once—without hierarchical order or strategic priority—that the antinomies of citizenship, and consequently the need for a democratic alternative, are being heightened.

But there are at least two figures—or, if you prefer, two symbolic modes of subjectivation—that can correspond to the idea of an insurrectional or insurgent citizenship. We must admit that they are heterogeneous. One is the deviant subject, considered from the perspective of the dominant norm. It is the figure of a subjectivity that resists the procedures of moralization and normalization imposed by the rationality of the neoliberal order, which are just as coercive, as we have seen, as those of the national-social state, even if it rejects the disciplines and methods of control its predecessor labored to perfect. What then is a deviant, rebel, or, in Deleuze's terms, "minority" citizen-subject?[79] It is a subject that invents and configures with others not so much utopias as what Foucault called heterotopias: spaces of autonomy that are also ways of actively protecting oneself from the nihilistic forms of negative individualism and self-destructive violence. This figure is distinct, both in its objective, social conditions and in its subjective aims, from the majoritarian subject of collective action, that is, in our political tradition, the militant who joins a movement or a campaign to serve a democratic cause. This is so even if, most of the time, such causes also have a moral dimension: protecting

the environment or solidarity with undocumented migrants whom a se-
curitized and militarized capitalist society tries to relegate and hunt like
dehumanized game after having forced them to leave their country and
forced them into illegality.[80] And of course the apparently most traditional causes, like defending the right to work or culture, or civic or civil
movements for gender equality, illustrate in particular the condensation
of different generations of rights.

By no means do I maintain that these two figures (which could be
called minoritarian and majoritarian) are radically separate in practice,
or can be realized independently of one another. The classical representation of revolutionary practice, conjoining revolt and transformation,
fused them into a single ideal type. But it is certain that, symbolically
speaking, they correspond to distinct forms of action, and are occasionally borne by different social practices rooted in the experiences and life
conditions of different groups, belonging to different sectors of society or
coming from different parts of the world that do not speak the same political language—or the same language at all. This is why the simple category of "the subject" (even conceived of dynamically, as a process of
subjectivation that goes on indefinitely) is not sufficient to think the constitution of politics, and we need many operative ideas (in my view at
least three: bearers, subjects, and actors). This is also why we must work
on inventing democracy, by thinking about the transitional unities that
can produce bearers, by becoming actors through certain forms of subjectivity, and not in terms of a preestablished harmony between social
conditions that exist "in themselves" and forms of awareness or political
organization that allow them to also exist "for themselves" from the perspective of historical progress. Unities of action or alliances are always
justified by the discovery of multiple forms of inequality or exclusion that
belong to the same system, and consequently can contribute to the same
process of democratizing citizenship (or, as some now say, the "democratization of democracy").[81] But they have no natural basis that one could
think in ontological terms or in terms of a moral destination. The sphere
of political action is not given or prefigured; it is "absent," like the people
itself, according to the formula from Deleuze I evoked above. This sphere
uses historically produced structures of communication and rights of
expression that it itself helps impose to engender a hybrid political actor,
situated in a determinate place where the world's conflicts meet in a

singular way, but is virtually effective on the transnational level (and always already cosmopolitical in this sense). It does not embody an empirico-transcendental type (the Worker, the Proletarian, the Colonized or the Postcolonized, the Woman, the Nomad, and so on) but is composed of differences, themselves formed by crossing visible and invisible borders. Its subjective task and its permanent problem consists in overcoming its own divisions and divergent interests as much as pushing back its adversaries. But are these two aporias really distinct? I do not believe so.

PART
ONE

THE STATEMENT
AND INSTITUTION
OF RIGHTS

THE PROPOSITION OF EQUALIBERTY

I would like to propose some formulations that will help orient us among the presuppositions of a characteristic discussion of the 1980s.[1] At once a subject for specialists and a matter of public debate, this discussion is marked by a tendency to substitute the theme of the relations between ethics and politics for that of the relations between the political and the social, and perhaps more profoundly to reinscribe the latter within the former. It sees—on the right, but also on the left—the question of revolution give way to that of citizenship, at least insofar as what is at stake at a deeper level is not a reformulation of the question of revolution in terms of citizenship, and thus also civic-mindedness and civility, whether one invokes a renewal of citizenship (going beyond the simple recognition of individual rights) or advances the idea of a "new citizenship."

This is why it is not surprising that a central theme of ongoing debates—quite apart from any coincidental anniversaries—concerns the unfolding and historical impact of the French Revolution, and more specifically its "founding" text, the *Declaration of the Rights of Man and*

Citizen of 1789, the meaning and nature of whose universality are again being questioned. In focusing on this text myself, I am conscious of the double risk of antiquarianism in relation to the interpellations of present history and of Eurocentrism or even Francocentrism that comes with such an approach to the problem of the political. But even if the question of "the rights of man" were only a mask or a lure, which I do not think it is, it would still be worth the trouble to try to assess the reasons for the gap between their statement in the past and a current democratic problematic. And even if this statement corresponds only to the fictive universalization of a particular society or culture, which I also do not think it does, it would be equally necessary to inquire anew into its reasons, unlike the intellectual movements and currents of social struggle that shaped the idea of "revolution" for us in the nineteenth and twentieth centuries.

I will address, in a more or less elaborated way, four aspects of this question.

First, if it is true that for us the statement or rather the series of statements of 1789 has long since lost the self-evidence it claimed, if it is true that a gap has emerged in many ways between the prerequisites of freedom and those of equality, which were previously inseparably associated, how should we interpret the reasons for this?

Second, how should we interpret the relation between the statement of the *Declaration* and the specificity of the revolutionary event? Should the collective practice that finds its expression and weapon in this institutional text be thought under the heading of a subject (humanity, civil society, the people, social class), or rather that of a conjuncture and a conjunction of forces? Without there being any question of proposing here an analysis of the character of the revolution of 1789–95, the choice of the second option will lead me to say a few words on the originality of the *Declaration*'s statements in relation to what is commonly considered its ideological "source," the classic theories of natural right.

Third, coming to what is probably the essential point, I will examine the status of the statement and the enunciation of the proposition that, it seems to me, is at the heart of the *Declaration* and allows us to understand its logic: the proposition that identifies—in extension and then in comprehension—freedom and equality. What interests me above all here is the truth of this proposition, which I will call the proposition of equaliberty, and on this basis the rupture it produces in the political field. But these are equally the reasons for its instability, the forms in which an incessant division has developed out of what had been produced as a unity of opposites. What follows from this is a system of reference, a topos for classifying and interpreting the different strategies, theoretical as well as political, that have confronted this dilemma over at least two centuries, and from which in reality we have not escaped.

Fourth and finally, though in an inevitably very allusive way, I would like to at least pose the following question. If it is true that the revolutionary proposition identifying freedom and equality constitutes the incontrovertible and in a certain sense irreversible statement of a political truth, if it is also true that the inscription of this truth in the very history that produced it is immediately characterized by instability and in a certain sense decline, and if it is true finally that its return in contemporary politics is at least a sign of the demand for a new practical inscription, under what conditions would that inscription be thinkable at the end of the twentieth century? Such a question will have to remain largely open, and no doubt aporetic. At least it will be possible to illuminate the reasons for this by negatively outlining what, in the contradictions of modern politics, has remained silent, and more fundamentally finds itself necessarily repressed in the topos constructed around the *Declaration*.

FIRST, THEN, WHEREIN LIES the contemporary relevance of the revolutionary statements? I said it a moment ago: in the paradoxical form of an apparently irreducible split between concepts or values that are felt to be equally necessary. No doubt this is *a contrario* witness to the interdependence of equality and freedom in the form of the periodic return of authoritarian ideologies positing that life in society, or human nature, requires both the imposition of hierarchy and the promotion of individual or even collective inequality. But the permanence of the critique of the rights of man, inaugurated at the beginning of the nineteenth century by counterrevolutionary thought, does not, conversely, make their own consistency self-evident.[2] Contemporary liberalism is not alone in positing that, beyond very strict limits (that have a juridical form), freedom and equality are mutually exclusive. This conviction is widely shared by socialism and more generally by the social progressivism of different minorities at the very moment that, practically, it appears that claims for freedom and equality condition each other, as we see in struggles for democracy in so-called socialist countries just as in anti-racist movements in western Europe or the struggles of black people in South Africa.

This profound contradiction feeds upon several ideas whose self-evidence is seldom questioned, in particular the idea that equality (or, more generally, "real" equality) is essentially economic and social—an elastic notion by definition that today tends to also include the cultural—whereas freedom is above all juridical-political and institutional. But at the same time there is another self-evidence or pseudo-self-evidence on which liberalism and socialism end up agreeing, even if they draw opposite conclusions—namely, that the realization of equality occurs through state intervention, since it essentially has to do with distribution or redistribution, whereas the preservation of freedom is connected to the limitation of this intervention, even to constant defense against its "perverse" effects.[3] It seems to me that this omnipresent but uncritical reference to the state, designated as a block, which constantly reproduces the difference between "formal" and "real" (or "substantial") rights as well as the representation of equality as an exclusively collective goal while freedom (in any case the "liberty of the moderns") would be essentially individual freedom, even in the realm of public freedoms (which would then best be thought of as public guarantees of private freedoms).

From this we proceed directly to the fundamental paradox, which is the split between the discourse of the rights of man and that of the rights of the citizen at the very moment a moralization of political life or its refoundation on ethics is asserted. Today the discourse of the rights of man (above all formulated as a defense, rather than conquest, of the rights of man) covers a very broad spectrum, from freedom of conscience or individual security to the claim to a right to existence or a people's right to self-determination. But it remains completely distinct from the discourse of the rights of the citizen, which itself oscillates between the proposal or claim to enlarge the political sphere to new domains (such as ecology) and that of revalorizing the political in the classical sense—a synonym for the collective institution of deliberation and decision—against the invasion of economism or technocracy. It seems to be very difficult, perhaps more and more difficult, to maintain the equation that is typical of the revolutionary statements of 1789, to which I will return: that of man and citizen, the consequence of which would be, among other things, the idea that the emancipation of the oppressed can be no one's work but their own. As if "man" were in fact nothing other than what remains when we abstract from the "citizen." There is nearly universal agreement on the fact that equating man with the citizen leads invariably to totalitarianism, to what is often called the imperialism of "the political" (*tout politique*). But the flipside of this agreement is the proclamation that the rights of man, however natural and universally necessary they may be, essentially represent an ideal—which is, if one thinks about it seriously, the exact inverse of the performative statement of 1789, which declared the immediate social relevance of those rights, posited the necessity and the possibility of putting them into effect, and materialized them in a constitution.[4]

One could—one should—investigate the reasons for this split, which becomes glaring the moment the reference to juridical universalism is renewed. Many well-known explanations are available. One invokes human nature: the gap between the "rights of man" and the "rights of the citizen" is the same as between the essential, theoretical goodness of human nature, without which true community would be impossible, and the practical malevolence of empirical individuals subject to the constraints of their passions, their interests, and the conditions of their existence. *Homo homini deus, homo homini lupus.* At the improbable point of equilibrium of this contradiction we find precisely law, which Jean-Denis Bredin recently suggested be defined as the "art of solving the insoluble question," rediscovering Kant's "unsocial sociability" as its basis.[5] Another common explanation is historicist: time has passed, so the material and cultural conditions under which the statements of 1789 could be constitutively self-evident no longer exist. We are no longer, no doubt, "men" of the eighteenth century, and it is doubtful that we are still "citizens" of the nineteenth. We are more than that, in one sense (for example, we live in a world of communications and global culture that relativize national citizenship, the unsurpassable horizon of the constituents of the revolutionary period); in another sense we are less, since our differentiated societies are organized not only by class, but above all by status. It is not impossible to combine these two types of explanation, emphasizing the original utopianism of the rights of man by positing that from the start their proclamation—which furnished political and social modernity with a means of asserting itself against the hierarchical social orders of the past and their own, above all, theological imaginary—only served to announce an ideal, that is, to crystallize a new imaginary.

I will privilege another mode of explanation, one that is more dialectical or, if you like, more intrinsic: it suggests that, from the beginning, the "founding" statements, by reason of their very simplicity and their revolutionary radicality, hide within themselves a contradiction that prevents them from becoming invested in a stable order. Or better still: the contradiction, to the second degree, resides in the instability of the relation between the aporetic character of the statements and the conflictual character of the situation in which they arise and which serves as their referent, so that every attempt to reactivate the statements of the rights of man and citizen, based on its very truth, cannot help but run into the effects of the development of its own tensions.[6] This path seems to me the most fertile, but it can be pursued in different ways that I will not discuss in detail. Here it is especially the interpretation of the development of the *Declaration* in the course of the revolutionary process of 1789–95 that acquires a differential importance, especially the comparison of the original text and its more or less abortive rewritings (which were not, however, without impact) of 1793 (the Montagnard Declaration) and 1795 (the Thermidorian Declaration). This development, with its characteristic oscillation between two readings of the relation between man and citizen, one plebeian and the other bourgeois, supported by antagonistic forces within the Revolution itself, already reveals the contradictions at work from the beginning.

In a remarkable book, *La révolution des droits de l'homme* (The revolution of the rights of man), expressing a neoliberal if not conservative perspective, seeking reasons why the Revolution is "finished" for us (but also what delayed this result for so long), Marcel Gauchet has followed what seems to him to be the development of a fundamental aporia from text to text: the fact that the kernel of the *Declaration* of 1789 was the establishment of an absolute notion of national sovereignty, the mimetic inversion of the monarchical sovereignty it opposed, in order to legitimate the representation of the people. For the "one and indivisible" will of the absolute monarch, the Constituent Assembly had to make a corresponding "general will"—equally one and indivisible, equally the depository of all authority, but founded in the last analysis only on the individuals who make up the nation. Such a notion is condemned to oscillate between direct democracy and revolutionary dictatorship. With the exception of the partial but determinate liberties inscribed in the American model of the Bill of Rights, it proves to be incompatible with the pragmatic institution of a juridical framework for modern politics, whether it is a matter balancing the powers of the legislature and the executive or state prerogatives and individual independence. This is why the Revolution was an immediate failure, while in another context, after a century of political confrontations and regime crises, its symbolic statements acquired the function of a more or less consensual regulatory ideal.

Symmetrically, in a series of recent articles, Florence Gauthier, rediscovering and renewing the tradition of revolutionary idealism (as it can be traced from Robespierre and Fichte to the young Marx and Ernst Bloch), has tried to show that a rupture took place between the Convention's Montagnard, Jacobin phase and its moderate, Thermidorian phase.[7] There is a continuity between the statements of 1789, centered on the primacy of freedom and the pursuit of its universality, and those of 1793, which develop the latent egalitarianism of this conception as universal reciprocity or the universal reciprocal recognition of freedoms, including the fundamental right to exist (the right to existence, with its economic consequences). They proceed from the classical, essentially Lockean idea of a declaration of natural right founding association or citizenship, which delimits the political sphere and the role of the state on the basis of human nature. On the contrary, with the Thermidorian Declaration of 1795, centered on the untouchable character of property and the reciprocity of rights and duties, a determinate social foundation is substituted for the natural, universal foundation of citizenship: there is a rupture, even a reversal. This of course expresses counterrevolutionary reaction to the development of social conflicts, and especially to the way the popular, nonbourgeois elements of the Revolution continually used the universalism of the rights of man politically, against the practical restrictions placed on them by their own authors—the distinction between active and passive citizenship on a censitary basis, and the exclusion of de facto equality from the domain of natural rights.

For my part, I will adopt exactly neither of these two ways of interpreting the intrinsic contradiction of the revolutionary moment. Both of them seem to me, for completely different reasons, to lack specificity: the specificity of the text of the *Declaration of Rights*, and the specificity of the revolutionary conjuncture, outside of which one can understand neither the immediate development of the statements nor their retroactive effects, which continue today. It is unfortunately impossible to go into all the details one could wish for. But, to put it schematically, I believe neither that the concept of national sovereignty forged in 1789 under the influence of circumstances is a simple reversal, within the framework of a fundamental continuity, of the concept of monarchic sovereignty, in a way substituting one transcendence for another, nor that the reference to man and the universality of his nature as founding the rights of the citizen can be traced back to the average content of its ideological sources, which can be generically designated as classical natural right.

As far as sovereignty is concerned, as I have tried to show elsewhere, the revolutionary innovation consists precisely in subverting the traditional concept by posing the highly paradoxical thesis of an egalitarian sovereignty—practically a contradiction in terms, but the only way to radically get rid of all transcendence and inscribe the political and social order in the element of immanence, of the self-constitution of the people.[8] From there, however, begins the immediate development of a whole series of contradictions that proceed from the fact that so-called civil society and especially the state are entirely structured by hierarchies or dependencies that are both indifferent to political sovereignty and essential to its institutionalization, even though society or the modern city no longer has at its disposal the means of the ancient city for neutralizing these contradictions and pushing them out of the public sphere, namely, the rigorous compartmentalization of the *oikos* and the polis.

As far as declared natural right is concerned, I believe that the revolutionary moment of the *Declaration* and its uninterrupted efficacy in the course of sociopolitical struggles is essential. In other words, I do not doubt that the materiality of this act of enunciation was the anchoring point for a series of claims that, from the day after the *Declaration*, started to claim it in order to demand the rights of women, workers, or colonized races to be incorporated into citizenship. But I in no way believe that it is inscribed in the continuity of classical natural right, be it Lockean or even Rousseauian, as its culmination, its realization, or simply its radicalization.[9] Historically and epistemologically, and whatever the self-consciousness of its authors, who were grappling with their own Ancien Régime intellectual formation, the core of the *Declaration of the Rights of Man and Citizen* does not come from preexisting ideologies. It is no longer part of the framework of theories of human nature as the foundation or guarantee of a juridical order that, from the sixteenth to the eighteenth century, formed precisely the alternative to theories of divine right and provided the opponents of absolute monarchy with the basis of their arguments. It only takes up—in part—their terminology in order to nullify their logic. So what it immediately determines is not the triumph but the irreversible opening of the crisis of classical natural right, the opening of a new ideological field in which the politico-philosophical ideologies of the nineteenth century will take their places, whether they express liberal, socialist, or conservative positions, and whether they derive epistemologically from positivism or historicism, idealism or political pragmatism.

Classical natural right is characterized by the extreme diversity of its conceptions of human nature and its schemes for the originary foundation of civil society, which correspond to as many strategies for reforming political institutions. The statements of 1789, the results of a veritable coup in the debates over national representation, which went on under the triple constraint of its own interests, the open but still not declared conflict with the monarchy, and the Great Fear of popular insurrection, are characterized, on the contrary, by a remarkable simplicity (what I called elsewhere a de jure fact), whose foundation, we will see, is purely negative, short-circuiting the problematic of the origins and modalities of association.[10] It is remarkable, notably, that the notion of a contract is absent.[11] But of course the complexity and heterogeneity of the classic theories of natural rights, be they contractualist or anticontractualist, statist or economistic, correspond to the relative homogeneity of a rising social class, which can be called the bourgeoisie, whereas the unitary simplicity of the *Declaration of Rights* represents in the field of ideas, or rather of words—words that immediately escaped the control of their authors—the real social complexity of the French Revolution: the fact that, from the start, it is not, is already no longer, a "bourgeois revolution," but a revolution made jointly by the bourgeoisie and the people, or the nonbourgeois and especially noncapitalist masses, in a constant relation of alliance and confrontation. It is a revolution immediately grappling with its own internal contestation, without which it would not even exist, a contestation that runs ceaselessly after the unity of its opposites.

LET US THEN COME to the core of the revolutionary statements. It resides, it seems to me, in a double identification, one explaining the other and giving it its content (although, as we will see, this content remains strangely indeterminate).

First identification: that of man and citizen. Here a choice of readings must be made, since a long, quasi-official, national, and international tradition interprets the content of the original seventeen articles as the expression of a distinction between the rights of man (universal, inalienable, subsisting independently of any social institution, thus virtual, etc.) and the rights of the citizen (positive, instituted, restrictive but effective), leading in its way to the foundation of the latter on the former.[12] And, no doubt, in order to be able to found these rights, it is necessary to distinguish between what founds and what is founded, but the whole question here is to determine whether, in the text itself, we are indeed dealing with the statement of a foundation.[13] No doubt, too, the duality of the terms "human" and "citizen" carries the possibility of a dissociation whose effects we will observe.[14] But it can and should be interpreted otherwise, in its context. Reread the *Declaration* and you will see that there is in reality no gap between the rights of man and the rights of the citizen, no difference in content: they are exactly the same. Nor, consequently, is there any difference between man and the citizen, at least to the extent that they are defined practically by their rights, by the nature and the extension of the rights to which they are entitled—but this is precisely the object of the *Declaration*. I recall that freedom, property, security, and resistance to oppression (Article 2) are enumerated as "natural and imprescriptible rights of man"—that is, exactly those that the rest of the *Declaration* will show are organized juridically by the social constitution.

What then poses a problem at this level? First of all, the presence of resistance to oppression. The least that can be said about this is that it is not very explicitly instituted thereafter. But it can also be said that it is the corollary of freedom, the guarantee of its effectiveness—to be free is to be able to resist any constraint that destroys freedom—and that it represents the verbal trace of the revolutionary struggle that imposes this freedom as a conquest.[15] On the other hand, the absence of equality. But this appearance should immediately be corrected—even if it is the trace of an internal vacillation to which we will have to return—by rereading Articles 1 ("Men are born and remain free and equal in rights") and 6 ("The law is the expression of the general will. All citizens have the right to contribute to it. . . . It should be the same for all. . . . All citizens being equal in its eyes are equally admissible."). These formulations do more than compensate for the absence of equality in the enumeration of Article 2; they reverse its meaning, making equality the principle or right that effectively ties all the others together.

The treatment of equality in the *Declaration* is precisely the site of the strongest and most precise identification of man and citizen. Indeed, no time was lost in reproaching it for this, and this was what very quickly led to the dissociation, in one way or another, of man and citizen, or the rights of man and the rights of the citizen, while we find here the confirmation of their coincidence in the revolutionary moment, from which the act of enunciation (the *Declaration*) is inseparable. Not only does the *Declaration* not install any "human nature" before society and political order as an underlying foundation or external guarantee; it integrally identifies the rights of man with political rights and, in this way, short-circuits theories of human nature as well as those of theological supernature, identifying man, individual or collective, with a member of political society. In a moment, I will specify this notion of the rights of man as political rights and vice versa by showing that it goes to the idea of the right of man to politics, to politically institute all human activity in view of a liberation and an equalization.

But before that it is not unhelpful to reflect on what radically distinguishes this from the "naturalist" statements of the tradition of antiquity. The equation of man and citizen in 1789 is not a revival of the *zôon politikon*. In fact, the idea of the zôon politikon, insofar as it really corresponds to the institutions of the Greek or Roman city, is not underpinned by the identification of equality and freedom, but by the completely different thesis of equality within the limits of freedom considered as a social status, founded, as the case may be, on a tradition, a constitution, or a natural quality of individuals (which makes them, for themselves and for others, masters). Here equality is only a consequence, an attribute, of freedom. There can be no reversibility between the two terms. Whence, right up to the texts that probe the democratic virtualities of the notion of citizenship most deeply, for example certain passages of Aristotle's *Politics*, the strange limitation of the concept—or at least what must appear as such retrospectively to the modern reader. Aristotle defines citizenship by the alternate exercise of the functions of ruling and obeying (*archein* and *archestai*), thus as a strong form of the generalized reciprocity of free, male, adult individuals (which is also the basis of their *philia*, a general concept of the "social bond"). From this reciprocity follows the anthropological and even cosmological position of the citizen between two limits of deficiency and excess that are, by the same stroke, the limits of the political: the subhuman in different figures (woman, slave, child) and superhuman in the figure of the wise man, the god, or the hero. But where we retrospectively see a contradictory combination, a suggestion of universality and an arbitrary limitation, there is in reality only the application of a different logic in which freedom represents a status, a personality, and equality, a function and a right of this status.[16]

Inversely, it would be just as erroneous to adopt, under the pretext of historical consciousness, the classical opposition that comes from liberalism. As opposed to the Greek (and even more, Roman) unity of the social and the political, the *Declaration* of 1789 would have instituted their "bourgeois" separation, founded on the distinction between the public and private spheres. That Marx, in a famous text of his youth, took up this reading on his own account does not prevent it from being essentially a complete misinterpretation in relation to the materiality of the statements. The man of the *Declaration* is not the private individual as opposed to the citizen, who would be the member of the state. He is precisely the citizen, and this recognition should, to the contrary, lead us to ask how it happened that the very notion of the state is so problematic in a revolutionary text that seeks to found a constitution whose goal—at least in the eyes of its authors—is to erect a new state. The answer to this question can only come from examining the subversive effects of a radically new idea bearing precisely on the relation of equality to freedom, announced universally.

What is this idea? Nothing less than the identification of the two concepts. Here is the extraordinary novelty and at the same time the root of all the difficulties, the nub of the contradiction. If one really wants to read it literally, the *Declaration* in fact says that equality is identical to freedom, is equal to freedom, and vice versa. Each is the exact measure of the other. This is what I propose to call, with a deliberately baroque phrase, the proposition of equaliberty—a portmanteau term, impossible and yet possible only as a play on words, that nevertheless alone expresses the central proposition.[17] For it gives both the conditions under which man is the citizen (through and through) and the reason for this assimilation. Beneath the equation of man and citizen, or rather *within* it, as the very reason for its universality, resides the proposition of equaliberty.

This proposition has the status of a self-evident truth, as the Americans said. Or, more exactly, it has the status of a certainty—that is, its truth cannot be put in doubt. How is it, then, that it is constantly put in doubt, albeit in forms of negation that never stop admitting its insistence, manifesting its irreversibility?

It cannot simply be by reason of the fact that we have here two words. Their formal distinction is obviously necessary to posit an identity of signification. Let us rather say that to be able to think freedom and equality as identical, it is necessary to reduce an initial semantic difference, inscribed in the relatively distinct histories of the words "freedom" and "equality" before the statement of '89 up to this meeting point, which changes the whole picture at a single stroke.[18] From another point of view, it is very simply the trace of the fact that the revolutionaries of '89 fought against two adversaries at once, and against two principles: absolutism, which appears as the negation of freedom (in the permanent fact of the prince, or what was called reason of state), and privilege, which appears as the negation of equality (in the abiding right of the stronger, that is, the right of the man of quality, or the aristocrat). The monarchy and the aristocracy, whose politico-social unity is immediately thought in the concept of the Ancien Régime—this amalgam which counterrevolutionary thought never ceased striking out at, even today, notably by distinguishing within the Revolution between a "revolution of freedom" and a "revolution of equality." But the Revolution of 1789 (and this is precisely why it is *the* Revolution, determining in an instant an irreversible mutation in the very meaning of the term) is both: it takes aim in an identical way against tyranny and against injustice (against an equality in submission and against a freedom identified with privilege). It shows that just tyranny (open despotism) and democratic injustice are equally impossible.

But what, more deeply, blocks the recognition of this radical thesis is what must indeed be called the Platonizing reading of these texts: one sees Equality and Freedom as Ideas or Species, subject to the law of the Same and the Other. One looks for the common nature of Equality and Freedom. One looks to where they would finally reveal their common "essence" (and one can be tempted to respond tautologically: this essence, this "nature," in a word this foundation, is man or the subject). There is also another reason. One senses that, in order to give this identity an empirical content, a positive reference, it would be necessary to indicate which freedom and which equality are identical—or rather, since what is manifestly characteristic of the statement of the *Declaration* is their universal identification, in all their forms, within what limits or conditions they are identical. In short, here one comes up against a stupefying indeterminacy.

In reality, it is a matter of two connected but distinct problems. For the first, the answer is simple but its implications are extreme, since it engages nothing less than the truth-status of the proposition of equaliberty. For the second, the answer is practically impossible—or, rather, it is destined to remain indefinitely open, indefinitely deferred by its very contradiction, which is no doubt of no less import, since what is at stake is very simply the application, the passage from theory to practice, of a proposition that comes from (revolutionary) practice itself.

Let us look first at the question of nature. My position is brutal: the reasoning that underlies the proposition of equaliberty (E=L) is not essentialist. What underlies it is not the intuitive discovery or the revelation of an identity of the ideas of Equality and Freedom, if only because they are completely transformed by the revolutionary equation. It is the historical discovery, which can rightly be called experimental, that their extensions are necessarily identical. Simply put, the situations in which both are present or absent are necessarily the same. Or, again, the (de facto) historical conditions of freedom are exactly the same as the (de facto) historical conditions of equality.

I am saying that, understood in this way, the proposition of equaliberty is indeed an irreversible truth, discovered by and in the revolutionary struggle—precisely the universally true proposition on which, at the decisive moment, the different forces making up the revolutionary camp had to agree. In turn, the historical effects of this proposition, however contradictory they may be, can only be understood in this way, as the effects of a truth or effects of truth. This does not mean that they are never forgotten or contradicted.

You will say to me: Where is the proof? Since it is a matter of a universal truth in this sense (an a posteriori universal or, better, a historical universal), it can only be negative. It can only have the status of a refutation—what Aristotle would call an *elenchos*. But it can be made at any time, in situations as diverse as one could want. It is, in fact, a negative proof: if it is absolutely true that equality is practically identical to liberty, this means that it is materially impossible for it to be otherwise—in other words, it means that they are necessarily always contradicted together. This thesis is itself to be interpreted in extension: equality and freedom are contradicted in exactly the same conditions, in the same situation, because there is no example of conditions that suppress or repress freedom that do not suppress or limit—that is, do not abolish—equality, and vice versa. I am not afraid of being contradicted here, either by the history of capitalist exploitation, which by negating in practice the equality proclaimed in the labor contract ends up in the practical negation of freedom of speech and expression, or by the history of socialist regimes that, by suppressing public freedoms, end up constituting a society of privileges and reinforced inequalities.[19] Clearly, the distinction between individual and collective freedoms, like that between formal and real equality, has no meaning here. It would rather be a matter of the degree of equality that is necessary for the collectivization of individual freedoms, and the degree of freedom that is necessary for the collective equality of individuals, the response being in each case the same: the maximum in the given conditions. Whence we arrive at yet another way of expressing the negative experience that constitutes the proof—the only possible proof, but sufficient as such—of the proposition of equaliberty: the diverse forms of social or political power that correspond either to inequalities or to constraints on the freedom of man-the-citizen necessarily converge. There are no examples of restrictions or suppressions of freedoms without social inequalities, nor of inequalities without restrictions or suppressions of freedoms, be it only to put down resistance, even if there are degrees, secondary tensions, phases of unstable equilibrium, and compromise situations in which exploitation and domination are not homogeneously distributed across all individuals. Such is the very mechanism of the formation of classes or elites, which inevitably transforms power into superpower or hegemony.

Indeed, if freedom is not equality, then either it is superiority—mastery—or it is subjection and dependence on some power, which is absurd. Thus, correlatively, equality must be thought as the general form of the radical negation of all subjection and all mastery, that is, as the liberation of freedom itself from an external or internal power that takes it over and transforms it into its opposite.[20]

One can then understand why the essential content of the statement of the *Declaration*, the circumstantial work of the bourgeois spokesmen of the Revolution, is not their own domination or control over the process in which they are participating. And one understands why a struggle is immediately engaged where what is at stake is the application of the principles of '89, that is, their universal extension or their limitation.

But one can also understand what I just suggested: that the signification of the equation Man = Citizen is not so much the definition of a political right as the affirmation of a universal right to politics. Formally, at least—but this is the very type of a form that can become a material weapon—the *Declaration* opens an indefinite sphere for the politicization of rights claims, each of which reiterates in its own way the demand for citizenship or for an institutional, public inscription of freedom and equality. The rights claims of workers or of dependents as well as those of women or slaves, and later those of the colonized, is inscribed within this indefinite opening, as we see in attempts beginning in the revolutionary period.

But here is the second aspect. An intrinsic part of the truth of our statement is its negative universality, that is, its absolute indeterminacy. Since we are speaking here about a truth and a truth-effect in history, it is more necessary than ever to articulate the level of the statement and that of the enunciation—or, if you like, the pragmatic relation between the signification and the reference. Its indeterminacy gives the statement all its force, but also the practical weakness of its enunciation. Or, rather, it makes the consequences of the statement themselves indeterminate: they depend entirely on relations of forces and their evolution within the conjuncture, within which it will always be necessary to practically construct individual and collective referents for equaliberty, with more or less prudence and precision, but also audacity and insolence against the established powers. There will be a permanent tension between the conditions that historically determine the construction of institutions that conform to the proposition of equaliberty and the excessive, hyperbolic universality of the statement. Nevertheless, it will always have to be repeated, and repeated identically, without change, in order to reproduce the truth-effect without which there is no revolutionary politics. There will thus be a permanent tension between the universally political signification of the rights of man and the fact that their statement leaves the task of producing a politics of the rights of man entirely up to practice, to struggle, to social conflict—in particular, to the development of the conflict that was already at the origin of its formulation. Let us simply note here that this tension is such that the politics of the rights of man and the citizen is in general what is most lacking in discourses of the rights of man, which are discourses of compromise and which sidestep or suppress the effective equation of man and citizen.

I NOW COME TO the last point of my exposition. I will propose the following hypothesis: to define equaliberty, or to inscribe it in practice at the price of struggles directed concretely against the historical negations whose negation this proposition itself represents, is to put its truth into effect. But such an effectuation depends on two factors: a determination of the real contradictions of postrevolutionary politics, that is, the given relations of forces and conflicts of interests in the successive conjunctures in which it is pursued, or even reconstituted, and a determination of the forms in which such real contradictions are thinkable within the ideological space opened by the revolutionary proposition—even, very simply and still more fundamentally, the very possibility of adequately thinking such contradictions within this ideological space, that is, naming them or formulating their solution as a realization of equaliberty. It does not follow from the fact that the proposition of equaliberty is universally true that it is the whole truth (a notion, to tell the truth, that is a contradiction in terms). It follows from this that in immediately determining the opening of a space of thinking, it also determines a closure—in other words, it immediately determines it as an ideological space.

Today it is exclusively the second aspect that will interest me in conclusion, and this for the following reason. Historical experience forces us to understand not only that different contradictions, different struggles for equality and freedom are not spontaneously compatible with each other in the field of revolutionary struggle, but also that they cannot be enunciated in the same language, in terms of the same discourse—which would, however, be a minimal precondition for their practical conjunction, to say nothing of their "fusion" in the same democratic or revolutionary movement. At least part of the reason for this situation, which suffices to account for the relative inadequacy of the revolutionary idea today, lies in the heterogeneity of contradictions we are dealing with here, and even more radically in the fact that it is not a matter of contradictions in the same sense of the word. To illustrate this idea it will suffice to mention what have traditionally been designated class contradictions and the contradiction of sexual relations (relations between men and women). To these, for reasons I hope to make clear, I will add for my part a contradiction that seems to me equally fundamental, and equally heterogeneous to the last two, and which serves to ideologically locate formulations such as the division of manual and intellectual labor, or the division between corporal and mental activity.

Our discussion will take the form of the construction of a configuration or topography of the ideological tensions of modern politics as restructured by the revolutionary proposition. It is within such a topography that we must try to localize the statement of contradictions in order to measure their heterogeneity and distance.

Here, schematically, is my working hypothesis:

1 The equation of freedom and equality is indispensable to the modern, subjective remaking of right, but it is powerless to guarantee its institutional stability. A mediation is required, but it takes the antithetical forms of fraternity (or community) and property (or commerce).

2 Each of these mediations is in turn the object of a conflict and finds itself practically divided, on the one hand into national community and popular community, on the other into labor-property and capital-property. The combination of these two oppositions is the most general ideological form of class struggle.

3 Each of these mediations, as well as their conflictual combinations, represses another kind of contradiction: on the side of fraternity-community, sexual difference; on the side of property (labor and/or capital), the division of "intellectual" knowledge and "corporal" activity.

The consequence of this formulation is that there are two completely heterogeneous types of contradictions, which not only cannot be reduced to a unity, but in a certain way must give rise to incompatible but rigorously inseparable discourses—at least as long as the discursive matrix of political action is founded on the concept of man the citizen, with which we began.

ALLOW ME TO COMMENT briefly on the three points I just raised, beginning with the question of mediations. We must again begin with the constitutive instability of the equation Man = Citizen, undergirded by the identification of equality with freedom, that is, the affirmation of a potentially universal right to politics. Elsewhere I have tried to show, following others (and, if one reads the texts carefully, the revolutionaries themselves), that this affirmation introduces an individual oscillation, induces a structural equivocation between two obviously antinomic politics: a politics of insurrection and a politics of constitution—or, if you prefer, a politics of permanent, uninterrupted revolution and a politics of the state as institutional order.[21] It is clear that such an antinomy divides the very concept of politics without ever being able to find a synthesis (which is perhaps the typical characteristic of modernity). It also signifies that freedom and equality will constantly tend to be dissociated, to appear as distinct principles or values that can be invoked by opposing camps or forces, at least that their identity—and especially their juridical identity—is not guaranteed or, if you like, founded by the introduction and the primacy of a third term. Then we would no longer have the immediate identity $E = L$, but a mediate identity: $E = L$ insofar as they are expressions or specifications of another principle, which would at the same time appear as their presupposition or common substance. By the same stroke, it will be ideologically possible to move from a negative, indeterminate proof to a positive, determinate one (but mediate and, as a result, productive of a simply relative truth).

Nevertheless, the fact is—no doubt because of the intrinsic ambiguity of any institutional mediation of the social, transindividual relation, but also because of the fact that any institutionalization of a revolutionary break is subject to the law of the prerevolutionary "return of the repressed"—that such a mediation cannot take a single historical form. Historically, it has assumed two antithetical forms: mediation by property (and property in oneself) and mediation by community (which was typically expressed during the French Revolution in the terms of the triptych Liberty-Equality-Fraternity, laid out on the three poles of a symbolic triangle, but the triangle Liberty-Equality-Property was no less decisive).

We can represent this configuration as follows:

$$\frac{\begin{matrix} F\,(C) \\ E \;=\; L \end{matrix}}{\begin{matrix} E \;=\; L \\ P \end{matrix}}$$

Let us pause a moment on this point. To be sure, none of the notions involved—freedom, equality, property or commerce, community or fraternity—is radically new. What is new is the way they are grouped, defined in relation to each other, and the tension that is established between the two possible "foundations" of liberty and equality, which are like two alternative ways of socializing the citizen: property, be it individual or collective; community, be it conceived as natural or historical, or even spiritual. Here we have the matrix of the political ideologies characteristic of modernity, from socialism and liberalism (each of which, in its way, places the accent on property) to nationalism and communism (each of which, in its way, places it on community, and notably in France on fraternity). Noting the insistence of this structure is also a way of clarifying the stakes of the contemporary discomfort concerning politics. It is believed that this discomfort concerns the terms of freedom and equality, but in fact it seems to have more to do with their complements. For, as an anchoring point for individuality and thus for the relation between men and things or man and nature, property in all its forms has today lost its self-evidence, its simplicity, and has become a complex, opaque notion. What is it, for example, to be the owner of an ability, a credit, or a right? Meanwhile, fraternity or community has lost both its univocity (for there is not one but many collectivizing socials, many competing groups or bonds of belonging with which individuals are called on to identify) and its consistency. There are social relations that, after having bound individuals together too well, no longer seem to bind them together at all: for example, the professions, the family, and no doubt the question arises more and more often for class and the nation itself. But we will see in a moment that the deepest reason for this vacillation of the foundations of modern politics is no doubt to be sought in the political emergence of differences that dissolve the identity of the property-owning subject as well as the communitarian subject as one of the major stakes of freedom and equality.

What is striking here—and is not only a formal symmetry—is that neither property nor community can "found" freedom and equality (and consequently the politics that are deployed around these rights of man the citizen) without an antithetical reasoning. This is what I will call the argument of the danger of the opposite excess. It will be said that the excess of community, the absolute primacy of the whole or the group over individuals, would be the suppression of individuality, which is why the relations of freedom and equality must be controlled, measured, by the principle of the guarantee of property, especially property in oneself, the property of the conditions of existence. Symmetrically, it will be said that the excess of property, the absolute primacy of the selfish individual, would be the suppression of the community. This is why freedom and equality must be defined essentially as expressions of the communitarian being of men, of the institutions in which the community pursues its own realization. As these systems become more complicated, one rediscovers the old dialectic of being and having: this is why the community undertakes to realize itself by means of a certain regulation of property, and property by means of a certain form of community, regulated by efficiency, justice, the general interest, etc.

But above all this dialectic cannot develop without each of the great mediations tending to split, to divide in two. This no doubt has to do with the fact that, initially borne by the convergence of completely heterogeneous social groups and practices, the notion of universal citizenship becomes the object of the confrontation between the dominated and the dominant, and also between violent as well as juridical or legal forms of politics. There is always, be it on the side of the dominant or on the side of the dominated—and without our being able to observe here a general rule, a disposition of forces and ideas established once and for all—the use of violence against the law, against juridical form, but also of legality against violence.

What then happens historically on the top half of the triangle (Liberty, Equality, Fraternity), in fact very early, beginning with the internal conflict of the Convention, simultaneously worked up by questions of war and public safety, but also by the patriotic revolutionary cult and the class differences that led to talk of a new aristocracy and new privileges? The system of Fraternity tends to be doubled into a national fraternity and, before long, a statist, revolutionary, social fraternity wherein extreme egalitarianism finds expression in communism. The meaning of the Nation changes: it no longer means all the citizens in opposition to the monarch and the privileged, but the idea of a historical belonging centered on the state. At the extreme, through the mythification of language, culture, and national traditions, it will become the French version of nationalism, the idea of a moral and cultural community founded on institutional traditions. Opposed to it, on the contrary, the notion of the people drifts toward the general idea of the proletariat as the people's people, the depository of its authority and its veritable communitarian aspirations. We see this ambivalence clearly in Michelet and above all in Hugo (*Les misérables*).

What happens symmetrically on the bottom half of the triangle (Liberty, Equality, Property)? There too a scission is at work, which turns around questions like the right to existence and the right to work. It could be said that there tend to be two ways of justifying the rights of the citizen with reference to property, and thus of thinking the individual as bearer of the values of freedom-equality: either by the property of labor (and especially the appropriation of oneself, of the means of existence, by labor), or by property as capital (whether it is a matter of money capital or symbolic capital, for instance entrepreneurial ability, know-how, etc.). On the ideological level, these notions are astonishingly ambiguous (as we saw a moment ago with "the people"). The capitalist is defined as a worker, as an entrepreneur; the worker as the bearer of a capacity, as human capital. The notion of property can be formally conserved in both cases, just as it appears to be common to ideologies of individualist liberalism and collectivist socialism, which formally agree in saying that what is socially decisive is property, the "commerce" of owners.

We also see that these two manifest contradictions in some sense fused politically very early. From 1789 to 1793, what was dominant was the question of the community of citizens, the problem of fraternity evoked in the complete statement of the Montagnard formula, which, once it was cut down to acceptable proportions, would become the republican motto: Unity, Indivisibility of the Republic, Liberty, Equality, Fraternity, or Death. From 1789 to 1795, and up to the Napoleonic Code, the other contradiction developed, resulting in the symbolic scission between bourgeois owners and egalitarian communists. Throughout the nineteenth century, what I have called the general ideological form of class struggle would develop: not simply the opposition between individual and collective property, labor and capital, but the addition of the two contradictions. The bourgeois camp is both, from an ideological point of view, to say nothing of material interests, one form of property against another and one form of community against another.[22] It is liberalism plus nationalism. And in the same way the proletarian camp is a form of property or appropriation—collective, social, or planned appropriation—plus a form of community: precisely communism, which inherits the revolutionary crowds' ideal of fraternity, and the idea that the only citizens in the proper sense are the men of the people, the workers.[23]

CAN WE LEAVE IT there? I do not believe so. And this is one of the reasons for what I have called the relative inadequacy of the idea of revolution at the end of the twentieth century, which goes back to its very origins. The contradictions we have just been discussing are manifest contradictions that have been made explicit for two centuries in the discourses that make up modern, postrevolutionary politics. This is to say that they are perfectly formulated in the language of freedom and equality, or if one likes, in the language of oppression and injustice. But today another type of contradiction or division is increasingly being noted, a division that is very difficult to formulate in this language (or that always bears an irreducible remainder to any formulation in terms of oppression or injustice). At least we have become more conscious of its existence. A sign of the times? Perhaps.

I believe that there are fundamentally two of them—which those of us who were engaged in politics in what used to be called the "revolutionary party" encountered as insurmountable obstacles to the formation of a community of free individuals struggling together against social inequalities. These contradictions or divisions of a completely different type, generally repressed out of political consciousness and discourse or mentioned only with shame, put in question the very notion of the individual, the model of individuality or, if one likes, "human nature," that is, the very possibility of presenting the individual in general as an example of the human race.[24] They are the division of the sexes (not only as a division of social roles, but more profoundly as absolute difference, the duality of man and woman that divides the human species, and with it any community, into two dissymmetrical halves without a mediating term) and the division between body and mind (this Platonic opposition of two sides of individuality, which Spinoza, to the contrary, tried to think as identical, and which is found from one end of the social field to the other as the division between manual and intellectual labor, technique and reflection, execution and knowledge, sport and art or culture, etc.).

No doubt it is a matter of inequalities, or more exactly of the foundations constantly invoked in order to institute inequality, and by the same stroke to limit or annul the freedom of an entire class of humanity. And yet behind these inequalities there is a kind of difference that cannot be overcome by the institution of equality, which does not mean that here too equality is not the formal condition of liberation, but that it remains purely external. And this difference itself is, in both cases, extraordinarily equivocal, combining a biological aspect with a historical aspect, a double articulation of individuality with the body and with language, a real aspect and an imaginary aspect. These are differences par excellence that announce the reality of the imaginary in human experience, and in this respect pose the question of the internal limits of politics, or of a transformation of politics that includes not only man the citizen, but man the subject of fantasies or desires.

Here, it seems, there is no political solution purely in terms of equaliberty, even if this is a necessary condition for the recognition of rights: neither the separation of groups nor their fusion. (The myth of the total man, manual and intellectual, is worth about as much as that of the androgyne—and, moreover, they are related.) These are repressed contradictions that haunt modern politics. In this sense, even if they are constantly presented as external to it, they are constantly present in the hollow of its discursive, legislative, organizational, and repressive practices. Perhaps we can date the beginning of their real enunciation only from today, to the extent that the inadequacy of specialized discourses on the family, education, and professional training is now becoming manifest.

Perhaps it is only now that we can ask about the mutation of politics that would be implied by the recognition, itself political, of sexual difference and cultural or intellectual difference, in their very difference—that is, an effective extension of the right to politics to women and to manual workers and other "uncultured" or "uneducated" people, abolishing the de facto necessity whereby they find themselves represented by others, or led by others in the political sphere. And yet these political differences have been constitutive of the political institution, as the sphere of government or the polity, from its origin, and they have been explicitly placed in question since the French Revolution, be it in the form of women's claims to citizenship or the apparently contradictory forms of rights claims to education and challenges to the power of intellectuals, spokesmen, and technicians. The two centuries that have elapsed since 1789 then appear to us at once as the age of the suppression of difference (to the home, to the school) and its irresistible expression.

What these two differences have in common negatively is that they are other than inequality, even if they are always already inscribed in a relation of power. More precisely, they are inscribed in a relation of collective inequality (men and women, elites and masses) that is reproduced, exercised, and borne out as a personal, singular relation, individual to individual, whereas modern society has formally abolished all dependence of one man on another. This is why they always appear backward with respect to the notion of an inequality of rights and status: short of or beyond the social, in the contingency of individualities or the necessity of transindividual destinies. What they have in common positively is that they have to seek their liberation as a right to equality in difference, that is, not as the restoration of an original identity or the neutralization of differences in the equality of rights, but as the production of an equality without precedents or models that would be difference itself, the complementarity and reciprocity of singularities. In a sense such a reciprocity is already virtually included in the proposition of equaliberty, but—paradoxically—it can only claim to be inspired by it on the condition of reopening the question of the identity of man and citizen, not in order to regress toward the idea of citizenship subordinated to anthropological differences (as in the ancient idea of citizenship), but in order to progress toward a citizenship overdetermined by anthropological difference, explicitly directed toward its transformation, distinct from both an institutional naturalization and a denial or formal neutralization (which in fact functions as a permanent means of its naturalization).

For all that, these two differences are not similar. The power they institute (and that appears as the universal expression of a transindividual force or power) does not subject the same individuals, or rather the same "classes" of individuals, and above all it does not subject them by the same means, even though it constantly operates additively.[25]

Thus, it could be shown that a monopolization of knowledge (or masculinization of knowledge, the institution of specifically "male" knowledges) is always present in the inequality of the sexes, to the extent that it concerns not only private, domestic behavior but also public behavior (or rests on a political constraint that makes it return to the private domain), and more fundamentally because it is inscribed in the everyday violence of a voice that dominates bodies. Equally, it could be shown—though with more difficulty, either because the mechanism is more deeply repressed or because in our contemporary technological societies the speech of the uneducated is harder to hear than that of women—that the political monopoly of instruction, expertise, and meritocracy always presupposes an implicit model of masculine domination in very ambiguous forms: the repression of "women's issues" outside the field of recognized intellectual disciplines, and above all the compensation for the "intellectual" power that some men exercise over others with the "corporal" power that these intellectually dominated men exercise over "their" women. But all this does not change the fact that in the last analysis the difference that forms the basis of these powers cannot be reduced to a single model.

With sexual difference we are dealing, as it were, with a supplement of singularity that prevents the same content from being attributed to the freedom of men and the freedom of women, and consequently either of them being reduced to the model of a common subjectivity. We can desire, as a condition of their freedom, that women should have equal rights, equal access to knowledge, the professions, and public responsibilities (which supposes a more or less profound transformation of the conditions in which they are exercised). We cannot think that they will then act as generic individuals. Equality here is not the neutralization of differences (equalization), but the condition and necessity of the diversification of freedoms.

On the contrary, in the inequality of knowledge, which is at once the differential reproduction of a mass and an elite, the use of educational institutions to compartmentalize and hierarchize social activities, and the legitimation of the "intellectual" way of life (even if only purely formally, outside the acquisition of any real knowledge) as a disposition and predisposition for authority to the detriment of the "manual" way of life, we are instead dealing with a subtraction of singularity. If we want to admit (here again, with a philosopher like Spinoza) that individuality is a function of communication, and that communication develops most not between predetermined social types or roles but between singularities, between practical experiences, each of which can learn something from and teach something to others, we must recognize that, paradoxically, the expansion of knowledge as a support of power is de-individualizing. The universality of the function of knowledge in modern societies, the positive condition for the constitution of a common language of politics (and also its secularization), is paid for by a restriction of the real possibilities for communication—the institutional form of which is precisely the specialized monopoly of communications. From this perspective, it is inequality that creates practically irreducible difference, but struggles against inequality can lead neither to the annulling of differences nor to their democratic reproduction in the form of a generalized selection of individuals. For greater freedom to develop, both for individuals and for communication itself, it would be necessary to institute at the same time a neutralization *and* a redistribution of knowledge, an equivalence of experts and the uneducated with regard to the right to expression in public space *and* a symbolic dissociation of the institutional equivalence between intelligence and knowledge. Truth be told, this egalitarian requirement has always been the aporia of the political utopias of intellectual emancipation.[26]

This asymmetry between sexual difference and intellectual difference is inscribed within the relations among the key institutions of modern politics as concrete politics, namely, the family and the school. This allows us to understand why, if the family (a constitutively inegalitarian institution) plays a weak, "private" role in the neutralization of intellectual differences as a source of power between parents, the school (a formally egalitarian institution) plays a comparatively large, public role in the liberation of women, albeit at the price of constantly tending to neutralize sexed subjectivity. The counterpart of this role is, obviously, the incomparably greater difficulty of relaxing the hold of male power for uneducated rather than educated women—despite the possibilities at times offered by work, unionism, and even organized politics.[27]

From these considerations I will draw the following hypothesis about the inscription of anthropological differences in the topography of equaliberty. No doubt one can maintain that sexual difference as well as intellectual difference is a function of community, whose conflictual character virtually contains the principle of the rupture of its unity, which at its limits manifests its "impossibility." And this contradiction reproduces itself in a circle. Is it because communication between men and women, or between intellectuals and manual workers, is in a sense impossible, that it must be imposed by an increase of communitarian organicity—a social division of roles, tasks, and honors that necessarily takes the form of inequality or power? Or is it because organic, identitarian community (society, the state, the nation, a class) confines equality within strict limits within which gender inequality and intellectual power can subsist or are even given free reign so that communication between singularities proves to be at the limit impossible? Here too, however, the analogy covers a dissymmetry. In effect one can, it seems to me, maintain that sexual difference has a privileged relation with respect to the institution of the community, whereas intellectual difference takes all its critical significance for politics from its relation to the institution of property.

Once all human individuals are deemed citizens, free and equal in rights, and virtually demand the effectiveness of those rights, the division of sexual roles directly becomes necessary in order for society to be able to represent itself as a community (and not as a juxtaposition of unconnected individuals).[28] One can certainly posit that every historical community, an institution that is at once both real and imaginary, rests on the relation between sexes (that is, on kinship, the division between male and female tasks and roles, the determination of the symbolic character of each as a repression of bisexuality). But the modern political community, not only because it is a state but because it is a state whose juridical structure is founded on the proposition of equaliberty, is never, as such, a sexed community. What underlies it, as a national community, is therefore not the simple relation of the sexes (except metaphorically, it is not an extended family), but practical and ideological sexism as a structure of the internal exclusion of women, generalized to the whole society.[29] It is thus the unstable equilibrium of the denial and the universalization of sexual difference. Thus, the affirmation of this as political power becomes the most sensitive point of the crisis of the community (or the communal identity crisis).

On the other side, intellectual difference maintains a privileged relation with property as a social mediation. It could be shown that the concept of an intellectual capacity (in the broad sense, including knowledge and will) has always been included in the representation of a human appropriation of things, precisely as (ontological) difference between a human personality and a body, which is itself only a thing. Its trace could be found *a contrario* in the constant legislation that identifies intellectual tutelage or derangement with an incapacity to possess. To possess things one must, in effect, first of all possess oneself, and this possession is nothing other than the generic concept of intelligence. Yet, when, in opposition to community, property—individual or collective—becomes the mediation of equality and freedom, the guarantee of individual humanity and the condition of citizenship, the meaning of capacity and incapacity changes. Here again, it leaves the purely private sphere and acquires a public value. All property is inscribed in the codes and equivalences formalized by the knowledge of political economy; every individual is a proprietor (and measured by his or her property) insofar as he knows the theoretical and practical science of exchanging values, or is (re)cognized by it (that is, is himself or herself inscribed in its account books). Individuals or classes relate to their being or having only through the intermediary of this abstract knowledge, which becomes increasingly autonomous and intellectual even as it becomes increasingly material. This process of the autonomization, intellectualization, and materialization of knowledge determines the exercise of property rights, and therefore of individuality, more and more directly. But at the same time it renders the identity of the proprietors, the identity of the subject of property, more and more uncertain.

This process intersects with class struggle. We know that the more capital is concentrated, the more (real or supposed) technical competence becomes the condition of its appropriation at the expense of principles like inheritance and personal activity. We can also ask ourselves if this evolution does not correspond to a complete reversal of people's property in things into property in people (and citizens) by the signs of value in motion (that is, money or its accumulation)—a description that is even more relevant for the capitalist than for the salaried employee. Correlatively, we know that the result of the exploitation of the salaried workforce is increasingly the impersonalization of the worker as part of a de-intellectualized mass, and that its condition is the accumulation of the intellectual power of production and exchange outside the activity of individual workers (today, in the self-reproducing ensemble of computer hardware and software).[30] In the deepest layer of his analysis of the property relation as a relation of exploitation, Marx precisely identified this scission between the intellectual and the manual as the point at which exploitation and domination (or alienation) fuse. For the worker whose work (and consequently whose training) is totally de-intellectualized, self-ownership or labor power has become a total fiction. But we must no doubt go one step further and designate the autonomization of knowledge beyond individual intelligence (and thus beyond the figure of the intellectual) as the opening of a potential crisis of any possibility for the individual or the collective to be represented as the proprietor of something or of itself. Then we are no longer dealing only with a mechanism for the division of human nature that practically contradicts the requirement of freedom and equality (and which one can endeavor more or less easily to confine beneath politics, in the economic, the social, and the cultural, all the while exploiting it to perpetuate the monopolies of political representation). Here what we have is a dissolution of the political individual. The rights of the citizen are deprived of their substance insofar as they must be exercised by proprietors, while the question of equality and freedom is led back to its original formulation, without a preestablished answer: Which men are citizens?

Thus, we can suggest that a second configuration, coming slowly to light, can be deduced from the first one, and that it is like its underside or the return of its repressed:

Men // Women
(masculine // feminine)

* *

*

$$E\ =\ L$$

*

* *

(intellectual // manual)
Experts // Uneducated

Instead of having the mediations for the institution of equaliberty and its ideological foundation, this topography has points of uncertainty for the preceding mediations and foundations, which are at the same time the points where anthropological difference causes modern individual or communal identity to vacillate. At these points, precisely the demand for equality and freedom (or equaliberty) is greatest, but the concrete forms (whether juridical or practical) for satisfying it are today the most aporetic. They are thus, par excellence, the sensitive points for remaking politics.

In situating these points in relation to the universal truth contained in the statement of the *Declaration* of 1789, we have thus finished setting out the historical and ideological dialectic of equaliberty, which opens onto not an end of history but a question posed in and by history in view of its continuation. This dialectic has allowed us to successively set out:

- the inherent alternative of revolutionary politics (not violence and law, but insurrection and constitution—or, if one likes, to speak with Lenin, the state and the nonstate);
- the post-revolutionary contradiction between the formal institution of freedom and equality and their realization in the

forms of property and community, whose most general form is class struggle (socialism against liberalism, communism against nationalism);

- finally, the anthropological differences that are returning to the political field and thereby producing its current uncertainty: the uncertainty of its language, its subjects, and its objectives.

We could also say that this dialectic allows us to set out successively three ages of politics: an ancient period, in which the concept of the city is subordinated to anthropological differences, to the unequal status of the free man and the slave, the sovereign and the subject, majority and tutelary humanity; a modern period, in which the concepts of man and citizen are virtually identified, opening the right to politics to all humans; and finally a postmodern period, in which the question is posed of going beyond the abstract or generic concept of man on the basis of generalized citizenship. Let us note here, however, that if these ages succeed or engender one another, they do not supplant one another like the scenes of a play. For us, and consequently in our relation to the political question, they are all still present in a disunified totality, a non-contemporaneity that is the very structure of the current moment—which means that we are dealing simultaneously with the state, class struggle, and anthropological difference. Our task is to construct practical conduct on all these levels at once, without being able to synthesize them. Yet this does mean that we are completely deprived of guiding threads. At the hinge between ancient and modern politics, we have the de jure fact implied by the revolutionary rupture: the proposition of equaliberty and its effect of universal truth. At the hinge between modern politics and the politics that is in the course of being born within and against it, we have a problematic of remaking: How do we move from universal truth to singular truth, that is, how do we inscribe the program and the name of equaliberty within singularities? From the fact to the problem there is not a continuity, a simple progression, still less a deduction, but there is necessarily a connection, since without the fact the problem could not even be posed.

THE REVERSAL OF POSSESSIVE INDIVIDUALISM

This essay arises from two conflicting intentions. One is to reexamine the idea of possessive individualism by restoring it to its original context, but also by submitting it to the test of an eidetic variation whose privileged figure is reversal. The other is to discuss the expression "negative individualism" or "negative individuality," proposed by Robert Castel in his *Metamorphoses of the Social Question* and some more recent interventions within the framework of his analysis of the effects of the crisis of wage-earning society and the process of disaffiliation it brings about.[1]

1. MACPHERSON AND "POSSESSIVE INDIVIDUALISM"

I cannot say if the expression "possessive individualism" was Crawford Brough Macpherson's invention. What is sure is that since he made the idea central to *The Political Theory of Possessive Individualism* (1962), it has had an extraordinary fate.[2] It is especially remarkable that it could be claimed at once by authors who see in it a summary of the negative traits of the present that must be criticized (the absolute reign of utilitarian values, the logic of profit and commodification, etc.) and by others who recognize in it a positive definition of the anthropological presuppositions that seem to them the necessary basis of social and political theory, such as Robert Nozick.

I recall that the term "individualism" was invented at the beginning of the nineteenth century, and that it served to translate notions like egotism, the English "self-love" or "selfishness" (in German, *Eigenliebe, Selbstsucht*), from a moral into an analytical register.[3] The question of whether all individualism is a consequence of the logic of appropriation, and whether, conversely, private property is the determining factor in the isolation and primacy of individuality, can be displaced onto other terrains. One will ask whether possessive individualism represents, within certain historical or cultural conditions, a principle of organization for society as a whole, if necessary with recourse to the great binary oppositions of the sociological tradition—*Gemeinschaft* and *Gesellschaft*, status and contract, solidarity of resemblance and differential solidarity, hierarchy and equality—or even if it characterizes a determinate domain of human behavior that can be more or less hegemonic or autonomous, but can never incorporate all behaviors, be it in the economic domain, around the notions of the generalized market and the autonomy of *homo economicus ratiocinator*, or in the juridical domain, deployed around the central category of subjective right.

Macpherson's theoretical material, we know, is made up of a corpus belonging to the period of the English Revolutions: Hobbes, the Levelers, considered as a collective across their tracts, Harrington, and Locke. It is a matter of extracting their common axiomatic and thereby showing that an *episteme* of the property-owning individual underlies the most contrary projects for founding political obligation in the inaugural crisis of modernity. Particularly important in this regard is the demonstration of the fact that the Levelers' democratism rests on the same foundation as the positions of their republican and constitutionalist adversaries: the individual's free disposal over his capacities as the basis for participation in the political collectivity, and the demonstration of the internal coherence of Locke's doctrine, which begins by founding the right to property on personal labor and ends up justifying capitalist accumulation.

At the end of the work, Macpherson puts forward an axiomatic of possessive individualism in seven propositions—what in another language could be called the metaphysics of classical liberal politics:[4]

1 What makes a man human is freedom from the will of others.
2 Emancipation means that the individual is free from all relations with the other except those into which he voluntarily enters with a view to realizing his own interest.
3 The individual is essentially the proprietor of his own person and faculties, for which he owes nothing to society.
4 Although the individual cannot alienate his property in his own person as a whole, he can alienate his labor power.
5 Human society consists in an ensemble of market relations.
6 Since freedom from the wills of others is what makes a man human, each individual's freedom can be legitimately limited only by the obligations and rules that are necessary to guarantee others the same freedom.
7 Political society is a constraint instituted to protect the individual in his person and his goods, and therefore to maintain the orderly relations of exchange among individuals regarded as proprietors of themselves.

These axioms were enunciated especially clearly by Hobbes. But it is with Locke that we find the full development of their consequences, particularly with regard to the reduction of the apparent contradiction constituted by the emergence of class differences in a society based on the generalized market and the equation of freedom and property in oneself. In order to test the originality and solidity of Macpherson's conception, we can proceed in different directions, external and internal.

After having been much invoked outside circles influenced by the Marxist doctrine of which it was considered to be a particularly representative product in the 1960s, Macpherson's theory was vigorously questioned, first of all from the perspective of its historical relevance. The most interesting of these criticisms came from the Anglo-American current of neorepublican historiography, whose most famous representative is J. G. A. Pocock.[5] He explained that the "property" that the classic authors made the foundation or even the substance of individual freedom, as the right to participate in the polity, was not property in movable goods circulating in the market, but traditional, landed or patrimonial property, which assures its master personal independence in the city, and thus a political status. This property is in a certain way inseparable from the person of the master, to whom it confers an authority or a specific quality expressed in the immediately evident play of words on *property* and *propriety*. One can respond to these criticisms, which are based on immense erudition and extremely close reading, in various ways. One can emphasize, as has, for example, Antonio Negri, that Pocock, who wanted to be more rigorously contextualist than Macpherson, paradoxically emphasizes the archaic elements of the classic authors' thought and language in such a way as to demonstrate the existence of a republican tradition that the development of capitalism would have left practically unchanged. One can also, as Macpherson no doubt would do himself, suggest that an axiomatic method, provided that it is applied with sufficient rigor, is the only way to grasp the articulation of profoundly enigmatic concepts like "property in oneself" with the differentials of historical tendencies and countertendencies. From this we are led to summarily evoke a second type of confrontation.

It has to do with the relation of Macpherson's conceptualization to other attempts to stylize what belongs to individualism, which is readily taken to be the defining trait of the modern period, in opposition to the "dependence" or non-separability that characterized ancient man, be it to the tribe, the city, or the feudal estate. Here I mention only one alternative by referring to Weber's thesis in the *Protestant Ethic*, which to my knowledge Macpherson refers to only once in passing, in order to recuse himself from the debate over the origins of capitalism while admitting the connection between Weber's model of social relations and his own.[6] Upon reflection, however, it seems that the divergence is very deep and of such a kind as to place the notion of possessive individualism at a veritable crossroads. What Macpherson considers central, we have seen, are the repercussions of the commercial principle of the alienability of goods for the person itself, or the constitution of the subject in the movement of appropriation. Accumulation clearly serves appropriation, on which is founded a new type of state power, or contractual political obligation. But the Weberian coupling of forward-looking economic rationality (which ultimately implies at least a formal separation of business property and personal property, and a very strong tension between their respective principles) and worldly asceticism (which completely replaces the ethics of self-control) seems to aim in a diametrically opposed direction. Here it is Weber who is closer to Marx, who in *Capital* places in the very mouth of the personification of capital the injunction: "Accumulate! Accumulate! This is the law and the Prophets!"[7]

Accumulation for its own sake, the constant risk and putting back into play of property—this is the heart of the capitalist ethos and its own asceticism. It is not certain that such a principle posits the subject of property, or the proprietary subject; it could, on the contrary, depose it, even disappropriate it, and we then enter already into the logical space of negations. Or, if one prefers, the subjectivation proper to capitalism is not that which aims at the appropriation of oneself but at the appropriation of the world, with the disproportion and perhaps the antinomy this objective implies. No one could be less proprietor of himself, then, than the Weberian individual. But let us leave this discussion suspended and return to Macpherson.

The most important comparison for our purposes is in reality that we can make with the author's other works, in which he explicitly tried to characterize the forms of the contemporary crisis of possessive individualism that resulted from the application of its principles to their last consequences, and thereby defined the theoretical framework in which this notion assumes its meaning. I refer here to his book *Democratic Theory* (1973), partly a discussion with Rawls, Nozick, Isaiah Berlin, and Milton Friedman, in which he defines the project of a political theory of property, for which the characterization of possessive individualism would be only a point of departure.[8] Here Pocock's objection is inverted, except that it does not have to do with the same concept of politics: it is not the *politeia* or belonging to the polity, but the articulation of rights and powers within society. Macpherson now defines property in general (as a concept and an institution) as "a man-made device which establishes certain relations between people," that is, a power relation whose field of exercise is access to the means of work (rather than the means of production). He sees the history of property tending to lead from classical right, defined as the right to exclude others from the use or profit (benefit) of certain things, to a juridical principle that emerges progressively in contemporary society: "Property is increasingly being seen again as a right to revenue . . . and for most people this must now be a right to earn an income, which is a right of access to the means of labour" by reason of the revenue it brings. This principle is called "democratic," and its logic leads to the recognition "that individual property must increasingly consist in the individual right not to be excluded from access to the means of labour, now mainly corporately or socially owned: so that a democratic society must broaden the concept again from property as an individual right to exclude others, by adding property as an individual right not to be excluded by others."[9]

An individual right to exclude others has become an individual right not to be excluded by others, both socially instituted and historically conditioned. Both are the object of a public guarantee, and consequently of a system of individual obligations and an organization of state powers. ("The state *creates* the rights, the individuals *have* the rights."[10]) Each form of property, consequently, in a certain relation with a type of state, is individualizing, but some in the modality of exclusion, others in the modality of inclusion. The first would have the function of inciting work, putting men to work.[11] The second leads to the idea of participation in the control of the use of accumulated capital and a right to the appropriation of what Macpherson calls "a kind of society," the set of immaterial things that is the "enjoyment of the quality of life."[12]

What is political here is perhaps less the intrinsic tenor of the general definition of property than the very idea of antagonism between the two forms of property that are marked out, even if the second is initially presented as an addition or expansion of the first. For they outline a radical alternative for the organization of society and power. "Social property" would in a certain way be a tautology, since all property is a social relation of individuation, but it is their differentiation that is political, or which is the political. Despite this, we see that Macpherson is not a Marxist, whatever might have been believed and said.[13] He does not propose to derive the structures of power from the organization of property or the social relations of material appropriation and exchange. What is important for him is not showing that political obligation serves market constraints so much as that it has the structure of a market, especially insofar as the subjects its implies are free individuals, defined by their property in themselves, who exchange a greater or lesser proportion of subjective right against objective security.

But the question of possessive individualism may, at the end of the day, be more complicated than simplified by being put in this perspective. Why? Not only because Macpherson is brought to write, "Property can and should become *again* a right to life and liberty," suggesting a political project of returning to the emancipatory sources of liberalism, but because the expression now goes on to oscillate between a broad and a narrow sense.[14] In the broad sense, it is the formal definition of property that includes all its historical forms, or at least the modern ones. From this perspective, with the right not to be excluded we are more than ever within an individuality based on property. The narrow sense is the exclusive adaptation of the individual to the logic of the market, whose axioms we have enumerated. At the heart of the difficulty is the functioning of the category of "property in oneself," its univocal or equivocal, variable or invariant character. For it turns out that this category is itself the source of a major difficulty with how Macpherson proposes to read the theorists of the classical age.

2. RETURN TO LOCKE: INDIVIDUAL, COMMUNITY, "PROPERTY IN ONESELF"

It is not very difficult to detect in the systematization of possessive individualism, around a common model, a series of difficulties or "forcings," the most important of which consists in reading propositions that belong to certain authors as generic. The most serious concerns the relationship between Hobbes and Locke. While in Hobbes the postulates of possessive individualism are immediately enunciated with maximal clarity and rigor, forming a system that allows the "body politick" to be represented as an association of individuals, each of whom pursues only his own interest, so that moral obligations are deduced exclusively from the competitive relations between individual powers, Macpherson also attributes to him the thesis or postulate of "individual property in oneself," implying that it could be alienated. We see that this is necessary to immanently secure the model, but one would have trouble finding this formulated by Hobbes. In fact, there are essential reasons why Hobbes would be absolutely opposed to "property in oneself": it immediately implies the possibility of the individual's withdrawal beneath the conflict of the two gods who fight for his membership or adhesion, temporal or spiritual. This pluralism of belongings and authorities on which each individual could play as he likes is exactly what Hobbes wanted to prevent. The Hobbesian is "free" to associate or not, that is, to live in security or insecurity, but this association must be unique. This is the explicit doctrine of *Leviathan*.

Shall we then conclude that, from the beginning, the notion stumbles on its central characteristic's lack of universality? I would rather admit that possessive individualism, though perfectly real, nevertheless only possessed unity around a conflict, an initial scission. There is not one possessive individualism; there tended to be two, but these two were from the beginning symmetrical, opposing each other term for term around a central divergence from which everything else follows. Let us say that it is a question of life and death, or equality in life and equality in death, which leads to the division of the notion of competition depending on whether it refers to the forms of war or those of exchange and the lawsuit. But no doubt things would be clearer still in negative form: no one can be expropriated from himself or herself. The limit of the political is therefore a resistance of the self to exclusion beyond its properties and outside the social world in which it makes them multiply, by a natural *conatus*. But in Locke's case this limit is a fullness (which will subsequently develop as the assertive natural rights of man, which are the rights to life a republican constitution makes into mutually guaranteed rights of citizenship, and which function as an internal limitation on power), whereas in Hobbes's case it is a potential void (a purely negative notion, arising from the thesis that every individual can resist in death, by putting his life at stake, a power he finds arbitrary—a thesis which adjoins in a frightening way the idea of an equality among individuals that resides solely in the capacity of each to threaten the others' lives, and consequently in the idea of a violent state of nature, repressed by the state but constantly underlying its authority).

If this opposition is meaningful, the notion of possessive individualism can be taken up in a constitutive dialectic. Its first moment doubtless consists in arranging the relations between *power, property,* and *proprietorship.* There is no doubt that the classic theories of possessive individualism always articulate a concept of power and a concept of property or appropriation. But it is no less clear that they do so in opposite senses, either by recognizing property as power or the power of property. If Hobbesian civil society has at least analogically the configuration of a competitive market, it is in the sense of a market in power, with property, as control over economic wealth, constituting only one of the ways of acquiring power. This is why, moreover, Hobbes has no need for long meditations to deduce the need for juridical constraint and omnipotent state regulation from the equal natural liberty of individuals. For power is by definition a surplus of power, a power to bend others to my will, for which the things I possess (wealth, office, skills) are so many means. The

Lockean model seems to me the opposite, and this is why it is favored by the theorists of *homo economicus*, even if at root it too is purely political. Property is not a component of power; power derives from property, and takes from its own socializing power the characteristics we are in the habit of calling liberal (the balance of powers, representation and majority rule)—in other words, the self-limitation of the political, which expresses the need to leave property free, or "preserve" it.

The question that then arises is whether in Locke the one who is fundamentally "free," or who distributes powers, is property or the proprietor. It seems to me that it is property, insofar as it constitutes the generic essence of the proprietor, his internal capacity to act that Locke himself calls his "life," and that in a moment we will rename his work.[15] Or, better, let us say that on this point Locke has to oscillate between two ways of understanding his own founding equation, whose terms come from what was already a long tradition: "Liberty and Property," being both other names for Life.[16] We can understand property as a precondition of freedom, and in that sense only the proprietor is independent, and thus virtually a citizen, which leads to measuring all political rights—eventually in order to limit them—by successive extensions of the property right as constituted property, already given within institutions or representations. But property can also be understood as the exercise of freedom, so that the free man (including the free man in the city, the citizen) is necessarily in some way a proprietor. It is then necessary to have in view a constituent property, not calibrated by preexisting institutions, that is individuality itself. It is from this perspective that one can say that property is free and not the proprietor, but only by showing how the individual (what we will then call the subject) can identify himself with this property that he *is*, or recognize his identity in his movement of appropriation and acquisition.[17]

One can attempt to derive two fundamental characteristics of Lockean individualism from this constituent figure of property: one that, already thinking in terms of a comparison with the problematic of Robert Castel, I will call a radical opposition between property and affiliation; and another that concerns the speculative paradoxes of "property in oneself."

On *affiliation*, let us recall that the *First Treatise* (written against Robert Filmer's *Patriarcha*) effects a systematic deconstruction of the confusions between the notions of political power, property, and paternal power or authority, which feed the justifications of absolutism. The most fundamental dilemma opposes an articulation of political power and property to an articulation of political power with paternity and filiation. In fact, by means of constituent property Locke achieves a veritable theoretical disaffiliation of power. It is not without practical consequences. No interference of familial (or genealogical) institutions with the operation of civil society can be legitimate, or only when it comes to technical conventions for assuring the transition of executive power. Here in particular it is important to distinguish this property that will return to the self in the form of work from the idea of patrimony, which is partly connected to the patriarchate. The individual proprietor-citizen is not an inheritor; his model is that of a divine work (Tully's thesis)—precisely God the maker and not God the Father.[18] Locke worked consistently to undo a certain conception of the relations between property and membership in order to define another in which the model for belonging is entirely removed from the genealogical order.

We will not therefore say that the individualism we are dealing with here is a negation of the idea of the community. But we will insist that we have the germ of a fundamental distinction between two types of community, whose interdependence or mixture will from this point forward be very difficult to think. Contract, representation, property, and freedom on one side, descent, inheritance, even tradition on the other, are henceforth of heterogeneous orders. Perhaps it is, moreover, this disjunction that specifically deserves to be called utopian.

The Lockean individual thus authorizes no one but himself, that is, his labor and his work, the power of appropriation of which he is the bearer. Let us try to draw out the paradoxes that result from such a situation, but that produce precisely the dynamism of the notion of property in oneself. Its difficulty comes not so much from a confusion of register between persons and things (as Kant will say, but also Marx) as from a difficult articulation between the available and the unavailable, the alienable and inalienable, which seems to affect the signification of freedom itself. In a sense this difficulty is nothing other than the unity of opposites that founds the modern subject, and there will be philosophers to theorize it. But the fact that Locke claims to draw political conclusions from it prevents him from retreating into the transcendental space of the pure condition of possibility of actions and responsibilities (like the Fichtean distinction between the "I" and the "Not-I"). The individual must be practically involved in his actions and in this sense alienate himself from them while remaining unaltered, and such a disposition seems very hard to understand—at least that it does not form the substance of the normative propositions on the responsibility of the subject that Locke has lodged at the heart of his conception of labor, the ultimate objective of which is to show how the field of freedom is constituted on the basis of the activity of reasonable individuals, including their interrelations in exchange and their representation within the state.

We are therefore not forbidden from reading the canonical definition of "property in one's person" that characterizes "every Man" in terms of his "Lives, Liberties, and Estates," not as a simple enumeration of objects, but as the progression of legitimate appropriation, the movement of life that descends into things and assimilates them. Property in oneself, in this sense, is not a contradictory thesis that would reduce persons to the order of things. It is rather the point of contact between *propriety* and *property*, the proper and property, on the basis of which persons and things are separated in order to confront each other. Locke does not say persons possess themselves, but man, each man, possesses his own person, which means that he has exclusive disposal over it, just as he has exclusive disposal over his life, his liberty, and his goods, and at bottom these formulations amount to the same. The subject resides on both ends: he forms a cause as well as an effect; he is in interiority as he is in exteriority. The secret of the Lockean formula is to have brought together, absolutely irreversibly, a discourse on the liberation of the individual from all slavery (in the *Second Treatise* the chapter on slavery immediately precedes the chapter on property, and forms its exact negative) and a discourse on the power of appropriation (and thus of transformation, acquisition) of the personal labor of this same individual, in such a way that he can consciously identify with the property that constitutes his raison d'être or his condition of possibility.

At this point, however, the difficulty of articulating the alienable and the inalienable begins. To say, as Macpherson does, that here we have the general figure of wage labor as the buying and selling of labor power only names the difficulty, which consists in considering the same thing, or the same person, as simultaneously available and unavailable, separable and inseparable, empirical and transcendental. We know that Marx himself experienced serious hesitations on this point before applying the model of a source of energy that is periodically spent and regenerated to the use of labor power over a given period of time. It seems that Locke had a different schema in mind: that of a force or capacity that would be entirely within his actions insofar as they are appropriated to a productive goal. Labor is the process in which the subject, the *self* and the *own*, continually change places. What is one's own can be alienated if the self always remains self-same. And the self can remain identical if it always returns to itself on the basis of its alienation. This implies, on the one hand, that all actions of the body in labor are doubled in a representation in consciousness that appropriates them to the one who perceives these actions as his; and, on the other hand, that this body forms an inseparable, undivided whole that expresses a person's life in the continuity and the diversity of the actions of "his hands." It is on precisely this point that Marx, in *Capital*, will undertake to show that industrial wage labor is indeed a new kind of slavery, and by the same stroke to problematize, at least in the course of professional activity and sometimes beyond, the appropriation of the actions of the productive body by thought.

We better understand, then, the architectonic function played by the notion of "property in one's (own) person" in Locke, which contemporary analytical philosophers turn into "self-ownership."[19] It is in effect what allows us to escape the dilemma of natural sociability and the transcendence of the political community. The individual constructs himself in the activity (and actuality) of work, but in work he also constructs the condition of commerce, that is, a fundamental form of community in which reciprocity becomes durable, and a precondition for the existence of the individual. In Hobbes we have a theological-political representation of the existence of the state in terms of a limit-experience, on the basis of an always-possible reversal of peace into violence or civil war. In Locke we have instead a virtual deconstruction and reconstruction of the community, whose principle is the property of the individual. Through labor the individual takes from the common (mythically identified with an originary property conferred by God on humanity as a species) the goods necessary for his conservation, but by the exchange that is its necessary development, he puts his productions in common, constructing the temporal, historical community. On one side he privatizes nature, on the other he socializes humanity.

3. FIGURES OF REVERSAL: ROUSSEAU, MARX, DERRIDA

I now want to address the reversals of possessive individualism, which, however, do not radically modify the problematic as it is exhibited above all in the Lockean figure.[20] Is there not always, at the basis of reversals, a concept of the negation of the negation, since it is a matter of showing that the positivity of individual property is constructed on the denial of an absence, or of a violent destruction? Obviously it is not the same thing to take as one's critical target the lack of property, or its non-universalizable, even intrinsically discriminatory character, the pauperization that results from the law of appropriation, and to designate property as a lack of being, the inversion of being into having, the reification of freedom. But in each case, according to different perspectives, the vacillation of the subject, its return in the form of subjection, constitutes the deepest stake of the debate on the possibility of community to which possessive individualism tends.

In examining Rousseau, Marx, and Derrida, I obviously want to suggest a system of oppositions and affinities. We need these three cases to discover the logic of the subjection of the subject that is at work here. The historical succession is important: Marx would not have been possible without Rousseau, and Derrida would not have been possible without Rousseau and Marx. Nevertheless, what is important to me above all here is not the succession as such, and still less the idea that it would illustrate a historical tendency or a transformation in the spirit of the times; it is the structure of variation as such, which unfolds in time through the works that respond to it, and which, for us, are now synchronic. Heuristically, I will return from Marx's expression, "the expropriation of the expropriators," and its enigmatic repetition in the "ex-appropriation" forged by Derrida to what seems to me their common interlocutor, the Rousseau of "dispossession" or "depropriation."

ROUSSEAU

The meaning of Rousseau's political anthropology is notoriously hard to determine, at least if one is looking for something completely coherent. Without pretending to resolve this difficulty, I would like to suggest the following interpretive key: the status of the particular property that is established in the *Social Contract* does not put in question the vehement critique of property developed in the *Discourse on the Origins of Equality*.[21] To the contrary, it radicalizes it, so that the juridical institution of property by the state for the benefit of the citizens is in reality also a dispossession. Under these conditions, the Hobbes-inspired term Rousseau uses to designate the mechanism by which the general will is formed, "total alienation," should be taken literally. In the formation of the state and the juridical institution, man is forever deprived of the possibility of possessing himself, or of rediscovering his "own," in his property. He exists only as the mandatory of that universal part of himself that is fused with all the others to form what Rousseau calls a "common me."

Private property is thus only the modality by which the people instituted as a state can force each other to be free. It has an essentially *public* function—whence the total ambivalence of the Rousseauian conception, evident in his legacy, with regard to the alternative of individualism and collectivism: individualism is never anything but a manifestation of the fiction and collectivism a way of changing the status of the "third," the Us or the people—the nation, if you like—from symbolic to real, stripping it of its ideality in order to project it into the real. It will be objected that the formulation that figures in the very next chapter, seemingly to warrant the idea of an exchange between the individual and the state, results in establishing the legitimacy of what the individuals in reality have never given away, their particular goods: "Each member of the community gives himself to it. . . . Thereupon the possessors . . . have . . . so to speak acquired everything they have given."[22] I think, to the contrary, that these formulations irreparably establish dispossession at the heart of property, provided one draws all the consequences from Rousseau's conception of the relation between possession and enjoyment. We might say that, from the original moment of taking possession, man—not only he who has been excluded from possession but above all he who appropriates something as his by saying "this is *mine*"—runs after a lure: that of effectively enjoying what he possesses. In this sense, the political institution says to him: you will never enjoy it. It prescribes legitimate property as the renunciation of private enjoyment.

Rousseau's formulations here mirror Locke's (and the confrontation is all the more inevitable since, shortly before, he had himself referred, in the *Discourse on the Origins of Inequality* as in *Emile*, to the Lockean notion of legitimation through personal labor).[23] Whereas in Locke labor constitutes the individual as an owner of things and of himself, inasmuch as he ceaselessly takes from the common the share of natural objects with which he has mixed his labor or which he has assimilated to his way of life, in Rousseau it is the community that, in a certain way, never stops taking from labor what it produces in order to symbolically attribute it to the individual-become-citizen, that is, an indivisible part of the sovereign. Indeed, Rousseau never stopped thinking, as he explains the *Second Discourse*, that "the Earth belongs to no one" and that the gesture of exclusion and enclosure is the origin of all the inequalities of status and all the violence that form the procession of the development of civilization. But he also declares (in the *Discourse on Political Economy*) that "the right of property is the most sacred of all the rights of citizenship, and even more important in some respects than liberty itself; . . . the true foundation of civil society."[24] Applying what Jean Starobinski rightly called the "remedy in the disease," he redoubles the alienation in order to symbolically annul its effects.[25] What appropriation or possession had deprived individuals of, namely enjoyment, the institution of property deprives them of definitively, making it the fictive mark of the belonging to the *res publica*.

This thesis of the irremediable division between possession and enjoyment is no doubt most explicit when, in the *Discourses* or the *Confessions*, then again in the *Nouvelle Héloïse*, Rousseau speaks of the "possession" of the sexes by one another, for its consequence would be the novelesque or autobiographical interpretation of all circumstances in which it seems that imaginary satisfactions are, in truth, the only ones possible. But we have no reason to think that the passage from sexual possession to economic possession here is a matter of metaphor. To the contrary, we have all the evidence we could want in the *Discourse on the Origins of Inequality* for the fact that the violence engendered by the possession of the sexes is of the same kind, and has the same historical impact, as the violence engendered by taking possession of the land, and that the latter brings no more real satisfaction than the former. In both cases, being and appearance are irreparably divorced. On this interpretation of the juridical or juridical-political moment, of property as forcing the division between possession and enjoyment—not so much as going beyond their opposition as its reiteration in a perpetual flight forward—we better understand the price the institution of civil society pays when it comes to sexual difference: a radical asymmetry of position, since one (the man) is assigned to the sphere of property and citizenship, while the other (the woman) is assigned to that of love and humanity. If we want to concede that Rousseau is, among all the Enlightenment philosophers, the one who thought sexuality most rigorously as a "differend" or an ambivalence internal to the constitution of the human subject, we see that in the institution of social property it is the very division of the subject that is sanctioned.

Are such categories foreign to the Lockean conception? One is tempted to think that they are rather suppressed within it. In effect they take us to the flipside of "property in oneself," which articulates the individual and the community insofar as they defer the unity or reunion with oneself that forms its condition of possibility.[26] Rather than think that here we are beyond the field of variations virtually contained in the axiomatics of possessive individualism, I therefore prefer to expand it to include the possibility of negation or of negativity. From now on individuality assumes the figure of a depropriation whose effects can be seen in the fundamental dissatisfaction of the subject citizen, but also in the incompleteness of the body politic itself. Perhaps here it is necessary to grant the full importance to the fact that the theoretical works that bear witness to it are themselves fundamentally incomplete—a mark of their implication in the object they seek to think from the inside.

MARX

The first book of *Capital* "unfinishes" with a famous formula whose political power, philosophical and perhaps also theological resonance, explain the divergent interpretations it crystalizes:

> As soon as the capitalist mode of production stands on its own feet, the further socialization of labour and the further transformation of the soil and other means of production into socially exploited and therefore communal means of production takes on a new form. What is now to be expropriated is not the self-employed worker, but the capitalist who exploits a large number of workers. . . . The knell of capitalist private property sounds. The expropriators are expropriated.
>
> The capitalist mode of appropriation, which springs from the capitalist mode of production, produces capitalist private property. This is the first negation of individual private property, as founded on the labour of its proprietor. But capitalist production begets, with the inexorability of a natural process, its own negation. This is the negation of the negation. It does not reestablish private property, but it does indeed establish individual property on the basis of the achievements of the capitalist era.[27]

We might think that here we find ourselves before the most elaborated expression of possessive individualism, since it undertakes to demonstrate that collectivization or communism results from the self-destruction of private property itself, according to its own logic. Broadly speaking, this interpretation is of course correct: it is the very meaning of the recourse to the category of the negation of the negation. The expropriation of the expropriators is the process from which results the appropriation that had been negated by capitalism (if it is true that appropriation is to expropriation as affirmation is to negation, a position to a suppression).

The text, however, includes several indications that the theoretical situation is not so simple. One of them is the personification effected by Marx, who does not speak of a generic process of expropriation of expropriation, but writes: "Die Expropriateurs werden expropriiert."[28] Let us content ourselves here with the following hypothesis: just as the objects of expropriation, in the final analysis, are persons or human individualities, the subjects of appropriation that result must be considered as persons. Let us then return to the question posed by the final formula, which is as striking as it is enigmatic: "It does not reestablish private property [*Privateigentum*], but it does indeed establish individual property [*das individuelle Eigentum*] on the basis of the achievements of the capitalist era." This formulation can be taken as an index of the contradictory way Marx relates to the tradition of possessive individualism, especially in its Lockean variant. It is as if he had undertaken at the end of the day to reconstitute the idea of "property in oneself," founded on the reciprocal implication of the appropriation of the self and the appropriation of things, but for the benefit of a new subject, the social or generic subject, whose historical figure is that of the proletarian engaged in the revolutionary transformation of the mode of production. But it is at the price of a radical critique of an essential postulate of Locke's, which is the strictly personal character of the activity of labor, which refers both to the responsibility of self-consciousness and to the indivisibility of the living body of which it is the agent (which in Locke cannot be divided, or cannot be exchanged, in order to make the community of exchange possible). Arendt, in her own Lockean reading of Marx (in *The Human Condition*), no doubt did not pay sufficient attention to this point.

I have already evoked the negative part of this critique: Locke did not see that the capitalist organization of labor splits and distorts the integrity of the body. In the phenomenology proposed by *Capital*, it is not only a matter of disciplining the body, as Foucault would explain after Marx while proposing this be generalized beyond production to all social practices, but of dismemberment, which at the extreme obscures consciousness.[29] To which we must add the set of developments that, perhaps in a partly fantasmatic way, suggests that the logic of capitalism leads toward the absolute integration of the workers' reproduction into commercial production, by eliminating all forms of autonomy in workers' consumption and completely conditioning professional qualification as a function of the needs of the New Leviathan, what Marx called in the unpublished chapter of *Capital* "real subsumption," and which unquestionably returns in the general concept of what Foucault would call biopolitics.[30] Except that it is not the doing of the state but of capital itself—in other words, the property of work pushed to its ultimate limit. Here we have the negative side of the process, where a devouring socialization coincides with the annihilation of individual autonomy. Marx explicitly interprets this in terms that echo Locke and his economic descendants, such as Adam Smith:

> The laws of appropriation or of private property, [*Gesetz der Aneignung oder Gesetz des Privateigentums*] law based on the production and circulation of commodities, become changed into the direct opposite through their own internal and inexorable dialectic. . . . Originally the rights of property seemed to us to be grounded in a man's own labour [*Eigentumsrecht gegründet auf eigne Arbeit*]. Some such assumption was at least necessary, since only commodity-owners with equal rights confronted each other, and the sole means of appropriating the commodities of others was the alienation of a man's own commodities, commodities which, however, could only be produced by labour. Now, however, property turns out to be the rights, on the part of the capitalist, to appropriate the unpaid labour of others or its product, and the impossibility, on the part of the worker, of appropriating his own product [*Unmöglichkeit sein eignes Produkt anzueignen*]. The separation of property from labour thus becomes the necessary consequence of a law that apparently originated in their identity.[31]

But the dialectic Marx puts to work here leads immediately to uncovering the positive of this negative, which reside in the absolutely anti-Lockean proposition of the *transindividual* character of productive activity, and consequently of the appropriation that results from it. We must give this thesis its maximum force to understand the conclusions Marx wants to reach. Not only is labor socialized historically, so that it becomes transindividual. Essentially it always was, insofar as there is no labor without cooperation, even in the most primitive forms, and the isolation of the productive laborer in relation to nature was only ever an appearance. There is therefore no possibility that the individual's personal (isolated and exclusive) labor could appropriate any part of the common for him, and the right to property cannot be established on this basis, except as an ideological fiction. Conversely, as more modern, socialized production develops, it is increasingly manifest that the collective subject of production, consisting in the solidarity and complementarity of all labor activities, including those crystalized in machines and past knowledge, realizes exactly this cooperation whose instruments have been forged against this collective subject, with a view to its exploitation. The most effective form of property in oneself is that which includes in its cycle not just the totality of exchanges and the infinite network of different human "commerce" it serves to support, the operation of "each and all" (*Tun Aller und Jeder*, as Hegel says), but the very process of transforming and humanizing nature that has no apparent given end.

But is this in fact a subject? Ultimately, the whole question is here, and there is nothing simple about it. The negation of the negation is carried out in the privileged figure of an effective recognition of the originarily social character of labor, or conscious planning, which is the organization (*bewusste planmässige Kontrolle*, Marx says elsewhere) made possible by the capitalist Industrial Revolution, which violently decomposed personal labor. This can again be expressed speculatively by saying that the expropriation of the expropriators is an appropriation by society and the individuals that make up the very means and forms of appropriation, or an "appropriation of appropriation." It is in this sense that it is, or rather becomes, eminent "property in oneself," or subjective property, replacing the *individualized* or *desocialized* individual ("der vereinzelte Einzelne," says the *Introduction* of 1857; "das einzelne Individuum," says chapter 11 of *Capital*, on cooperation) with the *socialized* (or "freely socialized," "frei vergesellschaftete Menschen") individual. The true society of individuals can only exist in their effective socialization. Individuals are only owners of themselves if they reappropriate their labor power and its use, and thus labor itself, but this is a process in which the only subject is the effectiveness of the social relation. It is not only Locke who seems to be reversed here, but also Rousseau, for whom the community paradoxically forms the necessary condition for the self-relation of the civilized individual—with the result that, through a negation of the negation, the negation seems to be reversed into an affirmation, dispossession, or depropriation into a new appropriation.

In fact, Marx never returned to his unyielding critique of any representation of society as a person, or as an imputed juridical and moral subject.[32] This is perfectly consistent with the idea that the anonymous structure of the "totality of productive forces," according the expression from *The German Ideology*, remains a multiplicity (not to say a multitude), unrepresentable with the simplicity and unity such a notion seems to imply. But Marx was a good enough Hegelian to find the solution to this aporia. It would suffice to think the subject not as a self-consciousness or an individual of individuals, but as an immanent reflexivity given only in the "thing itself"—its works or its process of realization, inasmuch as this is ordered by a single totality. Such a solution (which Althusser would represent as identifying the subject with the "process without a subject") constantly haunts Marx's development. Yet it seems to contain an obstacle that a symptomatic reading cannot fail to turn up in his statements about the communism of the future. It lurks in the uncertainty of formulations concerning the "end of the division of manual and intellectual labor" or the "intellectualization of labor" (the "general intellect" dear to Negri). Or again on the side of what I will call the remainder of production within production itself: the problem of the relation between the historically determined needs of the social laborer and pleasure or enjoyment in the Rousseauian sense of the word, that is, the agent's capacity to identify wholly with his collective operations, which ends up reemerging in Marx's text. This problem appears very precisely in certain passages of volume 3 of *Capital*, or the *Critique of the Gotha Program*, when it comes to determining the relation of labor time and free time: on the one hand, the idea that labor has become "the first human need," going from capitalist suffering to a sort of Fourierist pleasure in work; on the other hand, the idea that freedom and satisfaction can only be found in free time, and the progressive reduction of work in the realm of necessity.[33] From Marx's point of view, it seems that the argument leads to an impossible choice, not only for the future, but also for the present, where the question is what gives meaning and energy to the proletarians' struggle against exploitation. Is it the defense of the right to work, even joy in work? Or the demand for liberation from its ineluctable slavery? In the end, we would have here an indication of the fact that collective appropriation, in a contradictory way, is and is not representable as a process of subjectivation, or subjective individualization, at least if one does not prefer the opposite formulation: subjectivation is and is not thinkable as appropriation. This is the limit of the Lockean moment in Marx.[34]

DERRIDA

Shall we say that, if Rousseau undertook an anthropological reversal of possessive individualism and Marx a dialectical reversal, with Derrida we have an eschatological reversal? The formula only makes sense, it seems to me, if it incites us to think that Derridean deconstruction in reality makes manifest the eschatological element that was always already at work in the classic discourse of possessive individualism, and that it is in part linked to a general questioning of the function of eschatology through the whole of the metaphysical tradition. At the same time, this new strategy of reversal allows us to reveal the same elements of violence and antinomy within the subject associated with the idea of constituent property as within the idea of sovereignty. It thus folds back onto itself the very political construction of possessive individualism that opened the possibility of democratic sovereignty as the domination of *dominium*: that of the self-identical subject-owner responsible to himself/his own.

I confess that I have long found the expression "ex-appropriation," constantly used by Derrida (in *Spurs*, *Margins of Philosophy*, *Glas*, *The Postcard*, *Specters of Marx*, and *Given Time*) enigmatic, despite—or perhaps because of—its affinities with certain common formulations in the mystical tradition.[35] It is, obviously, an oxymoron that takes in its way the negative logic of "X without X" or "X that is not X," whose origin, we know, is in Blanchot.[36] Ex-appropriation would thus be a "property without property," a property that does not appropriate without expropriating, a process of appropriation whose object or effect is indefinitely frustrated. We could hear here first of all a reference to the transcendental tradition, wherein the singularity of the "proper" is immediately inverted into a universality that, as such, belongs to no one. But the most insistent references aim at an economy of the subject that Derrida explicitly identifies with the anticipation of a return (in both senses—but every [economic] return is first of all a return to the point of departure, to the source).[37] The process of capital is then, in general, as a substantial process, the model of all subjectivation, on which the very category of the subject itself depends. Every subject represents the anticipation of an accumulation or capitalization of properties. It is this logic that can then be opposed to the counterlogic of the gift, whose "incalculable" logic evades every expectation of the subject and consequently deconstructs the subjective economy from the inside. Here I will cite two characteristic passages from *Given Time*:

> The simple intention to give, insofar as it carries the intentional meaning of the gift, suffices to make a return payment to oneself. The simple consciousness of the gift right away sends itself back the gratifying image of goodness or generosity, of the giving-being who, knowing itself to be such, recognizes itself in a circular, specular fashion, in a sort of auto-recognition, self-approval, and narcissistic gratitude.
>
> And this is produced as soon as there is a subject, as soon as donor and donee are constituted as identical, identifiable subjects, capable of identifying themselves by keeping and naming themselves. It is even a matter, in this circle, of the movement of subjectivation, of the constitutive retention of the subject that identifies with itself. The becoming-subject then reckons with itself, it enters into the realm of the calculable as subject. That is why, if there is gift, it cannot take place between two subjects exchanging objects, things, or symbols. The question of the gift should therefore seek its place before any relation to the subject, before any conscious or unconscious relation to self or the subject. . . . One would even be tempted to say that a subject as such never gives or receives a gift. It is constituted, on the contrary, in view of dominating, through calculation and exchange, the mastery of this *hubris* or of the impossibility that is announced in the promise of the gift. There where there is subject and object, the gift would be excluded.[38]

But whereas only a problematic of the trace or dissemination can pose the question of the gift, and forgiveness, this does not imply that writing is *generous* or that the writing subject is a *giving subject*. As an identifiable, bordered, posed subject, the one who writes and his or her writing never give anything without calculating, consciously or unconsciously, its reappropriation, its exchange, or its circular return—and by definition that means reappropriation with surplus-value, a certain capitalization. We will even venture to say that this is the very definition of the *subject as such.* One cannot discern the subject of this operation of capital. But throughout or despite this circulation and this production of surplus-value, despite this labor of the subject, there where there is trace and dissemination, if only there is any, a gift can take place, along with the excessive forgetting or the forgetful excess that, as we insisted earlier, is radically implicated in the gift. The death of the donor agency (and here we are calling death the fatality that destines a gift *not to return* to the donor agency) is not a natural accident external to the donor agency; it is only thinkable on the basis of, setting out from [*à partir du*] the gift.[39]

And yet we may ask if here we are not still, more than ever, caught in the transcendental movement that tends to release or disentangle the subject (or the nonsubject, the subject beyond subjectivation) from its own given empiricity, that is, from the transcendental appearance that reduces it to an ontology (including the ontology of the substance-subject that is capital). It would then be a matter of rediscovering it beneath the purified form of its retreat, if need be under another, more impersonal name (*Dasein, Ereignis, différance,* "trace," or "gift") that would by the same stroke allow us to exhibit the antinomy lodged in the heart of the conditions of possibility of every subject. This gesture, as we know, is ceaselessly repeated in philosophy, not only since Kant (in the *Transcendental Dialectic*) criticized the paralogism of the substantialization of the subject's self-identity in the "I think," but since Locke himself undertook to rigorously distinguish personal identity and substantial identity.

But another hypothesis emerges here, which is indicated by the work's very title, *Given Time,* the paradoxical consequences of which it never stops displaying. It completes the previous one. If every subject is in fact a nonsubject, that is, negatively constituted by an ensemble of relations among human beings as soon as their "commerce" (*Verkehr,* "intercourse") exceeds de facto every commercial form (*Handel,* "trade"), every economy of calculating anticipation and return, giving rise to the antinomial possibilities of excess and violence, friendship and hospitality, is it not because time—no doubt including labor time—intrinsically resists appropriation? Is not time the un-appropriable as such, which never (or never really, completely) becomes the instrument of calculation or a subjective project? One would in this way encounter the idea that men or subjects in this sense are never *in the same time*, "contemporary" with each other, the authors of a work or a totality that is built in the present in their common "presence" (least of all in the *present future* of the end, of eschatology). Rather, they must indefinitely wait for each other, wait for the unpredictable coming of the community in which their respective singularities would exist for and with each other. For "property in oneself" as appropriation or return, putting an end to the loss of self or dissemination, to finally become possible, they would therefore need an appropriation of transcendental time itself—but this is precisely the impossible. And finally, since ethics as well as politics is suspended on the intelligence of this impossible, which evokes the risk and the very possibility of justice (which is irreducible to recognition, retribution, (re)distribution, etc.), the impossibility of "giving time" would also be, allegorically, a figuration of the radical negativity that ethics and politics cannot do without. And what was just said of time would hold equally for all "quasi-transcendentals": language, death (destruction), and therefore life.

Can one thus simply (too simply, no doubt) connect some of the major themes of Derrida's work? I am not certain. But I will nevertheless risk it in order to articulate a question concerning the relation of the series of terms "appropriation," "expropriation," and "ex-appropriation" with the signifying chain that can be located under the name "possessive individualism," expanding the sense Macpherson gave it and developing it dialectically.

In Derrida we find a first movement of overcoming, no doubt suggested by the Heideggerian associations between the proper (*Eigen*), property (*Eigentum* and *Eigenschaft*), and the event (*Ereignis*), but just as much by the doublet of "property" and "propriety," which plays a decisive role in classical English-language philosophy. We must go beyond the opposition of affirmation and negation and retrieve a more fundamental notion of "propriation"—almost the literal equivalent of the Greek (Stoic) *oikeiôsis*—that is, as such, neither ap-propriation nor ex-propriation. The constitution and self-identification of the subject, with its negative and positive sides, takes place precisely in the process of propriation. We have a beautiful exposition of this idea in *Spurs*, one of the texts in which Derrida departs from the Heideggerian denegation of sexual difference and arrives at the idea that a process of propriation precedes subjection as well as subjectivation, since it already commands, upstream, ontology:

> The conceptual significations and values which would seem to decide the stakes or means in Nietzsche's analysis of the sexual difference, or the "eternal war between the sexes," and "mortal hatred of the sexes," "of love," eroticism, etc., are all based on what might be called a process of *propriation* (appropriation, expropriation, taking, taking possession, gift and barter, mastery, servitude, etc.). Thus, in numerous analyses, . . . the woman's appearance takes shape according to an already formalized law. Either, at times, woman is woman because she gives, *because she gives herself*, while the man for his part takes, possesses, indeed takes possession. Or else, at other times, she is woman because, in giving, she is in fact *giving herself for*, is simulating, and consequently assuring the possessive mastery for her own self. The *for* which appears in the "to-give-oneself-for," whatever its value, whether it deceives by giving only an appearance of, or whether it actually introduces some destination, finality or twisted calculation, some return, redemption or gain, into the loss of proper-ty (*propre*), this *for* nonetheless continues to withhold the gift of a reserve. Henceforth all the signs of a sexual opposition are changed. . . . Should the opposition of *give* and *take*, of *possess* and *possessed*, be nothing more than a transcendental snare which is produced by the hymen's graphic, it would then escape not only dialectics, but also any ontological decidability.
>
> As a result, the question, "what *is* proper-ty (*propre*), what *is* appropriation, expropriation, mastery, servitude, etc.," is no longer possible. Not only is propriation a sexual operation, . . . because it is finally undecidable, propriation is more powerful than the question *ti este*, more powerful than the veil of truth or the meaning of being. Furthermore, . . . propriation is all the more powerful since it is its process that organized both the totality of language's process and symbolic exchange in general. By implication, then, it also organized all ontological statements. The history (of) truth (is) a process of propriation. And it is not from an onto-phenomenological or semantico-hermeneutic interrogation that proper-ty (*propre*) is to be derived. . . .

> [T]he question of proper-ty (*propre*) has only to loom up in the
> field of economy (in its restricted sense), linguistics, rhetoric,
> psychoanalysis, politics, etc., for the onto-hermeneutic interroga-
> tion to reveal its limit. . . .
> Metaphysical questions and the question of metaphysics have
> only to be inscribed in the more powerful question of propriation
> for their space to be reorganized.[40]

In all his texts, no doubt, Derrida appears more than suspicious of
reversals in all genres—or should we understand that it is only a matter
of those that are simple?[41] We can doubtless understand this, that expropriation will necessarily be a critical, paradoxical figure of this process,
which is characterized by endless dissimulation. The importance of this
question is greater still in *Margins of Philosophy*, where the Hegelian dialectic (and no doubt the dialectic in general) is criticized as an infinite
process of expropriation that results in (or tends toward) a (re)
appropriation—the very definition of a teleology. We then arrive at the
idea that deconstruction, insofar as it aims precisely at an essential articulation of the origin and the end, is always already essentially a deconstruction of the "proper," in the double sense of property and propriety.
Whatever its point of departure or its object, deconstruction is always
already this movement that would be designated by the paradoxical
name "ex-appropriation," in which the contradictory or dialectical movement is reproduced and, at the same time, detained or blocked. What the
essay on "The Ends of Man" tells us is "vacillating" or "trembling" today
is precisely this "property" or "co-belonging" of man and being (and thus
also of nature) that the metaphysical tradition had established at its
center, which finally found its absolute expression in the idea of the dialectical process.[42]

Yet at this point the idea of an undeconstructible element, subsequently introduced by Derrida to respond to accusations of nihilism and
skepticism directed against deconstruction ("everything is deconstructible
precisely except deconstruction itself"), begins to signal a return toward
the tradition from which it had detached itself.[43] If deconstruction is always deconstruction of the proper, or the unity of property and propriety, does this not mean that the possibility of the undeconstructible
(moreover identified by Derrida with the always antinomic possibility of
justice, a justice to come) comes very close to the Lockean identification

of property and identity in the idea, itself paradoxical, of property in one's own person? To say it comes close is not to say that it coincides. Perhaps it is to say, to the contrary, that it is like its *other*, inseparable and irreducible, that cannot let it survive as such. Yet what they have in common in their opposition is the form of the unity of opposites, the X without X. In Locke, property in oneself must be at once a process of alienation and a manifestation of the inalienable, the infinite expenditure of the subject into the economy of properties *and* a return or retreat of the subject into the inalienable (identity). Here the inalienable or the undeconstructible cannot be called "subject" or "agent" in the classical sense, since it is only its loss or abandonment that at the most marks it as the absence of the subject, its retreat into a "property without property" or a self that is essentially expropriated of itself.

But the question of the self (or the self of the subject) is not separate from that of the community. In a sense it is the same, as *Given Time* clearly indicates. If a term is "improper," the other is wholly other. Cutting short the detailed inquiry that would be necessary on this point, I will nonetheless recall that this was already the case in Locke—contrary to what hasty interpretations of his individualism suggest. Locke is also a philosopher of the community, and even of the eschatological community.[44] It is here that the messianic dimension of ethics in Derrida, itself announced in a critical modality ("messianism without messianism"), completes the idea of ex-appropriation. Ex-appropriation, as a negative characteristic that affects the subject (or deconstructs it and so "gives" it to the question of justice, and to the related questions of democracy and hospitality), communicates at least theoretically, speculatively, with a community that itself has no "property," and thus no common good (no *res publica* or common-wealth) to preserve, appropriate, or identify with. It can only be approached in terms of an injunction to make a place for alterity. It thus goes beyond (and challenges) reciprocity or recognition, but it aims at a community without community that has nothing in common but non-property, the resistance of its own members to identifying with some "proper."

There remains only a continual homology that enigmatically prevails between the way, in Derrida, undeconstructible justice is articulated with deconstruction as its limit (breaking-point) and its condition of possibility, and the way, in Locke (and perhaps more generally in theories of natural right), the inalienable is articulated as the limit and condition of possibility of alienation itself, and thus as its internal principle. This is what pushes me to speak here again of a "reversal," in an extended sense. To be sure, their intentions are opposite. In Locke, it is identity and the identical (or even, recalling Paul Ricoeur's basically very Lockean title, "oneself as another"), preserved as "oneself," that is found as the inalienable immanent in the process of alienation, and so can always make it return dialectically to itself in the form of appropriation; whereas in Derrida it is deconstruction as such, infinitely, that constitutes the undeconstructible (and thus never ends), excluding any form of return to the origin, property as appropriation or "expropriation of the expropriation." It then coincides with an infinite dissemination of identities and properties, where every identification is destined to perish. It is a matter of radicalizing the theme of alienation, freed of its negative connotations—what could be called an abyssal alienation (whose form, this time, evokes Rousseau). The opposition is complete, but I suggest that a certain form has been preserved that itself has the status of a trace, and which returns to the unity of opposites (loss and gain, having and losing). It is therefore perhaps not as surprising as we initially believed that the ethical, but also political, discourse of justice and judgment remains caught in a necessary relation with that of rights and exchanges whose object and norm is property, even if we have gone from a transcendental teleology to a radical aporia.

4. "SOCIAL PROPERTY" AND NEGATIVE INDIVIDUALITY

In this last moment of our journey, our task is to expand the theoretical formulations hypothetically proposed by Robert Castel—"social property," "disaffiliation," "negative individuality"—in order to examine their impact on the problematic of possessive individualism.[45] Very abstractly, what is at stake in the discussion seems to be the following: Is what we have in the contemporary phenomena presented and analyzed by Castel a real figure of the reversal of possessive individualism, which can be inscribed, at least virtually, in a dialectic like those I have just evoked; or is it a very different form of the intrusion of the negative into the movement of appropriation and property in oneself? Do we not have to use here another metaphor, for example that of a "turn-around" [*retournement*]?

Social property, as Castel describes it, certainly has characteristics of a "right to not be excluded," as Macpherson calls it. It achieves a true abolition of the distinction between "rights to" and "rights from" (which no doubt allows us to understand why it is always noisily opposed). And, as Castel notes in the second part of his book, it reverses the "contractual" tendency that can be observed in the whole "utopian" phase of dismantling corporatist institutions in order to create a free labor market, replacing it with a new form of status needed for the regulation of the social consequences of the generalized workforce by political authorities.[46] The effects of this institutional transformation (more or less completely achieved within the framework of the national-social state in the first two-thirds of the twentieth century) have above all been discussed in terms of the proclamation and effectivity of security as a fundamental right. (Here we can think of the definition of right John Stuart Mill proposed in *Utilitarianism*: "To have a right . . . is, I conceive, to have something which society ought to defend me in the possession of."[47]) But we also and above all have to ask what type of individuality or individualism it corresponds to. Here we find again the criterion of "property in oneself." Is it applicable to social property, and if so in what sense?

I will propose the following response: no doubt social property (as "propriety of transfer" or the attribution to the wage-earning citizen of guaranteed access to collective, but divisible, "services" that "temper private property to the credit of its social function") is irreducible to the notion of completely private property (not only in view of the enjoyment it brings, but from the point of view of the disposition or "power" it institutes over persons and things), and marks the limit of the validity of such a notion in the field of right as in that of the economy.[48] It is not for all that "transindividual appropriation" in Marx's sense, but (just as it corresponds politically to the emergence of a "third way" or a "mixed constitution" between the undivided domination of the capitalists and the revolutionary alternative of a reversal of domination) it gives rise to the new (or renewed?) figure of conditional property, which always already includes the mediation of a "third": the state, public services (perhaps also within elastic limits that are hard to determine, public economy).

It is here, notably, that the rapprochement not only with Durkheim, whose connections with the current of French solidarism are obvious, but more distantly with Hegel, who sought to refound the Lockean conception of property in oneself within the framework of the state's "moral constitution," would be worth exploring thoroughly. What is at stake is nothing less than lifting the abstract antitheses with which we began: *Gesellschaft* and *Gemeinschaft*, contract and status, individualism and "holism" (or communitarianism), etc. From a perspective that is no longer purely speculative and does not come before but after the great developments of class struggle around the condition of the workers, we have here a dynamic (or, if you like, open) correlation between the development of individuality and that of sociality, or the socialization of interests and behaviors—an institutional process of externalizing individual properties that is the condition of their "recognition" and consequently their appropriation. It is precisely this that has been put in question, on both sides, by the decline of wages (and the status of the wage-earner) since the 1970s. Disindividualization and desocialization (the expropriation "of the self" and the dissociation or dismantling of belonging) thus go together, conversely furnishing proof that the constitution of the self is inseparable, even indistinguishable, from that of material and symbolic relations with the "social body"—even and above all if they are fundamentally conflictual.

As Castel insists, we must attach a fundamental importance to the moment of the universalization of social security, which detaches it from all modalities of local membership or personal dependence on a particular enterprise, "nationalizing" them and thereby tending to transfer them to the side of citizenship, or at least posing again the unavoidable political question of their inscription in the very definition of the citizen.[49] But this universalization (which corresponds to the emergence of a wage-earning society) brings out all the more the relation of appropriation to work and the division of labor, which has become indirect or second degree (that is, political and not economic), since it is not a matter of appropriation through labor (be it individual, as in Locke, or collective, as in Marx), in its own sphere, but of appropriation conditioned by the formal equality of the laborer, established by statute, materialized at the point where society and the state intersect, and thus in a mixed zone that is at once public and private. We have, as it were, a three-part dialectical progression: the appropriation of rights, and through rights to services the appropriation of social services, and through services the "self" or the individual capacity to shape and preserve oneself by "taking from the common" the necessary means. It is first of all in this way that, at the very moment it aims to extend its form, the historical institution that interests us here starts to escape the paradigm of classical possessive individualism and its reversals.

But the displacement is clearer still if we are interested in the remaking of the relation between the alienable and the inalienable implied by social property. What becomes inalienable is henceforth no longer its personal basis (responsibility, consciousness, applied to the individual's disposition over his body). This is precisely what had made Marx's critique possible: the forms of the industrial division of labor in practice abolish the laborer's self-mastery and physically destroy its physiological basis, while the commodification of labor power ultimately absorbs reproduction, in a totalitarian fashion, into the cycle of the reproduction and accumulation of capital. What is inalienable is henceforth not the living, conscious substrate of activity, but the *remainder* (or, from another point of view, the *surplus*) of every use of the labor power, since social rights preserve the individual's existence wherein his economic function is suspended, or even ceases to exist (as in unemployment or illness); and since their combination (including housing, and thus the basis of family life, medical care, education) preserves the individual capacity to reproduce the labor force beyond the cycle of production by giving him a recognized social function in the service of the national economy.

Within this discrepancy of appropriation and labor (through the mediation of the state), which becomes the condition of their articulation, is obviously the basis of the contradiction that affects social citizenship—accurately expressed by the term "disaffiliation," with which Castel proposes to replace "exclusion." When the laborer becomes (or becomes again) a nonlaborer, even when he is a potential laborer, he still belongs to a quasicommunity of wage-earners, structured by the system of social and public services and the personalized relations of dependence (even if their modalities are bureaucratized) they establish between each individual and the democratically constituted political "body."[50] Castel goes so far as to speak of "negative individuality" and presents as a symptom of it different statements of the (paradoxical, and most of the time unrealizable) injunction to be an individual, that is, to individualize oneself by "becoming what one is" (owner of oneself), without for all that having access to the collective conditions of individualism. Such a paradox can perhaps be positioned along a theoretical line between two extreme manifestations: on the one hand, the fact that the state constitutes a pseudo-affiliation of individuals (a "second nature" that in practice is a nation), or develops on an ever-greater scale the mechanisms of controlled individualization, providing individuals with the means to construct their autonomy, but also making sure that they make good, "productive" or "normal" use of it (in a sense the reverse of what classic republican theorists like Rousseau imagined, for whom the formation of the individual served the production of the generic citizen); and on the other hand, the fact that public services and above all social services function with a view to the efficient mobilization of the workforce in production that remains completely capitalist. It is sufficient, then, that, conjuncturally or structurally, the economic circuit is interrupted and the workforce becomes useless or unusable (finally superfluous) for, tendentially at least, the teleology to be reversed. Just as utility descends from the institutions of social property to active "social citizens," uselessness rises destructively from a lack of work and new forms of assistance for the poor that make it "bearable" to the statist mechanism for the constitution of an individual self and appropriation of oneself. This reveals an essential fragility of social property, not only with regard to having or owning, but also with regard to autonomy and power—which is to say, being.

NEW REFLECTIONS ON EQUALIBERTY: TWO LESSONS

Thirteen years ago, on the bicentennial of the French Revolution, I gave a talk within the framework of the Conférences du Perroquet series, organized at the Théâtre de l'Odéon by Alain Badiou, Natacha Michel, and their friends, that I entitled "The Proposition of Equaliberty." I took the term "proposition" in the double sense it can have in French: a statement characterized by its meaning and its form, and an invitation or suggestion one makes to others. The text was then republished in French and other languages under the more conventional title, "Rights of Man and Rights of the Citizen: The Modern Dialectic of Equality and Freedom." Ever since I dared to forge a portmanteau word to suggest that the combination of the two key ideas of classical political philosophy constitutes the very heart of the representation of the citizen that has continually been claimed in modernity and which after two centuries has totally transformed our idea of "man," it must be said that the idea itself has not stopped seeming profoundly enigmatic to me. In any case, I have not stopped reflecting on the difficulties that characterize it. At the same time, however, others have found it illuminating and have imported it into different contexts, in particular to signal the possibility of an egalitarian alternative to the dominant conception of political philosophy, which rests on the primacy of the idea of freedom in relation to that of equality—when not on the critique of the "illusions" of equality and egalitarianism, in favor of the principle of freedom posed as an absolute. They have sometimes also suggested that the concept or notion of equaliberty could be a useful instrument for showing that an articulation is possible or even intrinsically necessary between the formal modality of the combination of freedom and equality (which is generally acknowledged as characterizing the constitutional systems that resulted from the bourgeois revolutions) and the material or substantial claims of the emancipatory movements of exploited classes, sexually or culturally dominated groups, and other "minorities."[1]

The fact that my formulations have been invoked in this way, in both theoretical and political contexts, has certainly convinced me that it is not a matter of mere verbal subtleties. But this has not, for all that, resolved the difficulties I saw in my account. This will thus be the occasion for second thoughts. Maintaining the idea of a "foundation" for political philosophy, at least to the extent that it has to do with historical figures of emancipation, I would like to reconsider the notion of equaliberty and the reasoning that underlies it.

These considerations will be divided into two moments, corresponding to two successive lessons. I will begin by briefly indicating their articulation. In each case, it will be a matter of taking up both the historical and the logical dimensions of the question of equaliberty. But in the first lesson I will be interested essentially in the dilemma that is inherent in the modern institution of citizenship: that which opposes a universalist notion of the citizen (such as is founded on the unconditional declarations of the rights of man) and a materialist notion of social rights (or "social justice"), whence proceeds the distinction (and generally also the point-by-point opposition) of formal and substantive concepts of freedom and equality. I will show that this dilemma can be related to an essential tension of political philosophy that Hannah Arendt in particular showed affects the very interior of the typically modern notion of revolution. This is also what I have tried to specify in other places by opposing a concept of politics as emancipation to a concept of politics as transformation.[2] In the second lesson, I will try, on the contrary, to return more

broadly to the anthropological determinations of the articulation between subjectivity and community as they are revealed by displacements
of the object and objectives of emancipation movements that demand
freedom and equality before and after the turning point of modernity.
Between these two lessons, which are formally independent, there is
nevertheless an articulation constituted by an interrogation of normality, which I will try to show constitutes the ethical counterpart of any
"majoritarian" conception of politics—especially a democratic politics,
made "by and for the people."

I

As I just announced, this first lesson takes up the examination of the
classical oppositions between freedom and equality from a formal and a
material (or substantive) point of view. For reasons I hope will become
clear as I go along, the accent will sometimes be on freedom more than
on equality, sometimes the reverse. But at the end of the day we will of
course have to come back to the logical interdependence that I suggested
in my earlier account can be thought according to the classical scheme of
an *elenchos*, that is, the simultaneous refutation of two possible negations, by suggesting that the negation of freedom de facto destroys equality, and the negation of equality de facto destroys freedom. This is precisely
why it is impossible to choose one against the other.

The distinction—generally understood as an opposition—between a
formal and a material conception of freedom and equality has a very precise origin in the history of political ideas. It appears as the immediate
consequence of the so-called bourgeois revolutions that were made in the
name of values that were at once universalist and individualist. They
gave a decisive impetus to what Gerald Stourzh has called the process of
the "constitutionalization of the rights of man" and set out the conditions of access to citizenship as full participation in political life that I
suggest we call "capacities" (a term popularized in French in the nineteenth century by the divergent works of Guizot and Proudhon, renamed
"capabilities" by such contemporary authors as Amartya Sen).[3]

In order to specify the significance of this origin, we can refer to the
presentation we find in the texts of the young Marx, where the formal
character of bourgeois political rights is criticized from the point of view
of the material substance of social conflict and the revolutionary claims

it provokes. We know that Marx's critique can be reversed and become a defense of the formalism of rights, as in the liberal and libertarian (in the Anglo-Saxon sense) tradition of the nineteenth and twentieth centuries, without really transforming the general problematic. An attentive reading of Marx's texts (especially *On the Jewish Question*) also shows that this debate is rooted in the dilemmas and conflicts of the bourgeois revolution itself (that it has to do with the Dutch, English, and French Revolutions, even the American), prefiguring what would soon become the "social question." In other words, this debate anticipates the new type of conflicts and dilemmas of the modern democratic state—the crisis of which we are experiencing today—and contributes essentially to determining its form and language. Let us immediately note, however, that the utopian and messianic form in which Marx conceived the future of the social question would profoundly influence the discourse of political emancipation; but for that very reason it has proven to be less and less adequate to its political figures and real developments.

The distinction between formal and material freedom and equality also has a theoretical content that cannot simply be abstracted from its historical conditions, but must be discussed in its own right. In my view, this content refers less to pervasive dilemmas in political and moral philosophy over many decades—individualism or communitarianism, the primacy of freedom or the primacy of equality, libertarian and egalitarian positions, etc.—which precisely remain abstract, than to subtler, "second-order" questions concerning the socially constitutive relation of individuality itself (or the "transindividual," as I call it in my own philosophical jargon). By defining individuality not only by citizenship, political status, active participation in the public sphere on the basis of enjoying certain rights, and belonging to a certain community or sharing certain capacities, responsibilities, and duties, but in a more active way, on the basis of how individuals confer on each other, reciprocally, these rights and capacities in order to construct the community, modernity crossed a decisive threshold. And one of the greatest interests of philosophy in this regard is to show that at the speculative level there is no such thing as a pure, unilateral theory, wherein the value of the individual would be affirmed at the price of an absolute renunciation of the community (even in the case of Robert Nozick).[4] Nor, for that matter, is there the reverse. The problem is always, for every great philosophy, to find a way to go beyond this abstract alternative. And in a sense the more philosophers insist at the beginning on the foundational value of one of the extremes, the more in the end they will insist on the necessity of re-constituting and practically determining the other.

But it is not only in philosophy that things happen this way. It is also true of the functioning and development of institutions—except that in this case, it is the tensions, ambiguities, and persistent conflicts between different versions, different vectors and polarities of the transindividual field opened up by the modern invention of the citizen that go on behind the scenes. Which means, fundamentally, that what I am calling here the transindividual is not on the order of an essence or a principle, and does not even constitute (unlike terms like "community," "humanity," "society," or "the social," whose meaning is close) a definite teleological horizon in a univocal way, but forms a problem. Better, let us say that what remains as an open problem and perhaps an insoluble aporia (but it is this aporia that feeds modern politics, and engages it in an infinite process of intellectual and practical invention) is the question of how one can *institute the transindividual*—find an institution of the political in which neither the individual nor the community, neither freedom nor liberty, can exist without its opposite.[5]

As we will have occasion to see, modernity is divided on this point. It has tended to evolve not only in the direction of a growing affirmation of the determinate political importance of the social question (and, as a consequence, of the resistance always reasserted against the political recognition of the social question), but toward a reversal in the use of terms "abstract," "formal," "material," and "substantive." From this point of view, too, Marx's formulations are symptomatic. They hold the line even at the point of reversal. Marx (here closely following Rousseau) explains that the universalist notion of the rights of man, from which the rights of the citizen with their own limitations are supposed to be derived, can in reality play two opposed roles in history. Sometimes one will see it as the true expression of movements that lead to radical emancipation; sometimes one will denounce it as an illusion or a mask, covering over and mystifying the bourgeois domination of property. It can therefore just as well designate an authentic recognition of the generic essence of man (*Gattungswesen*) as serve to constitute an alienated political community in which the conflicts of civil society are imaginarily overcome.[6] Marx insists, however, on the necessity of this philosophy of filling in the gap between the formal (what we could also today call symbolic) claim of equaliberty and practically putting this principle to work in reality (what German calls *Wirklichkeit*). This is why he proposes a necessary relation between "the development of a totality of capacities of individuals" and the form of association he identifies as "community," in which "the free development of each becomes the condition of the development of all."[7] These formulations are fully in line with the universalist tradition dominant in the first modernity and the Enlightenment, and the concept of citizenship to which it corresponds. They are rooted in the debates of the so-called bourgeois revolutions and in their most radical tendencies. It is the first modernity, in effect, that represented the meaning and end of history as a continuous process of the realization or materialization of formal (symbolic) rights, of which the combination of equality and freedom forms the essence, and consequently as a process that aims to transform the world. Not by accident, this formulation (whose origins must no doubt be sought in the thought of Bacon) passes literally from Kant to Fichte and from Fichte to Marx.

But we find in Marx another way of developing the significance and practical political bearing of the proposition of equaliberty that already heads in the direction of the second, postrevolutionary modernity, and implies a tendency to reverse the relation between the formal and the material, or the symbolic and the real. This is the case, it seems to me, when Marx advances as a political watchword the thesis according to which "the emancipation of the working class will be the work of the workers themselves," where the term "work" (in the original English version of the Inaugural Address of the International Workingmen's Association in 1864) refers at once to labor and activity. We must interpret this idea as signifying that the practice and its proper materiality are not to be added from the outside to principles in order to compensate for their formal character, to correct for their abstraction, or to fill their emptiness. Politics always already unfolds in the field of practice, and it is material conditions that give it its energy, its movement. All the same, we must also admit that at the heart of the materiality that is essential to practice (and which Marx derives, in the last instance, from the productive essence of man and society, of labor and the relations of production—what Saint-Simon called "industry"—as the determining factor in the constitution of society), the formal element represented by ideas, consciousness, and principles plays a decisive role. It forms the "subjective" moment, or what could be called the differential element of practice itself, what makes the difference at its heart, and thus the equivalent of what Hegel called "negativity." It is obviously no accident that Marx developed the idea of the self-emancipation of the working class in intimate relation with a contemporary workers' movement, wherein the names "citizen" and "citizenship" were mostly used to designate the type of equality and fraternity that prevailed among the revolutionary militants.[8] Here we do have not so much the idea of the material realization of ideas as the idea of the becoming conscious of contradictions, through which the latter engender the very subjective force that will bring their solution. It is thus already a characteristic expression of what I have called the reversal of the relation between the formal and the material aspects in the institution of rights and their constitution in a transindividual system— even if, by all appearances, it is neither the final stage nor the most historically effective, owing to the reticence with which Marx takes into account the element of law and his constant, intransigent, and undifferentiated critique of juridical formalism, or the juridical form of politics.

These preliminary considerations, subtended by a brief reminder of well-known Marxian themes, should help us undertake a more systematic comparison of two historical moments that I have respectively called "first" and "second" modernity, on either side of political revolutions and the Industrial Revolution.[9] No doubt there is no rigid separation between them. It is from the ideal of universal citizenship, or rather from its internal tensions, that second modernity results—the interpretation of rights as so many ways of transforming historical practice and its material conditions from the inside. And the program of realizing the rights of man and of the citizen formulated in the Enlightenment obviously does not stop influencing the history of the social question, be it only through the affirmation of the originary or fundamental character of social rights. It is thus only for the needs of conceptual analysis that we oppose the two moments. Before studying their practical interference, we must show that each modernity, each new way of thinking the reciprocity of equality and freedom, can engender its own consequences and its own problems, and therefore bears its own dialectic.

1. UNIVERSAL CITIZENSHIP: ANTHROPOLOGICAL DUALISM AND THE DILEMMAS OF THE FOUNDATION OF DEMOCRATIC POLITICS

I have called first modernity (before and during the bourgeois revolutions, which are themselves designated as insurrections of the rights of man, made by *insurgés*—in English "insurgents," in Spanish, *insurgentes*) the moment when the idea of citizenship stopped referring to a closed, privileged status and for the first time in history was related to the principle of a universal right to political participation. But we will see that, paradoxically, this in no way prevented it from remaining associated with the perpetuation of old exclusions and, what is perhaps more significant, with the rise of new principles of exclusion, in a sense more deeply rooted in anthropological essentialism than the earlier ones.

In order to understand the profound contradiction inherent in the universal citizenship (and thus the political universalism) of the first modernity, we must begin by distinguishing clearly between two ways of understanding universalism and applying it to the human condition. This tension is already present in what we are in the habit of calling universalist religions (essentially Christian and Muslim monotheism, perhaps also Buddhism, even if it is not a religion in the same sense), but it unfolds completely in the secularized form of modern ethics and politics. Universalism has an extensive and an intensive aspect. The former (which is hard to dissociate from a state-type institution) goes back to the idea of space without limits or borders, throughout the whole of which reigns a single principle or the same positive law. It is the empire of law. The latter, to the contrary, presents itself as the refutation or negation of differences.[10] And these are themselves of two kinds: constraints and discriminations. Intensive universalism is thus what rejects arbitrary power in the political field, which it calls tyranny or despotism, and abolishes privileges of status, rank, or caste.[11] Nonconstraint and nondiscrimination apply to every community, and notably to every nation, making each, in principle, an image of human community that is, in itself, the ultimate or absolute community. It is this principle of universality that I identified a moment ago with a universal right to politics—one could even say more precisely to active politics, the right to have rights of which Arendt spoke. This is why it tends at least virtually to identify man with the citizen, to (re)think man within a horizon of citizenship and political participation that makes him "autonomous," master of his own kind. It makes everyone a "citizen in power," disqualifying in advance the anthropological difference that, in the ancient city in particular, restricted access to citizenship.

This quick characterization of intensive universality, an idea that has become inseparable from modern citizenship, allows us to reflect afresh on the conflicts and antitheses that dictate the philosophical expression of the great systems of the Enlightenment (of which we are of course still the heirs): not only the dualism of institutional mediations through which the process of the constitutionalization of the rights of man develops (the state and the market, the political body and commercial civil society) or their formalization as citizen rights, but the anthropological dualism that derives from the tendency to oppose a discourse of *subjectivity* (in the sense of interiority) and a discourse of *individuality* (practically implying the primacy of a philosophy of exteriority).

We can indeed ask how it happened that the notion of the equaliberty of citizens, the practical implications of which are mostly the same in different legal systems or modern democratic constitutions, are based on two paradigms as profoundly different as utilitarian individualism and the republican community of citizens, when it comes to the representation of their philosophical foundations and corresponding institutional mediations. The reasons for this lie not only, in my view, in different national traditions (the pragmatism and individualism of the Anglo-Saxon tradition, the idealism or subjectivism of continental traditions, which are moreover heterogeneous) and political and social history, but in the importance of true metaphysical choices, on both sides, and what, with Foucault, we could call the "points of heresy" of the discourse and practice of modernity. As always, philosophers carry these choices to extremes, allowing us to see their stakes: on one side, Locke and Adam Smith, on the other, Rousseau and Kant—but the details are often less simple. Since these discourses did not develop independently of each other, they tended to internalize their own opposition, and there are unclassifiable figures. At the end of the day, it is a matter of understanding how the articulation of society and the state is "constituted," but for this we must reflect on the foundation of universality, or we must think the metaphysical origin of right, the political capacity of each person, their *becoming citizen* (what antiquity referred to as the education of the citizen—*paideia*, *cultura*—and should now refer to the very "formation" [*Bildung*] of the human within the person). In this sense, the mediations, both discursive and institutional, of universal citizenship *precede* insurrectional practice, the moment of revolutionary emancipation where modern citizens affirm themselves as such against despotisms and privileges, but they also *follow* it; they constantly inform its constitutional realization, and so they delimit it. What we have to try to understand, or at least describe, is how the anthropological basis is divided in two.

The guiding thread I propose to follow here rests on the articulation of two philosophical categories between which the philosophies of the Enlightenment can be divided, the categories of the *subject* and the *individual*, with two ways of hierarchically organizing the constitutive relation between society and the state (but also, we will see, their contestation): one that foregrounds the question of *community* and another that foregrounds the question of *property*. This was how, in my essay published in 1989, I proposed to schematize, in diagrammatic form, the symmetries of the discourse that thinks the equivalence of freedom and equality as the common good of the members of a community (a nation, but also a class, or a universal revolutionary class, on the basis of the notion of fraternity) and the discourse that thinks this equivalence as the reciprocity of conditions and rights between owners associated by the practice of exchange. We can specify this terminology, since the Enlightenment inscribed on one side the *subject*—the traditional correlate of the sovereign—within a community of citizens that could be a state (the typical formalization being here proposed in Rousseau's *Social Contract*) or something beyond the state (a communist or communitarian utopia), and on the other the *individual* or *agent* in a network of exchange relations (intellectual as well as commercial), for which we must take up the classical notion of "commerce" in its full extension.[12]

Rousseau is responsible for the mutation of the meaning of the subject in philosophical language to the extent that—by a drastic reduction of verticality—he identified individual "subjection" with participation in a collective sovereign. The Rousseauian subject is immediately a *legislator*, whose anthropological characteristic par excellence is a conscience that expresses in one's internal forum the difference between the particular and the general interest, and thus the individual will and the general will, submitting the former to the latter and affirming the superior rights of the community at the heart of individuality. In contrast, the Lockean individual, and even more, that of the classical economists (Smith), is an *agent* whose autonomy of decision rests on the idea, which Locke placed at the center of his political philosophy, of "property in oneself" ("proprietor of one's Person," which Macpherson called the principle of possessive individualism).[13] This individual is of course also characterized by self-consciousness, but it is essentially psychological, establishing a universal individual responsibility for his actions and their good or bad consequences for himself or others, as if it were juridically and morally doubling the indefinite movement of acquisition or the properties that make up the life of the individual.

The man of the first modernity, as citizen in power, thus has a double possibility in relation to social norms: a subjective possibility based on interiority and the internalization of the law within self-consciousness, and an objective possibility based on utilitarianism and the observance of rules and conventions. These are indeed two ways of articulating the individual and society, perceived as antithetical from the Enlightenment up to our own day. But we must immediately note that they are equally universalistic, and above all that both bear the possibility of exclusion inscribed at the very heart of the principle of inclusion. This possibility is now directed not at "strangers" to the community of citizens in general, but at individuals or groups who are perceived or declared strangers to the norm of humanity or its complete realization: women, children, criminals, the mad, representatives of "inferior races," etc. This has been strikingly exposed and interpreted by Geneviève Fraisse and other feminist historians when it comes to the anthropological roots of the exclusion of women from active citizenship in the constitutions of the Enlightenment (where it is clear that the trace is not always universally erased), which goes back not to a patriarchate or a traditional genealogical order, but to a doctrine of public reason, of differential access to the capacity to reason and to rationality itself.[14] This exclusion, along with other, similar ones I will return to, can be thought precisely either as a decline of subjectivity, a rise of the private "nonsubject" of reason in the very figure of the universal subject (or a reversal of the constitutive relation between the universal, transcendental subject and the empirical subject, particular and limited by its interests), or as a decline of autonomous individuality, of the capacity for action (agency). The question that is then posed is whether we can trace, in the paradoxical logic of Enlightenment universality, a clean border between the human and the inhuman (or the infrahuman), but above all, and more decisively from the perspective of the institution of citizenship, between the oppositions that would be in a sense dialectical, that is, that contain a conflict between right and fact (and thus imply a struggle between those who seek to maintain differences and those who aim to challenge them: masters and slaves, bosses and workers, men and women), and other oppositions that would be essentially nondialectical, which tend to refer back to nature, even to the naturalization of practices of exclusion relegating different "abnormalities" and "minorities" beyond human nature. This is the whole problem of insanity and criminality. It is perhaps even more the problem of childhood, the provisional exclusion of which only accentuates its natural character (no one imagines—or not yet—that children struggle against adults to leave their condition of minority, or claim equal rights).[15]

Classical Enlightenment universalism, whose emancipatory principle—which I have called "intensive"—rests on the idea of a universal right to politics, thus opens onto a dialectic of *capacities* and *exclusions* (often called precisely "incapacities" by civil and constitutional law), unfolding the paradox of a citizenship that can be demanded unconditionally and yet is subject to conditions. But these conditions are not historical (and thus cannot be immediately designated as transformable; it would later be the task of social criticism, closely tied to socialist thought, to try to make the larger part of them appear as epiphenomena of capitalism or material inequality). They go back to a deep anthropological level where human nature would limit or contradict itself, giving rise to the distinction between normal and abnormal, the human and its double, inverse, or perversion. These are all figures, let us note, that have been projected into the different "minorities" of classical citizenship, including women, but never without contestation or discontent. They work the paradoxical objective of instituting an acquisition of political rights that are de jure, always already acquired ("birthrights"), or, further, of preventing certain individuals from enjoying them even as they are thought of as universal and "imprescriptible."[16]

2. SOCIAL CITIZENSHIP AND THE QUESTION OF SOCIAL RIGHTS

I turn now to examine the second moment, which corresponds to what I hypothetically called second modernity, where the problem of citizenship appears inseparable from claims for social justice, and consequently from an infinite dialectic of universality and practice, or of social transformation, in which equality tends to appear as a historical construction rather than a given, and freedom as a material conquest rather than a principle.

Just as in the first part of this essay I associated the anthropological dualism of the subject and the individual with the way the Enlightenment constitution of equaliberty produces a figure of universal citizenship characteristic of the first modernity, I would now like to connect the tensions of the social question and debates typical of second (or late) modernity, which concern the constraining or nonconstraining character of what are called social rights, such as the right to work, the right to social insurance or education, rights to cultural goods, but also the rights of association and claim-making, with a figure of the citizen that, following T. H. Marshall and his heirs, I will call social citizenship.[17] I would like to suggest that we are dealing with a strict relation between social rights and social citizenship, so that we must necessarily discuss the two problems together, from a historical as well as a theoretical point of view. Yet I do not want to simply identify the two notions. Instead, I want to try to understand the dialectic of their interaction, which concerns both their mutual reinforcement and the way each is limited by the other.

In order to be able to fully describe this dialectic, however, to understand the new significance it confers on the idea of equaliberty and the aspects of the transindividual relation it brings out, we must also invoke a third term that escapes the simple discussion of ideas or constitutional perspectives and constitutes a historical force that really acts and becomes part of every relation between individuals and groups—even, as we will see, between individuals and themselves, as well as between groups and themselves (or, if you like, necessarily enters into the constitution of every individuality as well as every collectivity). I wish to speak of the state. For social rights to be defined and practically recognized, for a purely political definition to become a social definition (which of course is more than ever also a political way of defining citizenship, or corresponds to a politicization of the social as much as a socialization of the political), the state must transform itself into a (more or less democratic) *social* state. And here, of course, we have a political fact. But the state must obviously also not only expand its spheres of intervention in order to make itself the agent of a new social governmentality; it must be pushed, even forced. Consequently, it is necessary to sketch a new dialectic made up of the following moments: 1) We will have to recall schematically how the content of the critique of the formal character of public freedoms and civil rights changed under the influence of the social question, or more exactly the question of differences and class struggles. 2) We will have to look into the conceptual difference between rights, citizenship, and the state, over which the adjective "social" is now distributed, in such a way that the political as a whole is conceptualized in terms of processes and social conflicts. 3) We will have to show the decisive turning point that allows social or welfare policies to be instituted in the form of universalist social citizenship, as opposed to charity or humanitarian assistance, by examining the arguments that associate rights with activities or actions in this new configuration: the political status of labor, the articulation of the individual with the collective in revolutionary struggles, and finally the reconstitution of the concept of positive liberty (as opposed to the merely negative liberties of liberalism).

The critique of formal freedoms is, as we know, at the origin of the renaissance of the problem of justice in modern societies, even if it has a completely different meaning from that conferred on it by ancient theorists and theologians. In fact, this reactivation derives from the rise of the antagonism (division, inequality, conflict) of social classes, which forms an obstacle to the realization of universally declared rights, or constitutes a denial of their symbolic universality. From this flaw internal to the problematic of emancipation then proceeds the idea, which is also entirely critical (or is presented as a critique of the critique, in Hegelian terms a negation of the negation), of a politics of transformation (of society or social relations, if not the world). Class contradictions, for all socialist thinkers of the nineteenth century but also for some of their liberal and conservative adversaries, appear as structural contradictions insofar as, beneath the state or political representation, they are rooted in society itself. But it is precisely for this reason that they allow one to think the state dialectically or organically, not as an authority external to social relations, but as the very agent of their regulation and reproduction.[18]

For the most part, class contradictions also appear as consequences of how work is socially organized—not only industrial work or wage labor, but socially useful activity more generally, which can be expanded in the direction of domestic labor, managerial labor (even exploitation), or intellectual or artistic labor. What gives them a political and ethical significance is, first of all, the way they manifest phenomena of domination and alienation, of a struggle for recognition that extends to the whole of human life, but also the fact that, little by little, the conflicts and moral tensions that arise from labor lead to a categorization or classification of the whole of society.[19] The problem of justice is henceforth no longer posed in relation to the merits and demerits of the individual or the transcendent destination of society from an eschatological perspective, but in terms of immanent obstacles that must be overcome politically, through direct or indirect state intervention (for example, by means of education), for individuals and the groups or classes to which they belong to realize their capacities as completely as possible. The problem of social justice thus appears in a privileged if not unique way as the reformulation of the question of equaliberty, even if other terms are sometimes advanced to try to mark the difference between points of view (for example, "equity," "dignity," etc.—terms, it is interesting to note, that are all taken from a tradition prior to modern citizenship and invested with a new meaning).

Social rights, social citizenship, the social state, all interdependent notions closely tied to the problematic of justice, are not, however, synonyms. The most difficult term to grasp and define is precisely "social citizenship," since it constitutes the mediation between the idea, the claim, and the definition of social rights, which for their part are presented as unconditional, and therefore press to be admitted into what we can call, with Claude Lefort, the democratic invention—which is nothing other than a history of the universal—and the constitution of a new type of state that crystalizes relations of force and seeks to formalize them in a historical hegemony.[20] The decisive fact in this regard seems to me to be that the state we are dealing with here is always already a *national* state. The institution of social citizenship results, at least indirectly, from struggles and sometimes even insurrections, but it takes advantage of the nation-state's need to create a common national belonging beyond class differences—without, for all that, abolishing them (and even, in certain critical circumstances, through their revolutionary expression). And the national state also takes advantage of social policy and the mediation or displacement of social conflicts, in order to present itself as a common authority that represents higher interests. This is what I have elsewhere proposed calling "Machiavelli's theorem," referring to the chapters of the *Discourse on the First Ten Books of Titus Livy*, in which he describes the effects of the Tribune of the Plebes and the representation of the people's interests against the Senate in reinforcing the power of the Roman Republic.[21] The recognition of social rights (or some of them, from the right to work to the rights to education, health, and culture) is of course never won irreversibly; it remains the object of struggles and relations of forces. But to the extent that it forms a veritable system of social citizenship, incorporated into the legitimacy of the state, which by this very fact becomes a national (and) social state, it reinforces (and in truth reconstitutes, on new bases) the modern equation of citizenship and nationality.[22]

This equation, however, can always be read (and interpreted, invoked in the political field) in both directions. Above all, it bears an exclusive as well as an inclusive face. It subordinates the institution of rights, their recognition for individuals and groups, to belonging in the nation, and thus to the formation of a collective identity. But it also constantly puts this identity or these imaginary representations into question, since it bears an intrinsic reference to a form of human existence and an expression of individuality that possesses, again, a transindividual character and an unlimited potential for expansion: labor, or, more generally still, transindividual or cooperative activity. This means that social citizenship can appear as more national (and "nationalist," when it tends toward the idea of a "national preference" for the right to work and social rights) and less national (even "internationalist," from the implementation of ILO regulations and so on, to the internationalism of the workers' movement that defends it) than classical citizenship. In other words, it accentuates the contradictory traits of the idea of citizenship in general—whence a very strong moral and political tension.

Historically, the crucial debate in this regard is the one that took place at the moment the welfare state was established in western Europe, on the eve of and just after the Second World War. The question was whether social legislation (including unemployment insurance, the right to health care and secondary and postsecondary education) was to be defined on the basis of the segregation, exclusion, and stigmatization of certain social groups (the poor), or on universalistic, civic bases, in terms of the integration of the population as a whole. This debate, as we know, comes from the very beginnings of the social question. It runs from the enactment of legislation that was at once repressive and charitable for purposes of social control, which accompanied the English Industrial Revolution to the social-democratic, reformist revolution after the Second World War, illustrated in Britain by the Beveridge Plan—of which Marshall's theory was precisely the formalization.[23] This was how the givens of the debate between revolutionary Marxism and reformist socialism were transformed by the establishment of contradictory new conceptions of public service and the object of social policy. The national-social state instituted social citizenship in a more or less complete and conflictual way between two opposed ways of dealing with the social question, or rather beyond their symmetry: on the one hand, paternalist assistance to the poor in a tradition that was both statist and religious, which was assimilated to a disciplinary or even repressive order, on the other, revolutionary or emancipatory workers' solidarity, based on the idea of the autonomy of the working class in relation to the state and citizenship.

The theoretical consequences of this debate are considerable, and of course they have not expired—even if the current conjuncture in Europe and other parts of the world where the principle of social rights has been more or less exactly imported is characterized by a deep crisis of social citizenship, which we are in the habit of blaming on globalization and the policies of deregulation it favors but certainly also has internal causes deriving from the inherent instability of this institution. As I suggested, it is a matter of a new foundation for equaliberty, which also implies a completely different concept of activity. The first question is obviously the sense in which social rights and social citizenship are connected to labor as a historical and anthropological transcendental par excellence—that is, finally, what is "labor"?[24] We could also put it in the following way. As soon as labor becomes the fundamental social reference for the institution of the political, the question is posed—and complicated—of its "essence," its phenomenological marks, its typical bearers, when and how it appears and disappears (the theme of the "end of labor" may be as old as the political importance of labor itself). The concept of a "labor force" or an essentially human capacity to work that is simultaneously the foundation of rights, underlying social conflict and political life (and the formation of parties), is again both potentially *inclusive* (it is possible to expand the notion of labor or transpose labor into activity, depending whether one takes a socialist or liberal perspective, in a way that includes all of life, all interaction, excluding no one) or *exclusive* (in multiple ways: not only by distinguishing between useful and useless, active and inactive, or productive and unproductive workers, agents of social conflict and "protected" individuals and groups and those subject to discrimination). The centrality of the reference to labor, which derives directly from the effectiveness of class struggles, brings with it a series of well-known consequences: defining other individual social qualities as conditions for the reproduction of the labor force and conversely, centering exclusion on non-labor (more or less long-term unemployment or the inability to work).[25]

But the philosophical problem that is posed by social rights and puts the constitutional framework of citizenship in question is above all the fact that in a certain way they are neither purely individual nor purely collective, even if their liberal adversaries describe them as implying the downfall of the individual, who is absorbed into the collective, and the socialist tradition also inscribes itself within this dichotomy—more, it is true, concerning the repercussions for the right to property than for social rights themselves. It is obviously here that the existence of a conflictual relation between the state and social movements, and, at the end of the day, between the state and revolution, acquires an essential dialectical function. Foucault in particular showed that the modern state tends to "individualize the individual" through disciplinary mechanisms and forms of governmentality that replace transcendent sovereignty with the differentiated management of social practices.[26] But the opposite is not quite correct: social and revolutionary movements do not tend to "collectivize the collective" (or the group, the community). Instead, they tend to *subjectivize* it, which implies a strong tendency that could be called emancipatory, to associate individual resistance and solidarity (based on class or other groups that rise up to demand their rights), or collective *praxis*, in a reciprocal way. This is why it is so important that—as Marx never stopped saying—revolutionary movements and social movements more generally are themselves democratic, that they try to develop equality and freedom in an autonomous way, "beyond the state," as Althusser said, but precisely in a way that produces equality and freedom in the state and in society. This makes the militant or revolutionary a *citizen*, one of the historical figures of citizenship, in the full sense of the term. Equality and freedom thus appear not as birthrights of man, but as political constructions. Rather than anthropological foundations of modern politics, we must speak instead of (practical) constructions of politics, the anthropological implications of which are fundamental, since in a certain way they transform the very representation of "human nature."[27]

Ultimately, this can mean that it is the state that henceforth "makes" or "remakes" human nature, and it is this, it seems, that a whole current of liberal criticism has perceived. This is why the extreme, libertarian currents of liberalism perceive every social state as totalitarian and see in them the perverse matrix of the confusion between social rights and the rights of man. But, once again, it seems to me that we should instead open space for a series of tensions and alternatives. The recognition of social rights implies the emergence of a form of citizenship that makes their effective institution possible, and it is these rights that, as new fundamental rights, come to define the human. But this citizenship in turn presupposes the state, or presents itself in the form of belonging to a certain state. It is therefore indeed true that the state tends to conform to the human, as a second nature, by imposing the whole series of anthropological norms that are those of collective identity and statist normality.[28] But the state does not go, once more, without the antagonistic figure of the people, the multitude, or the masses, which it seeks to control as much as it dreads their insurrectional capacity, but which, as constituent power or counterpower, is sometimes able to control the forces of control themselves. Yet here we would still have to ask what authorizes us to imagine in the multitude a capacity that is subversive as such. Foucault, in particular, showing a deep libertarian pessimism unlike the revolutionary optimism perpetuated by Negri today, endeavored to show that the multitude often precedes the state itself when it comes to demands for normalization.[29]

To conclude this point, however, I would like to evoke an alternative presentation that can be found in the work of the great economist and philosopher of economics Amartya Sen, especially in *Inequality Reexamined*.[30] In an argument based on the study of problems posed not by the national-social state but by what is in many respects its historical counterpart in the Third World, the politics of development, it is as if Sen (who is by no means a Marxist, but who on the basis of classical utilitarianism develops a left critique of the social liberalism of Rawls in the same way Nozick had developed a libertarian, right critique) had thought the necessity of a new reversal between the notions of *rights* and *activity*. Sen's apparent objective is to correct what is at once formal, univocal, and global in the definitions of equality used in social philosophy. For him we must concretize the concept, arriving at a notion of material equality that is sufficiently determinate to furnish objectives for social development policy. But in reality Sen pursues a deeper objective: to reaffirm the proposition of equaliberty by reformulating it in a way that shows that freedom cannot be understood as mere negative liberty, even in the case of the classic liberties of opinion, expression, association, etc., but only as a positive power, a "capability" or capacity to act, or, again, a power of the individual to influence the collective choices on which his life and personal well-being depend. For the conditions of this capacity themselves reside in interactive struggle, in subjective effort and the action of public (political) institutions against multiple structures of domination and discrimination that contribute, each in its way, to constituting the concrete personality of individuals and giving them a place or status in society. The activity par excellence, from Sen's perspective, is therefore creating possibilities to act—or, as Spinoza would say, multiplying individuals' power of action on the basis of their social solidarities (especially in the fields of health and education). And this conception is all the more interesting for us since, provoked by the inadequacy of conceptions of social citizenship associated with the formation of the welfare state in social democracies of the North when it comes to development problems in the South, they can also appear, in a typically postcolonial configuration, as a basis for understanding and confronting the crisis that now affects this same welfare state as much as its philosophical and anthropological foundations. Let us note (before returning to it in the next lesson) that this conception is closely connected to a perspective of "normalization." Sen, it seems, never questions the association of the idea of action or individual activity (agency) with normality and rationality, but he clearly seeks to expand their criteria, in any case in comparison with the abstractions of official liberal political economy.[31]

To conclude this section, I propose three remarks:

1 There is a clear continuity between the insurrectional principle of equaliberty invested in the construction of classical citizenship and the subsequent developments of the concept of citizenship. This explains its persistent relevance. The politics of equaliberty implies an ethics of immanence or self-emancipation. But there is also a clear discontinuity or persistent tension between the two concepts of politics that I have schematically designated a politics of emancipation and a politics of (social, institutional) transformation. This is why, no doubt, the very concept of revolution—but this applies equally well to that of reform—remains a complex, even equivocal concept, as Hannah Arendt saw very clearly.[32]

2 The process I have tried to draw in broad strokes cannot be described as a movement of progress—not just because the relations of forces it covers do not evolve in a linear fashion, but because the Enlightenment alternative of the subject and the individual, and thus different concepts of activity, return in the representation of the social emancipation of individuals, and because, even if the typical antitheses of Enlightenment rationality are displaced in late modernity, the association of the idea of citizenship (in a community of free and equal citizens) with that of normality not only does not disappear; it recurs in an intensified and naturalized way.

3 The principle of anthropological exclusion that remains latent in the idea of the rights of man as the foundation of the rights of the citizen is not therefore abolished, but it is displaced and itself reinforced when formalism is questioned and social rights recognized as fundamental rights. I will return in the next lesson to discuss the question of the relations between minorities and majorities more explicitly. It must be clear from the start that this does not constitute a moral or rhetorical objection concerning the problematic of equaliberty. But it is certainly a problem that must be faced, and perhaps the most difficult of all.

II

SUBJECTIVITY AND CITIZENSHIP:
THE ANTHROPOLOGICAL DILEMMAS OF CITIZENSHIP

The last section carried some general lessons that I would like to begin by summarizing and reformulating. I presupposed that the general basis of modern democracy, or of the institution of politics in the form of generalized citizenship, a universal right to politics, was constituted by the proposition of equaliberty, which I defined as the perfect equivalence of freedom and equality. I explained that this equivalence can only appear as incontestable in the form of a refutation or a double negation: no freedom without equality, no equality without freedom. I suggested that we see in the historical statement of this proposition a double event, both political and philosophical, which seemed to us irreversible—which does not mean that it was never put in question, but that its opponents were themselves obliged to criticize the proposition of equaliberty in its own language, based on its own implications.[33] Nor does this mean that it does not bear internal difficulties. And of course it is these difficulties in particular that interest me. I have thus long been detained by two debates that, historically speaking, are not mutually independent, that constantly overlap and overdetermine each other, but can nevertheless be ideally attached to two successive moments of political modernity: before and after the rise of the social question in the center of the political space of modern states that aspire to be democratic.

The first of these debates concerns the anthropological bases of classical equaliberty, in other words, the presuppositions of the sentence that announces that "men are born and remain free and equal in rights." Here I would like to affirm that the problem of foundations, revived today especially within the framework of debates on the possibility of creating constitutional law for postnational or transnational entities (like the European Union), is not only of speculative significance. The problem of foundations concerns the construction of institutional mediations of equaliberty, notably in the form of legal systems. It therefore has entirely practical consequences on the national as well as the international level. I have emphasized the fact that, historically, there was not a single system of mediations but two partly competing systems: the first based on the hypothesis that man as a citizen in power is a *subject* in the Rousseauian sense, that is, an individual who frees himself from all external or transcendent subjection and thus chooses to freely obey a law he makes himself, as a member of a sovereign community of equal citizens. The second is based on the hypothesis that man as citizen in power is an *agent*, "proprietor of his own person" in Locke's sense, which means that he and his fellows have an equal right, and equivalent capacity, to engage in "commerce" in the general sense of this term (*Verkehr*, "intercourse") on the basis of his absolute disposal over his own person and the unlimited responsibility that follows from it.

I thereby wanted to suggest that, on the basis of the duality of the anthropological foundations of citizenship, we can account for different consequences in the history of ideas and institutions: the conflict of constitutional doctrines that see democracy above all as the expression of the general will or the sovereignty of the people, or, conversely, as the political regime that binds itself to respect certain fundamental human rights and institute guarantees for them.[34] Or we can observe the different ways the line, as decisive as it is paradoxical, has been drawn between humanity and inhumanity, which turns out to be the only possible way of restricting a universal (or universally human) political capacity from the inside, or of reversing it into an incapacity for certain categories of individuals or subjects. Clearly, it does not at all amount to the same thing to think this line of demarcation between the human and the inhuman in moral terms, by referring to "alienated" (*entäusserte*) subjects, or in pragmatic or utilitarian terms, by referring to "dependent" or "impeached" agents, those unable to act in an autonomous manner. And they do not have the same practical consequences.

I was then interested in a second debate concerning the institution of social citizenship or the transformation of the social question into a fundamental issue in relation to society and the state, the individual and the collective—what I (following others) call second modernity. I formulated the hypothesis that, throughout debates about class differentiations, class struggles, and social inequalities in general, and thus the division between active and passive participation in public affairs, the differential representation of social groups within the state and politics, a reversal was produced that affects our understanding of the relation between the abstract or symbolic notions of equality and freedom and their material realization, or the limits within which they are effectively put into effect. At the end of the day, these debates (in which Marxism is a player, but which include all social thought and sociology in the nineteenth and twentieth centuries) open onto a new interpretation of the proposition of equaliberty, a refoundation of the political conditions of democracy, at the center of which is the collective recognition of the social rights of individuals as fundamental rights of a new kind (from social security to the right to education to the collective rights of workers against employers, which can equally be collectives or public persons). These must also become political rights or politically instituted—and in fact if they are not political they have no reality, since only state intervention or a certain interaction of the state and civil society can bring them into effect. I recognize that here we are dealing with a complex problem. The fundamental and political character of social rights has no more been unanimously recognized than their content (including cultural rights and so on). But I want to describe a tendency, and to ask about its more or less irreversible character.

What I suggested in this regard is that the decisive historical turning point—what we could call the social-democratic revolution, in the etymological sense of the term "revolution"—was produced when the welfare state or the social state was no longer instituted only as a system of assistance or protection for the poor, immediately related to their stigmatization and relegation to diminished or second-class citizenship, but as a universal system for covering risks and a public program of development or of equal opportunity for all individuals, insofar as they all contribute actively to the life of society. (Again, of course, here we have a criterion that can be interpreted in very different ways in practice, and be the object of constant theoretical and legal disputes.[35]) And once again I wanted to indicate that this universalization of social rights can be given opposite foundations. However, although I was persuaded that the new dichotomy we are dealing with here, which opposes a language of revolutionary praxis to a language of the capacity to act and social justice, extends and reproduces, in its essential features, the dualism of the foundation of the rights of man in terms of communitarian subjectivity and individuality and "property in oneself," I think it is more important to study first of all its political side, which concerns the political relations between rights, citizenship, and the state, than its anthropological side. The anthropological side comes after the fact, as a necessary consequence more than in the form of declarations of principles. As a way of characterizing the two problematics we are dealing with here by attaching them to philosophical oeuvres, just as I earlier gave them the names Rousseau and Locke-Smith, I referred this time to the heritage of Marx on one side and to the contemporary propositions of Amartya Sen on the other. On Marx's side, that of the long-term, partly unforeseen and involuntary consequences of his ideas and action, I outlined a paradigm of praxis that follows from the intervention of social movements, revolutionary collectives whose practical effect is—in the best of cases, and for a longer or shorter period of time—to democratize societies and the state by practically anticipating the recognition of individuals as autonomous social beings and thereby helping make them such. On the other side, I invoked (even if too briefly) the analysis and theoretical propositions of Amartya Sen, who does not refer to the paradigm of praxis but to individuals' capacity for action, which has to do with increasing their possible choices, in other words, whose positive liberty must be promoted by systematically destroying the structures of domination that produce economic, educational, and cultural inequalities.

To conclude, I emphasized several points. First, there is a continuity in the claims and defenses of the proposition of equaliberty, that is, of the insurrectional principle that universally claims the right to have rights. This is what allows us to understand the persistent currency of this proposition in the democratic tradition—in any case in its radical formulation. But as its interpretation and its political translation also carry reversals and discontinuities, we are obliged to think the historicity of the proposition of equaliberty, whose history appears open and not complete or enclosed in its origins.

Second, we cannot think this history as simple progress, according to the teleological scheme the philosophers of the Enlightenment applied to it—the presupposition of which, in this respect, Marx shared completely, even if he thought its realization in a dialectical way, borrowing from Hegel the scheme of the negation of the negation. The dialectic of equaliberty is less linear and more complex than the classic philosophy of history thought. It saw the same anthropological dilemmas repeated in legal, social, and political debates—the proof being that the Marxian communist model follows in large part directly from the model of Rousseauian citizenship, and that the "heretical" or radically democratic utilitarianism from which Sen takes his inspiration proceeds in part from the Lockean model of individuality. But, on the other hand, we must recognize that the relation between the question of rights and the existence of the state—that is, for the whole past period, the nation-state—completely transformed the meaning of constitutional debates, which tended to mask the transformation of the relations of social forces.

Finally, it is necessary to emphasize that what I have called the *intensive* universality of the proposition of equaliberty is expressed in the institution of modern citizenship in the same way that its successive reformulations associating the claim of equality with that of individual or collective freedom are always subtended by a condition of *normality* (which also means, according to the context, morality or rationality). This is why citizenship is historically engaged in an uninterrupted process of the extension, deepening, and adaptation of norms. The social norm must be represented to individuals or subjects in order to be able to define or delimit the rights of man (humans) and social rights, that is, to identify their (transcendental) conditions of possibility. Critical philosophies as different as the Freudian tradition, the Frankfurt School, and the post-Nietzschean genealogy developed by Foucault contribute here in different ways to showing that this process of instituting norms is in no way external to the construction of the universal and the institution of modern citizenship.[36] The determination of norms of conduct or behavior is the hidden face of citizenship, but it is also a problem for citizenship that is constantly open. Perhaps we could therefore suggest here that democratic politics in its modern form has among its principles not only the idea of emancipation or the transformation of society, but also normality and normalization.

I would now like to relate this thesis to the fact that so-called universal rights and citizenship can only be claimed and instituted in an ambivalent way, at once inclusive and exclusive. Perhaps in reality the idea of a form of political universality that would be or become absolutely nonexclusive is an anthropological absurdity. The ethical problem politics poses is not that of choosing between inclusion and exclusion in an absolute way, without remainder; it is rather knowing who is excluded, why, from what, by what mechanisms. But, above all, I see here a characteristic of this typically modern, and thus typically insurrectional or revolutionary, form of politics that can be called *majoritarian* politics, of course playing on the different connotations of "majority," which we can find with different meanings in all the authors invoked above: Locke, Rousseau, Kant, Marx, Foucault, and others.[37] The criterion is furnished *a contrario* by the way a counterrevolutionary thinker like Nietzsche identifies normalization and democracy in the same loathing, and draws from it one of the great critical philosophies of modernity.

This is then the question that I would like to examine in the following by focusing on the relation between subjectivity and citizenship. I have already said enough to suggest that these two terms cannot go without a third, namely, community. Formally, we will have to ask what kind of subjectivity or, in more directly Foucauldian terms, what kind of subjectivation, that is, "passage" from passivity to activity, or of subjection to autonomous subjectivity, is implied in the construction of what Dominique Schnapper has called the "community of citizens."[38] This is also, conversely, the question of how the normative determinations of modern citizenship, which are deployed at once on the legal, political, and moral levels, affect the relation of the subject to the community and how the community requires subjectivation. These civic norms, which serve to found the definition of capacities and incapacities, have taken the place of what the philosophers of ancient politics (the Stoics and Cicero) called the statuses or roles (*personae*) of citizens, in relation to their functions or duties (*officia*). Let us put the matter differently by using a category that belongs to the lexicon of both Freud and Norbert Elias. Up to what point must we regard the subject as constituted by a process of civilization that allows the internalization of the moral norms that are constitutive of the community (or, if you like, can be represented as its "ego ideal," or its "ideal we," if this derivative expression will be allowed)? And what active or passive resistance, what dissidence is induced by the immanence of this moral norm to the community? Finally, this is also the problem of how an internal relation between subjectivity and community, which is also an ambiguous and conflictual relation, comes to overdetermine this characteristic tension between citizenship and secular political universality, the tension between the insurrectional moment and the constitutional one, or, if you like, between the moment of utopia, of infinite negativity, and positivity, or the institutional limitation that appears as the essential characteristic, always begun again, of its historicity. In the language popularized by the contemporary work of Antonio Negri, we could also say it is the tension between the constituting power and the constituted power.

I suspect that, starting from the moment we begin completely deploying the dialectic of community, and especially the normative anthropological presuppositions that complicate the symmetry of equaliberty, the emancipatory logic we saw at work in the constitution of a political community (a polity) must be placed seriously in question. Does this, for all that, lead us to the conclusion that citizenship is in a certain sense "impossible"? Does it lead us to demand of "citizens" (be they French, English, American, European, or Mexican) "another effort if [they] want to be republicans!," according to Sade's famous expression, taken up notably by Blanchot? Must we in a sense reproduce with regard to the citizen the sentence from Montaigne upon which Derrida commented at length, "Friends, there is no friend," by writing: "Fellow citizens, there is no citizen"?[39] I believe that this skeptical formulation is not inevitable, or more exactly that it can be read backward. Following the hint contained in Arendt's formula concerning the right to have rights and the probative value for the institution of the political represented by stateless individuals, which Agamben has sought in our own day to generalize, we could say that in a sense today the political subject par excellence is not the subject of the norm, but the refugee, the homeless or *Heimatlos*, the *sans papier* or stateless.[40] Or we could take up the proximate, but not precisely synonymous, suggestion of Rancière, who articulates the infinite character of the process of emancipation with an injunction to recognize the "share of those who have no share" within the instituted community. In other words, we can interpret the "impossible" or "impolitical" character of the community of citizens, not in the sense of a factual or material impossibility, but in the critical sense of the impossibility of constructing the community and constituting citizenship without simultaneously deconstructing the community as well as citizenship. It is precisely here that I would like to try to articulate a question concerning politics with a question concerning anthropology.

At the end of the day I will formulate this question in terms of the political status of anthropological differences, by showing that the articulation of the majoritarian politics inherent in the democratic tradition and a minoritarian politics—or, if you like, the articulation of the norm and the exception, the universal and singularities—is precisely "impossible," that is, affected by its opposite in its very realization. I borrow the term "minoritarian" or "becoming minoritarian" from Deleuze, the term "majoritarian" from Kant's text on Enlightenment and Foucault's commentary on it. As for the terms or expressions "equaliberty," "transindividuality," and "anthropological difference," although they have sources that are easy enough to identify, I take them in my own sense.

Given the impossibility of discussing the question here in all its concrete, legal, and sociological aspects, I will situate myself on a more general, metahistorical level by schematically comparing the status of anthropological differences before and after what I called modernity— that is, before and after the invention of universal citizenship as social citizenship, and thus before and after the formulation of the norms of natural humanity and social norms that draw a line of demarcation between the human and the inhuman, social being and asocial or desocialized being, in order to deduce from it the conditions of active citizenship or effective participation in politics. On one side (before), I will refer to the ancient world, whose relative conceptions of the city and human diversity extend up to the Middle Ages and the Renaissance. On the other (after), I will refer to the postmodern world, whose rise is precisely signaled by the importance increasingly assumed within political thought by different minorities defined by culture, sexuality, administrative status, but also biological or biopolitical difference. These minorities do not demand only "negative" rights or liberties, that is, the abolition of certain incapacities or repressive constraints. Much more fundamentally, they demand the possibility of contributing to an overhaul of the political, and by this alone they profoundly subvert the proposition of equaliberty. This also means that they project it in the direction of its own, partially unknown and unforeseeable future.

If I choose this approach, it is because I want first of all to correct the impression my previous presentation must inevitably have created of an articulation between subjectivity, community, and citizenship that would be perfectly coextensive with modernity (or rather with one of its faces or mediations). It is also because I want to introduce once again the idea of a history of citizenship that is open, just as the history of equaliberty is open. They have a past before modernity and its bourgeois or socialist revolutions, declarations of rights, etc., but they certainly also have a future after modernity, however we philosophically understand "future" or "after," which raise their own problems, and the taking into account of the past, without which the designation and recognition of a to-come (à venir), which in a certain way is always already there, would not be possible. It is finally because I want to try to start clarifying the reasons that led a philosopher like Foucault to convert to the study of antiquity in a way that was not without surprise for many of his readers.

The general idea I will develop can be put very simply: a "postmodern" problematic of citizenship (that is, a problematic that designates the contingent or aleatory future of modernity, and perhaps this is precisely what upsets many modernists and universalists, whom, for my part, I prefer to call backward-looking defenders of modernity and universality) is a problematic in which anthropological differences again become determining factors for citizenship, as they were in a completely different way in antiquity, both subjectively and objectively, morally and legally. When I speak of antiquity I think here essentially of the Greek conception of the *politeia*, the "constitution-of-citizenship." There is, however, a considerable difference between the before and the after, which could be interpreted in terms of a return of the repressed of (theological as well as secular) universalism, as well as in terms of the rise of new cultural models, new forms of civility or biopolitics. The difference comes from what in antiquity were anthropological differences. For example (following the Aristotelian typology), the difference between master and slave, man and woman, adult and child (which means, essentially, from the perspective of access to citizenship, father and son) were differences of status that also allowed human beings to be distributed among different spaces—public space (*polis*) and domestic space (*oikos*)—and distributed among different, hierarchically defined functions. The process of *paideia*, the civilization, emancipation, and reproduction of the citizen, requires precisely the complementarity of spaces and functions. To the contrary, in what I call the postmodern moment or the postmodern side of modernity itself (since with postmodernity we do not, strictly speaking, leave modernity; we discover its critical face, the process of permanent deconstruction) anthropological differences appear as ambiguous, problematic, and impossible to define and fix in their meaning. Despite all the institutions of discipline and enclosure (the army, the school, the family, the hospital, the prison, etc.), they are never really localizable or territorialized, confinable within boundaries, within simply dichotomous spaces. They are, as Foucault said in another context, essentially "heterotopic," since, at least officially and explicitly, they do not fulfill the positive role of reproducing the citizen, of actualizing the civic or political power inherent in human nature and human society.

Among what I call anthropological differences, of which I will not claim (what would ultimately be contradictory) to produce a final, exhaustive list and the terms of which are radically external to each other, I of course include not only sexual difference as differences of gender and sexuality, the "bio-social" difference of the "normal" and the "pathological" or health and physical as well as mental illness, the difference between the upstanding person and the criminal and also the differences of these differences (like that of the madman and the criminal), but "cultural" differences that have to do with the opposition between mind and body, manual or physical and intellectual competences, oral and written cognitive competences, etc., the division between ethnic or ethno-religious cultures, communitarian models of identification in Georges Devereux's sense, and so on.[41] Such differences do not enter into the process of reproducing the citizen—at least not in the first degree, since it is not the same for the institutions that undertake to control them. But they illustrate and demonstrate, like so many vanishing points, the dissociation or cleavage that prevents this reproduction from achieving its goals uniformly and universally (especially when it comes to education). Unless, of course, as minorities claim directly or indirectly and sometimes in an antinomian fashion, we take them as indices of the fact that equaliberty can only be realized through the *subversion* of norms, of the existing codes that institute citizenship and communication among citizens.

Incontestably, the Greeks themselves had a very strong notion of equaliberty, which they called *isonomia*. And in many regards *isonomia* (such as, for example, the passage of the *Histories* Rousseau cites in the first note of the *Discourse on the Origins of Inequality*, where Herodotus places the claim in the mouth of Otanes, who refuses "to obey as well as to command") also represents the insurrectional or revolutionary side of the Greek institution of the *politeia*. But *isonomia* or equality before the law did not exist and had no meaning for all but a small share of humanity, free male adult citizens who built among themselves a relation of *philia*, that is, reciprocity, friendship, esteem, or recognition. And above all it existed only as the condition of other humans, who were fundamentally unequal, among each other and with citizens—slaves, women and children—each fulfilling in their way a vital function in the creation of the individuality of the citizen, in service of his autonomy. It is precisely the complex arrangement of these anthropological differences that formed the domain of humanity or defined human nature by organizing it around the central figure of the citizen. "Humans" or "human beings" were thus precisely those who, as equals or unequals, contributed to the constitution of the sphere of collective autonomy, where the process of civilization (what the Romans would call precisely *Humanitas*) unfolded, and which in a more or less secure way distinguished human beings from other natural beings, such as gods and animals, who were ignorant of equality as well as inequality and were neither absolutely free nor absolutely deprived of freedom.[42]

The postmodern model of anthropological differences and its relationship with citizenship powerfully evokes this ancient model and its typical complexity. But in the end it differs still more radically, since the anthropological differences we are speaking of are essentially ambiguous and deterritorialized. What characterizes them is a permanent double bind: it is impossible either to deny their existence or to localize them exactly, or, if you like, it is both necessary and impossible to use them as fixed, purely dichotomous differences. What makes them necessary is that no one can imagine the humanity of human beings without the use of these essential differences: human beings are manual workers or intellectuals, male or female, healthy or sick, sane or insane, law-abiding or criminal, etc. To want to imaginarily suppress these differences (not to speak of the attempt to *really* suppress them, "in the real") is to suppress the humanity of human beings themselves, and sometimes to violently destroy it. It is only within the unconscious that in a certain way these differences are abolished, or more exactly constantly subverted and transgressed, that they trade places (and perhaps this, precisely as Freud sometimes suggests, is the constitutive phenomenon of the unconscious).

Yet no one can ever say exactly where fundamental anthropological differences run, and consequently what their essential content is. No one can really say what a "man" or "woman" is (except ironically, tautologically, as in the title of one of Godard's films with Anna Karina, *A Woman Is a Woman*) any more than one can say what personal identity is, what a mad person is, etc. It is only possible, then, to force identities corresponding to an ideal or institutional definition of differences in social or psychological reality by means of social categorizations and stereotyped, codified, "fetishized" models of behavior, symbolic references, and marks sometimes inscribed, engraved on the very bodies of individuals. This also allows us to understand why the social state, which we have seen organizes itself around the recognition of the social rights of individuals, constantly tends to transform unclassifiable minorities into social categories. Perhaps, moreover, the very term "minority" already has to do with this at once protective and repressive social and institutional categorization: here we are in the presence of a manifest limit to the process of the universalization of social rights, which leaves a permanent trace of assistance and stigmatization at the very heart of citizenship.

My real conclusion will therefore be the following. I do not know how to define and conceptualize a proposition of equaliberty that would thereby imply the reversal of the reversal—the utilization of anthropological differences not as so many internal obstacles to the universalization of the rights of the citizen and the becoming-citizen of the subject, but as a pressure point for the becoming-subject of the citizen in the active sense of the term, and I do not believe that anyone knows how to do it. But I assume (and I believe that we all assume) that this process is already underway, and that in this sense the very malaise of our political civilization must be read as evidence of the rise of new forms of transindividuality. Nor do I really know how majoritarian and minoritarian politics, whose attitudes toward the role of norms in the construction of the community are absolutely opposed, can be politically articulated—even if, abstractly or speculatively speaking, I believe I can affirm that there is nothing here that resembles a renunciation of the universal, contrary to what many believe or pretend to believe. To the contrary, we can and must see this (even if the expression is paradoxical) as a supplement of universality that corresponds to the incorporation of differences and singularities into the very construction of the universal—as the invention and institution of a system of "equivalences without a general equivalent," the translation and retranslation of the human to infinity in the ensemble of its variants.[43] But I can even say that this problem, along with other, closely connected ones, like that of violence (or extreme violence) and civility, forms the very horizon of political philosophy insofar as the latter remains bound to the elucidation of problems posed by its own fundamental formula.[44]

PART
TWO

SOVEREIGNTY,
EMANCIPATION,
COMMUNITY
(SOME CRITIQUES)

WHAT IS POLITICAL PHILOSOPHY?

NOTES FOR A TOPOGRAPHY

Let me begin with a few preliminary remarks.[1]

In the first place, all reflection on the past and present status of political philosophy brings into play different conceptions of the temporality of the alternatives they outline. Catherine Colliot-Thélène has suggested that, openly or not, all political philosophy in the modern period refers to a philosophy of history that reflects the articulation of rationality and Western modernity.[2] This remark holds equally for the returns to political philosophy we periodically witness, especially at this moment, in the form of what could be rightly called neoclassicism. This is why its primary theme is the critique of historicism or evolutionism. But here the tradition offers different models that do not lead to the same conceptions. It is not the same thing to reread Machiavelli while privileging the theme of *fortuna* or inscribing institutions and relations of forces in a cyclical temporality. Nor is it the same thing to revive Greek questions while aiming at a new theory of prudence, or to situate them within the horizon of tragedy. Such choices are nothing really new. Through the Nietzschean legacy they were already present in the Weberian critique of forms of domination and the conflict of ethics. We can also see them haunting Althusser's search for a critique of historical time that articulates the overdetermination and underdetermination of political action in a trajectory that leads from Montesquieu to Machiavelli by way of Marx (a very unusual Marx, truth be told, since he tends to boil down to one or the other of these two models).

In the second place, the debate between the adherents of social science and the adherents of political philosophy takes up antitheses that in reality predate the birth of sociology, whether we locate it in Comte, Spencer, Durkheim, Tönnies, or Weber. The designation of Montesquieu and Rousseau as "precursors of sociology" (according to Durkheim's expression) is a clear indication of this. In the same way, the continuity of the critique of contractual themes running through Montesquieu, Hume, Burke, and Hegel, which divides discourses concerning the origin of the state and the foundation of legislation, is a true "point of heresy" in modernity. But if there is conceptual continuity, there is also, from the first modernity to the second and beyond the revolutionary event (which is not only French, American, European), an effect of repression that, as Wallerstein rightly says, normalizes change.[3] If political philosophy in a certain way disappears in the second, postrevolutionary modernity between philosophies of the subject and theories of social evolution, it is tempting to think that its resurgence (with the crisis of modernity, after the world wars and the "civil war" of sociopolitical systems) corresponds to a closure of the revolutionary question (even an end of revolutionary "illusions," as François Furet says). In reality, it would be just as accurate to note that it expresses a new uncertainty concerning the meaning of the revolutionary event, with its tendential correlates (secularization or the disenchantment of the world, individualism and mass society, democratization and the rule of opinion, bureaucratic rationality, etc.), the description of which formed the heart of the discipline of sociology.

Finally, the unity of neoclassicism is absolutely problematic. If we locate it in the effort to restore meaning to the idea of the *city* (or the republic), independently of the evolution of social conditions, we see immediately that Leo Strauss's discourse cannot be made totally congruent with that of Hannah Arendt.[4] The critique of the subordination of politics to practico-theoretical sociological operators undeniably brings them together. But the diagnosis concerning the continuity of and rupture with tradition (which forms the reverse side of the philosophy of history), and thus the foundation of individual and collective rights, the anchoring of action in being or appearance, irrevocably opposes them. Here, too, consequently, there is no return without the reproduction of a point of heresy.

These preliminary remarks lead us to sketch what could be called a topography of discursive conflicts in which political philosophy then takes its place, and outside of which the very use of the term would be unintelligible. Political philosophy, of course, only exists as a multiplicity of currents and objects, as the object to which classical categories of community and conflict, rights and power, legislation, sovereignty, and justice, authority, representation, responsibility, etc., refer. It is probably an achievement of debates in the second half of the twentieth century (to which, from this perspective, thinkers as different as Arendt, Habermas, and Negri have contributed) to have reestablished the connection between political philosophy and philosophy as such, by way of categories such as action, judgment, rationality, and constitution. They did not do so, however, metaphysically, by deriving the political sphere from anthropological or ontological foundations, but rather through a reciprocal determination of reflection on political practice and reflection on the meaning of human existence or being in the world. This double affiliation no doubt draws on a complex history, but it can also be posed axiomatically, which gives political philosophy at least the apparent possibility of declaring itself self-sufficient. Conversely, it is precisely this self-sufficiency that is thrown in question in the *Methodenstreit*, which opposes the discourse of political philosophy and its critics. If you understand me, you will not for all that regard these criticisms as extraphilosophical. To the contrary, we will see in them the characteristic modality according to which, today, the political object and the difficulty of thinking it divides philosophy, thus helping to constitute it.

The first and most obvious of these criticisms, at least within the horizon in which we are situated, can be called sociohistorical. Whether or not it is connected to the prospect of transforming social relations (or their regulation, the adaptation of their transformation—this is the point of disagreement between Marxist and liberal critique, each of which claims to represent a "realistic" perspective), it explains the growing autonomy of the political as an inversion of the relations between the part and the whole, or between the expression and its condition of possibility. Beyond the political phenomenon (the state, institutions, the actors' subjectivity), it would be necessary to find the real ground of society and history. I will not develop this perspective, which is well known, any further.

But it is equally indispensable to take into account a completely different criticism, for which, following Roberto Esposito, I will reserve the name the "unpolitical" [*impolitique*].[5] Instead of opposing reality to representations, fact to values, it is a matter of going beyond the position of values (and especially juridical values, or ways of legitimating the law or the state, but also civil society or revolutionary action) toward their genesis or creation, and the antinomies they bear. It is a matter very specifically of genealogically going back to the moment of the constitution of the community (and the very idea of community), where violence and love, order and justice, or force and law, appear indistinguishable.[6] In this sense, it is a matter of deconstructing the autonomy of the political, not by relativizing it, subjecting it to an ontological destitution in favor of another sphere, but by reinscribing into its very center the non-sense or aporia it must, to constitute itself as a positive, normative, or simply analytical discourse, push to its edges, or to "another scene," as Freud said in his works on the theory of culture.

The term "unpolitical"—a recent usage in French—has different origins that stamp it with distinct connotations.[7] On one side, there are the *Observations of an Unpolitical Man*, published by Thomas Mann in the wake of the First World War, which represented his personal attempt to elevate himself above the conflict between socialism and liberalism in the name of "culture" and an ideal Germany (as he did allegorically in *The Magic Mountain*). On the other, there is Julien Freund's book *Politique et impolitique*, which opens by deploring the "distress of the political" in parliamentary societies, and was of explicitly Schmittian inspiration. In both bases, the connotation of the term is essentially negative. This connotation is suspended, or rather is subject to a radical change of value, in Esposito's usage. Here too the reference to Carl Schmitt plays an essential role, but only insofar as it exposes the crisis of political representation (and any possibility for the political community to be representable) as the culmination of the modern movement of secularization and the neutralization of the political. More profoundly, the term must be traced back to a Nietzschean inspiration and its extension in Bataille.[8] The question of the unpolitical is that of the negative or the nothingness that is lodged at the heart of politics, beyond which the substantial absolutes that order the hierarchy of values and organizational projects (the common good, the divine plan, the will of the people) are suspended or destroyed—without, for all that, transcending the problem of authority, justice, or sacrifice, which would simply abolish them in favor of the positivity of institutions or procedures for fabricating consensus. This explains, for example, the privileged role played here (along the lines of Bataille's texts) by the critique of the category of sovereignty. The problematic thus outlined unquestionably possesses an ethical dimension, but what singles it out is the formulation of ethical questions, not on the basis of anthropological idealities or formal imperatives, but solely from the limits or aporias of the political itself—its sacred or accursed part. In this sense it covers studies in which we could line up in whole or in part the work of authors as different as Foucault and Derrida, Negri and Lefort, Nancy and Agamben.

Without being able to go into all the details, I will proceed schematically in two steps. First of all I will briefly recall some themes of Esposito's work, making use especially of his collection *Nove pensieri sulla politica*.[9] Then I will sketch a comparison with certain themes from Jacques Rancière's book *Disagreement*, in order to better discern the conflictual "shore" of political philosophy we are dealing with here.

ON DIFFERENT OCCASIONS ESPOSITO uses a characteristic formula: "To place the limits of politics at its center, and thus to leave the presuppositions of political philosophy" (13, 25). This project opens, it seems, two large critical questions. One concerns the freedom that the community seeks to make its own foundation, going so far as to concentrate it in the "sovereign" figure of an authentic decision or absolute being in common (think of Rousseau: what makes a people a people, in other words, the general will). But freedom as an affirmation of singularities is radically absent of any positive institution of sovereignty, which can only concentrate it by turning it into nature or an ideal. And this is the principle of a forward retreat in which the succession of figures of power carefully avoids recognizing its own intrinsic relation to death. The other critical question concerns the representation—or rather, conversely, the unrepresentability—of the democratic principle, be it in the form of juridical equality, procedures of discussion, or the delegation of power. At best this means that democracy is essentially incomplete, that it only exists in the form of an infinite process, devoid of rules and guarantees. But it is necessary to see—and on this point too Rousseau is situated at the very point where political philosophy turns into its opposite—that this incompletion immediately calls forth the complement of myth, that of an organic, final, or original community. On this basis we can understand that the whole of political philosophy unfolds as rational myth, or a myth of communitarian, intersubjective reason.

This compensatory structure is already perfectly expressed in Plato, to whom Esposito refers here: "The actuality of Plato's reflection on politics is unsurpassed: insoluble antinomy, constitutive scission of power and the good, right and justice, form and value, which is projected into the heart of politics according to an inevitable discord that tears it forever and that no liberal humanism can make up for" (42). It is not a matter, for all that, of reconstructing Platonism. What the reference to Plato opens up is rather the alternative of metapolitics and unpolitical thinking—or, if you like, transcendence and an absence of the One that underlies every reference to community. The metapolitical thread is that which extends from Plato himself to the Marx of the "disappearance of the state" and communism, where "democracy is entirely subsumed, but also destroyed, in the power of its own myth" (47). The One is finally represented in the element of the social, the social practice that makes individuals engaged in a common "work" [oeuvre] communicate beyond their singularity. The unpolitical thread, to the contrary, attempts to assume completely the unsaid of the self-sacralization of the state as a "terrible concentrate of power and violence that exploded at its origins" (32). In other words, it runs through the theme of the irreducibility of conflict or division, such as we inherit from Machiavelli, Simmel, Marx, and Schmitt, but extends it into a negative politics whose fundamental thesis is that democracy is always still to come—what Esposito, referring to the work of Jean-Luc Nancy, in dialogue with Bataille, calls a "presence of the unpresentable."[10] This oxymoronic expression serves to designate a task or "responsibility" (63 and following) at the root of democracy: not exercising civic or political functions, but accepting an element of alterity or radical noncommunication, without which there is no communication, and thus considering community as the opposite of collective security or "immunity."[11] It is thereby situated in an insurmountable proximity of the common good with evil, and of political unity with death. The idea of the unpolitical is thus inscribed in a tradition of worldly asceticism that always attempts to "belong to its time against its time" (Bonhoeffer, Weber, Canetti) at the same time that it joins the recent propositions of Derrida (*Specters of Marx, Politics of Friendship, On Cosmopolitanism*) by making welcome the stranger, "the most unexpected host" (58), the criterion of democracy.

It is precisely on the basis of this theme of the necessary impossibility of democracy as a limit-figure of politics that resists its own institutional recuperation that it is tempting to make a connection to the recent work of Rancière. In *Disagreement* in particular, the subtitle of which is *Politics and Philosophy*, Rancière organizes his whole discourse around a dissociation of two terms that are at once infinitely close and essentially opposed: *politics*, which he relates to the demand for democracy, and *the police*—in the most general sense it had in the Enlightenment, notably studied by Foucault—which goes back to the institution of consensus. Here the common etymology (*politeia*) is symptomatic of the very problem with which political philosophy has endlessly been confronted, from its Greek origins to the recent development of globalized politics, for example in the attempt to give normative content to the idea of the international community on the basis of an opposition between identitarian violence and humanitarian intervention.

The police in general is a matter of claims. It tries to "give each its part or share" in the distribution of the common good by means of authoritarian or contractual procedures. The sole criterion of democratic politics, in contrast, is the "part of those who have no part," that is, the demand for equality *against* social identities or personal merit (and here we can recall the young Marx's famous formula in the 1843 manuscript: "Democracy is the (sole) truth of all constitutions," hearing in it a direct echo of the way in which the Greeks thought of *isonomy*: "the fact that the meaning of the law is to represent equality").[12] In other words, it demands the recognition of what, in fact or in the established order, initially appears impossible, and presents itself as a measure of the incommensurable: "In this way the bringing into relationship of two [unrelated] things becomes the measure of what is incommensurable between two orders: between the inegalitarian distribution of social bodies in a distribution of the sensible and the equal capacity of speaking beings. It is indeed a question of incommensurables. But these incommensurables are well gauged in regard to each other, and this gauge reconfigures the relationships of parts and parties, of objects that can give rise to dispute, of subjects able to articulate it."[13] In short, politics is constituted by an incessant encounter of its own egalitarian logic and police logic "that is never set up in advance."[14]

What reveals this encounter, and simultaneously leads it into a radical opposition, is of course the emergence of those whom the distribution of power and civil rights excludes in principle as bearers of the discourse of emancipation—those who appear not as "victims" of injustice, but as representatives of a "wrong" [tort] against democracy itself (depending on the circumstances and times: the poor of antiquity, the third estate and proletarians of bourgeois society, women and foreigners in the modern nation). This is again an essentially negative determination, even if it engenders a dynamic, a struggle.

> Not only does freedom as what is "proper" to the demos not allow itself to be determined by any positive property; it is not proper to the demos at all. The people are nothing more than the undifferentiated mass of those who have no positive qualification—no wealth, no virtue—but who are nonetheless acknowledged to enjoy the same freedom as those who do. . . . Now it is this simple identity with those who are otherwise superior to them in all things that gives them a specific qualification. The demos attributes to itself as its proper lot the equality that belongs to all citizens. In so doing, this party that is not one identifies its improper property with the exclusive principle of the community and identifies its name—the name of the indistinct mass of men of no position—with the name of the community itself. . . . It is in the name of the wrong done them by the other parties that the people identify with the whole of the community. Whoever has no part . . . cannot in fact have any part other than all or nothing. On top of this, it is through the existence of this part of those who have no part, of this nothing that is everything, that the community exists as a political community—that is, as divided by a fundamental dispute, by a dispute to do with the counting of the community's parts even more than of their "rights." The people are not one class among others. They are the class of the wrong that harms the community and establishes it as a "community" of the just and the unjust.[15]

On this basis we can see the distribution of resemblances and oppositions. There is indeed something of the unpolitical in the way Rancière develops his radical critique of consensus and the common good (*Commonwealth*), or the way he smashes unitary, identitarian representations of the community: "For politics, the fact that the people are internally divided is not, actually, a scandal to be deplored. It is the primary condition of the exercise of politics."[16] This also allows us to understand his antipathy for the notion of citizenship as it figures at the center of a tradition of political philosophy that goes from Aristotle to Hobbes, Rousseau, and, no doubt, also to Kant and Arendt. But Rancière's critique absolutely refuses the theological connotations, even if they are negative, of the idea of a "community of death," inherited from Bataille through a dense discussion of the function of sacrifice. In this sense, for him, the tripartition of negations or denials from which, in contrast, the originality of political discourse emerges is resolutely secular. He calls them "archipolitics" (Plato and the project of realizing a unified community, a *politeia* in which the order of laws would rejoin nature, or the organic life of the city); "parapolitics" (Aristotle and in his wake every "normal, honest regime of political philosophy," whose *telos* is "transforming actors and forms of action of the political conflict into the parts and forms of distribution of the policing apparatus" by looking for a best regime—one that contains in itself a principle for regulating or moderating conflicts, an optimal combination of freedom and stability); and finally "metapolitics" (Marx and in a general way any theory that localizes the radical wrong in a social, prepolitical structure—in this case class structure—for which the political language of equality is nothing but an ideological mask, destined to be abolished with the "end of politics").[17] We see that what is fundamentally important is not the unrepresentability of differences, or of the singularities that difference forces in an "immunitarian" way into a state institution, but the unrepresentability of conflict itself, or of the dispute around the quality of citizen at the origin of the community.

Here we have oppositions that cannot be philosophically neglected. It is no less the case that, by their very divergence, they signal a problematic limit of political philosophy that its return to the forefront after two centuries of the real or supposed primacy of historicism and sociologism only makes more palpable. Political philosophy, as a reflection on the constitution of the public space and the meaning of the kind of life that corresponds to it, can no longer devote itself to the categories of belonging and reciprocity as axioms, either in a "realist" or in a normative or "idealist" way. To the contrary, the uncertainty and, at the limit, the impossibility of giving them a univocal meaning must become the object of the thinking of the common, even as it sets out to determine modalities of the institution of citizenship. We find preoccupations of this kind in Herman van Gunsteren, about whom I have had occasion to speak in more detail elsewhere, whom Habermas wrongly believes can be classified as a "communitarian."[18] Van Gunsteren's notion of citizenship as "infinite access" (in the making) indeed presupposes that we begin by postulating that every political community (local or global) is a community of fate—not a community of destiny, as Ernest Renan and Heidegger each wanted in his way, but a community of lot whose members are at once radically foreign to each other (or, if you prefer, foreign to every common cultural presupposition) and unable to survive without each other. This amounts to transposing Hobbes's and Rousseau's problem of a fictive natural prehistory into a "post-history" that has dissolved borders without for all that instituting humanity as a political subject.[19] It is also what I myself recently tried to indicate, not only by identifying the question of democracy with that of its frontiers—in different senses of the term—but by characterizing the system of critical conceptions of politics that overdetermines the constitutional question of citizenship without an a priori principle of unity as emancipation, transformation, and civility.[20]

COMMUNISM AND CITIZENSHIP:
ON NICOS POULANTZAS

I

I will begin by recalling what I will term, without useless pathos, our "differend," which is, deep down, coextensive with the larger part of our discussions in the 1960s and 70s.

It could be situated as a variant on the opposition between a critical Eurocommunism and a more or less orthodox neo-Leninism. But these labels would express the way we tended to perceive one another more than the reality of our positions, and they have the inconvenience of obscuring two facts that, in retrospect, seem to me fundamental. One is our common participation in the enterprise of reconstructing Marxism in structural terms that, like it or not, remained one of the significant witnesses of its theoretical vitality on the eve of the collapse of state and party models deriving from traditional Marxism. The other is the fact that, in the tense conjuncture of the French political crisis of 1978, after the rupture of the Union de la Gauche, we found ourselves again in essentially the same practical position. This reunion was also personal, though it remained, alas, without a sequel. It was the work of Henri Lefebvre, whose memory I want to salute here. I thus prefer to set out this differend in terms of a debate on the central question of the state, which will lead me directly to questions of politics and the political today.

One can find the trace of this differend in Nicos's last book, *State, Power, Socialism*, in the form of two critical propositions.[1] The first says that the question of the lack of a political theory in Marxism is badly posed when it is understood as the simple demand for a general theory of the state, when what was lacking is a specific theory of the capitalist state. The other strikes out at "eschatological and prophetic dogmatism," one of the last clear (and, in hindsight, derisory) manifestations of which was the attempt by some of us to "defend" or "rethink" the dictatorship of the proletariat just as it was abandoned by Communist parties. To be sure, although I was cited by name (21, 124), this had nothing to do with an ad hominem settling of scores. But it was around these questions that deep cleavages opened up between us during this period. They concerned both the critique of the Marxist and Leninist concept of the state and the analysis of institutions or political forms in the framework of a new relation of forces just as the hegemonic state, that of the capitalist bourgeoisie, was shaken by the internationalization of capital (what we did not yet call globalization) and reacted to its declining economic efficacy by an authoritarian turn more or less accentuated and disguised by liberal discourse.

Poulantzas's thesis, which defined the capitalist state as the "material condensation of the relation of forces" between classes (expressing the strategic hegemony of one over the other, but also the opposition and resistance of other forces), crystallized these divergences to the extent that it seemed to some of us not only to minimize the historical materiality of state apparatuses (which Poulantzas denied), but to interpret its "autonomy" as relative independence in relation to the interests of the dominant class and, behind it, of capital. From this came two very different ways, not of valorizing the radical democratic element implicit in mass popular movements (on this point we were in agreement), but of thinking their impact on the form of the state in a possible socialist transition: either as a "break" of the apparatus, the emergence of a "nonstate" confronting the surviving state, or as a radical democratic transformation of its functioning correlative with the emergence of a new power relation and a new hegemony over fractions of the intermediate classes.

No one can know how Nicos's ideas would have evolved had he been given the chance to pursue his reflections. There is thus something arbitrary and perhaps indecent in wanting to add more arguments to those we exchanged at the time. But I can also take the theses and formulations he defended, especially in his last book, as indications of the fact that the stakes of certain questions persist, and I can ask aloud how I would assess them today, which is also a way of saying that they have lost nothing of their suggestive power.

I will therefore say, when it comes to the "condensation of the relation of forces" or the "relational concept of the state," that I have long since conceded this point to Poulantzas, first of all for a reason he himself mentioned while implicitly giving the basis for his difference with Althusser: only such a conception allows us to put an end to the myth of the exteriority of revolutionary forces (parties or movements) in relation to the functioning of the state in advanced capitalism. I will return at the end to the theme of exteriority and interiority, which seems to me absolutely fundamental in this case. And I conceded for a second reason that leads me to go even further than he did at the time in the direction of a dialectic, inherit in the state, of the translation and transformation of class conflict (and for this reason exposes me, even more than it did him at the time, to charges of "reformism"): in analyzing the capitalist state it is necessary to admit not only the strategic effects of class relations internal to the "power bloc" of the dominant classes or the "gains" in the struggle between the dominant and dominated classes, capital and the workers (for example, social rights), but also the institutional modes of the regulation of these struggles and their effect in turn on the very definition of classes, starting with the working class. (Whereas it seems to me that Poulantzas, owing precisely to a class position, maintained the idea of the constitutive function of the state in the formation of a power bloc, but did not speak about the determining function of state institutions in the historical formation of the working class, to use for the moment the language of E. P. Thompson.) This leads me, and I will return to this, to propose, within highly determinate limits, the category of the national-social state, to extend certain interrogations on the transformations of the political field to which Poulantzas devoted the greater part of his activity.

On the other hand, I will say that, when it comes to the theory of the state and the epistemological problem it poses, today I am tempted to push the idea of the "relational," or, if you like, structural, theory a notch further. Not only is there nothing like a substance or given objectivity of state power outside the "history of its constitution and reproduction" (25). The state is not separable from the configurations of social relations. Although the state never stops presenting itself as a driving cause (in order to be able to be perceived and perceive itself as a power of command; we know that in Greek the two notions coincided in the term *archè*), it is always only on the order of effects and chains of effects, even if some of them are very durable and all are inscribed within an institutional materiality. To which we must add: the social relations we are speaking of here cannot be reduced to class relations or relations of the production and reproduction of exploitation (which is not to say, conversely, that we could undervalue, let alone forget, them). It is also, in an autonomous—or, if you like, overdetermined—way, a matter of ideological relations. I would rather say, since the term "ideology" is loaded down with reductionist schemas, that it is a matter of symbolic relations constructed in the element of the collective imaginary, for the combined effect of class relations and symbolic relations in determinate institutional actions—what I once called the "double basis" or the "double scene" of politics in history—does not correspond to any invariant scheme, either in the long run or in the conjuncture. This point is obviously essential for our attempts to see clearly, for example, the modalities and current consequences of nationalism as an aggressive and defensive state practice (including what I call supranational nationalism, for example, in Europe). In the fullest sense, *the state*, one could say, *does not exist*—which is to say that it does not exist as a separate instance. What exists are forces and relations of forces (including symbolic or "immaterial" forces) materially combined in the form of the state.

II

These premises being established, I would like to proceed as follows. In a first step, I will recall some of Poulantzas's political propositions concerning the crisis of the state and state practices, which I will use to formulate some remarks on the omnipresence of this theme in the crisis of our discourse, as witnessed especially in Poulantzas's writings. I will then linger a bit more on the analysis of the capitalist state in terms of the national-social state, and its crisis as a crisis of the national-social state.

Finally, in conclusion, I will outline a response to the question I posed in my title: that of a politics of emancipation that would always have to refer to the double register of citizenship and communism.

Let us begin with some propositions announced in *State, Power, Socialism*. I will recall them in two groups, in keeping with the critical objective stated above, without entering into all the detail of the citations and references, but in a way that I hope will be recognizable and verifiable. First, I will do so around the question of the relation between the state and popular struggles and thus the place of the dominated classes at the very heart of the state and the consequences this place has for the history of democracy; then around the question of the national form of the state, and thus the relations between the state and capitalism—with, on the horizon, the question of the relations between revolutionary struggle and national form.

First of all, the state and the dominated classes. Poulantzas, as we know, insisted that this place must be recognized (contra instrumental or, conversely, transcendental representations of state power), but it can only be recognized in a dynamic way, in the mode of a historically evolving effect of class struggle that must be articulated with the totality of social movements. In relation to this dynamic, one could say that the form of the state is always both constituent and constituted, in an endless process. What is "theoretically urgent," Poulantzas writes, is thus the following: "*We have to grasp the mode in which the class struggle, and especially political struggles and domination, are inscribed in the institutional structure of the State . . . ; this must be done in such a way as to explain the differential forms and precise historical transformations of the State. . . .* In order to make a serious study of the State, we must therefore clarify its role with regard to both the dominant and the dominated classes" (125–26).

And, further on: "The State concentrates not only the relationship of forces between fractions of the power bloc, *but also the relationship between that bloc and the dominated classes. . . .* In reality, however, popular struggles traverse the State from top to bottom and in a mode quite other than penetration of an intrinsic entity from the outside. If political struggles bearing on the State traverse its apparatuses, this is because they are already inscribed in that state framework whose strategic configuration they map out (140–41)." And, a bit later still, rightly refusing the model of "double power" not only as schema for revolutionary transition but as a description of the tensions and contradictions of the democratic capitalist state, Poulantzas restricts the scope of this general thesis, or adds to it an asymmetry:

> The dominated classes exist in the State not by means of apparatuses concentrating a *power of their own*, but essentially in the form of centres of opposition to the power of the dominant classes. . . . [T]he material structure of the State [comprises] internal mechanisms of reproduction of the domination-subordination relationship: this structure does indeed retain the dominated classes within itself, but it retains them precisely as *dominated* classes. . . . [T]he popular classes have always been present in the State, without that ever having changed anything of its hard core. The action of the popular masses within the State as a necessary condition of its transformation, but is not a sufficient condition. (142–43)

We see that what Poulantzas refuses here are not only illusions concerning the neutrality of the state above classes, but also, more subtly, a certain Machiavellian schema that would allow us to think that the constitution of the state relies on the dominated classes themselves—or, better, on the dynamic configuration of their struggles and claims, and on the power they develop. This does not prevent him from, in the last section of the book and its conclusion—always from the perspective of a critique of instrumental Marxism—returning at length to how popular class struggle traverses the state, explaining notably that these effects are inscribed in the heart of "state economic functions" (which requires us to go beyond the representation of the welfare state as a purely "social" function supplementing the organic state inserted in the process of capital accumulation from the outside and making up for its deficiencies): "there cannot be *over here* state functions in favour of, and imposed by, the popular masses and *over there* pro-capital economic functions" (see especially 185 and following, 245, 254–55). Evoking the closeness of the "relations between *political democracy* and *social-economic democracy*" (215), he makes his way toward a general thesis that remains slightly abstract, even though it is obviously essential to his plea for "democratic socialism," concerning the historical connection that has always existed between the intensity of popular class struggle and the degree of development of political democracy, including representative democracy.

Let us pause briefly here to underline the absence of a key term from the political tradition in Poulantzas's terminology, a term whose usage today has again become omnipresent and that I will invoke myself in a moment, in order to try to avoid at least some of the confusions such an inflation would bring: the term "citizenship." Although one would expect to see it at least discussed in relation to the alternative of democracy and authoritarianism, it is carefully avoided.

Several reasons for this come to mind. I cite them in no particular order: a close association, probably, in Poulantzas's linguistic awareness of the term "citizenship," *politeia*, with a completely different historical reality, that of the Greek *polis*, and a refusal to extrapolate from its model or myth (others did not deprive themselves of it, for example Cornelius Castoriadis); closer to us, the crucial function of the notion of citizenship, or *Bürgertum*, in part of the Marxist tradition (that of Jaurès and Bernstein) that Poulantzas never claims as his own; the force in Poulantzas's works (all the more remarkable in that here he, unlike many others, came to see it from the inside) of the Hegelian-Marxist tradition of the critique of juridical formalism, and consequently of constitutional themes, in favor of analyses of relations of forces and social configurations; and finally, last but not least, a deliberate refusal to admit the idea of a regime of political equilibrium between powers and counterpowers that is an organic part of a certain definition of citizenship (notably in American republicanism), even in an amended form that takes into account the national framework of the development of class unionism.

But this leads us directly to a second group of theses. As has often been noted, reflection on the national form and character of the capitalist state, as well as the political consequences that follow from it, constitutes one of the originalities of Poulantzas's last book, in relation not only to his earlier work but to the larger part of contemporary Marxist and non-Marxist political science (with a few exceptions, it must be said). I can indeed admit here that it took me several more years, under the pressure of another conjuncture marked by the resurgence of aggressive nationalisms in Europe and notably in France, to identify this as the blind spot of Marxist theory, and one of the decisive fields for theorizing the political. I will simply recall here two of Nicos's formulations.

First of all, in the chapter devoted precisely to the nation, I will recall the extremely sharp critique of all attempts to "deduce" (*Ableitung*) the national form of the state from commercial forms or conditions for the circulation of capital. It is, Poulantzas tells us—deliberately very close to Althusser at his best—in the "process without a subject, the process of the class struggle" (115) or, again, in the political configuration of forces and factors of transformation that make up the historicity of capitalism that one must seek the secret of the articulation between capital, state, and nation, which means that these terms are always given together in practice, all the while remaining irreducible to one another. So that "the modern nation . . . tends to coincide with the State, since it is actually incorporated by the State and acquires flesh and blood in the state apparatuses: it becomes the anchorage of state power in society and maps out its contours. The capitalist State is functional to the nation" (99).

Next I call attention to Poulantzas's insistence that in the study of the national question, what must be called the point of view of the dominated or of the dominated class must prevail: "*The real problem, of course, concerns the relationship between the working class and the modern nation. This profound relationship has to a large extent been underestimated by Marxism*" (117–18). We know that this question bears not only on the analysis of the past, but on resolving burning strategic questions. And it is here that we open onto formulations that are at once Poulantzas's riskiest and, it must be said, his most equivocal (but this equivocity lies in the very question, and in no way in a personal weakness of the author), to the extent that they combine two theses that are on first view in conflict. On the one hand, we must affirm the importance of the national political formation as the framework of the process of social transition and confer a national content on socialism itself. On the other hand, we must see the internationalism of the working class or workers' internationalism as a fundamental characteristic of popular and democratic struggle—which, further, Poulantzas made more than ever a basis and objective of revolutionary practice by evoking the transnationalization of capital as well as the participation of immigrants in mass struggles of a new kind and in the forms of direct democracy they implemented. I think this difficulty of finding a stable formulation is explained in large part by the weight of the legacy of Comintern forms of organization, that is, the hijacking and perversion of internationalism in the form of an anti-imperialism that lost no time in reproducing fundamental characteristics of its adversary—which, in fact, historical Communism never overcame. But the fact is that the dialectical solution to the problem of a specific relation of the working class and its politics to the nation-form ends up taking refuge in little words like "certain," "correct," "genuinely":

> To set the national State as the prize and objective of workers' struggles involves the reappropriation by the working class of its own history. To be sure, this cannot be achieved without a transformation of the State; but it also points to a certain permanency of the State, in its national aspect, during the transition to socialism . . . ; national working-class ideology, both as a correct expression of internationalism and in terms of the impact of bourgeois nationalism on the working class: bourgeois nationalism could not have had such an enormous impact on the working class (leading it into the bloodbaths of national-imperialist wars) unless it rested on the materiality of the constitution and struggles of the working class, and unless it was linked to the genuinely working-class aspect of national ideology. (119–20)

It remains that the problem had been posed, and we ourselves are far from having solved it.

I would like to conclude this first point with the following remark. Between the two series of propositions I just recalled, those concerning the question of the place and effects of popular struggles within the state and those concerning the national form of the capitalist state, even if they obviously tend toward a single objective—establishing in concrete terms the necessity of socialist democracy and democratic socialism—a discrepancy remains, and consequently an unresolved tension. It seems to me that this relates to the fact that Poulantzas, even though he consciously pursues a "relational" conception of state power (which he himself helped establish), hesitates to think this strategic determination where the reproduction and resistance of the popular classes help determine the very constitution of the "bloc in power" (though he constantly affirms that "class struggle overflows institutions"), and to the fact that, on the other side, he tends precisely to suppress the nation-form's excess of signification in relation to the capitalist state over the working-class or popular component of nationalism (even as it is constantly at risk of being hegemonized by bourgeois nationalism). Or, if you like, on the one hand, he does not concede enough influence to working-class struggles in the history of the transformations of the capitalist state, and, on the other, he concedes perhaps too much autonomy to working-class nationalism in relation to bourgeois or dominant nationalism at the same time that he assigns this nationalism the enormous task of opening the way to its own overcoming.

I suspect, without being able to get into this new discussion, that this is not unrelated to the difficult and interesting terms used in Poulantzas's last texts to discuss the concept of crisis. Here we can see both a determined attempt to extend the apocalyptic formulations inherited from Romanticism (including Marx's Romanticism), the scheme that makes the worsening of the crisis itself the very cause and sign of the imminence of its solution (this is the case notably in his fine distinctions concerning the growing fascism of the state, dictatorial solutions to international conflicts of power, authoritarian statism, etc.) and a constant attraction to the idea of a "crisis of hegemony" or a "state legitimation crisis" inherent in its authoritarian drift, containing in itself the necessity of beginning a socialist transition, as we see notably in the workers' movement's resistance to its complete social-democratization.

III

I will thus now turn to my second point, where I will first of all try to explain why it seems to me useful to reformulate some of the questions posed by Poulantzas in terms of the crisis of the national-social state. I hope it will be clear that this is not a matter of an attempt at posthumous annexation, but of the continuation of a collective reflection, extended across time and distributed among many researchers. I will first of all try to characterize what I, with others, call the nation-social state, by way of two historically reciprocal propositions. One consists in noting that the regulation (and not, as is sometimes wrongly thought, the "integration") of class struggle by social policy and the institutions of collective security for at least some employees, set up under the name of the welfare state, *l'État Providence*, or *Sozialstaat*, has been absolutely indispensable since the end of the nineteenth century for preserving the national form of the state, and thus the hegemony of the state as such, which was threatened, at times mortally, by antagonisms and crises both internal (social, religious, ethnic conflicts) and external (wars, colonization). The nation has nothing like a "natural" permanence or inertia. It must be reproduced by a determinate policy, and this has been in essential part a social policy, partly imposed by the struggles themselves, partly decided from above in a Machiavellian fashion. But the reciprocal proposition is that the regulation of class struggles, and more generally of social conflict, in the last instance in the interest of the dominant class, would never have been possible without the implementation and imposition of this privileged form of community, at once sacralizing and secularized, that is the nation-form. (Think here of Gramsci's "national-popular will," or again of Benedict Anderson's "imagined community.") This is the virtuous circle that, no doubt at the price of much violence, constraint, and illusion, the political history of modernity has allowed to be established for at least a certain period, in certain places, and within certain limits. It is its institutional result that it seems in my opinion appropriate to call the national-social state, without concealing the provocative character of the expression—that is, not as a camouflaged variant of National Socialism but, to the contrary, as an alternative to the "solution" it represented within the same conjuncture. We thereby indicate that it has to do with an original phase in the history of the state, "organic" for a whole period of the history of capitalism (even if it is very unequally developed—a point I will return to), and that it produces irreversible effects, including for the very constitution of classes and the historical perspectives that can be attributed to them.

This proposition immediately calls for two clarifications that are fundamental in my view. One concerns the transformation of the question of citizenship, the second its relation to the opposition of the center and the periphery.

As concerns citizenship, it must first of all be said that the constitution of the national-social state led to refounding it and cementing its equivalence with nationality, which already tended to be inscribed in the very foundation of nation-states, especially those born of popular (so-called bourgeois) revolutions in the Enlightenment. But this was never achieved without a remainder or contradiction. This great, typically modern equation (ignoring precisely precapitalist formations), which the polysemy of a term like "citizenship," in American usage, admirably expresses, from then on contained not only the formal sovereignty of the people, but an ensemble of social rights that tended to be incorporated into citizenship itself (even if this incorporation never stopped being debated). Far from being opposed to political rights (as a pure liberal tradition would have it), social rights are in a sense the most political part of citizenship, transforming it into a social citizenship that is obviously all the more real the more their guarantee and progress depend on the extent of organized social struggles recognized by the state. National belonging, conversely, constitutes the basis for the attribution of social rights, from education, housing, and health (everything Foucault called biopolitics) to unemployment insurance and social security, even if the presence in the national space of a foreign, so-called immigrant, workforce, more or less completely included in the field of social rights but not political rights, created a very powerful source of tension and at times violence.

But it must be said above all that the realization of a new historical form of citizenship, social citizenship, in national form, and more precisely within the framework of a hegemonic national-social state, initiates the dialectic of relations between political and class struggle in new forms. It is here in particular that it is important to reverse the dominant point of view and study political form from below—in other words, from the point of view of those below—just as it is important, in order to study the complexity of relations between capital and the state, to abandon the idea of a "deduction" or a single mechanism. Moreover, the two go together. In different places, Poulantzas notes that the contemporary state carries out a process of individualizing subjects (see 65 and following, 105, etc.). Here it is a matter of a fundamental dimension of citizenship that Hegel had already placed at the center of his theory of the relations between civil society and the state. But what the development of social citizenship shows is that there is not an opposition but a strict complementarity between the process of individualization and the emergence of collectives, with their own consciousness and culture, most of which, when it comes to the working class, are historically connected to resistance and struggle. We see this, conversely, when the crisis of social citizenship engendered by a new phase of the superexploitation of the workforce that demolishes national borders engenders both a dissolution of collective memberships and a regression of individual rights, and ends up threatening personality itself in the forms of exclusion Robert Castel has sagely called "disaffiliation."[2]

We should finally note that the establishment of the national-social state displaces and accentuates the contradiction between several aspects of the universality characteristic of the modern political, which is always situated both on the symbolic level and in the real (or, if you like, the economic), neither of which is less determining. Here it is a matter of, if you like, a translation of the internalization of global contradictions. On the one hand, the emergence of social citizenship (or of a set of social rights included in citizenship that makes each individual the quasi-proprietor of part of the collective inheritance, even a very limited part) represents an original and decisive development of what we can call *intensive* universality, that is, in effect, equality—an equality that is not only formal, but has a very determinate material content. It is absolutely fundamental from this point of view that the collective social security regimes imposed after the Second World War, in effect conjugating the struggles of the organized working class (unions, Social Democracy) and its participation in a war effort that urgently needed its political sanction, were never conceived as regimes of assistance, methods of reverse discrimination specifically directed toward the poor and the workers, but presented as universal regimes that would have to benefit all citizens of the relevant countries, in any case all citizens engaged in paid work, which by this very fact was itself recognized as a basis of belonging in the "city." (This is precisely what mass unemployment and the expansion of neoliberal ideology now allow to be more or less profoundly put in question.) As Donald Sassoon rightly notes concerning the Beveridge Plan, this universalism (the principle of which never went without strong "workerist" resistance within unions and the workers' movement) is precisely what would sanction a recognition of the dignity of labor and workers within the national state, allowing them to escape the subaltern condition of a class receiving assistance and subject to tutelage, without for all that abolishing exploitation.[3]

But, on the other hand, the very fact that social citizenship existed, again in a limited way, only in the form of national "social pacts," within the framework of a national-social state of which it constituted the basis of reproduction, obviously implies a limitation of its universality—or, if you like, a particularism from the perspective of *extensive* universality. The time has indeed come to emphasize a constraining material condition that goes back to the division of the global economy into center and periphery. Even and above all if the national-social state became for a hundred years an ideal model (and an idealized one, to which especially the development policies sparked off by decolonization tried to attach themselves, as well as reformist movements in the countries of the East), it is clear that it was only ever established in more or less complete form in the countries of the imperialist center (and again, not to the same degree: it is striking in this regard that the United States was not at the head of the movement but rather at its tail, owing to characteristics that already anticipated those of forms of current globalization). And this limitation on the universality of the national-social state and the inequality of development that underlies it (105 and following) brings about dramatic consequences in the new phase of globalization, consequences that certain capitalist policies aim to accentuate and deliberately exploit in the direction of a massive re-proletarianization of the working class, but that—for reasons I evoked above, since the emergence of social citizenship was inscribed in the heart of the equation of citizenship and nationality and the process of reproduction of the nation as a hegemonic state form—also endanger the constitution of the state and the institutionalization of the political. It is indeed no longer a matter only of the gap between living conditions in the center and the periphery, developed and underdeveloped countries, working classes that have tended to pull out of proletarianization and working classes kept in superexploitation, created by international tensions on the global level that crystallize along certain frontiers (like those that both separate and unite the former colonists and the former colonized, as we see clearly in the case of the Franco-Algerian or the U.S.-Mexico border) and to invest certain social and demographic processes, like immigration. It relates to the fact that *Wohlstandsgefälle*, "well-being differentials" (to borrow the German economist Georg Voruba's expression), now widen within each political unit and throw the dynamic equilibrium of their reproduction into question to the extent that the center-periphery (or, if you like, in another language, North-South) distinction stops cutting simply *between* national formations, but also starts cutting, in a decisive way, *within* the same formations.[4] Not only, under the combined effect of the import of cheap immigrant labor more or less completely deprived of civic and social rights and policies of deregulation and the dismantling of social protections, do traditional national states re-create within themselves a disparity of living conditions and forms of exclusion that are the negation of the idea of social citizenship (and obviously presuppose the constant weakening and systematic delegitimation of organized class movements, especially unions). We can go so far as to suggest the following hypothesis: the supranational political-economic units that tend to be established both to relativize the national framework, and thus to circumvent the national-social state, and to reproduce state mechanisms for integrating social conflicts at a higher level, as is typically the case with the European Union, are systematically constructed on gaps in living conditions or *Wohlstandsge-fälle*, mechanisms of inequality or internal exclusion. It is not a question of reducing these but of extending them for a certain time, if need be by means of new expansions of the European community, and despite the ritual announcements of a common social policy that would in the end have to include monetary and security policy.

A situation of this kind reinscribes the "dangerous classes" at the heart of the political space. Or, more generally, it inscribes the full specter of organized violence in political space, from racist discrimination and the law-and-order management of social exclusion to ethnic reactions and delinquency, which in turn heighten the militarization of the social order, and so on. We can thus push a notch further Poulantzas's reflections twenty years ago on the emergence of authoritarian statism. The crisis of the national-social state correlative to globalization and the re-proletarianization that constitutes both its result and one of its objects from the side of the dominant classes (of financial capitalism) gives rise to a whole series of national or international political initiatives that relate to what could be called a *preventative counterrevolution*, even more than neoimperialism. For the objective is not to conquer zones of territorial influence, which has lost its point in the age of constant outsourcing of production and extraction of surplus value; it is to create and, to the extent possible (with all the risks of such a policy of the sorcerer's apprentice brings), to provoke a "war of all against all," a generalized situation of endemic violence and insecurity, in which the constitution of a transnational, multiethnic, multicultural movement turns out to be practically impossible.

The whole question is whether a policy of this kind, more or less deliberate but perfectly observable in its effects, which combines financial, military, and humanitarian aspects and which I believe can be characterized as preventive counterrevolution, elicits a revolutionary response, or, if you like, a counter-counterrevolution, according to the schema of "going to extremes" that was largely shared among Marxist and Leninist representations of the socialist transition after the experience of the insurrections of the nineteenth century. It is indeed, I repeat, a matter of a policy, which one could assign to the pursuit of the interests of the dominant class, or a fraction of it, which means in particular that the effects of the re-proletarianization of the global working class are by no means an economic fatality (we could even think that they are in part econom-ically counterproductive). But this policy cannot be simply reversed, in mimetic fashion, by social forces: workers, oppressed peoples, revolu-tionary intellectuals, and other emancipatory and resistance movements that make up everyone the progressive tradition calls the left or "the people." The dramatic historical experience of the twentieth century—what Eric Hobsbawm has called the Age of Extremes—can serve at least to teach us that, precisely because political realities are strategic, there cannot be symmetry between the strategies of the dominant and those of the dominated.[5] This was also, already, the lesson of Machiavelli. And this is what I would briefly like to come to in conclusion.

IV

Even if the constitution of the national-social state has only been a fact limited in space and time (but inscribed in the center of the capitalist system), it constitutes a historically irreversible fact. The cunning of his-tory is not in the process of reversing direction, despite all the phe-nomena of regression, or more exactly of the cyclical reproduction of mechanisms of exploitation and oppression, that characterize it. It must be remembered, in particular, that it is largely in order to enter in their turn into the sphere of citizenship that the peoples of the countries of the East, subject to what I have elsewhere called the "dictatorship over the pro-letariat," put an end to the Soviet-style regimes, and not to enter the sphere of savage liberalism. And the fact must also be recognized that the phe-nomena of extreme, exterminist violence that today characterize global politics and are inextricably combined with economic-demographic vio-lence tend toward the physical elimination of populations that have become "useless" for exploitation, with ideological, ethnic, or religious violence, massively express the *impossibility* of constructing a national-social state, and thus in many cases of constructing a state as such, in a large part of the globe, affects the social situation, the possibilities of col-lective representation and political organization, the very notion of the rights of the individual, from the inside, everywhere in the world. This is why the question today is, as has been said, *both* defending and extend-ing a social citizenship that has been profoundly called into question (it is, moreover, impossible to defend it without extending it) *and* inventing new forms, a new concept of citizenship that in particular allows it to overcome the deep contradictions of the national-social state. It is clear that this situation places us before dilemmas that are very hard to solve in practice, and even to formulate.

I see evidence for this in the way that, in Europe in particular, a process of fragmentation is taking shape within the socialist tradition into two types of discourse, each like the negative of the other. On one side (as we see, for example, in Habermas or left Habermasians), the idea is advanced of a "postnational politics," the engine of which would be the extension of human rights and the juridical form of collective negotiations across borders, but on an essentially moral basis and independently of effective social mobilization. On the other, we see forming, not astonishingly, movements to defend the gains of social citizenship that focus on the guarantee of the state (or, as one says in France, the Republic), but that by this very fact become movements in defense of the nation and the sacralized and idealized principle of national sovereignty (which occasionally leads them, in what has been called a red-brown combination, to practically or theoretically join demands for a "national preference" and justify discriminatory policies against immigrants). It is this alternative that we must try to escape by combining the defense of social citizenship with the invention of new forms of citizenship, and thus progressively constructing an alternative to the national-social state.

For my part, in a nonexclusive and provisional way, I will say that such an alternative must include at least three fundamental dimensions.

First, it must include a drastic reduction of *Wohlstandsgefälle* that pit regions of the planet, sometimes of the same continent or country, against each other, and that end up taking the form of a gap between zones in which national and human resources are devastated and others in which lifestyles are managed. Here it is a matter of a concerted (planned) struggle against underdevelopment and ecological catastrophe. But it is also a matter of, in a new sense that overcomes the old antinomies of city and country, or recent antinomies of industrial and residential space, a policy of urbanization, or of civilization as urbanization, without which there is no reduction of collective, state and antistate violence. (One could argue convincingly that the violent campaigns of ethnic cleansing in the former Yugoslavian space were in many respects wars against the city and urbanity.)

Second, this alternative has to include a dimension of transnational (rather than postnational) citizenship, which in my view always proceeds from below rather than from above (even if it is destined to one day give meaning to still-technocratic formulas like European citizenship). That is, it has to include the democratization of borders, coordinated management, negotiated with the interested parties and the countries of origin, of the fluxes of immigration, the recognition of the civic and political rights of immigrants (or let us rather say, resident foreigners) in each country, the recognition of cultural pluralism and its contribution to the development of each national culture.

Third, an alternative must include a movement beyond the forms and limits within which the national-social state establishes the protection of individuals, or the satisfaction of their demand for emancipation, which most often implies a sociological categorization, a transformation of ethical or anthropological differences (gender, health and sickness, age and educational difference, etc.) into quantitative and essential social differences, as we see very clearly in the case of women's rights or minority protections. It is largely against this categorization (what Deleuze called "coding," "territorialization," the "society of control") that the so-called individualism or spontaneism of contemporary social movements has developed. We must therefore find ways, without renouncing the principle of social protection and its extension, of freeing social citizenship from its own sociologism, its own bureaucratic tendency to reify categories of individual social belonging.

Are these objectives democratic? Incontestably. They even extend the secular movement of the invention of democracy or of new fundamental rights, without which there would be no democracy but only the corporatist representation of society within the state. Are they "socialist"? Perhaps, at least in part. But I would rather insist on what they articulate of the permanence and renewal of the *communist* political idea, beyond a century of official, orthodox or heretical Marxism, which enclosed it within the limits of a program of socialist transition or a "transition to socialism," that is, a pure alternative to capitalism—when it was not a simple inversion of capitalism.[6] And since we are discussing these questions today in memory of Poulantzas and trying to profit from his incomplete work, and since, on the other hand, the idea of communist politics is philosophically an ethical idea that cannot be presented in an impersonal way, I will pose the question in the form of a triple interrogation to which there is only one answer. In what way is a communist position indispensable to the revival and refoundation of citizenship beyond the national-social state? In what way can we say that Poulantzas himself was a communist, through and through? Who, today, are the communists?

I will speak, then, about Nicos Poulantzas's communism, and I will speak of it in the singular. For it is not a question here of *Was* (*Was ist der Kommunismus?* What is communism?) but of *Wer* (*Wer sind die Kommunisten?* Who are the communists?). In this formulation, which flirts with a theme made famous by Nietzsche and Heidegger, I also invite us to hear the legacy of the *Manifesto of the Communist Party*, wherein Marx in effect asked himself, within a given conjuncture, *who* the communists were, could be, and must be. ("The Communists fight for the attainment of the immediate aims, for the enforcement of the momentary interest of the working class; but in the movement of the present, they also represent and take care of the future of that movement. . . . In short, the Communists everywhere support every revolutionary movement against the existing social and political order of things. . . . [T]hey labour everywhere for the union and agreement of the democratic parties of all countries.") To be sure, the signification of what Marx called a party in 1848 has been totally reversed over 150 years. It is therefore necessary to return to his idea while shifting the accent. In all political movements, social or cultural struggles, the communists "represent"— that is, *practice*—the plurality, the multiplicity of interests of emancipation, which are irreducible by reason of their very radicality. They claim and put to work freedom, not as the isolation of individuals and groups, equality, not as uniformity, but equality and freedom as the reciprocity of individualities, or as the community that individual and collective singularities offer or provide each other. Here there is of course (as was the case with Marx) an essential connection with citizenship, but against the statist form of managing pluralism through formal rules and administrative constraints.

At the conference at which this paper was presented, Annie Leclerc called Nicos Poulantzas a *cosmopolitès*, or, better, a *philoxenos*. I too see Nicos's communism this way, beyond his fundamental democratism (coming from a country under military dictatorship) and his attachment to socialist politics (whose history and variations throughout Europe he studied), and as the very condition of their union. Or, if you like, in the conjunction of two elements:

- his *practical* (even more than theoretical) internationalism, his unremitting quest for the meeting and communication between emancipatory movements beyond frontiers, illustrated particularly sharply by the opposition between the notions of communism and communitarianism;
- his insistence, in the pure tradition of Marx's communism, on the necessity of overcoming the difference between manual and intellectual labor as a way of eliminating the roots of state and party bureaucratism and making possible an open dialectic, without foreseeable end, of representative, institutional democracy and direct, associative or popular democracy, without which there would be no new citizenship.

We must of course recognize that globalization, the concentration of economic and cultural power, and, in reaction to this, religious or secular nationalism, have multiplied the obstacles facing these two necessities. They are the same obstacles that block our escape from the crisis of the national-social state.

I will say, intentionally playing on the expression, that Nicos Poulantzas was a typical "internal communist," not only internal to his country (although he lived outside it), but internal to social, intellectual, and political practices, as we must be today, even if the idea of an external communism has lost all referents in the real (though not in the imaginary, since phantoms die hard). Poulantzas ironically theorized this highly particular topology of communist struggle as immanent within struggles and circulating among them (against the idea of "double power" that was emblematic of external communism of the Soviet type): "To imagine that political struggle can ever be located wholly outside the State" (260). It is a matter of the outside of the state, outside institutions, but still more outside the practices that underlie them. A bit later he in fact writes, dialectically: struggles for "radical transformations of the state"—or, as I would say myself, for active citizenship—and which, for this very reason, cannot be external to it, are nevertheless necessarily situated in a *"global perspective of the withering away of the State"* (262). Today Poulantzas and others are no longer there. But communist citizens, citizen communists or communists of citizenship, are always there—"invisible," since they are neither an army nor a camp nor a party nor a church. It is their way of staying alive.

HANNAH ARENDT, THE RIGHT TO HAVE RIGHTS, AND CIVIC DISOBEDIENCE

Every great oeuvre has its history, internal and external.[1] It reflects an intellectual development that sometimes includes ruptures. It responds to historical changes that force it to reorient itself. We could imagine that this is particularly so in the case of a philosopher like Hannah Arendt, who, trying to make intelligible (to herself) that political action deals with the unpredictable, the *new*, confers a central function on the category of the event.[2] More than any other contemporary thinker, we are tempted to say that she never wrote the same book twice, nor any two books from the same point of view. But this does not mean that we are not dealing with strong continuities, the recurrence of insistent questions, on which the expansion of her philosophical horizon and displacements of her analysis precisely depend. It is based on this conviction that I will take elements from moments in her work that are very far apart, inscribed in different contexts and heterogeneous styles—history, speculative reflection, politically engaged essays, journalism—in such a way as to reconstruct what seems to me to be a central problem (perhaps *the* central problem) for her: that of the politics of human rights and its foundation, or rather its absence of foundation, its unfounded character.

A HIGHLY PARADOXICAL CRITIQUE OF THE RIGHTS OF MAN

Where does the persistent difficulty Arendt's discourse on rights, at least from a philosophical point of view, come from? First of all, it seems to me, from her combination of one of the most radical critiques of their speculative anthropology, and thus of the classical theory of human rights as a foundation of the juridical edifice and corresponding political practice, with an intransigent defense of their imprescriptible character (at least for some of them), which practically identifies their neglect with a destruction of the human. How is it possible at the same time to reject the idea that there are fundamental human rights (as well as the majority of our democratic constitutions and universal declarations that postulate their anteriority and primacy in the normative order) in theory and to place an intransigent politics of the rights of man at the very heart of the democratic construction? How is it possible to negate on one side what one seeks to put into practice on the other?

The discourse Arendt develops in what is, at least in appearance, her most systematic philosophical treatise, *The Human Condition* (1958), does not make the task any easier—quite the contrary. The word "condition," which figures in the title, is the exact antithesis of "nature."[3] It doubly repudiates any metaphysical or speculative theorization of human nature. On the one hand, it does so by reiterating in its way the proposition announced by Marx in the sixth thesis on Feuerbach: there is no such thing as a universal or formal human essence housed in each human individual (for example in the modality of a cogito), but only, if one can put it this way, a plurality of human individuals, and thus a plurality of more or less conflictual relations among them, which are constitutive of their common "world."[4] On the other hand, this time at the antipode from Marx, it does so by allowing the deeply alienating conflict to be named that develops between two sets of conditions: those that could be called natural, since they concern the reproduction of life, and those that could be called political (or civic), since they concern the formation of a public space, where the common is recognized by the plurality of human beings as their end.[5] Arendt sees, as we know, a typical characteristic of modernity and of the alienation proper to it (alienation from the world, and not just from the self or the subject) in the fact that the growing technicization of processes for reproducing life in "mass society" allows humans to represent reproduction as their activity par excellence, and to substitute this for the pursuit of the good life—that is, the construction of political relations based on the irreducibility of each person's position.[6] Paradoxically, the development of growing artificiality thus tends to naturalize the political domain at the same time that it socializes the world.[7]

To put it in Derrida's terminology, the counterpart of such a radical alienation seems to be the task of inventing a cosmopolitics "to come" as the sole modality of emancipation that offers humanity the means to reconstruct, differently, what has been lost in its history. But we must at the same time be careful here not to contradict Arendt's many warnings against any idealization of the past, including the Greek past, which is nevertheless the origin of our concept of the political, and the epistemological lesson implicitly contained in her historical pessimism and her reticence about prophesizing the future.[8]

We are thus led to reformulate the question posed by this concept of the politics of human rights, which links different moments of her practical philosophy, from the analysis of the tragedies of contemporary history to the republican ideal of the *vita activa*, by giving it the form of the most brutal possible dilemma: how to hold together an extreme form of institutionalism, explicitly connected to the critique of theories of natural right we can find in Burke, and a critique of world-alienation, which is hard to imagine without reference to an idea or model (*Urbild, Vorbild*) of the human, precisely by reversing the anthropological and metaphysical presuppositions of the Enlightenment?

ARENDT AND HER CONCEPT OF THE POLITICAL

It will be said that the escape from the verbal embarrassment is not so difficult, and can be found in the author's contemporary commentary in the essay *On Revolution*: it has in fact become a commonplace that for Arendt the rights of man cannot be conceived as an *origin* to be rediscovered or restored (as was postulated in their name by the revolutions of the Enlightenment), but only as an *invention* (one of the meanings of *auctoritas*) or a continuous *beginning* (*archè*).[9] It is by following this thread that we can most readily identify Arendt's trace in a whole current of contemporary political philosophy (or nonphilosophy, even "antiphilosophy," which rightly shares her concern with demarcating itself by means of a critique of the originary, conceived in historicist as well as transcendental terms).[10] By criticizing the classical revolutionary ideologies and simultaneously vindicating the "lost treasure of revolution," Arendt distanced herself from the explicit or latent representation that makes revolution a restoration, the rediscovery of a birthright or an originary state of freedom and equality while by the same stroke making constitutions essentially systems of guarantees for preexisting rights (as Locke had perhaps announced more perfectly than anyone else).[11] She sought to insist, to the contrary, on the idea that revolutions institute or, strictly speaking, invent what is human, including the principles of reciprocity and collective solidarity, and for this reason exert a durable effect or inaugurate a permanence in the life of republican political systems. They therefore do not derive from a foundation and do not derive their legitimacy from their universal, a priori character; rather, they introduce the universal into history. Philosophically, nothing is opposed to what we call the "groundlessness" (or the absence of foundation, *Grundlosigkeit*) of this way of articulating the practical and historical character of human rights, which precisely reverses a certain way of founding the political on a metaphysical essence. It is in fact such an idea of groundlessness that alone can authorize the identification of human rights with a practice (or a pure activity)—at the price, no doubt, of recognizing their historically contingent or aleatory character.[12]

I endorse this interpretation, which has become classic, without reservation, but I believe it is incomplete. We must take a further step to expose what gives Arendt's thesis its extreme radicality. Following the dialectical model of the *coincidentia oppositorum*, she is not content to make the institution the source of positive law but sees it as a construction of the human as such, and pushes the idea of a politics of human rights so far as to make dissidence—in the specifically modern form of "civic disobedience"—the touchstone of the founding reciprocity of rights. She is therefore in no way "historicist" (or "relativist"), even if she presents the construction of systems of individual rights as entirely immanent to history. And, while legitimizing the notions of power and authority, she finds a means of lodging a paradoxical principle of *anarchy*—of "nonpower" or the contingency of authority—at the very heart of *archè*, or the authority of the political. We are thus led to reinterpret the absence of foundation or groundlessness of rights not only as a logical thesis, but as a practical thesis that is itself political, even if in an essentially antinomic mode. Every political construction implies the combination of a contrary element (which we could call "unpolitical"), and thus—at least virtually—the permanent recreation of the political out of its own dissolution, and in the end the practical impossibility of separating once and for all the construction of the human through political institutions from its destruction or deconstruction (which results specifically from the historical collapse of institutions, but sometimes also from certain aspects of its most everyday, banal operation). For this combination of collective action with its own opposite is, in fact, the political itself.

I do not conceal from myself, of course, the fragility and imprecision of these formulations. This is why I would now like to return to Arendt's texts (or at least some of them) to see if we can find in them such a dialectic of opposites that would coincide with her own concept of the political, her *Begriff des Politischen*. To begin, it will deep down only be a matter of naming or locating the problems in the hope that this basis will be sufficient to expand the discussion to other aspects of Arendt's oeuvre. My point of departure will be the relation between the now-famous expression "right to have rights" and the critique of the nation-state, and what I call "Arendt's theorem"—its position against the current of modernity when it comes to the relation between man and citizen. From there I will return to the highly particular way she lays claim to the Greek model of democracy, or rather (for she never stops reminding us of how important the original terminology is here) the concept of *isonomia*—which is not, contrary to what we still sometimes read, equivalent to "democracy" (which had strongly negative connotations in Greek debates), but rather the origin of a series that passes through the Latin translations *aequum ius* and *aequa libertas* and arrives at our "equal freedom"—not a regime, but the principle or rule of the constitution of citizenship.[13] This detour will allow me finally to return to how Arendt uses antinomy, or develops an "unpolitical" conception of the political. I will insist in particular on the anti-theological modality of this usage, which has to be associated with the depth of Arendt's moral and aesthetic connection to Greek tragedy, and consequently with a notion of law that is systematically detached from the heritage of sovereignty, even under positive and secularized juridical forms.[14]

What, then, is what I called Arendt's theorem, and what is its relation to the notion of the right to have rights? We know that in the last chapter of part 2 of *The Origins of Totalitarianism*, "The Decline of the Nation-State and the End of the Rights of Man," Arendt developed a provocative thesis based on her observation of the tragic consequences of imperialist wars, which resulted in the appearance of masses of stateless refugees and superfluous human beings. The common characteristic of all these humans, who are in a sense "too many" but remain physically present in global space, is that they are progressively deprived of all personal protection by the destruction or dissolution of the political communities to which they belonged—despite the efforts of international organizations created precisely in an attempt to respond to this unprecedented situation—and permanently threatened with elimination. This must be seen as a perverse consequence of the history of the nation-state, which served as the historical framework for the universal proclamation of certain fundamental rights of the person, but also rigorously identified belonging to a community with possession of a nationality or the status of a national citizen. This situation refuted de facto the declared ideological foundation of the nation-state (at least in the democratic and republican tradition), whereby the rights of the (national) citizen appeared as a secondary construction, instituting or recognizing preexisting natural rights. In turn, human rights gave the political institution (in practice, the state) that transformed them into civic rights a universalistic principle of legitimacy—not in the sense of *extensive* universality, potentially including all humanity, but, much more significantly, in the sense of *intensive* universality, which corresponds to the absence of internal discrimination and the equal freedom of nationals. Under these conditions, we would have to admit—with practically the whole modern juridical and philosophical tradition—that human rights have a broader extension than civic rights. The former are logically independent of the latter and thus provide a basis for recognizing the dignity of people who do not belong to the same political community but only, so to speak, to the natural (or essential) community of human beings. This is why their protection would have to be organized internationally, since national solidarity no longer applies—especially in wartime, when national communities enter into conflict and exclude one another.[15]

But in practice the opposite happened: when the civic rights and corresponding guarantees are abolished or historically destroyed for whole masses of individuals, so are their human or personal rights. Arendt speaks here of a "bitter confirmation of Burke's critique" of the rights of man in the name of a principled anti-individualism and the primacy of the historical institution over transcendental universalism.[16] What we are offered here is a typical *elenchus* (or *reductio ad absurdum*), where the impossibility of the consequence refutes the theoretical premise. This is what I call Arendt's theorem, in order to emphasize that her argumentation does not only have empirical value but significance on the level of principle. It is by no means a matter of maintaining that since the consequences of war and imperialism are incompatible with the universalistic ideological claims of nations, we must find an equally practical compensation or counterweight (for example, an internationally recognized humanitarian politics), which would mean that at the level of principles or moral ideals, human rights could still be conceived of as the foundation for civic rights, whose evolution contradicted them in fact. The direction of the argument is exactly the reverse, and this is what makes it so provocative (a bit like how the arguments of the ancient Sophists appeared as provocations against reason and tradition). If the abolition of civic rights is also the destruction of human rights, it is because in reality the latter rest on the former and not the reverse.

Here there is an intrinsic reason, inherent in the very notion of rights and their relational character—or, better, in the idea of reciprocity that is inherent in them. Rights are not properties or qualities that individuals each possess on their own, but qualities that individuals confer on one another as soon as they institute a "common world" in which they can be considered responsible for their actions and opinions. From this comes the crucial importance of the formula "right to have rights": the right to have rights is precisely what the stateless, and more generally excluded individuals and groups who are multiplying in contemporary societies, are deprived of. And among the rights individuals are thus deprived of, we must of course include the fundamental political right to demand or claim their rights, the right to petition in the classical sense. The reciprocal thesis that follows from this is that the first right is precisely the right to have rights, taken absolutely or in its indetermination (I will return to this point), and not some particular statutory right. It is in this sense a matter of a right without an a priori foundation, as contingent as the political community itself—or, better still, the existence of a community of political actions, the simultaneous engagement of individuals in common political action.[17] Paradoxically (at least from the perspective of a meta-physical doctrine of foundations), this right to have rights is at once absolute *and* contingent. It is what in modern history the nation-state, in a violently contradictory way, has alternately guaranteed and suppressed, not only for distinct groups (for example, for the citizens of colonial powers and their colonial subjects) but sometimes for the same people (thus, in Europe, for Jews emancipated in the Enlightenment and dena-tionalized and then exterminated in the twentieth century, but also to varying degrees for other categories of stateless persons).

To gauge the full weight of this proposition, we must turn to the next section of *The Origins of Totalitarianism* and its interpretation of how the totalitarian state became exterminist. Here Arendt draws all the conse-quences from the fact that, on the universalistic (and thus humanist) conception of citizenship claimed by nation-states, there was at bottom no means of excluding someone (or some category) from the enjoyment of civic rights other than excluding them from humanity itself. Let us recall that what she is discussing here is not the situation of foreigners insofar as they find themselves already (or from a certain point, follow-ing a rectification of borders) outside the political territory of the state, but the ongoing production of the excluded within the state itself—a process that begins with the deprivation of civic rights, continues with the systematic destruction of the moral personality of individuals who command the respect to which they have a right (and which they them-selves bear), and culminates in industrialized mass murder that destroys individuality, or the "human face," as such.[18] So we understand why Ar-endt's institutionalism has most deeply nothing to do with the long tra-dition that extends from Burke and Bentham to legal positivism. The idea implied in Arendt's critique of human rights is not that only institu-tions create positive rights (along with obligations and sanctions), which would mean that outside institutions the notion of right has no meaning, individuals have no specific rights, only natural (biological, psychologi-cal, even cultural, etc.) qualities. Nor is it, despite certain appearances that are used to include Arendt in a neoclassical current that would also include Leo Strauss, a return to the ancient idea of the *zoon politikon*. It is a much more radical and philosophically opposite idea: outside the institution of the community—not, of course, in the sense of an organic community, another naturalist, symmetrical myth, but in the sense of the reciprocity of actions, what Kant called "commerce" or "reciprocal action"—there are no human beings. Humans do not exist as such, and thus they are not, strictly speaking.[19]

Nothing is therefore more erroneous than reading Arendt as if she sought to abolish or relativize the connection between the idea of humanity and that of rights in general, for it is instead a matter of reinforcing it. Arendt does not seek to relativize the idea of rights (or human rights) but, to the contrary, to make it indissociable and indiscernible from a construction of the human that is an internal, immanent effect of the historical invention of political institutions. We must say that strictly speaking human beings *are* their rights, or exist through them. But this notion covers over a profound antinomy, for we are forced to note that the same institutions that create rights—or, better still, by means of which individuals become human subjects by reciprocally conferring rights on one another—also constitute a threat to the human as soon as they destroy these rights or become an obstacle to them in practice. This is made very clear in the history of the nation-state (and its imperialist, colonialist, and exterminist derivatives), but it is certainly also true of other political forms constituted in history—including the Greek *polis*, whose privilege does not reside in some immunity from this tragic contingency but perhaps from the fact that its way of presenting and justifying exclusion, which was not that of modern universalistic discourse, was much less ideological or dissembling.

ARCHÈ AORISTOS

We thus find ourselves on the threshold of the questions posed by recourse to the notion of *isonomia*. This is precisely its first meaning: an institution by which individuals confer rights on each other in the public sphere, starting with the right to speak on a footing of equality (*isègoria, parrèsia*), which allows them to claim or legitimize all the others and is thus the concrete anthropological figure of the right to have rights. Be it in *The Human Condition* or in *On Revolution*—in reality two complementary books written during the period that follows the Hungarian revolution against Stalinist dictatorship and ends in the triple catastrophe of the 1960s: the U.S. war in Vietnam, the global student revolts of '68, and the Six Days War between Israel and the Arab countries, leading to the occupation of East Jerusalem and the Palestinian territories—she never stopped insisting on the typically "sophistic" idea that it is not the case that social and political forms replace a natural human freedom and equality with such and such a degree of inequality and tyranny, but, to the contrary, that the institutions of the city, insofar as they rest on *isonomia*, give birth to equality in the public sphere and by the same stroke to freedom in relations with power and authority in place of preexisting hierarchy and domination. Not only is the institution the origin of a second nature. It is not preceded by any real first nature, or only by an indetermination and a possibility that remains virtual.[20]

Here a philological and philosophical episode takes place that is at once subtle and rich in consequences. In both *The Human Condition* and *On Revolution*, Arendt does not refer initially to Aristotle's classic definition of citizen (*politès*) in terms of the reciprocity of command and obedience (*archein* and *archesthai*, whence proceed the places of the *archôn* and the *archomenos*), but to the (undoubtedly fictional) episode reported by Herodotus in book 3 of his *Histories*, concerning a debate among the Persians as they chose an heir and at the same time decided the form of government after the murder of the imposter who had taken power after the murder of Kambyses, following an aristocratic plot.[21] Let us note first of all that the same episode plays a crucial role for Rousseau, who could be called Arendt's intimate enemy in her project of redefining the political against the tradition of political philosophy, in the negative moment of his critique of inequality prior to trying to imagine a constitutional order analogous to our lost nature.[22] In the story, each of the three Persian princes who could be named to refound the state (Otanes, Megabyzes, and Darius, who is chosen in the end, definitively setting Persia on the opposite course to that of the Greek city-states) makes a plea for one of the typical regimes: *isonomia*, *oligarchia*, and *monarchia*.[23] The first is defined as "government of the mass of the people" (*plèthos archon*), in the sense, first of all, that "affairs [of state] are placed at the center" (*es meson katatheinai ta prègmata*), and then that offices are drawn by lot with the obligation to account for how they are discharged, with the "public" retaining the say in the last resort (*bouleumata panta es to koinon anapherei*). After the Persian nobles reject this extreme solution (a kind of anticipatory night of August 4), Otanes, in the form of a personal claim, delivers the formula that expresses his political ideal: *oute archein oute archesthai ethelô*, I want neither to command nor to obey.[24] Clearly, Aristotle (and, following him, the tradition of political philosophy centered around citizenship) never saw the definition of civic virtue in such a formulation: for there to be citizens, there must be an *archè*, a principle of authority, even if that authority is divided or circulates among the citizens. Otanes's principle, taken literally, is thus an anarchist principle. When it is taken into consideration (by Arendt or others), we are obliged to ask ourselves what place the anarchist moment has in a determinate conception of the political.

What I am maintaining here is of course not that we should classify Arendt herself as an anarchist or that she did not differentiate between democracy and anarchy. (She defended herself on this charge, in particular in her essay "On Civil Disobedience," to which we will return, and in the German interviews she gave at the end of her life.) It is rather that she deflects all positivism by including, at the origin of political institutions—or, better, in the indeterminate neighborhood of this origin—an imprescriptible moment of an-archy that has to be constantly reactivated precisely if the institution is to be *political*. The construction of the political, and thus the definition of the citizen, can thus only be antinomic. No doubt disobedience and obedience to the law are not equivalent; they cannot put on the same level by institutions. But the fact is that without the possibility of disobedience, there is no legitimate obedience—a thesis that does not refer (as in classic formulations of a right of resistance) to an imprescriptible and inalienable human nature, but to the pragmatic experience of the birth, history, and decadence of democracies (and "constitutions of liberty" in general).

This thus leads directly to what Arendt argues in her essay on "civic disobedience," provoked by the debates around the Vietnam War and the dissidence it set off in American society.[25] Her thesis, as we know, is far from simple. It relates in particular to the relation she maintains with contemporary events that serve as a framework and within which she tried to intervene in a specifically theoretical way. It is not a matter of forging arguments for or against this policy, even if Arendt in fact takes sides, but of returning on the basis of conjunctural problems to the republican principles at stake, and by the same stroke—taking note of the contingency of the history to which they belong—correcting or reworking our understanding.

Arendt does not give the name "civic disobedience" to simple objections of individual conscience based on a subjective reaction to the abuse of power (or what is perceived as such).[26] She speaks of "organized minorities" and even of "masses" (if not of mass movements) that present problems for public order and the recognition of state power.[27] But neither does she aim at the simple fact that a regime gripped by a legitimacy crisis has to face phenomena of insubordination and growing illegality. In a sense it is just the opposite: it is a matter of collective movements that, in a highly determinate situation with objective limits, abolish the vertical form of authority in favor of a horizontal association so as to re-create the conditions of free consent to the authority of the law. It is thus a matter, in the end, not of weakening legality but of reinforcing it, even if this way of defending the law against itself (or against its discretionary application by the government, the administration, the magistrates) can only be legally considered illegal, even criminal—at least from the classic institutionalist perspective for which there can be no difference between the legal order and the state order.[28] What is particularly striking in her analysis is her insistence on the idea of the risk civic disobedience implies. What is at stake is not the legal risk that is run (the punishment logically implied by breaking the law or disobeying the constituted authorities), which goes without saying, but the political risk—that is, of an error of judgment on the situation and the relation of forces that constitutes it, such that the aim of recreating the continuity of the *politeia* or the conditions for the existence of the active citizen could very well turn into their opposite, by a ruse of reason or rather of history, symmetrical to that of Hegel, resulting in their definitive destruction.

It is striking that here Arendt again cites Tocqueville's notion of "dangerous freedom" and refers to the "perils of equality" that are inseparable from democracy. These ideas are at the center of the political dilemma inherent in movements of dissidence and civil disobedience, caught between the authoritarianism and conservatism of the state and the possibility of an essentially totalitarian internal degeneration:

> No doubt "the danger of civil disobedience is elemental," but it is
> not different from, nor is it greater than, the dangers inherent in
> the right to free association, and of these Tocqueville, his admiration notwithstanding, was not unaware. . . . Tocqueville knew that
> "the tyrannical control that these societies exercise is often far
> more insupportable than the authority possessed over society by
> the government which they attack." But he know also that "the
> liberty of association has become a necessary guarantee against the

tyranny of the majority," that "a dangerous expedient is used to obviate a still more formidable danger," and, finally, that "it is by the enjoyment of dangerous freedom that the Americans learn the art of rendering the dangers of freedom less formidable." . . .

We do not need to go into the old debates about the glories and the danger of equality, the good and the evil of democracy, to understand that all evil demons could be let loose if the original contractual model of the associations . . . should be lost. Under today's circumstances, this could happen if these groups, like their counterparts in other countries, were to substitute ideological commitments, political or other, for actual goals. . . . What threatens the student movement, the chief civil-disobedience group of the moment, is not just vandalism, violence, bad temper, and worse manners, but the growing infection of the movement with ideologies (Maoism, Castroism, Stalinism, Marxism-Leninism, and the like), which in fact split and dissolve the association.[29]

That is to say, it would deprive it of its capacity to gather together an internal pluralism of tendencies into a common dissidence, a distilled model of what could be a society of citizens, a public square. These problems are obviously far from obsolete today.

But the idea of contingency or indetermination (opening the necessity and risk of judgment) that inspires these considerations can also be formulated "in Greek," for example by retrieving the first definition of citizenship proposed by Aristotle in the *Politics*, which characterizes it as the bearer of an "indeterminate" or "unlimited" *archè*, according to the translation we choose of *archè aoristos*. (But no doubt it is necessary precisely to retain both connotations, especially if we do not want to immediately return this to a simple institutional function, whose content would be participation in deliberative and judicial assemblies, and thus to the exercise of judgment in decisions and accounting, *bouleuein kai krinein*.)[30] This definition—the first of three—is fundamental; it commands the whole logic of what follows. What is more, let us not forget that it is precisely what Aristotle wants to get beyond as quickly as possible, no doubt because of the danger it poses of an uncontrollable oscillation of democracy and tyranny. Nevertheless, it does not disappear in favor of better ordered or better defined notions (especially the second definition of citizenship as the alternation of authority and obedience: *archein te kai archesthai dunasthai*) without leaving a trace that is periodically re-activated in the construction of the *politeia* as the "balanced" or "perfect" regime (as far as is humanly possible) because it neutralizes the inconveniences and cumulates the virtues of the others (in practice just two: democracy and aristocracy).[31] This is the case every time it is necessary to reactivate the foundation of the city in the "domination" or "mastery" (*kurios einai*) of that which constitutes it (the uniform mass of citizens), which means that every regime is in a sense democratic (or better: a regime cannot be antidemocratic).[32] Arendt's thesis, by comparison, would be that *archè* has to again become unlimited or indeterminate (*aoristos*) in the negative form of civic disobedience, for this annuls the privilege of power, or returns judgment to the side of "whatever" citizens. The problem that is by definition insoluble (as was constantly objected to by Arendt), which she treats as the challenge that is the test of the truth of democracies, is to incorporate into institutions their opposite: it is to institute disobedience as the ultimate recourse in the face of the ambivalence of the state, which makes it the destroyer of liberties and of lives at the same time that it is their guarantor.

HOW TO ESCAPE VOLUNTARY SERVITUDE?

It thus remains to take into account a crucial dimension of this antinomic conception that we can associate with a certain tragic model of the groundlessness of rights. The fact of combining in this way a negative thesis—what I have called Arendt's theorem—that identifies the construction of the properly human relation with the possibility of a right to have rights in the framework of a political institution that takes the form of a historical community, with a positive thesis, which makes the inclusion of a principle of disobedience or dissidence at the heart of obedience itself the condition of the existence of the political (and thus reverses the idea of the closure, the completeness inherent in it into openness or incompletion), places any purely legal (or legalistic) understanding of right itself in question. It is opposed to the sovereign tautology: the law is the law (*Gesetz ist Gesetz*), which also means that its own "nonviolence" (in the highly particular sense Arendt gives this notion) poses a limit to the violence of tautological propositions that descend from theology to the political.[33] What can seem strange here, at least for those with some familiarity with dialectics, is that the negative proposition (reduction to absurdity or impossibility) in reality announces the sole condition of possibility of the institution, and the content of the positive proposition is the idea of a negative dialectic inherent in the life of the law, which accompanies all its existence to the point at which it is applied (and is not limited to a founding insurrection of the juridical order as a whole or to the exercise of a constituent power destined to be effaced in the constitution it produces).

Arendt did not meet the question of obeying the law and how it is conceived by the dominant positivism (which is organically united with the operation of the modern state, including the rule of law) abstractly, but in the course of what, for historical and personal reasons that are easily understood, was probably the "crucial experience" par excellence in her life as a public intellectual, namely the Eichmann trial. Here the chapter of *Eichmann in Jerusalem* on the "Duties of a Law-Abiding Citizen" must be very carefully reread, noting the effect of generality produced by the formula abstracted from its context, but also without prejudicing the relation Arendt finally establishes between the state of exception and the normality of the *Rechtsstaat*. The chapter closes with a provocative interpretation of Eichmann's zealous behavior, which, during the decomposition of the Third Reich, while some Nazi leaders responsible for the Final Solution attempted to "moderate" its operation by negotiating the exchange of safe-passage for groups of Jews slated for extermination for strategic goods (or in hope of personal accommodations with the victors, which they sometimes obtained), led him to demonstrate an intransigent "conscience" in executing the Führer's annihilation order, running the risk of coming into conflict with his immediate superiors. Arendt shows that we need not see here the signs of particular ideological fanaticism nor of Eichmann's exceptional cruelty, but an illustration of the inevitable consequences of a certain conception of law and legal obedience constitutive of what she calls in the same work the "banality of evil."

Three main traits seem to characterize the law understood in this sense: its *universality* (the fact that it cannot allow exceptions, and thus is "without prejudice" in its application); its *imperative* character (the fact that it requires unconditional obedience to the letter, not interpretation or discussion on the part of the citizen whose obedience it prescribes); and its *absoluteness* (this is the most problematic point, for in the case of the legal system of the Third Reich the ultimate source of law was not a constitutional order or the general will of the people expressed through its representatives, but the very words of Hitler, including those that remained unwritten, which had the force of law, since he was supposed to be the incarnation of the German people). What Arendt described as "the moral, juridical, and political phenomenon at the center of our century" thus resides in taking to the limit certain intrinsic characteristics of juridical formalism that invert it: from a function of the construction (or conservation) of the common world to a function of destruction, without for all that altering its form. Neither the guarantees of juridical form itself (the fact that the law was promulgated according to rules) nor the mechanisms of moral defense—conscience and humanity—were sufficient defenses against this reversal. They presuppose, Arendt tells us, that the problem is solved, for the problem lies in the very significance of the idea of law as command or expression of sovereign will.

> And just as the law in civilized countries assumes that the voice of conscience tells everybody "Thou shalt not kill," even though man's natural desires and inclinations may at times be murderous, so the law of Hitler's land demanded that the voice of conscience tell everybody: "Thou shalt kill," although the organizers of the massacres knew full well that murder is against the normal desires and inclinations of most people. Evil in the Third Reich had lost the quality by which most people recognize it—the quality of temptation. Many Germans and many Nazis, probably an overwhelming majority of them, must have been tempted *not* to murder, *not* to rob, *not* to let their neighbors go off to their doom (for that the Jews were transported to their doom they knew, of course, even though many of them may not have known the gruesome details), and not to become accomplices in all these crimes by benefiting from them. But, God knows, they had learned how to resist temptation.[34]

What on one side (that of obedience) appears banal, as the sense of duty executed to the letter, thus appears on the other side as "radical evil," following the critical usage Arendt makes of this Kantian category, simply by pushing the identification of the law with an expression of will whose autonomy can turn from good to evil, to the extreme.[35] And, in the same way, voluntary servitude (in which the individual's "good will" in a way turns against the capacity to judge for himself) appears as the other side of the totalitarian process of the institutionalized destruction of the human through the production and elimination of superfluous humans.

Here it would be necessary to attempt a genealogy of the expression *Gesetz ist Gesetz* or "the law is the law," which furnishes the tautology of right with its typical expression. Its origins are murky, even if one could try to trace a line that goes back to certain maxims of Roman law (*dura lex, sed lex*), or, very differently, to debates in the Jewish tradition on obedience to the Torah (which Spinoza recalls in chapter 4 of the *Theologico-Political Treatise*). But the crucial problem seems to reside in the transfer of absolutism to the law itself, which was the work of jurists at the time of the institution of the nation-state, in particular Bodin (and, following him, Hobbes), and thus of the *internalization* of the sovereignty of the will to the form of law itself, which impersonalizes it or renders it independent of the particular person of the sovereign and the circumstances of his decision.[36] The important point is obviously the fact that in the conception of the law as expression of the sovereign will (be it that of a prince or of the people) that subjects "each and all" to a single juridical order, one is led to do without the subjects' consent (and consequently their capacity for contestation through representatives or intermediary bodies, as they had been variously preserved by feudal monarchies). At the same time that the state acquires, according to the jurists' expression, "decisional and procedural autonomy," the law becomes *unilateral*, which means that it presumes the subjects' obedience or makes it into a prior obedience. Not only is "the privilege of the law to be obligatory without the agreement of its addressees"; "the act of sovereignty is imposed unilaterally as soon as one is in a position to distinguish between its authors and its addressees (third parties), who are subjected to a prior obedience. It may be that the law of the Sovereign runs up against the active opposition of certain subjects, but in law it is valid as soon as it is juridically perfect, and thus it is valid if need be against the will of the addressees. It is essentially constraining since the refusal to obey it can imply enforcement."[37] This holds more than ever as soon as the sovereign is no longer an individual prince but presents itself as the body of the citizens themselves, and thus independently of the modalities of the exercise of legislative power.[38] And this leads immediately to distinguishing between norms that are contestable (acts of magistrates, particular government decisions) and those that must always remain incontestable (laws against which, as soon as they are promulgated, there can be no appeal—but can only be changed through a new act of sovereignty).[39]

We can now return a last time to Arendt's analysis (here more than ever "thinking without banisters," as she claimed) in order to specify at once where the line of demarcation falls between the normal, conservative institution of law and its perverse or criminal institution, if it can even be drawn cleanly, and by which byway or change of paradigm Arendt tried to draw the political (and therefore also unpolitical) consequences of highlighting a grey zone where these two extremes paradoxically meet.[40] Here the notion of voluntary servitude is unavoidable, not because it would bring a solution (which would only be a repetition of the enigma), but because it poses the problem in a radical way—at least if we read it not as a simple empirical description of situations in which to varying degrees subjects consent to servitude or subordination—as soon as this cannot be explained simply by relations of forces, but as an interrogation without an immediate or definitive answer on the conditions of possibility, within the very constitution of the will, of unconditional obedience, or the *will to obey* without which there would be no absolute power.

It is precisely this problem that absorbed Arendt's attention as soon as she took seriously Eichmann's reference during his trial to the Kantian categorical imperative and how he applied it to his own "dutiful" obedience. Not only did she not see it as a ruse plain and simple; she related it to what in contemporary jargon would be called a process of subjectification inscribed in a certain way of interpreting the citizen's relation to sovereignty through the intermediary of the universality of the law.

> And, to the surprise of everybody, Eichmann came up with an approximately correct definition of the categorical imperative: "I meant by my remark about Kant that the principle of my will must always be such that it can become the principle of general laws" . . . He then proceeded to explain that from the moment he was charged with carrying out the Final Solution he had ceased to live according to Kantian principles, that he had known it, and that he had consoled himself with the thought that he no longer "was master of his own deeds," that he was unable "to change anything." What he failed to point out in court was that in this "period of crimes legalized by the state," as he himself now called it, he had

not simply dismissed the Kantian formula as no longer applicable, he had distorted it to read: Act as if the principle of your actions were the same as that of the legislator or of the law of the land—or, in Hans Frank's formulation of "the categorical imperative in the Third Reich": "Act in such a way that the Führer, if he knew your action, would approve it" . . . Kant, to be sure, had never intended to say anything of the sort . . . But it is true that Eichmann's unconscious distortion agrees with what he himself called the version of Kant "for the household use of the little man." In this household use, all that is left of Kant's spirit is the demand that a man do more than obey the law, that he go beyond the mere call of obedience and identify his own will with the principle behind the law—the source from which the law sprang. . . . Much of the horribly painstaking thoroughness in the execution of the Final Solution . . . can be traced to the odd notion, indeed very common in Germany, that to be law-abiding means not merely to obey the laws but to act as though one were the legislator of the laws that one obeys. Hence the conviction that nothing less than going beyond the call of duty will do.

Whatever Kant's role in the formation of "the little man's" mentality in Germany may have been, there is not the slightest doubt that in one respect Eichmann did indeed follow Kant's precepts: a law was a law, there could be no exceptions. . . . No exceptions—this was the proof that he had always acted against his "inclinations," whether they were sentimental or inspired by interest, that he had always done his "duty."[41]

The expression "household use" that Arendt employs here is not, of course, secondary. It does not simply signify "personal" or "private," but is opposed to the *public* use of practical reason that, in the true Kantian doctrine as Arendt understands it, makes the discovery of principles (or maxims) of action conform to the law of the exercise of judgment. This is why invoking the "voice of conscience" cannot serve here as a banister, but finds itself carried away in the same movement of perversion as the categorical imperative itself. But the most delicate point of this interpretation (which tried to think to the extremes the virtualities of a certain concept of law) clearly resides in the proposition concerning the subject's ideal identification with the legislator. We can illuminate this by connecting this passage to developments in the third part of the *Origins of Totalitarianism* on the relation between the Leader and the members of the movement:

> The supreme task of the Leader is to impersonate the double function characteristic of each layer of the movement—to act as the magic defense of the movement against the outside world; and at the same time, to be the direct bridge by which the movement is connected to it. The Leader . . . claims personal responsibility for every action, deed, or misdeed, committed by any member or functionary in his official capacity. This total responsibility is the most important organizational aspect of the so-called Leader principle [*Führerprinzip*], according to which every functionary is not only appointed by the Leader but is his walking embodiment, and every order is supposed to emanate from this one ever-present source. This thorough identification of the Leader with every appointed subleader and this monopoly of responsibility for everything which is being done are also the most conspicuous signs of the decisive difference between a totalitarian leader and an ordinary dictator or tyrant. A tyrant would never identify himself with his subordinates, let alone with every one of their acts . . .
>
> This total responsibility for everything done by the movement and this total identification with every one of its functionaries have the very practical consequence that nobody ever experiences a situation in which he has to be responsible for his own actions or can explain the reasons for them. . . . The real mystery of the totalitarian Leader resides in an organization which makes it possible for him to assume the total responsibility for all crimes committed by the elite formations of the movement *and* to claim at the same time, the honest, innocent respectability of its most naïve fellow-traveler.[42]

There is thus perfect symmetry between the way the Leader, the source of all legitimacy, incorporates the actions of the all the subjects, and the way they internally identify their will, in what distinguishes the "inclinations" and "sentiments" Kant called "pathological" (that is, deriving from the empirical arbitrariness of each) from those of the "legislator," who is now the Leader.[43] But we are also closer to the way that de La Boétie, in his *Discourse on Voluntary Servitude*, questioned the mechanism by which, in a perfect tyranny (what he calls the power of One), "the despot subdues his subjects, some of them by means of others, and thus is he protected by those from whom, if they were decent men, he would have to guard himself."[44] Here, too, we find a process of identification that makes each individual with a certain power a "little One"—or, as de La Boétie says, a "little tyrant" (*tyranneau*), an exact replica of the sovereign One:

> whenever a ruler makes himself a dictator, all the wicked dregs of the nation—I do not mean the pack of petty thieves and earless ruffians who, in a republic, are unimportant in evil or good—but all those who are corrupted by burning ambition or extraordinary avarice, these gather around him and support him in order to have a share in the booty and to constitute themselves petty chiefs under the big tyrant. . . .
>
> . . . For, in all honesty, can it be in any way except in folly that you approach a tyrant, withdrawing further from your liberty and, so to speak, embracing with both hands your servitude? . . . The tiller of the soil and the artisan, no matter how enslaved, discharge their obligation when they do what they are told to do; but the dictator sees men about him wooing and begging his favor, and doing much more than he tells them to do. Such men must not only obey orders; they must anticipate his wishes; to satisfy him they must foresee his desires; they must wear themselves out, torment themselves, kill themselves with work in his interest, and accept his pleasure as their own, neglecting their preference for his, distorting their character and corrupting their nature . . .
>
> . . . What condition is more wretched than to live thus, with nothing to call one's own, receiving from someone else one's sustenance, one's power to act, one's body, one's very life?[45]

To return to the situation Arendt describes—which, according to her, constitutes the difference between a tyranny, even an absolute one, and totalitarianism, strictly speaking—it is necessary that, on the one hand, the particular will ("pleasure," "interest") of the Leader is replaced by the universality (or, rather, the form of universality) of the law, and, on the other hand, that the process of identification extends to all subjects, in the minimal exercise of power each makes to command himself to obey, or to identify his will with that of the legislator.

We then better understand, perhaps, the dilemma that resides at the heart of the critique of law-as-expression-of-will as a political absolute that runs through all Arendt's reflections on contemporary history and her attempt to rediscover, with the help of the Greeks—and, more fundamentally, to invent, "without testament"—an interpretation of the institution (of *nomos*) on which the collective exercise of judgment, which is rooted in freedom of speech and tests itself to the point of risking disobedience, would not constitute just the ideal foundation of legislative power, but the everyday reality of its exercise and control by the community of citizens. The tautology of legal positivism ("the law is the law") is essentially unstable. Either it requires a supplement of conviction or a sense of duty on the part of individuals, who can—under the extreme historical circumstances of totalitarianism—be transformed into zealous collaborators with the execution of legal crime, or it has to be corrected with all the risks this carries by incorporating a right to disobey into the constitution itself (in the sense of the material constitution, that is, a *practice* of public institutions, not a normative text). It would, to be sure, be a bit hasty to suggest that each of us, as citizen, only has a choice between becoming a potential "little Eichmann" and transforming himself by resisting authority (into a citizen against the powers that be)—just as it would no doubt be illusory to imagine that a state or a society in which civic disobedience figures among the fundamental rights would in itself be immunized against totalitarian degeneration. And yet, at least as a regulative idea, this is indeed the choice that, according to Arendt, should orient our understanding of the political.

POPULISM AND POLITICS: THE RETURN OF THE CONTRACT

The translation of Ernesto Laclau's book *On Populist Reason* is an important event to which I would like to do my best to call attention.[1] Coming after several others, sometimes very far removed from the publications that made for the author's international renown, it will give a new dimension to the reception of an important body of work in contemporary political theory. The work should provoke discussion. It is in fact rather rare to find a project of such ambition, aiming at nothing less than rethinking the coordinates of "the political" as such, combined to such a degree with a vast comparative inquiry covering two centuries of problematic articulations between democratic institutions and mass mobilizations, and finally an intervention that aims to reformulate the terms of debate on the most worrying phenomena on the current political scene. It arrives at a moment when the question of populism provokes heated controversies, whether concerning how we should evaluate the growing popularity of xenophobic ideologies in different parts of the world (including Europe) or the reasons for the dynamic in favor of certain candidates in American electoral campaigns, the media style adopted by certain politicians, or the critiques of the "democratic deficit" periodically noted in the functioning of national and transnational bureaucracies. Such a tangle of references could discourage theory, or it could function as a symptom that calls for a radical overhaul. Laclau has sought to meet the latter challenge on bases his works have long been preparing. Within the limits of simple review, I would like to draw attention to what seem to me to form the main elements of his construction, and outline the discussion they gave rise to around some key points.

Laclau's highly structured work is divided into three parts. The first examines the fate of populism in contemporary political theory, which finds the means at once to disqualify the notion and to use it to stigmatize movements or ideologies considered ruinous for the search for rationality or the promotion of the common good. Upon further consideration, this denial goes back to the very origins of political philosophy (Plato); it is correlative with a constitutive contempt for the very category of the people. But it includes exceptions. It is by drawing on these that Laclau proposes to reverse this judgment, radicalizing the thesis they suggest by fully assuming it—namely, that the confusion or contradiction inherent in the idea of populism does not mark a failure of conceptualization, but rather an intrinsic characteristic of historical-political reality. Above all, he shows that the question obsessed the modern critics of democracy, especially in the form of crowd psychology (from Gustave le Bon to Gabriel Tarde to William MacDougall), only to be the object of a growing reversal, to the extent that the denunciation of revolutionary pathologies threatening society with disintegration gave way to a differential analysis of crowd phenomena and public opinion, and the process of identification or collective mimetism appeared constitutive not only of the "excess" of political and social life, but of institutions and public order. This movement culminates with Freud, whose theory of the masses Laclau studies in search of the lineaments of a "political constitution of the social" in terms of the production of homogeneity (or "equivalence") that "collectivizes" both representations and affects. Independent of its application, this reading is very interesting in how it brings together Freud's way of thinking with that of Antonio Gramsci (which would finish by opening later onto the idea that psychoanalysis and politics do not really have distinct discursive objects insofar as both challenge the antithesis of the normal and the pathological, and consequently the rational and the irrational).

The second part of Laclau's work, which takes up the construction of the people, is more ambitious and more complex. I cannot entirely do it justice, since it would be necessary both to fully unwind its axiomatic and to reconstruct the movement by which it is progressively enriched. Apparently highly formalistic, it nevertheless never loses sight of the delicate objective of redefining the relation that unites democratic demands with the popular identities by means of which they are transformed in practice. Democratic demands are all claims for equality, recognition, or inclusion that come from particular groups whose commonality lies in confronting the resistance (and, at the limit, the repression) of an established power. Popular identities are the imaginary equivalences among claims that, around the signifier of "the people" (which becomes emptier the more it is extended or acquires greater universality), allows subjects to *name* themselves in a homogeneous and collective way by rejecting outside their community the enemy they identify as the obstacle to their affirmation ("privileges," "power").

The theoretical instrument Laclau uses here is itself progressively elaborated. It has to do with a "generalized rhetoric" whose operations (derived from the classic pairs of structuralism, metaphor and metonymy in particular) bear not only on discursive significations, but on the affective investments they crystallize, and consequently on the ontological modalities of the construction of collective individualities in the very movement of their opposition and extension. In the last chapter of this part, the question of the construction of the social being as a product of a political logic is taken up again in the form of a discussion of the classical dilemmas of representation. Laclau shows, then, not only that this does not form a secondary characteristic of institutions (unequally developed according to the regime), but constitutes symbolic structures that institute the reciprocity between the representatives and the represented, "the people" and incorporation (with or without charismatic leaders). In a dense discussion with Claude Lefort, he thus goes from the idea of a totalitarian deviation that would be inscribed as a virtuality at the heart of any institution to that of a "constitutive populism," without which there would be no political relation or space, since the condition and result of politics is the existence of a hegemonic collective subjectivity (in other words, a majoritarian "we"). Populism, rethought and generalized according to a modality that is no longer normative but ontological, is not a marginal, still less a pathological, phenomenon. It is a presupposition of politics itself. If it includes a dimension of excess, this excess has to figure at the center of the operation, constantly reiterated (and always thrown back into question), of the formation of a collective individuality. Its denial—for example in the form of a purely procedural conception of democracy—thus appears as itself the effect of society's blindness to its own bases.

While I have only evoked the content of this construction in very broad outline, I will draw out three moments in particular that seem to me to be of great interest.

There is first of all the idea of the symbolic collectivization of claims in the modality of a "discursive construction of a void," which means that every popular community, far from being the result of a preexisting essence or expressing a historical necessity, is essentially contingent, and depends on how it is traced by the discourse of an "internal border" between the camp of the people and that of its adversaries, which is solely a question of the imaginary or representation. Here Laclau summons several historical examples, whose function is to show at once how such a configuration emerges and how it dissolves. The most interesting is English Chartism. (There would be a further counterexample in the inability of Italian Communism to become a national party after the Second World War, even if its policy was based on the scheme of hegemony elaborated by Gramsci.) Taken to its conclusion, this thesis leads us to see that the fact that a "people" constructs itself as right or left, and at the limit whether democratic claims totalize themselves in a liberal or fascist form, is equally contingent (which is not to say arbitrary, but dependent on circumstances). From this perspective, the oscillations of electorates in periods of social and institutional crisis between the extremes of the political spectrum seems entirely logical—which does not make them any less worrying.

There is then the idea that the internal border between parties, the object of an incessant displacement, is the stake of a conflict of rival hegemonies (the heirs in Laclau's analysis of the Gramscian notion of a "historic bloc"). It is thus inseparable from an *antagonism*, which itself must be read on two levels: on a first level as an antagonism between the "we" of popular unity and the "them" of the adversary, against which the border is defined; and on a second level, between competing ways of defining popular unity, and consequently of characterizing its enemy or its other. Here the "empty signifier" of unity equally becomes a "floating signifier" in search of appropriation. One could worry here whether Laclau, in much more sophisticated terms, is not reproducing a formalism of strategic games, applicable especially to the constitution of electoral coalitions in parliamentary systems. But this is not the case, especially owing to the very nice use he makes of the category of heterogeneity, borrowed from Bataille, which he takes up to rethink certain political schemas derived from Marx and detached from their initial relation to class struggles: first of all that of the "universal class" (the excluded group or *pleb* that, claiming to incarnate opposition to the established order in its totality, identifies itself with the people and gives itself its name); then that of the *Lumpenproletariat*, or society's "unclassifiable element," whose displacement from one extreme to the other of the ideological spectrum forms in a sense the flipside of hegemonic conflicts.[2]

There is finally the analysis to which Laclau proceeds by combining two logics for treating the heterogeneity manifest in every social and historical conjuncture: that of "difference" and that of "equivalence," neither of which is tenable in an absolute way (the absolutization of either always leads to its collapse, to political crisis). In this analysis we find again the antitheses elaborated on the basis of the reading of Freud, but above all some of the keys proposed to understand the ever-present alternative of the hierarchical recognition of differences by the state (especially the social or welfare state) and their horizontal neutralization by a populist logic, itself susceptible to diverse modalities, that includes a more or less latent subversive dimension. Here we have the touchstone for identifying, among contemporary political currents that call themselves or are stigmatized as populist movements, those that truly merit the name. (In a long analysis in the third part, Laclau denies that this is the case with Berlusconi in Italy—in comparison, for example, to what Peron established in Argentina during his first period in power.)

The book's third part is no less interesting than the preceding ones, but it is still more difficult to summarize, for it takes on the "variations of populism," and thus rests essentially on the analysis of examples. What is up for discussion are the limits within which the category is applicable, regarded as conditions of possibility and impossibility for the construction of "the people," and thus the historical vicissitudes of populist politics. An especially interesting, and current, development concerns the difference between nationalism in general (whether it is from above or from below) and the ethno-populisms illustrated by the history of eastern Europe in the twentieth century (up to and including the wars in former Yugoslavia). Laclau shows that here the "internal border" is replaced by an "external border," including the designation of internal minorities as "foreign bodies" to be symbolically or physically eliminated. Paradoxically, this substitution of the internal enemy with the external enemy (which in many respects, following Chantal Mouffe, constitutes a return to the esoteric Carl Schmitt at the expense of the exoteric Carl Schmitt) is at the same time a way of posing the question of the conditions under which populism can be regulated or internally self-limiting, to the extent that an internal enemy can be transformed into an "adversary" in order to avoid the self-destruction of the community of citizens.[3]

In conclusion, Laclau distinguishes his theses from those proposed by some other contemporary theorists, in particular Slavoj Žižek, from whom he has borrowed the bases of a theory of nomination as a performative operation, in contrast to descriptive semantics à la Saul Kripke, but whose attachment to the idea of the "determination in the last instance by class struggle" he denounces as inconsistent with regard to the logic of the signifier; Hardt and Negri, whom he reproaches both for the borderless universalism of their conception of the multitude and the substantialism of their idea of revolt, always still connected to a mystique of labor; and finally Jacques Rancière, to whom he feels closest owing to the affinity between the "part of those with no part" and the operation of transforming the *plebs* into the *people*, but whom he reproaches for underestimating the intrinsic ambivalence of identifications and for believing that activist equivalences can only serve emancipatory objectives.[4]

All this, to be sure, poses many problems, and the most difficult ones. I will briefly mention three that seem to me insurmountable and to which, if need be, it will be necessary to return. The first concerns the way the alternative of order and disorder is introduced (or rather reintroduced on the ruins of the conception of populism as a pathology of the social body). Laclau repeatedly notes that anarchy or anomie is unsustainable, and that for this reason populist movements seek to recreate an order, at the limit *any* order. One is compelled to speak here of a return to a contractualist thematic. Of course, this return is effectuated beyond the collapse of the ontology and anthropology on which the scheme of the contract was based by the classic authors. It nonetheless (or even just as much) takes the pure form it took notably in Hobbes. Laclau concludes, moreover, by recognizing this, multiplying the allusions to the formal identity between his logic of the "production of emptiness" and the way Hobbes, for his part, thought of the making of the multitude into a people by externalizing an individual transformed into a sovereign, to whom all the citizens are identically connected but who on their side are not connected to each other. He notes the affinities of this scheme with the Freudian construction of identification (at least in the case of the leader), and even, implicitly, with the Marxian construction of a "general equivalent."[5] But this highly striking reprise (which is at the basis of the idea of a "constitutive populism," or forms the quasi-transcendental condition of possibility of politics itself) is accompanied by a reversal (that we could also regard, here again, as bringing to light the esoteric side of the author of *De Cive* and the *Leviathan*). What for Hobbes forms the more or less threatening flipside of the construction of the people, namely the violence of the war of all against all, now takes center stage in the form of conflicts between hegemonic equivalences that rend apart the possibility of naming the people.

This introduces a second problem. What is highly striking in Laclau is the way he reduces to nothing the distinction between politics and the political, so prized in contemporary philosophy, which is sometimes normative and sometimes ontological. Even if he also refers to a dualism of the "ontic" and the "ontological" (that is, of substantial identity and practical, discursive identity), the former category plays practically no role for him.[6] As a result, the "nature of the political" is nothing other than the logic of the operations of politics as a discourse or language game. More precisely, the nature of the political is identified with this essentially contingent construction of the people, the modalities of which are constantly repeated and varied. But this equation can be read in both directions. It signifies that the characteristics of politics (conflictuality, ambivalence) affect the center or essence of the political, but it also signifies that the category of "the people" is practically equivalent to a foundation, or refers only to its own construction. And depending on whether we privilege one or the other of these readings, we will obviously arrive at different orientations concerning certain dilemmas of contemporary politics.[7] The question is all the more sensitive because, as Laclau himself indicates, these problems are posed in the context of capitalist globalization,

which forms not the logical but the historical condition of conflict between different hegemonic initiatives, for the categories of conflict and
ambivalence (in "chains of equivalence") seem to be generalizable to any
space at all, without preexisting limits. In contrast, the category of the
people, however empty the signifier to which it refers, seems to be usable
only within certain limits, the narrowness of which are clearly shown by
the vicissitudes of the European construction. What would be a populism at a global level? Here external antagonism takes precedence over
internal antagonism, the exoteric Schmitt over the esoteric Schmitt, and
the framework within which the politicization of democratic claims tends
to pull back to the nation or its substitutes.

From which we arrive at the third problem. Obviously, Laclau's conception of the people inherent in populism is profoundly different from
communitarianism. One of the fundamental points of his work is to explain that totality as such is unrealizable, and that consequently popular
unity can only take place in the form of an "absent presence" or an "empty
plenitude" that is essentially metaphorical. But this is at the bottom
the means of reinforcing the autonomy of the political by displacing it
from an institutional (and *a fortiori* statist, as in the Schmittian tradition strictly speaking) referent to a practical referent, a language game of
the Wittgensteinian type. Does this mean that for Laclau the political
has no outside? Not exactly. His polemic against the idea of class struggle
and more generally every attempt to think the political as the expression
of sociological tendencies or preexisting social interests does not do away
with the idea of a given social heterogeneity, without which the very idea
of democratic demands prior to the appearance of the logics of difference and equivalence (or of classification and homogenization) would be
meaningless. But it pushes it back beneath the properly political construction or formalization, which makes it at bottom the equivalent of a
Kantian thing in itself. About this heterogeneity, and thus about this demand for equality and freedom, without which there would be no initial
"shock" for politics, at bottom we can say nothing except that it must
exist. This is no doubt why Laclau has to add (at the end of chapter 4) an
appendix to respond to the question: "What makes some demands (and
not others) democratic?" It is perhaps here that it would be necessary to
begin again in order to try to elaborate—if only in view of discussion—an
alternative to Laclau's construction that would endeavor to reverse the
terms of the problems: not by identifying the properly political moment

for the hegemonic incorporation of heterogeneous democratic demands into the (relative) uniformity of a popular construction, but by reflecting on the conditions under which essentially ambiguous popular demands can be democratized, and thus serve emancipation.

In any case, this discussion has the advantage of showing that the *demos*, the eponymous category of democracy from which it nevertheless initially seeks to distance itself, can only operate as a schismatic notion, either divided against itself or reinscribed in a rhetoric of the universal, constantly suppressed (this is one of Rancière's axioms, which I have also tried to analyze under the heading "the fear of the masses"), performatively reiterated to effectuate the critique of its institutional realizations, which are so many alienations. This is why—and Laclau would have been right to remind us of this, in his way—by taking sides by means of theory, the differend of populism and democracy (one divides into two, two fuse into one) is indeed its intimate secret.

PART THREE

FOR A DEMOCRACY WITHOUT EXCLUSION

WHAT ARE THE EXCLUDED EXCLUDED FROM?

My intention here is to submit for discussion some of the implications of the categories of *social exclusion* and *internal exclusion,* which political scientists as well as sociologists and philosophers increasingly use to think about racism (and especially the emergence of postcolonial "neoracism") in the European and North American context.[1] First suggested by liberal theorists as an alternative to analyses based on class difference, exclusion has also become an instrument of critical thinking for those who try to analyze persistent forms of discrimination and violence after the category of race has been officially disqualified. The result is a paradoxical situation in which the forms of institutional racism that characterized both colonial imperialism and fascist regimes, or ones based on segregation or apartheid, have been dismantled without racism's ceasing to exist in the functioning of institutions, or more generally in social relations. It is this real complexity of "racism after races" that we must try to illuminate.[2] But an epistemological dilemma immediately arises. On the one hand, it can seem that exclusion designates a circumscribed set of social practices occupying a more or less central place in a series of historical formations that can be called racist or neoracist. It would allow us to identify the thread that links different degrees of stigmatization and discrimination, leading at the limit to mass phenomena that relate to physical or symbolic elimination.[3] It is essentially a matter of accounting for the fact that certain groups, social categories, or types of behavior are represented as foreign to universal norms, to the rules of the community, and consequently fought or in any case pushed into a position of inferiority as the butt of constant repression.

But it is also at the same time a matter of accounting for other phenomena in which all the *limit situations* that imply for individuals or collectives an extreme degree of weakness or incapacity to act on their own conditions of existence tend to return. The very possibility of resistance and organized struggle thus becomes unthinkable or takes self-destructive forms, as if violence suffered without the possibility of retaliation turns back on itself. For such situations arise in the context of extremely varied domination—whence the extensive use of the category of exclusion: with regard to women in relation to power or political representation; migrants or ethno-cultural minorities in relation to citizenship and social recognition; the poor in relation to employment, housing, and, more generally, urban life; the handicapped and sexual minorities in relation to careers and cultural expression; "ethnic" minorities, from the perspective of protecting their languages, cultures, and ways of life; and finally whole continents, in relation to globalization and the construction of a new international order. We are thus caught between two types of usage, one characterized by extreme specificity, the other by an indefinite extension of analogies that creates a fear of conceptual confusion, but also allows us to deploy transversal criteria with a general political bearing, precisely like "impossible resistance" or the denial of the "right to have rights," which have an undeniable resonance across multiple, heterogeneous experiences.[4]

My intention here is not, of course, to undertake an exhaustive analysis of the current uses of the term "exclusion" and its correlates or partial synonyms, nor is it to describe all the situations that could be considered situations of exclusion. This is a program that defies the imagination, but also prejudges some elementary conceptual distinctions. In particular, it seems to me that we cannot discuss degrees of exclusion without at the same time posing the question of the model of belonging they cover, even if we must at once admit that social realities are composite and that models overlap or interfere with each other, giving rise to cumulative or overdetermined forms. (One thinks of the example, which has almost become too easy, of the nonwhite, poor, single mother in the United States.) The idea of exclusion can refer to a pariah condition situated at the bottom of a system of competitive social hierarchies, or to finding oneself cut off from a community conceived as a national or cultural "totality." It reflects a whole phenomenology of visible and invisible forms of violence. At the limit it is exhibited as such or, to the contrary, practiced shamefully. It exists according to distinct ontological models when it is directed at "real" groups, institutionally deprived of rights or confined to segregated spaces, or "only" (and it is not certain that the resulting violence is less) at *idealities* such as cultures cut off from the progress of "civilization," collective histories suppressed in the grand narrative of universal history, discourses that the norms of the dominant form of communication, with its own grammar, renders impossible or inaudible.

All these distinctions can be encountered within the phenomenon on which I want to focus my attention here, internal exclusion, the formal characteristic of which is that the excluded can be neither really accepted nor effectively eliminated, or even simply pushed into a space outside the community. Such paradoxical situations could exist throughout history. It was that of heretics and persecuted religious or moral minorities, but above all that of women confined to the private sphere by reason of the inequality of the sexes. It seems that to different degrees it concerns many other groups in so-called postindustrial and postnational societies, especially in Europe. I would like to call attention here to the fact that this model of internal exclusion, characterized by an institutional contradiction that engenders double-edged policies of integration and repression, of positive discrimination but also stigmatization, in fact covers two heterogeneous logics.[5] Here we must understand at once the difference in principle and the combined effects in practice: on the one hand, a logic of commodification of individuals on the capitalist market (such as the most recent development of globalization tends to configure by "liberating" them from social regulation and corresponding juridical constraints); on the other, a logic of racialization that derives from the essentialist representation of historical (especially but not exclusively national) communities, where intolerance of the other they project or identify in their midst exacerbates a fantasy of purity, homogeneity, and unity that is all the more virulent for being undermined by ongoing processes of communication and transnationalization.[6]

When these two logics are superimposed, the superexploitation of a workforce bought and sold on a capitalist market governed by global competition, where the mass of direct producers is reduced to a subsistence level or even below, combines with the defense or constitution of fictive political identities that are supposed to have existed for all eternity and to guarantee social cohesion precisely by virtue of this transhistorical eternity. One thus arrives at precisely the forms of internal exclusion, material as well as symbolic, that are characteristic of the contemporary world. And when their extreme violence also tends to be formalized in juridical statuses, we can have what Giorgio Agamben has characterized in a deliberately paradoxical way as a "normalized state of exception," combining an inspiration from Carl Schmitt (who supplies its justification) with another from Walter Benjamin (who attempted to criticize it).[7] This is typically the situation that the double mechanism of class and racial exclusion imposes on a growing mass of undesirable refugees and immigrant workers (and their families) within European society (which I take as an example, but of course is not the only one). This situation can perhaps equally be perceived as the inverse of the European citizenship that is emerging for better and for worse at the same time that the European construction acquires a political and institutional character, which I have characterized elsewhere as *European apartheid*.[8] I am trying to better understand the complexity of this specific exclusion by referring to a double series of causes or structural determinations, and at the same time to explain what makes it so that it could never be isolated from other social phenomena, implying in turn discriminations that aim at other groups of subjects. The political implications of this are obvious.[9]

In speaking of two distinct logics—commodification and communitarian racialization, and thus the *reification* and *identification* of subjects, even if they are convergent—I take up the formulation proposed and elaborated by Alessandro Dal Lago in his great sociological, philosophical book on "nonpersons."[10] The first logic proceeds through the transformation of human beings into things, that is, imported and exported goods that can also become redundant or disposable, having lost their use-value.[11] The second proceeds via the transformation of outsiders (not only *foreigners*, defined by their nationality, but *strangers*, defined by their culture or behavior) from merely relative Others into absolute Others and thus enemies, and especially into enemies "by race."[12] Here we could content ourselves with taking up what the classics teach with regard to the antithetical forms of *Gesellschaft* and *Gemeinschaft* (or, better still, in Weber's terms, *Vergesellschaftung*, or "socialization," and *Vergemeinschaftung*, or "communitarization"), considered in view of their negative effects.[13] These two processes, typical of modernity, which can be connected to the development of the capitalist labor market and to the essentialization (even the sacralization) of the nation-state, respectively, each bear a normative modality of the individual's association to the collectivity, having as its inverse exclusion from social recognition or full citizen status.[14] This would not be, from this point forth, without political consequences, especially for understanding the development of processes of resistance to exclusion—claims for equality or rights that are denied or taken away from some at the same time they are recognized for others. But it is necessary to be more precise and more concrete. For here we are not talking about just any labor market. After what Polanyi called the "great transformation" at the beginnings of capitalism, and under the influence of democratic movements but also the differential advantages offered to Europe by imperial conquest, this market was regulated through the institution of social rights.[15] Its purely competitive character was thus subject to limitations and even partially nullified by social legislation and national policies to reduce inequalities. It is this whole institutional system that is today being progressively dismantled, tending to return, despite resistances, to forms of savage competition that prevailed before the institution of what I call, along with Robert Castel, the "national-social state."[16] As for the nationalist policies and ideology on the basis of which we are trying to understand the formation of neoracisms in the age of globalization, they cannot be considered atemporally. The exclusive nationalism historically constituted by the passage through the colonial situation and its postcolonial reorganization tends to become a reactive "postnational" nationalism, surviving the nation-state's loss of sovereignty and compensating in the imaginary for its slow but irremediable decline. It is above all important here, I believe, to understand that in all European countries, whether they are on the west or east side of the former division into blocs, the discourse of what are called "populist" (and are in fact racist) movements targeting immigrants and refugees is not simply a continuation of colonial traditions and a reprise of orientalist stereotypes, but also constitutes the displaced or projective expression of mutually xenophobic feelings for which immigrants serve as scapegoats, and which the oligarchic and bureaucratic character of the supranational political construction can obviously only encourage.

These historical specificities must thus be examined very closely. If it is important to shed light on the intrinsic duality of the phenomena of exclusion at work in the contemporary reproduction of racism, it is precisely because of the paradoxes and contradictions they correspond to. A deregulated labor market that progressively generalizes insecurity and precarity more than a century after the historical development of forms of social regulation incorporated into a model of social citizenship, imposed by class struggle within the framework of the national-social state, is not at all the same thing socially and politically as the capitalist market formed in the age of the Industrial Revolution on the basis of the dissolution of the peasantry and precapitalist artisans. To be sure, it leads to the reconstitution of a sort of proletariat insofar as it recreates conditions of radical insecurity for the working class (what official terminology euphemistically calls "flexibility"). But its forms are new and extraordinarily heterogeneous. It is not even possible to apply here a univocal concept of poverty. Immigrants belong to the excluded in this sense (especially "illegal" immigrants, which is in fact to say those illegalized by the constantly evolving play of legislation and mechanisms of police control): their lives unfold under conditions of insecurity connected to *forced mobility* that prevents them from settling permanently, where family life could restart or begin in the place of immigration.[17] But, in a way opposed to this deterritorialization, we are also dealing with poverty that is perhaps less visible (except when it manifests itself electorally in the growth of the populist vote): that not of foreigners but of nationals and even locals, victims of what Robert Castel calls "disaffiliation," that is, the loss of citizenship and the collapse of social property through long-term unemployment and the deskilling of trades. Here it is not a matter of forced mobility, but rather *forced immobility*, which is felt physically as well as culturally in a world in which mobility is becoming the norm. These two groups can coexist and even partly overlap, but they do not merge; they have neither a shared social identity nor a common imaginary, but are virtually hostile. It is precisely this latent or open hostility that explodes in the *banlieues*, where it is transformed into destructive and self-destructive violence. Both are racialized; both arise from class racism, but following opposite stereotypes inspired in one case by a discourse of "barbarism," and in the other of "degeneracy."

Things are no less complex on the side of ethno-cultural racism, where we see a projection of and compensation for the crisis of nationalism as an organic ideology of the nation-state that globalization has rapidly thrown into a zone of existential uncertainty in the countries of the North as well as, in their own forms, those of the South. The complexity of the internal contradictions should not in my view prevent us from speaking of racism or racial exclusion, since, more than ever, a genealogical schema is at work here. It includes differentiations on the basis of color, culture, and name, which are then regarded as hereditary. And this is exactly what happens when foreigners or immigrants are regarded as such perpetually, and the fact of being a foreigner can be inherited (or transmitted)—which is on first glance a contradiction in terms. Thus the children of immigrants in France are still so designated in the third or fourth generation, exactly as in slave-holding or even abolitionist America "Negroes" remained "Negroes" indefinitely, despite mixing and forms of legal emancipation. This *hereditary trace* is sufficient to transform those affected into "internal enemies" and to ensure that, fantastically, the alterity that is projected onto them is perceived as their own work, responsibility, or indelible defect. Yet here too we should make room for displacements and contradictions. Bodies and marks of corporal difference, the stigmata invented by nineteenth- and twentieth-century biopolitics, have not stopped informing the representation of differences,[18] but the dominant obsession is increasingly *culture*, cultural difference being all the more insistent the more it is invisible and the more reality in practice is made up of mixing, hybridization, and cultural standardization. For the insistence on cultural factors and the instrumentalization of cultural difference for purposes of discrimination also produces a defensive and reactive use of identity that cannot be designated as "counter-racism" (since here we have a fascist slogan, and one that is moreover increasingly widespread—"anti-white racism," etc.), but oscillates between the poles of *self-exclusion* and *cultural resistance*, associated according to the case with practices of irony, aesthetic parody, and more or less mythic constructions of origins and "authentic" traditions threatened by deracination.

Here, as we know, we are dealing with an especially sensitive matter, but one that cannot be easily evaded, especially when we have to take into account what are called "secondary contradictions" among the excluded themselves, that is, internal conflicts to which the victims of racialization fall prey. No doubt the hardest problem to formulate, since it really is complex, but also the most decisive from a political point of view, is that which results from the asymmetrical effects of racialization on men and women, or boys and girls from the immigrant youth. It is never possible to completely separate racism and sexism, which have in common precisely the same genealogical scheme.[19] Yet racism and sexism are not only additive (as in the case of the "black woman"); they can also come into conflict and produce a specific contradiction. This is what happened in the famous episode of the Islamic veil, to which repeated conflicts in the French school system and their repressive treatment by the state have called attention (while in practice the punishment for young Muslim girls for refusing to take off the veil, to which they clung for diverse reasons strongly connected to personal and collective identity, has been exclusion from the school system).[20] As a general rule (but every rule of this kind entails numerous exceptions), internally displaced and excluded minorities are more repressive and oppressive toward "their" women in the name of ethnic, cultural, and religious customs, whose communitarian defense is inseparable from that of masculine power, than "modern," "secularized," or even traditional societies.[21] But it is striking that European societies react to this discrepancy—in the name of modernity, secularism, and republicanism—by instrumentalizing *the other's sexism*, blinding themselves to their own, and making it an additional means of racist stigmatization.[22] The European societies that originated the exclusion essentialize and dehistoricize the other as well as themselves. They develop secondary forms of nationalism that continue to rest on the paternalist control of minority women's freedom of choice.

If I had to provisionally conclude in a word these, in my view, essentially preliminary considerations, which I give at most as a program for research and discussion in the field of political philosophy (and not only sociology or social psychology), I would do so by invoking and generalizing the concept of *exclusive democracy*, applied by Geneviève Fraisse to the condition of women in the French republican tradition.[23] Better, let us say that the question here concerns the institution of an exclusive democracy. Such a formulation is obviously paradoxical; it can only refer to a system of historical contradictions. The term "institution" is taken here in the active and passive sense. It designates both a process of materially constituting the political community, in the singular, and a plural set of juridical and technical systems of subjection and power that traverse the frontier between civil society and the state. In this sense, the regulated or deregulated labor market is just as much an institution as the school system, city planning, or the distribution of public services. But national or supranational borders, like those of the Schengen area, and the policing of foreigners are equally institutions that play a central role in the real operation of what we call democracy.[24] To various degrees and in highly differential ways depending on the social groups we are considering, all these institutions contribute both to including *and* excluding; they are, consequently, those that produce internal exclusion in the first place and crystallize its constitutive violence. The aporia of exclusive democracy, and thus also the dilemma to which every project of citizenship that seeks to confront its negativity theoretically as well as practically, resides in the fact that the processes of exclusion can be considered both as the other side of inclusion or integration into the community of citizens, which reveals its true signification, and as the set of limits we must get beyond in order to meet its universalistic ideals, thus marking the imperfection of every historical democracy, the fact that it never completely or durably institutes equality and freedom. Equality and freedom therefore have to be imposed by the revolt of the excluded, but also reconstructed by citizens themselves in a process that has no end.

DISSONANCES WITHIN *LAÏCITÉ*:
THE NEW "HEADSCARF AFFAIR"

The debate over the prohibition of the Islamic headscarf and other "visible," "conspicuous," or "ostentatious" signs of religious belonging in public schools, revived by the conclusions of the Stasi Commission, the intervention by the president of the republic, and the introduction of a "simple and clear" bill by the minister for education, has seen no end of opacities and displacements.[1] The contradictory implications of the demand for a legislative intervention, which its promoters sought to ignore or imagined would be easily mastered, have proved to be uncontrollable in the national as well as the international sphere.

All this would be laughable, especially if one takes a bit of distance from the self-absorption of members of the French political class and intelligentsia, convinced that the terms in which they define the facts of the problem are universal. In fact, the contrast is glaring between, on one side, the thinness of the pretext (a small number of cases not settled by the ruling of the Conseil d'Etat, the intervention by the Education

Ministry's mediator), the stereotyped quarrels between partisans and adversaries of a law setting disciplinary norms in schools (a tired remake of the great republican battles of the Third, Fourth, and Fifth Republics), and, on the other side, the enormity of the principles at stake (the constitutional secularism of the state, the equality of the sexes, France's mission as defender of the Enlightenment in the world), but also the gravity of the social situations that overdetermine every political gesture touching on gender relations, the postcolonial heritage of the French nation, religious forces and currents around the world, the future of the educational institution—in short, politics.[2] But the debate, or pseudo-debate, can acquire another function: it exposes the crisis, no doubt irreversible, of an idea joined to the construction of the national state. The dissonances within *laïcité* are not new.[3] Indeed, they are one of its conditions of possibility (since *laïcité*, which has been reshaped and moderated many times, is, de facto, essentially a social and political compromise).[4] But the form they take today clearly shows that this typically republican institution is at a crossroads, that it is its principle that is in question.

President Chirac's initiative is supported by the party advisers who represent his electorate in 2002 (the conservative Union for a Popular Movement and the Socialists in particular), but divides the teaching profession, promises schools endless controversies over dress codes, opens a road to Islamist clerics who are elevated to defenders of freedom of conscience and the dignity of stigmatized Muslims, feeds anti-Semitism, substantiates Le Pen-inspired fantasies about foreign subversion, makes French legislators ridiculous, elicits incomprehension in international public opinion, and, to top it off, will probably turn out to be impracticable or ineffective.[5] It is charged with solemnly affirming the principles of *laïcité à la française*. It would not be the least of the ironies that in reality it brings its coup de grâce.

The first headscarf affair began in fall 1989 when two students were expelled by the principal of the Collège de Creil. It was pragmatically settled at the behest of the Jospin government by an opinion of the Conseil d'Etat, which is not always easily applied, but has proved manageable aside from a few exceptions.[6] At the time, some of us already tried to point out the flagrant contradiction inherent in expulsions: one claims to defend young girls against religious fundamentalism, of which sexism is an intrinsic part, by banishing them from school, that is, making them personally—in their lives, their futures, their bodies—bear the penalty for the injustice of which they are the victims, and sending them back to the communitarian space dominated by precisely this religious sexism.[7]

In the period that followed, although the frequency and intensity of school conflicts fluctuated from year to year, three facts in particular emerged:

1 The individual motives of young girls who wear "veils" are extremely diverse within and outside Europe. This is not the only element to be assessed politically, since before being the object of a choice or a custom, the *hijab*, in its different variants, is a cultural, religious, and increasingly a political symbol, which the law will naturally accentuate, but it is one which, from the standpoint of democratic education, one cannot abstract away from. These motives are inscribed in a framework of more or less physical and psychological violence, but they can express forms of personal emancipation and feminist striving (exemplarily, Afghanistan on the one hand, Turkey on the other). In Algeria, a fundamental reference point for French debates, they cannot be disassociated from the pitiless struggle that opposes those who uphold the patriarchal order (symbolized by the family code limiting women's civil rights) and claims for the equality of women. In France itself, these motives range from adherence to forms of militant Islamism, to submission to family and social pressure, to personal attempts to silently express a difference the dominant society seeks to suppress or manipulate.[8]

2 Part of the teaching profession, increasingly called upon by the state and families to alleviate the effects of social suffering while the conditions of its work are undermined by the accelerated devaluation of its social status and educational purpose, is turning toward a law-and-order ideology that combines feelings of powerlessness, appeals to state authority, and fear of the transformations of the contemporary world. This ideological tendency is exploited and amplified by a republican intellectual lobby of the right and of the left (in which there are unfortunately a good number of philosophy professors), for which *laïcité* and "the French exception" serve as ready-made ideas at the level of principles.[9]

3   Stigmatization and discrimination, inveterate in French postcolonial society and directed above all against populations of Arab-Muslim origin, also promote the development of political-religious fundamentalist ideologies that, though in a tiny minority, constitute a threat to democracy (symmetrical to that represented by the Front National, but in the end tending in the same direction). If it is important in this respect not to allow oneself to be recruited in the war of good against evil that is being fought or declared by fundamentalist currents of Islam and the neoimperialist West, one must not be so naive and foolish as to ignore the resources and objectives of the political, religious proselytizers who operate in the European-Mediterranean realm.[10]

Under these conditions, we renewed our criticism of repressive legislation and exclusionary practices, notably by associating ourselves with the petition "Oui à l'école laïque, non aux lois d'exception" [Yes to the secular school, no to exclusionary laws].[11] I see no fundamental reason to revisit this position today, which has moreover been joined by others marked by a political concern to return the debate to the terrain of national and international realities and to protect the educational institution from instrumentalization by strategies that resolve social divisions by symbolic means (which also implies warning it against its own fantasies of disintegration).[12] But this principled position is by no means sufficient. It leaves open a number of problems that turn theoretically around the current meaning of the idea of *laïcité* (obliging us to reexamine its principles, origins, and history), and practically around the question of the role of the school in the ideological conflicts of the contemporary world. Among these questions, and without any pretense of being exhaustive, I would like to schematically raise four.

The first concerns the distinction between "the political" and "the religious." It is well known that one of the Stasi Commission's proposals—not kept by the government, but very popular among teachers—was to extend the prohibition to political symbols. The discussion that followed showed that many of those who advocate the prohibition of the Islamic veil (and of religious symbols generally) oppose its extension to the political, regarding the permission of political expression in school (which is in fact only a generation old and accompanied by restrictions) as a democratic achievement. This means that they believe in the existence of a rigorous line of demarcation between the political (which would be fundamentally *laïque*, or "secularized," at least in "our" societies) and the religious (which would be religious).[13] But it also showed that this line of demarcation is doubtful or called into question in practice precisely at the sensitive point: Islam, and secondarily Judaism.[14] Some bright minds explain that the principal danger is not religion but its political use by clerics influential among immigrant Muslim youth, or else the aggressive projection into France of ethno-national solidarities, in particular those connected to the conflict between Israel and Palestine—thus to a political problem, but one in which religion is immediately enrolled and instrumentalized (the Jewish state, the Holy Land, Sacred Places, etc.).

In fact it would be necessary to admit that there is no natural distinction between the political and the religious, but a historical one resulting from decisions that are themselves political. In modern states, extreme forms of this permanent tension correspond to the existence of parties officially inspired by confessional ideologies or interests (Christian, Muslim, Hindu, etc.), but also to the powerful religiosity that animates antireligious political ideologies—sacralized secular struggle, as in France, socialist or nationalist messianism, etc. This tension gives rise to all kinds of combinations, which are not equivalent, but it never disappears. The two terms have never been, and are now less than ever, exterior to one another. In the current period, for reasons involving the circulation of populations and mixing of cultures connected to globalization and the crisis of the symbolic bases of the nation-state (sovereignty), this tension has entered a new phase of intensification and transformation, leading at once to the mobilization of institutional authorities and the interventions and claims of citizens, and consequently making politics more than ever a site in which religious beliefs are invested, and the place of religion in the public space a political matter. Many discourses on *laïcité* as a French exception (subtext: the ideal and definitive solution to the problem of "spiritual power," as Auguste Comte said) are underpinned by the illusion that this Pandora's box can be kept closed, or its opening indefinitely postponed—whereas, as such, they are themselves ways of opening it. There are neither intrinsic grounds for nor intrinsic ways of separating the expression of political opinions from that of religious opinions.

The existing conceptions of *laïcité* are in fact a way for the state to impose a double definition of limits: limits to acceptable ideological conflict, based on a certain institution of consensus or civil peace (but always privileging certain interests or social forces), and limits to the translation of religious beliefs into political positions, based on a certain institution of truth (which plays a greater or lesser role in official scientific proposals and the principles of natural, argumentative, communicative, etc., morality). We cannot claim that these conceptions do not have their reasons, or that doing away with them as such would produce a liberation of politics. But neither can we indulge in the illusion that the institutional forms connected to parliamentarism, the juridical monopoly of the nation-state, and thus nationalism, the translation of social movements into the language of natural right or secular hope in the historical context of the universalization of European culture, will suffice indefinitely and without alteration to constitute political conflict or codify its institutional limits—including in Europe and in France. The question will inevitably arise (in fact it has already arisen) of the terms in which the state defines political or political and religious expression so as itself to benefit from the constituent force of ideological conflicts, which are citizenship itself (the "right to politics" for all), without, for all that, perpetuating civil war or a "state of exception."[15]

THIS FIRST QUESTION IMMEDIATELY leads to a second, which concerns the "neutrality" of the public space and the presence at its heart of marks of identity, and thus marks of social, cultural, and more fundamentally anthropological difference. Here again, allegedly self-evident and natural thresholds turn out upon examination to be wholly conventional, which also means shot through with strategies and norms, with relations of forces among groups, subjectivities, and powers, dictating the very meaning of the categories "public" and "private." This is why we should not be surprised by the rise of discussions about the length (and very existence) of beards, nor by the comparison of the problems of propriety raised by the veil and the thong, nor by proposals to reestablish uniforms, nostalgically evoking the republican school of the nineteenth century and classic utopian models for representing the citizen—the unity of the two coming from the fact that the school has always furnished the privileged place for implementing utopias of citizenship. And we should not be surprised that, in the sudden emergence of trouble in the relations between *representation* and *publicity*, religion (belief, communitarianism, subjectivation) and sexuality (the ultimate but "obscene" anchoring point of controls and affirmations of identity) appear inextricably mixed.

Here we should start with two propositions. First, what is the relation between state neutrality and neutrality in education? This question can be illuminated by the debate between those who maintain that *laïcité* should be interpreted as the school's neutrality with respect to religious beliefs (and thus equal respect for their expression) and those who insist that religious beliefs must be suspended within the school walls (two interpretations that reflect different philosophical models of secularism). Both are correct and incorrect. In our society, the school (particularly the public school, detached from the family and reattached to the state, above parties and governments) is essentially a place of transition between the space of private existence and the existence of public space—but one legally situated within the public space itself. This imposes contradictory imperatives between which it must negotiate. The school must be a closed space, but one in which information and representatives from the outside circulate. The school must prepare (and thus anticipate, simulate) the relativization of social belonging, beliefs, and ideologies in order to facilitate individuals' entrance into the political sphere, citizenship; it thus has to virtually detach individuals from their primary identities (which is in fact a very violent process—a sort of dismemberment, a separation from their identities, that then ideally allows them to reclaim these identities, but from the distance implied by the primacy of the second, common political identity).[16] But the school must also give individuals the means to represent their ideologies and belongings in political life, though without itself being political, that is, without speaking the language of politics except indirectly and metaphorically (through history, literature, philosophy). Holding these contradictory imperatives together, and *a fortiori* holding them together in an egalitarian way, would evidently require highly favorable circumstances. It can be expected that practice approaches them only very incompletely, or attains them only at the price of successive conflicts (which it is just what is happening at the moment). What is demanded of the school is not that it simply be "neutral" like the state, but that it carry out a neutralization or constitute an additional neutrality between two nonneutral spaces— what we call "private" and "public"—in a way that avoids confusing them.

BUT THIS BRINGS US to another proposition: What should be the marks of the public space in general, and more particularly of the educational space that duplicates it? There is no simple answer to this question, which has a tendency to deny itself (a mark of neutrality or uniformity is a sort of contradiction in terms), but what is certain is that there cannot not be marks.[17] The marks of neutrality are obviously themselves not neutral, either in terms of their visibility (to say nothing of their ostentatious character) or in terms of their meaning (since they embody a history, sacralized traditions, and refer to a symbolic sovereignty—that of the nation, of the people). It must be said that the hierarchy of marks, their dominant or dominated character, the modalities of their visibility, are the object of permanent conflict, sometimes of ideological war.

The ideal (republican) school would accept no marks other than those of neutrality, those that proclaim that the students' bodies and minds are entirely docile, available for learning, those of the teachers (for whom, let us not forget, the problem also arises, as we see in Germany, where the question of the headscarf was raised not with regard to students, but a teacher in Baden-Württemberg) solely oriented to accomplishing their educational mission. The real school tolerates a greater or lesser number of individual or collective marks, which are spontaneously interpreted as eccentricities, privileges, preserves, resistances, or provocations (long hair, eccentric clothing, insignia or flags, taken to be "lax" or "indecent").[18] But a common feature of all marks is that they are applied to the body and showcase it. This is why sexual determination is omnipresent in the war of marks. A conflict that calls into question the double allegiance of certain students in relation to the nation and religion, and the degree of independence of one in relation to the other, would not crystallize around an article of clothing charged with sexual symbolism (the visibility of certain parts of the female body) if republican schools had not become mixed in the course of the last half century, and if this mix had not made the sexual difference (and different ways of instituting or controlling it) a problem for the school that cannot be settled by pure secular doctrine. Hence wearing the veil also functions as a claim of sexual identity, according to a certain modality (which can be deemed "alienated" or "servile," but what of others?), and (selective) prohibition as a denial of the insistent presence of desire in the relations among the subjects of the educational institution, or in any case as a confession of the difficulty of controlling it. It would also be necessary to think about the relation of this hystericization of marks of political and religious belonging to a context in which the "ostentatious" exhibition of desire is deprivatized, invades the public space, but is also commercialized, banalized, and finally dulled. One can note that it is not certain whether girls with tight jeans or girls with the Islamic veil are more "sexual" (I do not say "sexy"), and it is this that creates a problem—as much as and more than imagining their submitting their history or philosophy lessons to the censorship of the Koran (unless it is the reverse). It is also here that it would be necessary to investigate the meaning of the spokesmen of Islam's claim (often made in the place of the interested parties) to demand modesty in a society that constantly exploits the female body in advertising. The imams' indifference to sex is no more credible than that of the clerics of any other religion, and their insistence on modesty is more suggestive of obsession than protection.

THE THIRD QUESTION THAT arises, then, concerns the intensification of cultural conflict around the liberation of women in the postcolonial context. It is not certain that what is central here is the divergent ways different traditions conceive of the relations between private and public. Or rather, this aspect of the matter can only be analyzed in relation to a concrete historical context in which the delayed effects of decolonization, like the conflicts that rage around the world (including and spilling over into Europe, west and east, north and south) around the abolition of patriarchy and the equality of the sexes, are no longer really separable. We must guard against instrumentalizations, but it must also be said that the contradiction between two equally universal emancipatory claims is total: those that fight ethnic discrimination, cultural racism, the hegemony of the old imperial nations, and those that fight the subordination of women and the violence and denial of equality to which they are subjected. Such a contradiction seems practically insoluble, save in the very long term. This is why none of the symmetrical discourses that seek to erase it is credible: neither that which presents women's struggle and that of oppressed peoples (or minority ethno-religious groups) as spontaneously convergent (although their conceptions of community are antithetical), nor that which presents the institutions and values of the West as the model and vehicle of women's emancipation everywhere (especially in the Muslim world)—although the West has developed its own massive forms of subordinating women, and a whole part of its feminism begins by denying any validity to the speech of minority women, and calling for legal assistance and coercive state intervention against them.[19]

We must take account of the tragic character of a situation in which young women, somewhere between childhood and maturity, become the stake of a merciless struggle for prestige between two male powers that try to control them, one on behalf of patriarchal authority wrapped up in religion, the other on behalf of national authority wrapped up in secularism. Whatever the intentions and the ruses by means of which young French (and other) Muslim women sometimes (but not always, it must be said) negotiate their autonomy, it is intolerable to see them directly or indirectly forced by their families (and especially by the violence of their "big" and "little brothers") to symbolically veil themselves in order to be "respected" (which is to say held in contempt in another way).[20] The spectacle of a "spontaneous" demonstration of veiled women against the law in the streets of Paris, solidly ensconced by men who prevent any of their "sisters" from communicating with passersby or journalists (and coinciding with similar demonstrations in cities around the world), provides food for thought. But it is just as intolerable to see the school system, men and women together, fomenting a civilizational conflict, making the unveiling of Muslim women in the republican institution par excellence a point of honor, unknowingly repeating (but this ignorance has its own history—that of colonial bad conscience) the gesture that French soldiers perpetrated on the bodies of their mothers and grandmothers during the Battle of Algiers.

How can we escape this vicious circle? First of all, evidently, by conferring a maximum of freedom of choice on those involved, knowing that there is no absolute freedom, no doubt, and that freedom includes the possibility of "voluntary servitude" as well as revolt, but also that they grow up in a transnational society where the omnipotence of the patriarchal family is shaken, and where alternative models exist (which is not to say that the equality of the sexes is assured). Secondarily, by demanding that the French Republic make some efforts of collective historical memory regarding its own reticence to grant women anything less than educational and civic equality.[21] Finally, last but not least, by insistently posing the question of the origins of social exclusion, which promotes religious fundamentalism and regression toward patriarchy (in the defensive form typical of what historians call "the invention of tradition," whereby communities suffering discrimination try to maintain their solidarity), but also aggravates competition between the generations and sexes. Here, for reasons that are well known (including the power of stereotypes stigmatizing the Arab male, but also the will of girls to use the educational system and a professional future as a means of emancipation), girls are advantaged vis-à-vis boys in academic life in particular, provoking as an indirect consequence the aggressiveness of many of the latter, who are destined for "preferential unemployment" by attending inferior schools.[22] It is true that here there is no reason to be optimistic. A society in which the idea of social equality has become an empty slogan (elections regularly turn on talk of a "social rift"), and the idea of "positive discrimination" an anathema, has little chance of looking in the face the causes of regression and violence it attributes to the inferiority of certain cultures.[23]

FINALLY, THE FOURTH QUESTION we have to examine—perhaps the most important of all at the moment—concerns the dilemmas of discipline, of authority and freedom, in the schools. A recent poll reveals that a majority of secondary school teachers support the planned legislation, and even want to extend the ban to all "visible" symbols of a political or religious nature.[24] All polls need to be interpreted, which does not always go without saying and depends on a number of conjunctural factors. My current interpretation is that the determining factor here is the disciplinary problem. Teachers profoundly destabilized by the crisis of the schools are not much concerned about the influence of Islam or its interference with their teaching (a situation that could perhaps change if they are really required to incorporate the "religious fact," amounting in the end to a certain positive conception of *laïcité*). And I do not believe that many of them (there are of course exceptions) are concerned with the liberation of women, or believe they can contribute to it through school regulations. On the other hand, they *are* concerned with what they experience as the collapse of the authority of their position: at once in the concrete form of the rise of indiscipline and illegality in the schools (especially in *zones difficiles*, a euphemism for the pockets of poverty in French society in which large parts of the immigrant population, but also many French Jews repatriated from Algeria, are concentrated), in the form of a loss of professional prestige and an inability to resist the claims and pressures of families, and more abstractly (though neither least importantly nor least painfully) in the form of a generalized uncertainty about the power of knowledge and its bearers in contemporary society.[25] It is certain that the meritocratic ideology of French society has led to the overestimation, even the mythologization, of this power, but it is also certain that it has now become the object of a concerted attack by both the market and the state, and that in this case this is experienced by teachers as a sort of betrayal.

The failure to take this dimension into account seems to me to be the great weakness of our criticism of the exclusionary legislation—which we could say, forcing the issue a bit, by displacing it and offering an inadequate response prefabricated by political power, reveals the existence of a situation of exception in the school system that has gradually taken hold in the last twenty years (who will speak of the responsibility of Socialist governments in this regard?), and has drastically reduced the teaching profession's own capacity for initiative (even if, here again, there are exceptions). It is in this context that teachers see no other remedy for their impotence than symbolically reaffirming the power of the state for which they work, which they reckon will reestablish a ruined equilibrium to their advantage. *Laïcité*, however defined, is not the aim but the instrument of this corporate reflex.

Here, too, however, in order to avoid stigmatizations ("It's the teachers' fault!") and laments ("What happened to the 68ers?") and move beyond moral exhortations ("Beware the Lepenization of the mind!"), a theoretical detour is required to understand how a crisis whose conjunctural causes are clear enough has also taken root in the inherent contradictions of the institution itself, which is suddenly brought to the limit of its capacities or deprived of the compromise formations that sustain it. Clearly, this means that the function of authority, without which there is no practice of teaching in the academic form we know (and which liberal pedagogical reform or libertarian contestation can at most attenuate or mask, but not abolish: that would amount to destroying the Ideological State Apparatus), has always necessarily had an impure, heterogeneous source. In part, it draws (and believes it draws) on the power of knowledge itself, which is to say on its capacity to transform the thinking of individuals, and thus their lives. This power of knowledge is in part the source of the interest it arouses, of the desire to know (and to teach) it awakens and maintains (on the condition, among others, of appearing accessible, appropriable, and transmissible with effort). But it also in part draws on, and visibly takes root in, more or less interconnected social powers: age or experience, credentials, social prestige, and especially that of the teaching profession, which collectively embodies a hierarchical and disciplinary institution, even if in a subaltern position—one of the organs of public power. The school and its functionaries evidently fulfill all sorts of functions on which the transmission of knowledge is based and which exceed it: functions of professional training, cultural and civilizing functions, "hegemonic" functions in the formulation and critique of the dominant ideology, the civic function of transforming the private individual into the political citizen. But none of these functions can be dissociated from authority. This is why there is a necessary tension, not to say a contradiction (but one that can lead to thought and action), between the authoritarian side of the teaching function and its democratic side, which consists at once in equality of opportunity and conditions that try to promote it, and in equal right to expression (and thus, at an elementary level, the right to politics), which it tries to provide to all through the mastery of language and knowledge, and which it can, within certain limits, try to institute at its heart.

This is also why it is tragic that, confronted with a political conflict on its own terrain, at once delimiting and gradually calling into question most of its functions and the conditions of its exercise, on this point the teaching profession doubts its own capacities and its future, hastening to reduce them to their most restrictive, least intellectual dimension, implicitly entrusting their theorization to doctrinaire ideologues who brandish their Condorcet or their Kant the way others brandish their Bible or their Koran, and demanding a fictive solution from a political power whose concern for the general interest today extends little beyond the reading of opinion polls.

IT WILL HAVE BEEN understood, I think (and I hope I am not alone), that a chance has been missed to rethink the history of the idea of *laïcité*, the place of the institution of teaching (and in this sense of the power proper to knowledge) in the articulation of the political and the religious, the marking and demarcation of public and private spaces, the status of sexual difference with regard to citizenship, and their collective evolution. In short, a chance has been missed to think and deal with political questions politically. It thus remains, since nothing has been settled, to prepare the elements for a resumption of the debate on other bases and under different conditions (which will probably be no more serene, but which could make the stakes more visible).

This can only be done, it seems to me, on the condition that we deepen the questions of which I have proposed a preliminary list: that we renew the debate on freedom of expression and democratic practices in the schools—but this renewal itself has all kinds of conditions, inside and outside the school, first of all the struggle against exclusion, which can turn back psychological insecurity and despair ("negative individualism"); that we revive the movement for equality, and reflection on its internal contradictions (especially those that set different emancipatory movements, or different forms of resistance to discrimination, against one another); that we reconstruct the idea of universality in a way that does not simply make it the formal envelope of legitimate political communication, but the stake and result of a confrontation of *all* the political discourses (including theological-political ones) that, in the contemporary world, within and across national frontiers, express viewpoints on the universal. This deepening is unlikely to come from national republicanism (which would now have to be called national republicanism-secularism), just as it is unlikely to come from a religious or theocratic worldview, even one of the left. But a social, cosmopolitical, antiauthoritarian democracy could attempt it.

SECULARISM AND UNIVERSALITY:
THE LIBERAL PARADOX

The product of a tormented history, the concept of *laïcité* is often considered specifically French.[1] Its meaning cannot be reduced to the general process of secularization that affected modern societies and political systems to varying degrees. It is inscribed in institutions that embody a certain historical compromise between social forces, but also a figure of citizenship. It is profoundly marked by the heritage of a certain ecclesiastical and administrative tradition, as well as by the imaginary of a certain imperial project. As soon as we no longer take for granted that it expresses an achievement of modernity, all the questions concerning its relation to universality reopen. This is not to say either that we return to clericalism or that we can make communitarianism the law of the city. But we must confront the difficulties of politically regulating belief and belonging, and in the end the question of constructing the universal in a given historical place, such as Europe, in a new way.

Here I would like to contribute to formulating problems for which I have no simple solution, and which I even suspect are not susceptible to a "solution" in the absolute sense of the term. This does not prevent them from requiring that citizens take positions, make decisions, and undertake initiatives. I will defend a "liberal" conception and practice of the principle of *laïcité*. But I will also try to locate the arbitrary elements that are concealed by the ideal of a juridical norm, based on the distinction between the public and private spheres of religious convictions guaranteed by the state. It is up to politics, as judge and party to the case, to confront and try to regulate this knot of necessity and contradictions.

AN INSTITUTION OF HEGEMONY

Laïcité, as has often been observed, articulates a two-fold series of facts, problems, and practices. We feel that they must be distinguished, but we know that they never stop overdetermining one another. Émile Poulat said (and wrote), there is "republican *laïcité*" and the "*laïque* Republic."[2] We refer to the *laïque* philosophy, which, before degenerating into taboos and dogmas, represented the outcome of an invention that comes from the Enlightenment (in which positivism plays a role, which one would do well not to vilify without knowing). But we also refer to the constitutional value of *laïcité* in France, which, even if in practice it sometimes conceals ignominious compromises, helps confer a democratic form on citizenship.

These two sides, to be sure, have to do with universalism, but in different senses. This means that *laïcité*'s principle of universality, like others, is essentially equivocal. It is this double face of *laïcité* that for a certain historical period gave it a hegemonic structure, in the sense Gramsci gave to this term. For in the idea of hegemony there is at once domination and the regulation of conflict; there is normalization, the suppression or exclusion of the forces of rebellion and anomie, and the production of the positive conditions of social individuality, to speak with Robert Castel. In other words, this means that under the name of *laïcité* we place a historical universalism, distinct from and in competition with religious universalism, closely related to equal freedom as an ideal of citizenship. But we also know that this universalism cannot be dissociated from the structures of power it helps legitimize and operate. The "*laïque* Republic" in which "republican *laïcité*" is constitutionalized is not itself the pure reign of the "rights of man and the citizen." It is a bourgeois republic, an imperial republic that survives even if the empire is no longer more than a phantom.

These characteristics determine the constant tensions, even the violent splitting of the ideology between the legitimation of power and the transgression of the established order. This is the deepest sense of the idea that *laïcité* is a struggle. But this struggle itself rejects those "without part," as Jacques Rancière would say, who all the more have no part in the "*laïque* pact"—we know that this is especially the case for the large majority of colonial populations. And it includes an unthought element of unresolved problems and suppressed conflicts. What is the relation, at a given moment, between the fact that *laïque* universalism expresses certain emancipatory tendencies and the fact that it ignores or refuses others? Here is a crucial question that can end up surfacing over time, even if not necessarily under conditions that render it fully intelligible. Is this not what is happening with the weakening forms of state and national community (which does not mean their disappearance), the exhaustion of the representative capacities of certain democratic (especially parliamentary) institutions, the crisis of models of education, the revolution of communication technology and modes of public-opinion formation, the return and above all the mutation of "the religious," the provincialization of the geo-historical space of Europe?

THE STATE, JUDGE AND PARTY

But the institution entails a more embarrassing paradox. I will express it by saying that, necessarily, an enunciation of the universal is situated at once *above* particular ideologies and convictions and *within* their conflictual space, just as a juridical rule is situated at once beyond particular interests, which allows them to be reconciled or regulated, and in a relation of antagonism or compromise with them, and thus on the same level as them. The state is the figure par excellence under which this double game crystallizes, this double inscription of juridical universality that constantly exposes it to contestation, constantly demanding a surplus of power and sacrality from it that is summed up in the category of sovereignty. It will therefore not astonish us that *laïcité*, which in France is a constitutional principle, legitimating the nation-state by refounding it on the sovereignty of the people, detaching it from its dependence on religious institutions, at the same time tends to be constituted as an *antireligion*.

For, be it on the side of conviction or that of constraint, antireligion can take on a whole series of forms that are those of religion itself, or, as is sometimes said of monotheism, Christianity, or Protestantism, of a "religion of the exit of religion"—but everything happens as if this "exit" is indefinitely deferred.[3]

I do not say that this characteristic is sufficient to define *laïcité*, but it forms a typical realization of the paradox inherent in the institution of the universal. For it entails perverse effects. Not only does *laïcité*, as a political program for transforming society, administration, and morals, require an adversary, from which it takes its justifications and which oscillates between various designations: intolerance, the "temporal" hold of religion on political government, religion itself (or *this* religion) insofar as its propensity for intolerance would be inherent. Not only can it be bid up by various political forces that want to benefit from the aura attached to its intransigent defense, analogous to patriotism. But it could be that, when its dynamic is weakened by the crisis of the civic values with which it is historically associated (equal opportunity, public services), it finds no other way of perpetuating itself than by identifying new adversaries, for example new religious fanaticisms. Let us say more cautiously that the divergence will be accentuated between the perspective of those for whom *laïcité* is an absolute form, who are all the more determined to make it prevail by particular means, and those who see it as one democratic instrument among others, and who ask how to preserve, expand, or adapt it. The paradox of the universal that is at once beneath and within social struggles, judge and party of the political process, is present in both cases, but in the former it tends to be denied, whereas in the latter it can be recognized and negotiated.

These are the preliminaries that seem to me indispensable. They put in question the relation of discourses, ideologies, and even state philosophies. Our reflections on *laïcité* are also reflections on the form of the state, and on its model of developing what one is tempted to call "legitimate belief" (in comparison to the "legitimate violence" inscribed at the heart of sovereignty).

LIMITS OF LIBERALISM

We are thus led back to the European model of freedom of conscience and opinion as religious freedom and freedom with respect to religion in a space in which the political functions of churches is neutralized. It is in fact in this form that, especially in France, a fundamental individual and collective freedom is codified that is at the same time a public freedom, which means not only that it is exercised in the public space, but that it configures that space, making it the place of conflict of political forces. In this sense it is inseparable from an institution of politics in which the general interest cannot be deduced from any preexisting norm, but emerges through successive, indefinitely revisable approximations in the clash of opinions. Historically the constitution of this sphere of relative equality among forces that claim to represent the interests of the community, a space of freedom in relation to transcendent definitions of the common good, supposes a dissociation of temporal power from spiritual power— what Hobbes and Auguste Comte, taking up Cardinal Bellarmin's expression, called the *potestas indirecta* of the theologians. It is more conflictual but also more visible, more distinct, when the church appears as a hierarchical, centralized organization (which is singularly the case of Catholicism), but it exists everywhere secularization affects the political as such. It brings about a cleavage in the functioning of the religious community, a cleavage between two modalities of belonging and subjectivation, which means that the Christian people (*laos*) changes its modality of obedience to authority. Those citizens who remain faithful to a religion become "faithful citizens," which is not equivalent to inherited or prescribed obedience and is never without internal conflict. Conversely, for citizens who are no longer faithful to one church or another, there is a constant tendency (sometimes claimed as an objective) to fuse belonging to the community of citizens with belief, be it in the mystique of the *res publica* or in a secular religion that comes from politics itself.

But this historic dissociation is soon accompanied by a reinscription of religious convictions in the public space as ideological forces and models that allow collective identifications and social movements, thus contributing to the formation of public opinion, with or without confessional political parties. The suspension of the religious monopoly thereby clears the space for ideological pluralism, the play of which feeds the endless dialectic of dissensus and consensus. In this sense, the democratic construction appears equally inseparable from liberal rules and practices—here we cannot oppose the two terms. And the fact that the prototype of conviction anchored in the interior forum of each individual is first of all what one calls "the religious" signifies that, far from being external to the definition of liberalism as a political form, the internal transformation of religions and their recycling as authorities in the formation of morals and public opinion, among others, constitutes one of its conditions of possibility.

It is this that confers on such a political liberalism, what I am tempted to call "real liberalism," a rather strange characteristic in its use of the great dichotomy of public and private, which structures the application of legal norms.[4] Many definitions of liberalism that place the accent on the primacy of civil society, private exchange, and their self-regulation independent of public action in fact represent its denial. We must rather understand how real liberalism is also paradoxical liberalism, which does not rest on the withdrawal of the state outside civil society, but on its constant intervention into social space to determine the limits of the conflict of freedoms and to guarantee equality. But we must also discuss the complex place of religious convictions in this game, where they are at once central and thrown off balance in relation to their historical traditions, since they can only be inscribed on the condition of an internal transformation or, in a certain sense, being "denatured."[5] It does no good to deny the violence, at least the symbolic violence in Pierre Bourdieu's sense, that can to various degrees pervade this process.

FRONTIERS OF THE RELIGIOUS

This leads us to ask ourselves about the uncertainty, the displacement of frontiers, that both intertwines and differentiates, on one side, the religious and the cultural and, on the other, the religious and the political, as they are commonly defined. Here we have the heart of the tensions that have been present since the origin of the idea of *laïcité*, updated today. Liberal principles are not necessarily accompanied by liberal practices; to the contrary, nothing is more common than an authoritarian or discriminatory practice of liberalism. This is what happens when the state, charged as a public power with instituting the confrontation of opinions, itself intervenes in their definition, rediscovering and extending the classical notion of sovereign's *ius circa sacra*, or seeks to control with one hand what it frees with the other.[6] It is, moreover, what the state can find itself pushed into, not only by the strategies of power but also by the resistance of ideologies, especially religions—namely, to be internally transformed so as to become "constitutional" agents of opinion formation, actors in the civic space. To the idea of the self-regulation of civil society, I, for my part, will therefore oppose that of the self-limitation of the state, the extraordinary difficulties and constitutive fragility of which I do not conceal from myself, but which I also think can be aided, even imposed, by the movements and struggles of public opinion itself. In order for convictions, and especially religious convictions, to constitute constructive forces in the public space, the state has to intervene in civil society, and it begins to do so by *imposing freedom*. It continues to do so by guaranteeing and creating it, depending on the case, especially by teaching, but also by various policies of emancipation and social promotion that expand the political capacities of citizens, by giving dominated or excluded social groups access to information and knowledge, the means of positive freedom—that of communicating and thinking on a footing of relative equality.[7] But the counterpart of this intervention, which is at once formal and material, is the political imperative of self-limitation. For this is not—this is the least one could say—a spontaneous tendency of administrations, and it is not even a tendency inscribed by nature in the logic of legal systems.

Another struggle thus appears here, for which we can return, in a sense contrary to its initial use, to the expression *laïcité*—or, better, we can apply it reflexively to its historical instrument: it is a matter of secularizing the very authorities of social secularization, especially the school. This struggle runs against the tendency of the state and the law to sacralize their own operation, to dogmatize knowledge, to reconstitute, in acting as arbiter or guarantor of liberties, a principle of sovereignty that is not immanent in the activity of the citizens but rather exhaustively represented by authority.

This is the source of the complexity of the terms in which, radically in our day, the double frontier between the religious and the cultural, on one side, and the religious and the political, on the other, appears. We cannot forego these regulative distinctions, since they contribute to the definition of a civil norm for distributing opinions and convictions between the private and public poles. But it must be conceded that, strictly speaking, they are only ever defined arbitrarily, by a political decision that can itself be liberal or repressive. We will never find an indisputable criterion for distinguishing a religious tradition, assuring the fidelity of a community, a tradition, or an ensemble of cultural models to itself across time when it comes to work, sexual ethics, or the symbolic distinction of social groups. Talal Asad is right to insist on this point. But neither will we ever find rigorous criteria for separating the religious from the political, a religious movement from a political movement, or vice versa. And this holds both for the political dimension of traditional religions, their capacity to intervene in what could be called the choices of society or civilization, and for the religious dimension of political movements, or some of them, insofar as they include a bedrock of spirituality, militancy, or messianic expectancy, for the most active are those that are most able to maintain the dialectic of consensus and dissensus without which the notions of public opinion and the public sphere are only empty forms.

What I would call "real," historical *laïcité* has systematically used these conceptual distinctions to circumscribe the private moment of religion, which would also mean, from the perspective of national hegemony, applying religious traditions to the constitution of a system of common cultural references, excluding or delegitimizing other cultures or denying them access to the space of visibility and public expression, especially those of colonial and dominated postcolonial populations. Strongly aided in this, moreover, by a distinction inherent in Christianity between internal and external religion, and thus by a certain Western form of religious subjectivity, real *laïcité* has used them to impose the private-public distinction within religion itself, that is, to institute a threshold, a subtle but decisive semantic distinction between various kinds of political theology, in its diverse forms, and religious culture, with its multiple fields of investment. At this price it was possible to transform theological principles into moral and ideological values, which enter as symbolic references into the programs that participate in democratic competition—and with them the masses who identify with them. We see this clearly in the history of unions or Christian Democratic and Christian Social parties. Yet this practice of regulation based on the double differentiation of the religious and cultural, on the one hand, and the religious and the political, on the other, which constitutes the other face of liberalism, carries limits, which it in fact runs into under certain circumstances. It is the very possibility of putting the liberal norm into effect that is thus shaken, forcing institutions into a painful choice between defensive, exclusive reactions and the collective work of regeneration, lifting the repressions inscribed within *laïcité* itself, and reactivating democratic conflict.

UPRISINGS IN THE *BANLIEUES*

I address the events of November 2005 on the French urban periphery not as an expert on urban violence or the sociology of the French *banlieues*, but because, as a French citizen, I feel obliged to clarify—to the extent that I can—what I think about events that have an immediate impact on our present and our political future.[1] The commuting academic I have become believes in the importance of comparison and dialogue as instruments for understanding the world we live in, and you have offered me an opportunity. This does not replace fieldwork. But it will allow me to try, on the basis of the information available to me, to engage in a distantiation that is no less necessary, first of all in relation to words and concepts each of us use at home.

In order to remain open to correction and discussion, the reflections I offer here take the form of a series of "files" attached to seven symptomatic words or expressions: names, violence, postcolony, religion, race and class, citizenship and the Republic, and politics and antipolitics. They constitute a progression, but not properly speaking an argument. I have no thesis to defend. I am looking for hypotheses, or the best way of formulating them.

1. NAMES

It was James Chandler, specialist on the urban scene of the Romantic period and director of the Franke Institute at the University of Chicago, who suggested my bilingual title, which I have taken up in my own way: Uprisings in the Banlieues. Both terms are problematic, as we see when we expand the series to which they belong and look for equivalents in the other context. It is a matter of confronting heterogeneous perceptions of the situation, which obviously arise from divergent, if not antagonistic, ideological presuppositions.

The natural equivalent of "uprising" in French would be *soulèvement*. Hardly anyone in France spoke of a *soulèvement* with respect to the events of November 2005, at least publicly. Bordering on insurrection, the term strongly connotes a revolutionary tradition ("the people rise up against their oppressors") that seems irrelevant or exaggerated here.[2] The French press oscillated between the idea of *révolte* (rebellion) and *émeute* (riot). Sometimes it was a question of *guérilla*, especially to describe the clashes between "gangs" of youths and detachments of anti-riot police (BAC, CRS). Or, in an apparently more neutral way (but only apparently, in a context of denunciations of "insecurity"), of *violences*. The young, car-burning demonstrators defying and being chased by police were sometimes characterized as *rebelles*, sometimes as *casseurs* (hoodlums) and *dealers* (and thus assigned to the register of criminality). The apparently undecided question is one of intentions and consequences, but more deeply one of logic—political or, to the contrary, criminal, supposing that the two are contradictory in a context of radical social as well as symbolic exclusion. Some observers were tempted to see the riots or revolts in French cities and suburbs not only as an illustration of the functions of illegalism in modern society, but as the resurgence in the postpolitical (and also postdemocratic, postcolonial, postnational) age of the archaic figure of "bandits," regarded by historians as characteristic of a prepolitical age—that is, of the recurring social crisis that preceded (and in certain respects explains) the formation of the modern state and its (national) monopoly on legitimate violence.[3]

The term "*banlieue*" poses completely different problems. We cannot consider it the equivalent of the American "suburb" (from the Latin *suburbia*, which would correspond more to *faubourgs* and evokes wealth or at least prosperity), given by the dictionaries; the sociological equivalent would rather be "inner cities," owing to inverse urban logics. The already-old debate on the problems that lead to conditions of exclusion and the double movements of social and racial exclusion in European and American society almost imposes the *banlieue*-ghetto analogy. Owing to the importance of the postcolonial dimension and the way it tends to reproduce a sort of apartheid in Europe on the level of citizenship that sets apart populations of immigrant origin, I would propose the equivalent of *townships*, in the sense the term had (and retains) in South Africa. But perhaps at bottom it is a matter of a specifically French reality. The important thing would then be the fact that, in our current usage, *banlieue* connotes not only a conflictual, divided reality, but the proximity of extremes. This point is politically important. For there are *banlieues* and *banlieues*, often geographically very close to one another but separated by a social abyss and a permanent antagonism (which feeds the policies of territorial management and municipal and local power struggles). Some are rich, even very rich (former Interior Minister, then president Nicolas Sarkozy belongs to one of these, Neuilly-sur-Seine, and has made it his fiefdom and showcase); others are symbols of poverty, the decline of public services, the relegation of ethnic minorities and poor whites, unemployment and stigmatization, and communal tensions. In many respects, even if the riots extended to other urban areas (especially outside Paris), this clash within the *banlieue*, between the two worlds it contains, was characteristic. Not only do unacknowledged frontiers separate one kind of *banlieue* from the others; the *banlieue* as such is a frontier, a border-area and a frontline. It forms a periphery at the very center of the great metropolitan areas. It materializes what I have elsewhere called the displacement of frontiers toward the center.[4]

And yet, revealing as it is, this semantics of the French-style *banlieue* is not wholly satisfactory. It conceals two other dimensions that dramatically short-circuit the local and the global and are characteristic of the contemporary world. On the one hand, we must, in effect, descend to a lower level. What burns concretely (cars, public buildings) and metaphorically (is ignited with rage) is never a municipality, but a *cité* or *quartier* (housing project or district), like the Cité des Bosquets, at Montfermeil, or the Cité du Val-Fourré, at Mantes-la-Jolie. It is the *cité*, with its history and its solidarities, that is the subject of violence, claimed by the young rioters as a place of origin, stigmatized by politicians, police, and employers, chosen as a target of social policy and the terrain of police raids. It is what can be usefully compared to a ghetto—with necessary specifications of degree and history.[5] But, on the other hand, at least in the French context, precisely these ghettoized *banlieues* (and within the *banlieues* the *cités* built to contain and isolate heterogeneous populations) correspond to what, from another perspective, Saskia Sassen has called global cities.[6] We would have to speak of global *banlieues*, whose demographic composition and movements reflect the contradictions of globalization and their local projection, which also explains what at first glance seems to be the disproportionate resonance of the events outside France in 2005. They seem to illustrate a type of revolt, perhaps of struggle, that is being generalized transnationally—a "revolt of the excluded," if not a "molecular civil war," that forms the horizon of the "great migration."[7]

2. VIOLENCE

It is necessary, however, to return to the characterization of the violence that was produced in November, insofar as this term, which is now used constantly (we live, it is said, in an age of the multiplication of violence and insecurity), is used in a highly selective and in any case never neutral way. A series of problems gravitates around the level and forms of violence; they are decisive for understanding the political meaning of what caused the French *banlieues* to rise up. For if there can be no doubt that it was a political *event*, it is not obvious that it was a (collective) political *action*. Who were its actors? Whom or what were they aiming at? With what intentions and—possibly very different—effects? To what extent is this violence the symptom, indeed the mirror of the functioning of the French political system?

It is necessary, first of all, to ask whether this violence was spontaneous or, to the contrary, provoked, even deliberately planned. To be sure, as is said, the local materials were highly combustible and the preconditions for a new explosion (on the model of 1982 in Minguettes, 1990 at Vaulx-en-Velin, 1991 at Mantes-la-Jolie, etc.) had long existed. The government knew this perfectly well—so well that, observing how riots were set off (taking up and amplifying a well-known scenario of vandalism by out-of-school, out-of-work youths) by the interior minister's "challenge" and the tragic outcome of a manhunt typical of routine police practices, we have to ask if it did not in fact seek to touch off an episode of "criminal" violence to boost its own legitimacy and law-and-order propaganda.[8] When speaking of the government, let us not forget that it was riven at the time by an implacable rivalry between its two heads, Prime Minister Villepin and Interior Minister Sarkozy. Each had his own strategy, partly directed against the other, but converging on the ground in a single series of provocations. The Villepin strategy was a parody of civil war. Its visible (and risible) element was the proclamation of a state of emergency based on legislation dating from the Algerian War (1955), previously used just once (in 1984, on the occasion of neocolonial clashes in New Caledonia).[9] Here it was a matter of stirring up typically illegitimate violence, associated with the figure of the internal-foreign enemy (facilitating deportations in particular), in order to stage a simulacra of reestablishing state authority and the monopoly of legitimate violence. Obviously this is a dangerous game, prone on the one hand to ridicule, on the other to slipping out of its instigators' control. The Sarkozy strategy, subsequently extended in the struggle against illegal immigration, has entered into memory above all through the interior minister's "inopportune" statements: generalizing insults and repeated appeals to the racist sentiments of poor whites. This also helped amplify the violence, the better to take credit for mastering it, but with another accent— that of realism, even responsibility. The same minister with the petty, macho posturing presented himself as the architect of a solution to the problem of ethnic diversity and religious intolerance, pleading for a certain recognition of the fact of multiculturalism, choosing Muslim notables as interlocutors and intercessors, and trying to enroll parents against their children in the name of defending authority and social order.

But having noted the element of provocation and calculation that played a not inconsiderable role in the unfolding of the events, it is necessary to return to a more enduring and decisive reality: the endemic violence of relations between the police and "*banlieue* youth" (itself a stereotyped category that always includes racial stigmatizations of blacks and Arabs, though not only them). This violence, sometimes compared to a war or urban guerilla warfare, is a polymorphous phenomenon that constitutes the most visible face of the condition of violence in which the populations of the ghettoized *cités* live, rooted in structural causes like the accelerated deterioration of the urban environment and public services, massive, long-term unemployment, ethnic and geographical stigmatization (to be from Sevran or even from the 93rd [Seine-Saint-Denis, immediately northeast of Paris] is to see the doors closed to employment, recognition, and social mobility from the start), delinquency (including the drug economy), both practiced and suffered. Undisputed studies have shown the extent to which the behavior of the police in the *banlieues* toward the residents they harass, and who provoke or resist them, bears a mimetic dimension. At the limit, police squads act like gangs fighting other gangs in an escalation of virile exhibitionism—the difference being that they are armed, sent by the state into hostile territory, and that their own disproportionate violence (insults, beatings, shootings, arrests, detentions, threats) is inscribed within a more general process of intimidation, profiling, and harassment of legal and illegal immigrants (ethnic profiling).[10] Here the incivility so often invoked as a social scourge is for the most part on the side of the state and its representatives. This combination of social suffering and the instrumentalization of the values of order and legality, this tendential substitution of law and order for the social and the economic, this perversion of the notion of the rule of law explains another important aspect of the situation in the *banlieues* that must never be lost from view: the resistance of families in solidarity with their children, although they are constantly called on to denounce them, and the activity of associations, municipal representatives, and teachers, or some of them.[11] Violence is not the whole of life in the *banlieue*—or, more precisely, the *banlieue* creates other forms of struggle against violence than police repression.

Finally, what is striking in the development of violence in the *banlieues* is a paradoxical, hard-to-define combination of contradictory predicates. This violence, it is often said, is in part self-destructive. People asked, more or less ingenuously, why "they" burn their neighbors' and parents' cars, "their" schools or those of the little brothers and sisters, "their" sports facilities, "their" means of transportation. And the notions of exclusion and despair are fused with those of nihilism and depersonalization. Here it is necessary to rigorously discuss the meaning of terms. The target of destruction is in large part a thing from which the young rioters are contradictorily excluded as noncitizens, to which they only have limited, illegitimate access, but of which they are themselves a part, that in a way is part of themselves and their identity. This is why they can be characterized neither as absolutely outside nor as really within the social system, but only in the paradoxical terms of an *internal exclusion*, which must have effects at the deepest levels of subjectivity. Here we encounter the idea of the permanent state of exception, proposed by Giorgio Agamben, on the basis of his reflections on limit-situations in which the law is said to suspend its own effectiveness.[12] This model seems more satisfactory, in the event, than that of nihilist violence developed by Hans-Magnus Enzensberger, or even violence without an addressee, proposed by Bertrand Ogilvie, regarding manifestations of extreme violence in our societies that exceed the means-end schema we are accustomed to making a cornerstone of our conception of rationality.[13] Rather than a pursuit of nothingness or the dissolution of any political objective that can be represented or expressed in a rational way, it would be a matter of violence in search of targets and adversaries that, in part, escape it or take a shape that is itself contradictory, ambivalent. We will find this confirmed in the way institutions—whether they have to do with the state, municipalities, public administration, but also civil society as a complex of public opinion and networks of belonging—react to violence directed against the urban environment. They themselves inspire feelings of revolt, hate, or fear, but all these modalities of passion are overdetermined by the feeling that it is not a matter of an isolable danger, but, to the contrary, an expression of the becoming or the manifestation of what we ourselves are (and that much more worrying for this reason). I will return to this point in conclusion.

On the basis of this deep ambivalence we can then try to isolate other striking features of the violence of November 2005. First of all, its relatively narrow limits. Without going so far as to suggest that it was subject to internal control, which would suppose a degree of organization and premeditation that was manifestly absent, we must note that, compared to other historical episodes that were immediately invoked (the Brixton riots in London in 1981, and above all the riots in Watts and South Central Los Angeles in 1965 and 1992), and contrary to what television coverage suggested, this highly spectacular violence remained relatively limited in terms of its destruction and victims: three dead (including the two youths, whose indirect murder by the police lit the powder), but no or very few attacks on persons.[14] Instead, consumer items and symbolic places were destroyed (among which, we must not forget, cars and buses that are subject to periodic assaults within the framework of the generalized violence I spoke of above). This spectacular character, however, was in no way secondary. It marks the advent of a new age in which the means of mass communication acquire the role of passive organizers of social movements. Very quickly after the first episodes a national competition emerged between *cités*, towns, and regions to appear on French and even international television with the most spectacular possible scenes of civil war.[15] It is very hard to say who is using whom in this process at the limits of the real and the virtual.[16] But what should be taken from this virtual violence is that it transforms real, endemic social violence, to which it responds, into spectacle, thereby at once making it visible in its intensity and invisible its everydayness. It expresses a desperate will to affirm not so much a cause or a project as an existence that is constantly forgotten or denied by the surrounding society, using means proper to the experience of reality in contemporary society. (There is no recognized existence other than that which can be represented, reproduced by the media.) But these means are double-edged, or they return against those who use them by imposing a certain identity on them. In this sense, reference to the "practico-inert" and "stolen praxis," according to Sartre, is as useful as reference to Debord's "society of the spectacle" or Baudrillard's "hyper-reality."

3. POSTCOLONY

It is by design that I now refer to this term, which radicalizes the notion of a postcolonial period or culture, popularized by the work of the African philosopher Achille Mbembe.[17] The need to combine an internal perception of the events unfolding on the French scene (where necessary correcting the historical and institutional inaccuracies of distant observers) with critical distantiation, an external view and a transnational perspective, is obvious. In this case it is also a matter of finding codes to interpret the typical short-circuit between local determinations and actors, on the one hand, and the global significations I alluded to above, on the other.

But before coming to Mbembe's intervention, it seems useful to refer to two others, almost contemporary, that also try to decenter our perspective, and in many respects complement Mbembe's. The first is Immanuel Wallerstein's in his essay "The French Riots: Rebellion of the Underclass." Wallerstein regards the French riots as typical of a phenomenon ineluctably produced by the combination of racism and poverty in the peripheries of the world economy (of which the *banlieues* are a sort of reproduction within the very center), where the contemporary politics of capitalism create growing social polarization. The reason we do not see riots everywhere all the time is nothing other than the vigilance of the dominant classes and the preventive repression they practice, especially against youth, who, since they have been pushed to despair and are likeliest to openly defy the established order, have nothing to lose. If there is a French specificity, it comes from the paradoxical combination of two factors. On the one hand, in a way that extends over centuries, France is a country of immigration, whose population has grown through successive admissions, in the past from elsewhere in Europe, today from the whole world and especially the former colonies. On the other hand, France—whose political system has always drawn its legitimacy from the revolution of the rights of man—thinks of itself as *the* country of universal values, where discrimination as such is unthinkable. While this double characteristic could ideally lead to the invention of a form of multiculturalism equal to the challenges of the contemporary world, it generates, to the contrary, remarkable blindness about its own history and social contradictions as well as an inability to question the founding myths of Jacobinism and state secularism (as recently shown by the famous Islamic headscarf affair). There is, however, no symmetry in these matters, since, as Wallerstein rightly notes, religious identity claims and conflicts between political and religious allegiances (such as those produced by the Israel-Palestine war) played practically no role in the revolt of the *banlieues*. "The French rebellion was a spontaneous class uprising"—a conclusion that clearly indicates where he places the accent.

This choice is reversed by Rada Iveković in successive contributions that see the uprisings in November 2005 as, above all, a return of a "colonial boomerang."[18] Her remarks are stamped by deep disillusionment with French universalism, the reality of which turns out in her eyes to be a barely veiled provincialism in which the nostalgia for imperial domination and the illusion of bearing the Enlightenment legacy (in a sense by birthright) bars any capacity for self-criticism or analysis of the social and cultural questions posed by the end of the colonies. Unlike Germany, which at least in principle has confronted its history of nationalism and anti-Semitism in order to understand the roots of Nazism, official France has never really undertaken a return to the history of colonialism, its intellectual wellsprings and its legacy. Iveković thus emphasizes the stubborn resistance, ideological as well as institutional, of the French university and intellectual class to considering the postcolonial problematics now discussed elsewhere, especially at the two extremes of the Anglophone world, India and the United States, where subaltern studies have developed. She sees this as the consequence in particular of the French illusion of speaking an intrinsically universal language, which is in fact deeply imbued with historical particularisms and Eurocentric paternalisms.

It is striking, however, that the main problem that (rightly) preoccupies Iveković in her interpretation of the riots in the *banlieues*—namely the internal (and in no way secondary) political contradiction they contain, combining a revolt against the stigmatization of cultures of "native" origin in the former metropole with a traditionalist reaction that crystallizes, above all, in the field of gender relations—obliges her to take into account French specificities that do not fit easily within this one-sided presentation. Iveković herself emphasizes that the groups of young rioters who face off against the police share a violent, "macho" culture, one expression of which is rap.[19] And she notes that France was the setting of one of the most significant recent feminist movements, which also came from the *banlieues*: the protest of girls and young women (organized by the association Ni Putes ni Soumises [neither whores nor submissive]) against the sexual oppression and violence practiced by gangs of male youths who seek at once to restrict women's sexual freedom and to benefit from it themselves. They are often the same as those who revolt against pervasive racism. We must thus suppose that, despite its lingering provincialism, the scene of the French *banlieues* reflects the sharpest contradiction affecting postcolonial culture in general, namely the conflict between affirming the identity of immigrants and their descendents against institutional racism and their own oppressive violence against women, the subaltern par excellence.[20] As elsewhere, in France this conflict has been instrumentalized by the dominant culture, which eagerly presents itself as the protector of women and stigmatizes the sexism of "people of color" and "Middle Easterners" or "Asians" while throwing a hypocritical veil over the sexual inequalities of Western society. But less than elsewhere, perhaps (owing precisely to the latent subversive capacities of a certain universalist discourse), can this be reduced to a Manichean choice between the cause of the indigenous and that of women's liberation.

Achille Mbembe lost no time intervening in the debate on the violence in the *banlieues* with two essays circulated on the Internet: "The Republic and Its Beast: On the Riots in the *Banlieues* of France" and "Figures of the Multiple: Can France Reinvent Its Identity?"[21] The dark "beast" of which Mbembe speaks is race, which is to say not only the object of diffuse institutional racism, periodically stirred up by political demagoguery, but the reproduction—beyond the independences and recolonizations hidden by the "community" of interests between France and its former African colonies—of a social mechanism of discrimination and separation of human beings into unequal "species" that includes both ends of the migratory chain (France and black Africa). Mbembe insists, as does Wallerstein, on the socially inegalitarian character of globalization, and as does Iveković, on the power of the repression of colonial history, which prevents French society from understanding what has now blown up in its face in the form of an explosion of urban violence. But he adds a further thesis. There is correlation and constant exchange between state racism at home and neocolonial policy in African countries that remain dependents of the former empire (with the complicity of corrupt bourgeoisies and military castes)—what he eloquently calls the "geography of infamy." We thus witness a resurrection of the Code de l'Indigénat (natives code) that once governed the subjection of colonial peoples in the form of laws of exception, the development of a "penal state," and quasimilitary methods applied by police and public administration to deal with *banlieues* populated by the descendents of the formerly colonized.[22] They reenact the race war and inscribe it in the global context of clashes between the civilizations of the North and the South, on the basis of a very French colonial tradition whose administrative habits have never been eradicated.[23]

Mbembe thus takes up, as does Iveković, the critique of the blindness and deafness of the French establishment (including the larger part of its intellectuals) to the postcolonial critique of the ideological functions of universalism, but instead of concluding that it is necessary to go beyond this universalism as such, he shows that it is rather a matter of an open contradiction within it ("universal citizenship and radical equality cannot live together with the practice of state racism").[24] To "imagine the beyond of race" it is therefore necessary, following the thinkers of Negritude (Léopold Senghor, Aimé Césaire, Édouard Glissant), who made a critical return to universalism in order to open up a "passage to cosmopolitanism," to confront the French republican ideology with its own democratic requirements, with no possibility of escape. This is also the responsibility of the "natives" themselves: violence without political objectives (aside from expressing rage) is "unsustainable." It is necessary in France to create a new, nonviolent civil rights movement inspired by the American and South African examples, and at the same time to work toward the emergence of a *métisse*, or "creole," intellectuality and a political common sense it would catalyze. This presupposes the rise of a generation of French intellectuals of all races who interrogate French culture from its margins: the *banlieues*, the overseas territories, the former colonies, the Francophonie.

We see from these three examples that it is impossible to reflect on how class, race, and gender combine in the alchemy of the revolts in the French *banlieue* without overcoming the epistemological obstacle of a purely French perspective, locked within the conventional boundaries of the hexagon. But it is just as impossible to define its singularity (the current moment), its causes, as well as its solutions or consequences, without considering its social and institutional specificity. The postcolony haunts the French situation—in many respects it is repressed—but it cannot supply the exclusive key, especially in forms that have been defined on the basis of another historical and linguistic world.

4. RELIGION

The texts I have just examined (to which others could of course be added) put the emphasis on determinations like class and race, as well as, in counterpoint, gender, but tend to ignore or separate the religious factor, which is, to the contrary, highlighted by analyses inspired (even critically) by the model of a clash of civilizations. Is this a mistake? And if we must integrate this dimension, either when it comes to the motivations of the rebels/rioters or their representation in public opinion or by state officials, in what terms should we do so? Let us not forget that among the factors that aggravated the tension in the first days was the fact that the forces of order—intentionally, according to some, mistakenly, according to others—fired a tear gas grenade at the entrance of a mosque, or that in the following days the spokesmen of the National Council of the Muslim Faith, called on by the French authorities who control them as strictly as possible, but also moved by a feeling of responsibility to the community they represent, which they feel is periodically threatened by the development of Islamophobic racism and the repercussions of the "war against terror," repeatedly called for calm.[25]

We should therefore be on our guard both against a reductive interpretation of the fact of religion that makes it a mere cloak of "real" social processes when it is in fact a component of them, and against the temptation of a religious (or culturalist-theological) reading of current conflicts that, for its part, conceals real dynamics and projects them into a prefabricated ideological world. Religious readings have tended to reproduce the stereotype of a global confrontation between Christianity (Catholicism, in particular), on which, despite its official secularization, the dominant French culture is still based, and Islam, to which some (but not all) of the youths burning cars belong by virtue of family origin.[26] This is readily associated with a reference to Jewish-Islamic antagonism by adverting to the existence of a tension between Jewish and Muslim communities in some French *banlieues* and cités, periodically triggered by events in the Middle East, and it is asked how to compare the French riots with the events that simultaneously shook Britain, apparently calling into question its "communitarian" model for organizing interethnic relations in a postcolonial space (the participation of young Britons of Pakistani origin in the London terrorist attacks of July 2005). Even authors who (like Mbembe) do not make the religious question an essential key have spoken of the Intifada of the *banlieues* and a "Palestinianization" of the revolts and their repression. In this way, references to the sociological reality of Islam and the often fantasmatic representation of its global role are combined in a confusion that must be untangled.

If we ask why, contrary to declarations and expectations, explicit religious discourse was so negligible in the events of November 2005—aside precisely from among ideologues and spokespersons of the French right—we can cite two heterogeneous but not radically contradictory kinds of reasons. The first is the weakness of what is called "political Islam" in the French context, despite periodic cries of alarm or intimidation.[27] This weakness in particular means that for youths of North African origin (whose parents or grandparents were immigrants from Algeria and Morocco) the reference to Islam functions essentially as the assertion of a collective identity experienced as discriminated against and stigmatized (whence the continual reference to the lack of respect for their religion and the provocative role of episodes like that of the grenade in the mosque). It has no political function and no necessary connection to religious practice. (Everything seems to indicate that most youths of Muslim origin practice as little as other French youths, and more generally that the codes of mass communication and scenarios of urban violence and political fiction spread by television have more influence on their discourse and imaginary than religion, as is the case for many other French people.)[28] The second type of reason is that the main function of religion and religious culture—from a point of view that conforms entirely to the juridical schemas of French secularism and is subject to the same difficulties—is organization in the private sphere. This is why it focuses (like Catholicism not long ago) on control of the family and in particular on the relations between the sexes. In a situation of pauperization, discrimination, and the crisis of identities connected to work, education, and traditional culture, the reference to religion functions as a refuge and a substitute for social recognition. It comes to the fore when the conflict between incompatible values is acute within the revolt or the demand for recognition, as shown by the veil affair, and, on a completely different level of seriousness, sexual or clan violence against girls. The fact that it remained in the background in November 2005 is a crucial indicator of the limits of the politicization of the movement and also of its orientation. It did not renew intercommunal clashes, especially Judeo-Arab ones (thankfully), but also did not question sexist stereotypes (regrettably).

This perspective amounts to regarding religious discrimination, in the French context, as essentially a component of more general racial (or neoracial) discrimination—which is not to minimize its seriousness. To say that religion functions essentially as an index of racial identity, marking its minoritarian, illegitimate character from the perspective of the dominant culture, that it allows people to be subjected to the mechanism of internal exclusion, is not to contest that it can play an essential role in how all actors in the conflict identify themselves and present their (and others') identities, but it is to insist that the conflict as such is religious neither in its origins nor in its stakes. It is also to point out the extent to which the political treatment of religion, especially the effective recognition of Islam, as it in fact is today, the second religion in France and perhaps the most vibrant, constitutes a fundamental democratic and civic objective, even from the point of view of a secular state. Here it is a matter of both fighting a crucial aspect of institutional racism and guarding against an ideologization of social conflict that is for the moment negligible, though not unimaginable. We cannot help but note that, deliberately or not, part of the discourse of the intelligentsia is going in exactly the opposite direction.

5. RACE AND CLASS

We thus return to the idea that the fundamental complex is the intersection of class and race, each being taken in its most extended, evolving sense, at once subjective (the mode of identification of oneself and the other) and objective (the effects of social relations and historical conditions). The revolt of the *banlieues* and the way it has been suppressed, and later, in the best administrative tradition, buried beneath a torrent of announcements and promises without guarantees, bears witness both to the depth of the carefully repressed racial conflict at the heart of French society, and to the development of massive class inequalities in employment, education, security, housing, and the "right to the city" (to use Henri Lefebvre's expression, which is more current than ever). While many commentators and especially state spokespersons want to separate these two determinations, we must to the contrary carefully hold them together.[29] But is it enough to observe that the addition of these two factors of discrimination, whose effect is at once to bear the stigma of foreign origin, as "immigrant," and to live in zones of deindustrialization and "preferential unemployment" (10 percent in France as a whole, 20 percent in the *banlieues* affected by the revolts, up to 40 percent for the youth of these districts) generates a reinforced exclusion, which in turn is transformed into a stigma and a social handicap in an apparently endless spiral? Perhaps it is necessary to take one more step and try to characterize the singular place that results from the double exclusion of class and race: an essentially *negative* place, the effect of which is to constitute those who occupy it as eternally displaced, out of place persons, the internally excluded—pariahs, not in the sense the term had in its original context (a caste outside the system of legitimate castes) but that it acquired in modern Western society (via theorists like Max Weber, Hannah Arendt, and Pierre Bourdieu): groups that find themselves denied, in principle or in fact, the right to have rights (that of having them or having the use of them, and above all, that of claiming them).[30]

The combined effects of race and class are covered by the single administrative term "discrimination" (now official at the national and transnational level: the European Union has set up programs to fight discrimination, the president of the republic has recognized the role of discrimination in setting off the riots, etc.).[31] Or else they are indirectly signaled by euphemisms ("identity crisis," "social divide") that always refer to two rival hermeneutics, while the experience of the youths of the *banlieues*, what provokes their revolt and drives them to despair, is precisely one of overdetermination, in which each stigma prevents them from freeing themselves from the other, ruining their individual and collective futures. The negative place thus defined then becomes equally the public place where the pariahs stand up to declare, in a way that is itself negative, the decomposition of the social order of which they are the result. I will return to this in conclusion.

This omnipresence of the negative, what could be called the rise of a *negative community*, on the model of what Robert Castel has called negative individualism (and of course the two phenomena are correlative), should not prevent us from positively identifying the contemporary characteristics of the condition of class and the ascription of race.[32] What predominates, it seems to me, is on the one hand the scheme of heredity, and on the other that of disaffiliation (in Castel's sense)—whence comes a violent tension, a condition that negates or destroys itself.

Racial ascription, and beyond it all the stigmas of color, religion, and culture, goes back in a privileged way to a fixation on familial relations, when it comes to the self as well as the other. Witness the institutional phobia of family reunification, the administration's stigmatization of "broken families" that have given up authority over their children and therefore need to be reeducated, even punished, and the reappearance of the orientalist phantasm of polygamy.[33] It culminates in the construction of a juridically and humanly monstrous social category: the hereditary status of immigrant. Once an immigrant, always an immigrant, generation after generation, whatever nationality is acquired—and hence foreigners in their own country, since they do not (or no longer) have any other.[34]

The condition of class, for its part, is no longer defined principally by one's place in the division of labor, even if the great antitheses between income from property and income from work (albeit hidden by the extension of the category of wage-earners) or manual and intellectual labor (albeit displaced by universal education and computerization) are still significant. Today it runs, above all, between relatively protected and precarious jobs.[35] Such a frontier is by definition unstable, constantly moving, the stake of a constant relation of forces, at once global and local, the object of a perpetual, apparently irreversible forward retreat (as irreversible as globalization and the "outsourcing" it brings). It gives rise to a fierce new form of competition, competition between territories, as much among continental or national spaces that seek to attract investment with tax incentives, lower labor standards, and the dismantling of social rights, as among urban spaces that are treated as development zones, reservations, even dumping grounds.[36] Some *banlieues* thus appear as veritable designated living areas for a new proletariat, whose insecurity is maximal, having a choice only between precarious work and unemployment.[37] Imprisonment in an ethnic genealogy (a past of domination) is thus combined with being prevented from leaving a space of relegation (to build a real future). It is this double knot that is truly explosive, that is too much.

But it is also here that the question arises of the political meaning of a revolt that takes its energy from despair, whose destructive aspects themselves can be interpreted as a way of rising up to reach another place, that of representation, recognition, and participation. Does this revolt mark (at least symbolically) the ultimate limit of the regime that (in France) calls itself the republic and presents itself as the institution par excellence of a community of citizens, which has now become impossible? Or does it entail another force of democratization, and under what conditions? Let us examine these questions in two steps.

6. UNATTAINABLE REPUBLICAN CITIZENSHIP

I will proceed here once again by way of critical confrontation. The discourse developed by the Indigènes de la République collective since its foundation, in January 2005, has the merit of asking what has allowed "race" to be reconstituted and thus reproduced beyond the abolition or profound transformation of the material conditions and ideological reference points of its initial constitution, and of the fundamental role of the republican state in this reproduction.[38] From this perspective, it can be evaded or dismissed only at the price of considerable hypocrisy—thus the privilege I accord it here. But there is a downside to looking for the logic of internal exclusion or banishment, whose structural necessity it points out, in a simple repetition of the colonial form in the social formation of contemporary France, and consequently a downside to seeking to overcome it through a metaphorical rebirth of the anticolonial emancipation movement and a settling of the republic's accounts with its past, which would allow it to achieve internal decolonization after external decolonization—the last, hardest, and riskiest stage, without which the previous one is in a sense nullified. This second aspect, which is insistent in Indigènes' discourse, albeit with nuances and debates, is in my view an obstacle to fine-tuning the analysis. We must try to call it into question without neutralizing the virtues of the first aspect.

It is correct to abandon a problematic centered exclusively around immigration (even while maintaining that it has become the "name of race," as I did two decades ago), since immigrant origin in its turn has become a hereditary stigma, returning to the structural invariant of historical racisms.[39] This allows us to interpret both the apparent renewal of racist discourse (passing from the biological to the cultural, the religious, etc.) and the permanence of the genealogical schema, which allows it to be articulated according to conjunctures of class, familial sexism, and religion, presented as so many substantial, transgenerational identity constructions.[40] The republic is certainly accountable for the discrimination and violence that results—not only because this contradicts its constitutional principle, the equal access of all citizens to education and social promotion, jobs and professions, equal treatment by public administration, etc., but for a more specific political reason.[41] In France over at least two centuries, the republic has been constituted and reconstituted, sometimes after long eclipses, by demarcating itself in a more or less revolutionary way from other regimes characterized precisely by the limitations they placed on citizenship.[42] This traces a line of demarcation and sets conditions of legitimacy for institutions that can also be invoked against their internal deviations. Of course, the reality has never corresponded exactly to this principle, and the list of French subjects institutionally excluded from citizenship (or from *full* citizenship) by various republics is long, from women (before 1945) to the natives of the colonies.

This is why what is important is the direction in which the frontiers of citizenship evolve, toward expansion or restriction, and how the contradictions that emerge with changing relations of social forces, institutional facts, and the symbolic features of real citizenship are dealt with. From this point of view, the savage critique of the Indigènes and their insistence on the murderous effects of the French nation's long repression of its recent colonial past allows them to call attention to the retrograde direction in which the contradiction resulting from the combined mechanisms of naturalization (the French Republic is in principle attached to *jus soli*), the legal or illegal importation of labor (which has not ceased for at least two centuries), and the transnationalization of the political space (which for us takes the form especially of the construction of Europe) is handled today. This has to do not only with the fact that, as in all European countries, a two-speed citizenship is being created, with a zone of exclusion reserved for the foreign workforce (even if this phenomenon could be compared to an apartheid).[43] It also has to do with the fact that the same state (and, behind it, national political community) confers and takes away citizenship, that it includes—even imprisons—certain individuals in the political space *and* prohibits them from participating.[44] There is thus indeed a political analogy (and not just a continuity of methods on the side of the administration and the forces of repression) with the way that, in the colonial territories, two populations with radically unequal rights found themselves brought together and set apart. But the institutional mechanisms and political effects are not the same. The trace of colonization is one of the origins and permanent conditions of possibility for the denial of citizenship that, in the revolt of the *banlieues*, came back to hit the French Republic like a boomerang, but it is only one of them. This is why we must insist on the double determination of class and race in phenomena of exclusion, and on the void of belonging that it produces. The colonial (and especially precolonial) past of earlier generations can constitute a symbolic reference, even a retaliatory weapon against French national good conscience, but not, properly speaking, a schema or model for constructing contemporary political identities. History does not repeat itself.

Without the trace of this past, however, we would not properly understand the radicality of the exclusion of youths of immigrant origin, and by extension of the urban territories where, by administrative policy as much as by reflexes of kinship and mutual assistance, they are confined. Better, we would not understand what makes this exclusion singular and leads its difference from other, partly similar ones to be translated into racial language, thus producing the effects of an antagonism among the excluded themselves. It is not sufficient here to suggest a symmetry between the radicalization of the youths of the *banlieues* and the drift of a growing part of the pauperized, precarious working class toward racist ideology, as witnessed in the rise of the Front National vote in the *ban-lieues.*[45] We must, it seems to me, go deeper into two (obviously connected) aspects of the crisis of democracy in the French social-political formation: on the one hand, the tendency to substitute a racial phantasm for failing political representation, and, on the other, the blockage and potential derailing of the transition that leads to democratic insurrection, properly speaking, in the absence of adequate representation. We must try to connect these two points in order to outline a reflection of the *becoming political* of the revolt of the *banlieues* and to shed light on its uncertainties.

In the French Republic as it is perpetuated today (through a daily republican pact to which each of our practices contribute), citizenship is not just imperfect, as the best theorists of democracy and the crisis of the bourgeois nation-state have maintained.[46] It is increasingly unattainable. This is to say that it is refused to many of those who would have to benefit from it for it to deserve the name of democratic citizenship, while for many others it is reduced to a formal, limited status. In the ferment exemplified by the riots in 2005, fed by rage at suffering from the double systemic discrimination of race and of class and thus the place they define, it is of course tempting to see an *insurrectional capacity* to refound or reactivate citizenship: at once by the irruption of the plebs into the affairs of the city, where they claim, in Rancière's now indispensable expression, "the part of those who have no part," and by the performative declaration that there is no community of citizens without minimal recognition of the rights of all, starting with the right to existence and access to basic common goods.[47] But for this we would have to be able to see the revolt of the *banlieues*, beyond the sign or political symptom it supplies for those observing from the national space or outside, as a moment (however fragile, uncertain, reversible) in the unfolding of a political process (or, as one now says philosophically, political subjectivation) that belongs to the consciousness and action of those who are its bearers.[48] The problem here is not violence as such; for even if this form of action is not intrinsically connected to the insurrectional uprisings citizens repeat when their rights are denied (they can be nonviolent), historical experience shows that is very often necessary to weaken the discriminatory system, to pierce the blindness and deafness of the good citizens who live in it. The problem is to know what, under given conditions, can be done politically with violence as well as what effects and reactions it will bring.

7. POLITICS, ANTIPOLITICS

It has been endlessly repeated that the violence of the *cités*, briefly unleashed and as it were thrown in the face of French society and the state by youths who are of course minorities (adolescent, male, undereducated, for the most part from immigrant families) but also at the limit representative of the general condition into which their social, familial, and generational environment has been plunged, was *infrapolitical* violence.[49] But this formula can mean two things: either that the riot did not (and will not) reach the level of collective political action, be it because that is not its aim or because, as such, it has no aims aside from a cry of rage, or that a riot is still far from political action, separated from it by several steps that have yet to be taken, and that it does not in itself contain all the conditions (consciousness, ideology, organization, tactics and strategy, etc.). In both cases, the questions of illegality and confronting repression (which are closely connected, since repression takes its pretext from illegality, draws its legitimacy from it and thus favors it as much as possible) play a crucial role. A movement's continuity and its becoming political depend on its capacity to transform the meaning conferred on illegality by the dominant system and to resist repression (or to turn its effects back on those who practice it). But in both cases we have an abstract, dangerously linear schema that makes the political a simple surpassing or outcome of spontaneous social conflict. It is important, in my view, to complicate this schema in order to see how politics can also occur through its opposite—what I will call *antipolitics*—and thus emerge from the very conditions of its impossibility, but also, of course, find itself blocked by its internal contradictions.

Should we identify antipolitics with a failure of representation? Yes and no. On the traditional bourgeois representation of politics, as exemplarily embodied by liberalism (which in France has always been organic liberalism, based on the hegemony of intellectuals, experts, and the social establishment, what used to be called *les capacités*, in close association with the state), representation is a function of the political system itself, which proposes representatives to the groups that make up the nation, and in particular to the popular classes.[50] A situation in which the political class not only refuses to represent the interests of a social group but denies it the right to be represented as what it is, and thus to belong to the legitimate nation (the community of citizens), is a limit situation, though one that recurs periodically and in the end would appear structurally necessary for the functioning of the system. The political class (of the right or of the left) could not monopolize representation (in what Althusser some time ago called an Ideological State Apparatus) if all social contradictions were regarded as representable and effectively insisted on being represented. Yet political representation, as a process that has a history and makes history, does not only have this passive face, conferred from above (oligarchically, technocratically, hegemonically); it also incorporates pressure from below that transgresses earlier prohibitions and imposes other types of representatives (not necessarily parliamentary, to the contrary, to begin with they are generally activists, organic intellectuals of all professions) or forces the existing representatives to convey (but also to try to appropriate) the speech and claims of those outside the law in an open dialectic. Under these conditions, what would seem to be characteristic of the conjuncture in a country like France (and, not for nothing, obviously, in the loss of legitimacy of its political system) is the exhaustion of its ability to represent and speak for its popular classes and its excluded (of whom the young, unemployed "immigrants" of the *banlieue* are eminently a part). The republican form indeed increasingly deprives a whole part of the social realities it informs and the conflicts it subsumes of representation—another way of saying that citizenship is emptied of its content. It is for this that we can reserve the name "antipolitics."

No doubt to interpret such a situation it is necessary to refer not only to a Marxist schema of class struggle, but also to a schema we can call Hegelian.[51] Originally conceived before the political organization of the working class and the institution of conflict within the framework of a national-social state, today it paradoxically regains its pertinence beyond the emergence and development of their crisis (which is already well advanced).[52] Significantly, Hegel used two distinct terminologies to mark out social groups, their interdependence, and their conflict. The inheritor of a tradition that was still premodern, he called recognized groups, incorporated into the state by corporate or parliamentary representation, "estates" (*Stände*, like the estates of the Ancien Régime) and reserved the name "classes" (*Klassen*) for *internal-external* or *marginal* groups, the bearers of a capacity to subvert or disrupt the system—the "rabble" (*Pöbel*), pauperized by the Industrial Revolution and living on assistance, and, on the other side, finance capitalists, whose wealth and transnational activities exceed the possibilities of state control. Today this terminology has shifted. Because the political system was refounded in the nineteenth and twentieth centuries by integrating class struggles and notably by giving revolutionary movements a "tribunal function" within the bourgeois state, thus putting limits on social conflict without suppressing it completely (obviously in a highly variable way, according to period and relation of forces), the term "class" has tended instead to designate a category integrated into the economic and political system. We must therefore look for other terms to designate that which escapes its representative mechanisms, even threatens to dissolve them. This is one of the functions of contested and contestable categories like the *underclass*, in English, and the *exclus*, in French, which always oscillate between repeating the stigmatizations they are subject to (delinquency, dangerousness, risk, incivility) and recognizing the phenomenon they betray: the fact that what exceeds representation—its remainder—has reappeared and occupies a growing place, throwing politics off-balance, boring a void within it or exposing it to catastrophic mutations (of which fascism is the great historical example), short of refounding the institutions of conflict on an expanded basis.

We see clearly, then, the function of the overdetermined fusion of racial and class exclusions on which I insisted above: precisely to precipitate, and to sanction, the exteriority of the new populace in relation to the political—all the more effectively to the extent that class discrimination is assumed not to exist (or is still to be made up for by exhausted welfare-state mechanisms) and racial discrimination is declared absolutely illegitimate (allowing one to deny its existence, or to pretend not to see it where it is practiced in new forms). But it is still more interesting to underline the reconstitution in renewed form of the scheme of the double exclusion of the extremes outside the political: those who are "too rich" and those who are "too poor," the owners and executives of multinational capitalism, on the one hand, and the subproletariat or underclass of the insecure, immigrants, and especially youth, on the other. Except that if the former are tendentially located outside representation, it is voluntarily, because they no longer have an interest in playing the game of national politics and accepting its relative constraints (common taxation, education, and medical care, participation in a certain social consensus), but only in bringing the logic of the global market to bear on the state and, by means of one state or another, obtaining favorable conditions for exploitation and access to workers. Whereas the latter are pushed or left outside representation, which prevents their existence and their rights claims from finding any, necessarily conflictual, expression, since they are deemed unmanageable by the system and the other classes, including the popular classes—even the poor, who are convinced or find reasons to believe that their security comes at the price of others' insecurity, or that their membership in the collectivity, their identity, would be threatened if other memberships, other identities, were recognized and added to theirs. The former set themselves up, materially and symbolically, beyond the distinction between the national and the foreign (which, in French society, continues to formally dictate citizenship), while the latter are, by force, treated as *internal foreigners*, threatening or superfluous. This symmetry is thus like day and night, always favoring day.

Here we find again the idea of a void, already evoked in different shapes above (the void of the space of the *cité* as the setting of the revolt, the void of the institutional place where determinations of class and race are superimposed), but this time as a void of representation at the heart of the political institution (including in the provoked form of criminalization, disqualification, and preventive evacuation). But this void is destined to be filled, or at least displaced. And it is here that another type of political representation enters the scene, produced essentially by the interaction of the law-and-order policies of the state and the images manufactured and circulated by the means of mass communication (above all television): a paradoxical representation, obviously, itself antipolitical, since its function is to replace real actors (especially those of the revolt) with fantasmatic actors who combine the characteristics of pathology (drugs, disintegrating families, unruly behavior in school), criminality (sexual violence, petty delinquency), and cultural or ethno-religious alterity, in order to embody the community's foreign body in the imaginary.

On this basis, we can then try to interpret the political ambivalence of the significations and effects of the revolt of the youth of the *cités*. As I remarked at the beginning, following many others, the rioters deployed a *spectacular* violence. One could think that here it is simply a matter of a passive, mechanical effect of the development of mass communications. But one could also think that this effect produced something like a passive organization of the revolt, giving it the character of movement at a distance, even if its development depends strictly on the medium that sends it its own image back to it.[53] Their violence was thus in part real, the result of intolerable conditions and directed against material targets (their surroundings, the police, the state), but in part mediatic, aiming to embody society's phantasm, to produce what it, and especially the state, had already described as their essence. This is why it combined a narcissistic dimension (including the self-destructive form already mentioned) and, conversely, a dimension we could call ironic, in the sense that true irony, as Baudelaire emphasized, is always addressed at once to the other and to oneself. It thereby managed to trap for a time the power that had provoked it by unleashing for its own purposes a representative machine whose power it believed it controlled—paradoxically recreating a political dialectic within the element that, in our societies, is meant to radically neutralize it. And this political power, in order to put a stop to this, could not be content with repression; it had to utter certain words ("discrimination," even "racism"). But it also eventually prepared counteroffensives on the same terrain. Today we see clearly how the same interior minister (having become in the meantime an official candidate for the presidency) instrumentalizes television to stage hunts for illegal immigrants or police raids on the hideouts of young delinquents.[54] Who knows, in the end, who will outrun whom in this competition?

But the scheme of a void can also, finally, help us establish the bases of the great problem of the becoming political of the revolt—I am tempted to say, in the sense recalled above, of its becoming insurrectional. This problem is the possibility or impossibility of a *collectivization*. Let us understand by this not just a repetition or a contagion (creating a series of similar revolts, as we saw in the course of November and as we could say more generally of the episodes that have followed one another over the years), but an articulation with other rights claims or protests against injustice, heterogeneous among themselves, and thus constitutive of a virtual citizenship within a democratic framework. On first glance, the practical implications of the existential, social, and political void are just the opposite, for how could association and communication emerge from exclusion and its doubling, secession or provocation? What constitutes an insurrectional movement—be it the American civil rights movement and black power in the 1960s and 70s, the student movement in '68, or the movement of *piqueteros* in Argentina in the 2000s—is both its radicalness and its transversality, its ability to express or echo other revolts in its own code.

The radicality of the revolt of the *banlieues* is indissociable from its power of refusal. Here the absence of objectives expressed by the repetition of incivility and violence is not a failing, even if it could eventually turn out to be a weakness. It is only to see how the university, the press, and the state devote themselves to defining it, circumscribing it, making it the essential characteristic of those who revolt in order to prevent it from disseminating wildly throughout the social environment. It makes the destructive void, the "nonright" of the condition produced for the pariahs of postindustrial society, "return to sender." It is not exclusive to one or more languages and therefore bears an interpellation (rap, whose identitarian function for the youth of the *cités*, beyond the phenomenon of gangs I recalled above, has this role among others). But this radicality is very hard to separate from a culture of isolation and defiance in all directions, another form of refusal—as if, rather than a guerilla or civil war, the revolt mimed the "exodus" of part of the youth, of which the primacy of clashes with police (obviously sought out by the police) is the most striking symptom. Of course this isolation is in part fictional and remains highly relative; this is why it is so important to note that at the height of the riots, familial and even institutional solidarities (relations to associations, be they secular or religious, and contact with social workers, behind whom stand some public services and certain municipalities) were not totally broken. It is not true in reality that youths are isolated in the *cité*, expressing their despair through their illegalism or violence; at least this isolation does not go without its opposite. Nor is it true that the *cité* is totally isolated from society and the city, even if barriers are erected to separate them.[55] This is why much will depend, from the perspective of individual lives but also that of politics, on how they appropriate (or not) the part of themselves that is their urban territory (with its institutions, from which Loïc Wacquant shows they are inseparable), against which their rage is in part directed.

The opening up of the youth revolt within the world of the *banlieues*, and more generally in French society, whatever its highly uncertain modalities, is a major challenge that concerns us all. It means nothing less than defeating the law-and-order project, or the reduction of politics to the police, borne alternately by the forces of the opposition (Jean-Marie Le Pen) and components of the powers that be (Sarkozy), but that more fundamentally constitutes one of the tendencies of the evolution of capitalism and contemporary public administration. This project tends to establish a permanent segregation of social space, especially in the most conflictual regions, of "dangerous" groups, without well-defined limits, but identified by racial characteristics and a whole set of cultural, social, and urban stigmas in a way that concentrates the mistrust, hostility, and resentment of whole parts of the population, especially the popular classes—those closest to them in urban space as well as living conditions. It thus justifies and reinforces state violence in advance. In a narrowing circle, demands for repression from below, what Gilles Deleuze called "micro-fascism," corresponds to spectacular or everyday operations of control and repression, which we know change little in the state of general insecurity (when they do not reinforce it), to say nothing of its structural causes, but mask the government's powerlessness and lack of representativeness behind a show of authority, sustaining the illusion among a share of the dominated and the exploited, whose living conditions are ever harder, that the state protects them and takes care of them—since it harasses and strikes others who can be identified as internal foreigners.[56]

There is doubtless no way of defeating such a political project (which is broadly shared today, to varying degrees and more or less openly, within the dominant class and has become popular among a large share of public opinion) other than by isolating it within the city, this time in the broad, constitutional sense of the term. But for this it is necessary to transform the power of the negative and the violence of exclusion little by little into a dialectic of convergence and mutual recognition of all kinds of resistance that the system of representation and generalized social competition subjects to a regime of "dismemberment."[57] Since November 2005, the extreme difficulty of this conversion has been repeatedly emphasized, sometimes by forcing sociological realities, for example during the anti-CPE movement of French students that followed the revolt of the *banlieues* by a few months (March 2006), whose political codes reflected completely different logics inherited from working-class trade-unionism or May '68 and its aftershocks in the 1980s and 90s.[58] This difficulty is very real. It would in fact be necessary to lay bare and confront all the contradictions within the people that the riots served to reveal (between young and old, insecure and relatively protected workers, nationals and foreigners or those regarded as such, and perhaps above all boys and girls among youth, who certainly do not make up two antagonistic worlds, but who clearly have quite different cultures of relating to institutions and imaginaries of action).[59] And it would be necessary that, still from within, all the mediations constitutive of civil society that bear active citizenship (of which teams of social workers, but also resident associations, be they secular or religious, form a part) be mobilized and articulated in practice.[60] Obviously I have no recipe to propose from the outside in these matters. I limit myself to interpreting the signs that reach us and trying to transform them into questions.

TOWARD CO-CITIZENSHIP

Allow me to begin with a statement with which I try to provoke us to leave the beaten track: Is nomadic citizenship possible? This means both: If such a citizenship in the age of migration is possible, under what conditions would it also become thinkable? And, if it has become necessary as an object of thought, under what conditions would nomadic citizenship also become possible as an institution?

These conditions, obviously, would be multiple and improbable. They have to do at once with law, politics, the economy, culture, and even philosophy.[1] If they were united, they would be equivalent to a revolution in the history of an institution—or, better yet, in a principle of the institution—of the city or the political, which has already undergone many revolutions in a history marked by disappearances and rebirths. They anticipate certain demands for transformations—still barely outlined—of the political in the world in which we live, but also go against some of the most deeply rooted structures, which are not all, far from it, structures of oppression or domination, nor can they be reduced to them, and which have to do with collective consciousness but also with a certain transindividual unconscious. They thus form at once conditions of possibility and conditions of impossibility.

I propose to examine them here under four headings:

1. the idea of the right of freedom of movement as a fundamental right;
2. the ontological paradoxes and anthropological effects of globalization;
3. the territorializing and deterritorializing of the citizen, which conjure up at once the structures of sovereignty and the elision of "the people" (thinking of Deleuze's question, "What people to come?");
4. the perspectives and instruments for instituting mobility as mobile or traveling citizenship (*civitas vaga*).

1. THE RIGHT OF FREEDOM OF MOVEMENT AS A FUNDAMENTAL RIGHT

This right has been gradually recognized (not without conflicts and tragedies) as a fundamental right, and is expressed in the Universal Declaration of the Rights of Man of 1948, along with its correlate, the right of residence.[2] This poses a double problem: that of putting it into effect and that of its status as a principle or foundation.

Among the obstacles to implementing the right to freedom of movement, some have to do with required facts or conditions, which make a complete liberation of the movement of persons difficult or impracticable. Jurists tend to consider these contingencies external to the juridical form; realistic politicians consider them historical necessities going back to the formation of nation-states, that is, to power relations anchored by control of populations and their movements. More deeply, they reflect contradictions that affect the very idea of an absolute freedom of movement, whose status must be examined in comparison to other fundamental rights, for example, that of freedom of expression and communication. We know that from this point of view there are considerable differences between states, even democratic ones, especially between Europe and the United States. Whereas freedom of opinion and expression is considered a constitutional principle, no one (except perhaps for consistent anarchists) thinks it is possible to say everything under any circumstances or to any audience, including insults, threats, and provocations. The same would go, *mutatis mutandis*, for the right to free movement. There is a point at which uncontrolled freedom destroys itself.

This is the source of the problem posed by the status of the right to movement as a principle or fundamental right, which in our modern states implies its constitutionalization.[3] Ultimately, it is a matter of knowing to what extent the more or less inevitable restriction of the principle's bearing by the conditions of its application does not finally result in its negation. The same problem holds, to be sure, for other fundamental principles, starting with that of the sovereignty of the people instituted in the parliamentary, bureaucratic forms of the "constituted power." If the restrictions or regulations that the institution of a right imply in fact empty it of its substance or reduce it to practically nothing, its statement or proclamation loses its political and even juridical value. The Marxist and revolutionary critique of bourgeois democracy and its abstraction has never stopped insisting on this point, and even exploiting it in order to propose alternatives.

These two problems are obviously connected. To account for them, it is sufficient to return to the way the Universal Declaration of Human Rights, speaking universally or *sub specie universitatis*, performatively declared the right to freedom of movement: "1. Everyone has the right to freedom of movement and residence within the borders of each state. 2. Everyone has the right to leave any country, including his own, and to return to his country" (article 13). Comparing this statement to other, more or less closely related ones in the declaration, we can make a number of observations:

a The statement of the right to freedom of movement has a
   structure that could be called antithetical or antagonistic,
   illustrated in particular by article 15 ("1. Everyone has the right
   to a nationality. 2. No one shall be arbitrarily deprived of his
   nationality nor denied the right to change his nationality."),
   which considers two inverse liberties as correlative and seeks
   their unity or equilibrium (in this case, leaving one's country or
   returning to it).[4]
b The right to freedom of movement constitutes an application
   of the right to legal personality proclaimed by article 6 ("Everyone
   has the right to recognition everywhere as a person before the

law"), which could be designated, in Arendtian terms, as a statement of the right to have rights. It is obviously significant that these texts all belong to the same immediate postwar conjuncture as the attempt to forbid the deportation and denationalization of entire populations—not to mention their extermination, which, as Arendt emphasized, supposes that individuals once belonging to a political community and thus, in practice, to a state are first deprived of their legal personality.[5] But this application is directly accompanied by a determination, and this is what begins to pose the problem of negation (*determinatio negatio est*).

c The determination turns entirely around the pivot role of the notion of a country. Everyone has "his country," in the sense of the genitive (a *membership* and a *belonging*: I belong to a country, this country is mine, it belongs to me at the same time that it belongs to others who are, owing to this fact, its co-owners), which is no obstacle—to the contrary—to changing it, by changing both one's location and one's membership, according to certain procedures. This exception confirms the rule. The double, antagonistic right defined as a principle is thus an *articulation* inside and outside the country—in other words, the national and international status of a person. Not only does this therefore not abolish the border as an institution; it legitimizes it or gives back to it a democratic and liberal legitimacy it was deprived of by policies of forced denationalization (which are being revived today under the name of ethnic cleansing).

d The right to freedom of movement is in this sense correlative to a certain territorial institution of the sovereignty of the people as announced in article 21 ("1. Everyone has the right to take part in the government of his country . . . 2. Everyone has the right of equal access to public service in his country. 3. The will of the people shall be the basis of the authority of government"), which takes all its meaning in this context from the struggle against totalitarianism and nascent decolonization, as well as the coming struggle for civic rights against institutional segregation in the United States, South Africa, etc. Let us retain from this that the right to freedom of movement so defined is inseparable from a belonging strongly stated with reference to his "country," but without the conditions under which an individual can consider a country "his" ever being defined.

Notwithstanding their letter, these texts allow us to anticipate four types of difficulties that would become more evident with time:

- Some would be tied to the relativization and even the blurring of borders, and thus the difference between being here and there, being from here and from elsewhere, with the rise of populations that could be called "nomadic" in a new sense, or, better still, ubiquitous (since they divide their time and their residence, and thus their lives, between several places, several territories belonging to different states, a condition that bureaucracies of course hate and try by all means to render unlivable, even if in reality these displacements are both regulated and regular).
- Some would be tied to the degeneration of the sovereignty of the people as an effective constitutional principle with the increase of the oligarchic and technocratic character of democracies themselves and the monopolization of political power by bureaucracies that escape popular control (which, to be sure, even the partial transfer of decision-making to a supranational level does not attenuate but reinforces).
- Some relate to the fact that the liberal-democratic legitimation (or re-legitimation) of the border as an institution (following, as we know, terrible forms of changing borders, involving amputation, partition, the change of status of whole nations and enormous territories in all parts of the world) clearly rests on a primacy of the individual (a sort of practical methodological individualism) in the relation of the individual to the collective (group or community). This brings processes of rights claims and conquests or inventions (as Lefort says) of fundamental rights or the politics of human rights. But behind the individual hides the (nation-)state, which is alone charged with recognizing these rights or guaranteeing them to individuals. These texts tend to refer movement to individuals and identify residence with "collective belonging." Individuals move and collectives are settled by the state. The reality of refugee problems and population movements as Arendt thought of them in her study of the

crisis of the nation-state (in the second part of *On the Origins of Totalitarianism*) already contradicted this presentation. This is all the more the case if we take into account types of migration that concern masses, not individuals (even if it is always, it must be noted, the individual whose life or death is at stake in the attempt to cross borders). This also means that one of the objectives of the Declaration is to categorize such collective or massive movements as catastrophic or exceptional by treating them as aggregates of multiple individual journeys. All this is fully coherent with a liberal representation of labor migration, whereby massive, regular, and even organized movements are reduced to the statistical effect of large numbers of individual trips that just happen to be along the same path.

- Finally, some difficulties are embryonically present in the fact that the Declaration, in a general way, does not limit itself to the notion of a formal right, in the sense of a proclamation of principles without efficacy, but invokes a material or effective right—that is to say, poses it without the means of achieving in reality a fundamental right that strictly speaking does not exist. This is also the case with the right to property, freedom of expression, the right to family and religion, etc., and even the right to work (article 23). For it falls, as it were, on both sides of the legal norm (in Hans Kelsen's sense)—universality of form and particular conditions of effectiveness—between the two spaces separated by a border (which also has the effect of making it a sort of universal a priori schema for interpreting the rights of man). Article 19, the meaning of which can be generalized, upholds the form "regardless of frontiers" ("Everyone has the right to freedom of opinion and expression; this right includes freedom to hold opinions without interference and to seek, receive and impart information and ideas through any media and regardless of frontiers"), while article 28, which defines a certain "order," shows clearly that its effectiveness depends on the state (that is, the nation-state), which is the "subject" of social and international obligations and thus responsible for implementing the law or realizing the principles ("Everyone is entitled to a social and international order in which the rights and freedoms set forth in this Declaration can be fully realized").

2. ONTOLOGICAL PARADOXES AND ANTHROPOLOGICAL EFFECTS OF GLOBALIZATION

These grand philosophical terms need not elicit dread. By "ontological," I refer to putting in question the classical opposition between *persons* and *things* on which our juridical thinking is based, the disjunctive application of which (in the sense of an *exclusive* disjunction: everything that is must be either a person or a thing, and cannot be both at once) ends up producing an increasingly inescapable paralysis of social practice (which it formalizes less and less well). "Anthropological" refers to the fact that the different treatment of individuals or groups (individuals and communities) concerning movement is not only a social and thus political problem but more radically puts in question how globalized national and international society institutes "the human," how it categorizes and hierarchizes it in such a way as to control its selective reproduction, making certain social relations possible and others impossible or very difficult, which is to say risky (making them, as it were, into "social relations of risk," as one speaks of "risk society").[6] This is radically the case with travel, not so much because of terrorism or international banditry as because of the hunt for certain travelers organized by the police forces of receiving countries.

Why do I feel the need to appeal to these philosophical abstractions here? If we begin from the idea of fundamental rights that call for regulation (like freedom of expression or association), we will ask whether the transformations of the contemporary world (commonly designated almost tautologically as "globalization") do not end up emptying the universally proclaimed right to freedom of movement of all content, whether the implementation of the principle does not in reality betray it by making it ineffective. We would have to ask whether this is because the very idea of a universal right to freedom of movement is contradictory, or whether it is because the necessary conditions for the validity of a universal principle when it concerns a very large number of human beings, or a multitude, have not been created. But we would also have to ask whether this is new: What was the reality of the right to freedom of movement, the freedom to move, in different periods, regions or civilizations, and social groups? Whence the fundamental importance of a comparative study of both the quantities and the qualities or modalities of movement. And we will have to ask whether the current transformations can be regarded as unexpected. Were the formulations of the Universal

Declaration of Human Rights not initially a fiction covering over a completely contrary reality, namely, the massive and restrictive control of freedom of movement, especially in collective forms (labor migrations, the exchanges and displacements of populations connected to the end of colonization)? Here we touch on a reflection on the performative political function of metajuridical enunciations of fundamental rights.

I will begin by recalling two phenomena that are characteristic of contemporary capitalist globalization: on the one hand, the disparity among *objects* and *subjects* when it comes to the *laissez passer* of liberal principle; on the other, the inequality and thus the profoundly discriminatory character with which it is applied to persons of different social status (of which belonging to nations and nationalities of unequal status, unequally recognized at the global level, forms an integral part).

Here, too, all sorts of preliminaries are required. The concept of movement is much too undifferentiated—we would have to subject it to a categorical elaboration that itself would have an ontological and anthropological meaning.[7] This is what jurists, geographers, and urbanists do, but perhaps sociologists, political philosophers, and political scientists have not done enough. It would be a matter of articulating, in counterpoint to a topology of the world's regions (which today can no longer be reduced to oppositions as simple as center and periphery or North and South), with its routes and its borders, movement and communication, migration and travel, mobility and residence, displacement and settlement, etc., with their complementarities and oppositions.[8] Any discussion of the freedom of movement is also of course a discussion of the configuration and material constitution of global space and its transformations. Political spaces and the politics of space correspond to a politics of movement and regimes of movement whose history is no less decisive for a general anthropological history.[9] In reality they cannot be separated, as the works of Nigel Thrift, Saskia Sassen, and Manuel Castells have shown over the last years.[10]

If we assume that the contemporary globalized world is governed by liberalism, where the principle of *laissez faire, laissez passer* reigns, we will no longer understand why the disparity between movements is so large, since "the dominant view among both classical and neo-classical economists is that both the free mobility of capital and labor is essential to the maximization of overall economic gains."[11] To the contrary, it is necessary to adopt the perspective of a capitalist world system, as Wallerstein defines it, in which social inequalities between regions are essential for the production of rents (or superprofits, and thus profits themselves; contemporary capitalism is less than ever in search of mere profit, but rather of superprofit), and those where the political structures that control the workforce, split into things and persons, has imperatives that serve economic logic wholesale and in the long term, but contradict it retail and at the moment, a present that has no foreseeable end. We see this paradox very specifically in the border regions or "semi-peripheries" in Wallerstein's sense of the world economy, where global equalities and their anthropological consequences are concentrated. It suffices to visit the U.S.-Mexico border or the southern Mediterranean, where astonishingly similar barriers are now being constructed to block the movement of persons.[12]

The characteristic disparity of laissez passer that delimits the right to freedom of movement today is not at all reducible to the opposition of persons and things, since there is a growing number of intermediary, transindividual beings, which are neither persons nor things but participate in both. In a sense they are reactivating the third category of Roman law (and, in the background, of the Stoic ontology that underlies it), that of *actions*. But they are actions without an agent, or in any case without a unique, individualized agent who is the exclusive owner of these actions and guarantor of their "propriety" (*conventia*), responsible for their effects. What is intensifying today is the movement of goods, capital, and money, but above all information (which is largely commodified, and to which the movement of capital is in many regards related), while what is limited is the movement of persons—both under the pretext of economic protection, of preserving national identity (even if, as in France or the United States, it is defined in universal terms), and of security in a time of war, terrorism, and subversive threats. In fact, it is the movement of certain persons, as we shall see. The ontological dilemma of persons and things is in crisis, since information is neither. Its introduction has to do with a hypercirculation that, on the one hand, replaces the movement of persons by compensating for their immobility with the ubiquity of their work (through the outsourcing of computer services to India, the Philippines, etc.) and, on the other, intensifies restrictions on movement. Those who have access to computers no longer have to look for work abroad, but those who do not are doubly excluded from circulation (see, for example, the populations of the deindustrialized areas of Europe, treated in the films of Bruno Dumont and the novels of Dominique Manotti).[13]

This leads to the second aspect: the enormous inequality in the right of freedom of movement and the mobility of persons. A whole phenomenology of persons' unequal relation to transnational mobility could be developed. It proceeds by means of asymmetry (in the delivery of passports and visas, so that certain borders can be passed in one direction and not the other) as well as differential repression (and from this perspective clandestine legal and police status would appear as a true economic institution of globalization, a job and workforce regime). It includes the double constraint of forced mobility (at the risk of one's life: see the boat people of Malta, the Canary Islands, and Lampedusa) and forced immobility, which is culturally conditioned, in the case of the re-proletarianized workers of Europe. The synthesis is the derisory offer made to the workers of Moulinex and Aubade when their factories were closed: "If you want to stay with the firm, accept 200 Euros a month and move to Malaysia!" This inequality, which would have to be compared to other correlative ones (the restriction of the right to freedom of movement is no more unjust than that of the right to housing, but it is also no less), is destined to grow and have more serious consequences, along with the security problems and social conflicts it engenders—especially, no doubt, with the effect of climate change, an aspect of globalization whose effects are still incalculable.[14] The consequences are counted in the destruction or destructuration of human groups, in situations of permanent insecurity, in conflicts that generate racial hatreds.

We can already try to point out the cosmopolitical consequences of these transformations. In the first place, there is the explosion of the category of "commerce" (*Verkehr*, "intercourse") common to Montesquieu, Adam Smith, Kant, and Marx, on which the classical cosmopolitan utopia was based—the idea that the intensification of contacts within the human species, resulting from commercial exchanges, would engender cultural and intellectual progress, and at the end of the day the political unity of humanity. In the second place, the reproduction of a new economy of race, or of sedentary and nomadic races; in this regard it would be necessary to return to, complicate, and historicize what I said earlier about the category of the immigrant as a new name for race in postcolonial society.[15] Finally, there is the tendency to reduce the undesirable foreigner to the enemy (social, cultural, possibly political), against whom we need to erect a new social defense. This is not so much a radicalization of the logic immanent in the institution of the nation-state, according to the Hobbesian perspective (for which civil societies, that is, nations, are like individuals in the state of nature, in other words virtually at war) than a radical reversal of its political function. The foreigner (more exactly, the foreigner of a certain type, one whose figure of foreignness is reinforced, intensified, essentialized) is not one with whom we can or, depending on the circumstances, must make war, but one with whom we can no longer make peace. He or she is the *nonperson* of whom Alessandro Dal Lago writes.[16] We are seeing the development of a fantasmatic negation of the process of recognition and the internal dialectic of alterity and foreignness that is constitutive of classical nationality, which defines citizenship in and belonging to a state. Hannah Arendt suggests that this negation is the kernel of nationalism itself, for there is no nation without nationalism. But the globalized world in which migrations are massive and constant (despite their cyclical fluctuations) no longer seems to make room for the foreigner as a person, distinct at once from a commodity and an enemy.[17] This is why we are seeing the massive production of what Sidi Mohammed Barkat calls an "exceptional body."[18] But the consequences are no less spectacular for the constitution of the juridical order of nation-states: the presence of foreigners as such within and outside their borders (thus more or less freely traversing their borders) is in fact no less necessary to their legitimacy than popular sovereignty. (This is why, moreover, militant actions, if need be in the form of resistance or civic disobedience, that tend to prevent the state from reducing foreigners to the status of commodities, disposable objects, or essentially suspect public enemies are in fact actions to preserve the legitimacy of the state.)[19]

3. TERRITORIALIZATION AND DETERRITORIALIZATION OF THE CITIZEN

The blockage or internal collapse of the category of the foreigner on the basis of the restriction of his right to freedom of movement in the context of an intensification of the circulation of things and actions (or messages, meanings) opens, or rather reopens, fundamental dilemmas of the right to the city [*droit de cité*]. This poses the problem of the origins, functions, limits, and exceptions of the fundamental connection between the state, nation, sovereignty, territory, and population. And, beyond this, it calls into question a whole conception of *civilization* connected to the idea of a line of progress going from nomadism to settled life, or toward the submission of the "nomads" to the "settled." This is why, even if they tended to take these terms in a metaphorical sense, the work of Deleuze and Guattari is important. It signals the reintegration of the distinction between nomads and the settled, and at the same a rediscovery of its complexity, at the heart of political anthropology.[20]

Reading the great theorists of sovereignty—from Bodin to Schmitt, but also other, less sulfurous constitutional jurists, such as Georg Jellinek, Alberto Donati, and Hans Kelsen, in short, the whole of the great tradition of theorizing the rule of law and the public power's monopoly of legitimate force and/or violence—shows that there is a triangular interdependence between sovereignty, population, and territory.[21] More precisely, there is an interdependence between national sovereignty, the population (or multitude) instituted into a community of citizens (even before the sovereignty of the people, whose proclamation it in a sense prepares), and the constitution of a relation of exclusivity between individuals and territories (the fiction of reciprocal belonging to which I alluded above) by means of borders. This relation is no doubt open to considerable differences from the perspective of the right of persons, between ethnic states (like Israel, where the land itself belongs exclusively to an ethnoreligious group, basing the political territory on the appropriation of land and producing a discrimination between first- and second-class citizens parallel to that affecting population movements: the opposition between the right of return of some and a prohibition on return for others) and liberal states of the Euroamerican type, where private property is free and income can be relocated—within certain limits and, here again, with considerable social inequalities (large incomes can be relocated for tax purposes, small ones cannot). But the triangular structure *de jure* includes all these variations. From this point of view, all modern nation-states are also territorial states; they define and represent themselves as communities of sedentary citizens, rooted or established on the territory.

This ternary structural relation signifies that, as Enrica Rigo shows in her book, borders and individuals' relations to borders are constitutive of citizenship. What the nation-state is doing today, be it directly or through the intermediary of a union it constitutes with others, is opening the right to freedom of movement for some and closing it for others. The type for this is the Europe of the Schengen agreement, which does not include all the E.U. member-states but includes others that are still only candidates for membership by way of anticipation. The citizen here is not only defined by habeas corpus and the right to vote, by being subject to taxes and military service, but as the holder of a right to move inside and outside. This also means that the radical separation between inside and outside, the space of freedom and the space of constraint, even if necessary to the very definition of the nation, is becoming increasingly virtual and hard to maintain. We have an illustration of this point in the paradoxes of the European construction: more and more policing of foreigners is required because the enlargement of the internal space of free movement automatically introduces a rising population of illegal European citizens, who are in many respects future citizens of Europe.

It is at this point that the anthropological and political inquiry must be relaunched. It would bear first of all on the question of the right to the city. Is it originally territorialized? Is it, through difficulties connected to the shifting of borders and changes in their function, headed toward a virtual reterritorialization? We have learned (it is the history, I will not dare say myth, of Clisthenes' reform and the institution of the *demos*) that at the origin of the ancient right to the city there was a territorialization of belonging that was a limitation of the functions of membership by lineage (the *genos*) at least symbolically connected to nomadism, or to an intergenerational bond preserved with a name, independent of residence, that survived migrations and diasporas.[22] At the current turning point of the right to the city, a conflict of principles is emerging between the territorialization of political participation and a deterritorialization that would also be a reterritorialization in virtual space, that of individuals who maintain ties and common, public interests, rights and duties, through their displacements (what we could call *civis vagus*).

This leads to a second, juridical or meta-juridical problem: that of the correlation between the territorial monopoly of the state and the constitution of subjective rights (which takes us back to the initial problem of the effectiveness of fundamental rights). As Catherine Colliot-Thélène, among others, has shown in some of her recent contributions to the philosophy of law and the state, to the extent that it relativizes, or even eliminates, the function of communities and belonging to so-called natural communities (that is, simply, traditional ones, those that preceded the state and that it opposes), it is the state that institutes the subjective rights of individuals or paradoxically makes them bearers of a right that can to a certain extent be opposed to the state.[23] But this institution is only possible to the extent that territoriality is a presupposition of sovereignty. From the perspective of the statist construction, peoples still tend to be nomadic; individuals are territorialized. Or better: the state virtually decomposes "the people" as a preexisting, "nomadic" community (the *ethnos*) and recomposes it as the *demos*, that is, as its own community.[24] The grand narrative of the barbarian migrations that preceded the state, the halting of which made the state possible, fits within this schema (and is reactivated by the current image of masses of immigrants attacking European territory). The state, like the city before it, liberates individuals from their dependencies or their servitude, on its territory, within its walls.

As soon as relations between nomads and the settled are torn apart by changes in the regime of communication and migration, the sovereignty of the people appears impossible, in any case, in its previous forms. (This is a strong point of sovereigntist discourse, which insists on the connection between the closure of national territory and the opening of the public space to all, a condition of imagining that within these limits the democratic action of the citizen still exists, not only as a phantom.) The sovereignty of the people, already mediatized, delegated, expropriated, and thus rendered more and more fictive by the transformation of modern bourgeois nations into democratic oligarchies, is itself well and truly threatened with dismemberment by the problem of governmentality that is posed to states. How can a heterodox population of nationals or supranationals, foreigners or temporary residents, be governed? How can the fiction of a *demos*, the equality of whose rights rests on exclusion, and thus on privilege (even if this privilege is partly imaginary), be maintained?[25] But in fact these new nomads themselves belong to antagonistic social classes. More generally, the question is becoming unavoidable of how to go in practice (and especially institutional practice) from citizenship always already considered as a *status* to citizenship considered as a *social relation*, a relation of politically instituted reciprocity.

4. FROM THE INSTITUTION OF THE RIGHT TO MOVEMENT TO DIASPORIC CITIZENSHIP?

Let us begin again with the idea of a principle of applying or realizing fundamental rights. All freedom presupposes regulation, restrictions, both in order not to harm their beneficiaries and not to contradict other rights, but, as I have said, only if this regulation does not represent its abolition. As soon as the implementation of the principle of territoriality inseparable from national state sovereignty as a veritable "exclusion from movement" for some results in the progressive destruction of the ideas of representation and sovereignty of the people, is it not necessary to try to invent and elaborate, on the contrary, something like a *nomadic* citizenship, or at least partly delocalized citizenship independent of territory?[26] Such a citizenship, incorporating a whole set of subjective and objective rights, including the right to freedom of movement and its correlate, the right to residence, under reasonable conditions that do not render it unrealizable, could then appear as a new stage in the progressive history of citizenship according to schema inspired by T. H. Marshall (even if we do not retain the detail of his formulations and especially the rigorously linear order of its three moments: civil rights, political rights, social citizenship).[27] This would be to place citizenship in a cosmopolitical perspective, at an equal distance from a simple ethical demand, such as the demand for hospitality (included by Kant in his project for *Perpetual Peace* and radicalized in our day by Derrida) and the project of a world state. (The Habermasian idea of *Weltinnenpolitik*, or "global domestic policy," which would virtually abolish any distinction between political spaces from the perspective of the efficacy of fundamental legal norms inscribed in a constitution, seems at least formally to tend in the latter direction.)[28]

Certain republican or neorepublican considerations, which are no less fundamental for being negative and now form part of the cultural basis of movements that strive to democratize liberal democracies (by underlining their hopelessly oligarchic character), certainly seem to go in this direction. Is the people constitutive of the community of citizens in republican states like France (and other comparable ones) not in the process of coming apart? I have spoken in this regard in earlier essays of an inverse application of "Hegel's theorem," which, beyond the now completed history of the national-social state, is rediscovering the problems he posed in his *Philosophy of Right* (1821) (problems Marx thought he could overcome once and for all by radicalizing the idea of class struggle). At two extremes of the social and political body, groups tend to find themselves excluded from the democratic polity: the excessively rich and the excessively poor—in this case, the new class of owners and managers (executives or CEOs) of multinational financial capitalism on one side, and the subproletariat or underclass of precarious workers, the excluded, immigrants, and especially young people, on the other.[29] Except that if the former tend to be situated outside representation, it is because they no longer have an interest in playing the game of national politics and accepting its constraints, but only in asserting the logic of the global market outside national states and using the means of one or another of them in the competition of territories to obtain fiscal privileges and get access to exploitable workers. Whereas the exploitable workers are pushed or left outside representation in order to prevent their rights claims from finding a necessarily conflictual expression that is deemed intolerable by the system and other classes—including the popular classes, even the poor, who let themselves be convinced or find reasons to believe that their security must come at the price of the precariousness of others. The new class of owners and managers, I have said, establish themselves, materially and symbolically, beyond the national-foreigner distinction, while the workers are forcibly treated as threatening or superfluous internal foreigners.[30] At the (much expanded) margins of the class compromise borne by political representation are thus two tendentially "externalized" groups: nonnatives excluded de jure or de facto from full citizenship, and the new transnational capitalist class, which offshores its residence and taxes along with its businesses, save for preserving control of certain essential organs of government.

But, conversely, the postnational, neorepublican perspectives are undermined by powerful objections we must be honest enough to recognize, of which I will here recall at least two:

a   The abolition of borders (or at least of state control over borders) would probably only correspond, in a world like ours (and for the foreseeable figure), to forms of what Deleuze called the "society of control" or globalized police governmentality. If we geographically and geopolitically deterritorialize the rights of the citizen, will it not be necessary in compensation to create a gigantic global system of surveillance that would constantly follow persons and even precede them, controlling their identity and movements in advance? We would then have gone beyond the figure of the foreigner only to replace it more surely with that of the potential enemy as a universal internal enemy, the object and justification of law-and-order globalization. Not only will individuals have their passports and visas; they will have their genetic fingerprints registered in a global database and—why not?—a permanent electronic bracelet.[31] The risk here is of paying for the generalization and liberalization of the right to freedom of movement with a radical restriction on the right (or power) to change one's identity or function, what we could call, with Sandro Mezzandra, the "right to flight," but also the right to a mask, to be incognito, and to multiple personalities—so many varieties of the "right to disappear" (certainly, it too, a fundamental right awaiting recognition if not institution or constitutionalization), already severely limited by current states.[32]

b If we admit with Arendt that the "right to the city" is without foundation (whether we consider it natural or cultural), without any foundation other than political activity itself, the reciprocity of rights and duties that the members of the community of citizens recognize in one another, then the transnationalization of subjective rights is a question that concerns not only "nomads," but also the voluntarily or involuntarily "settled," and presupposes their attributing to themselves *in common* a power of control over the usage of the immaterial good that is movement. Overturning the Hobbesian solution of delegating power to an eminent sovereign who dictates the law and imposes it through fear of the police, we are carried to the aporia of a democratic representation without a preestablished people, which "creates the people" by the very movement of what Rancière calls the recognition of the "part that has no part."

We can, however, imagine loosening this aporia on the basis of specific claims that bear a dynamic of universality (or, in other words, from the perspective of recognition). I am thinking on the one hand of the universalization of rights of residence and movement under conditions that make them effective (especially the development of transnationalized educational institutions), thus making them "opposable rights," in the sense that comes from being revived by controversies around the right to housing.[33] On the other hand, I am thinking of the contractual democratization of borders and how they are crossed, which includes a self-limitation of state sovereignty and will indeed one day be organized by means of an equilibrium of public powers and social counterpowers (as the rights of labor were in their time, and must periodically be balanced anew through the dynamic conflict of the state, entrepreneurs, and unions)—as the case may be, states, international organizations, and associations of migrants and their advocates.

You will understand why under these conditions, at the end of the day, I prefer the expression "diasporic citizenship"—or, on the local level, "co-citizenship"—to that of nomadic citizenship (though it is perhaps in part a matter of convention), designating not so much "citizenship of the world" as a totality as "citizenship in the world," that is, a movement of expansion and relocation made up for by symbolic and institutional relocations.[34] At the same time such a citizenship will reproduce the structure of polarity or antagonistic equilibrium that we have seen in the abstract in the normative statements of the Universal Declaration of Human Rights with a new content, determined by the anthropological and political configurations of today's world. In this sense it cannot mark a rupture, but more a recasting and concretization. Yet it is from such a dynamic, whose improbable character and highly conflictual tenor in a world dominated by national and transnational capitalist interests I emphasize once again, that we must expect a relative deterritorialization of citizens belonging to the community they create through their participation. The common actions of resistance, but also of claim-making—even, perhaps tomorrow, of the participation of nationals and foreigners (and thus of human rights activists and migrants with or without papers) in the same political space—are a fundamental component of this developing belonging that is one of the laboratories of what we can today call, beyond utopia, "cosmopolitanism."

RESISTANCE, INSURRECTION, INSUBORDINATION

Who is speaking here this afternoon, ladies and gentlemen?[1] Not, alas, the little boy who, almost fifty-five years ago, entered this very hall wide-eyed to see and hear, year after year, *Macbeth*, *Lorenzaccio*, or *Mother Courage* performed by Vilar and his comrades against the background of trumpets and the mistral winds—even if, no doubt, that little boy still accompanies me. But if you will permit me, today it will be a "dear professor" who has strayed far from his office and his classroom. And this is why I would like to refer to this formulation that formerly served to designate one of our teachers.[2]

In June 2006, with many other writers, artists, and teachers, I signed an appeal elaborated in agreement with the Groupe d'Information et de Soutien des Immigrés and the Réseau Education Sans Frontières calling on the government to stop the arrests of students without proper immigration papers, who are sometimes sought out even at school in order to be expelled from French territory.[3] This appeal essentially consisted of a long citation from Robert Antelme's book *The Human Race*, published after he returned from the camps, in which he recalled that those who invented them had not succeeded in their project of dividing humanity into several species according to criteria of color, custom, or class, and that for this reason their system had finally been defeated. From this evocation, my cosignatories and I took the argument that we must be on guard against any policy—for example that of "chosen" or selective immigration—that would reproduce, in its own way and on its own level, the idea of unequal access to fundamental rights based on naturalized social and anthropological differences. Commenting on this extrapolation at the press conferences at which our text was presented, I indicated that in my eyes there was, to be sure, an immense distance between the economic, political management of immigration instituted in our societies and the mechanism of selection and elimination at work in the Nazi camps. And yet a certain thread runs from one to the other, which we run great risks by ignoring. I would conclude that it is legitimate and coherent to envisage acts of resistance as soon as we think we are partaking of this logic, that is, as soon as it takes shape. Some days later I received at the university a letter signed by the then interior minister, who roundly reproached me for my stance. Justifying the government's policies and bills in the name of national interest and public security, Mr. Sarkozy affirmed that the measures of control and expulsion were in conformity with the law and with republican principles, declared the proposed analogy between historical periods ignominious, and concluded with these words: "Monsieur le Professeur, you have dishonored yourself."

This is why, along with others, having gratefully accepted Frédéric Fisbach's invitation to contribute to the circle of his production of *Feuillets d'hypnos*, I decided to take as the subject for my lecture these three ideas, or rather these three words: resistance, insurrection, insubordination, in the full extension and consequently the full uncertainty of their usage. It is not a question of honor but of intellectual exigency, which I am perhaps not the only one to feel.

IT IS ESPECIALLY IN France, it seems to me, that the need to clarify the usage of these terms is making itself felt, even if it is obvious that we do not have a monopoly on this. Our national history is punctuated by episodes in which disobedience toward the established powers, and especially the state, has made possible or precipitated changes of political regime, even if it received the retrospective sanction of a legal procedure. This was the case for all the republican regimes since the First Republic, born in the taking of the Bastille in 1789 and the mass mobilization of 1792, right up to the Fifth, born in the coup of May 13, 1958—a rather brutal way of connecting events, I admit, but one that will suffice to show how uncertain political judgments on the revolutions of history are, even after the fact. Our history is rich in insurrectional moments, days of barricades and bloody weeks, but also general strikes and communes, in which some of the political myths were forged that pass from one generation to another and still elicit, depending on the case and individual, exaltation or execration. Finally, they include—in part, mixed with precedents—a series of moments I will not call "mystical," despite the shadow Péguy's famous distinction casts over this discussion, but simply "moral," in order to mark that these two orientations of action, that which looks to a value judgment and that which looks to an analysis of political effects, are not simply opposed, but intersect and determine each other. The Dreyfus Affair, in which a certain tradition of left intellectuals see the true foundation of the Third Republic, or in any case the event that neatly cuts it off from the preceding, more or less authoritarian or oligarchic regimes, is a symbolic figure for all these moments. In my generation, we readily associated it with the moment of protest against colonial war and torture in Algeria, the institutional effect of which was in a certain sense the opposite, since it helped strain the legitimacy of the Fifth Republic in a way that remained incompletely resolved.

Revolutions and coups d'état, insurrections and rebellions, resistance and insubordination—you will guess that the list would be long of events, large and small, that demonstrate that politics cannot be reduced to right, least of all to the execution of the law, without for all that our being able to simply distinguish between what reinforces this and what overwhelms it, even restricting ourselves to modern and contemporary history. Why, moreover, this restriction, as if the comparison of the similar problems faced by the ancients and moderns had not been, since Machiavelli, at least in the background, the main thing in the reflections of political philosophy as soon as it interrogates the paradoxes and, at the end of the day, the enigma of citizenship? And why only take French examples, as if the American or Russian revolutions do not have as much to teach us about the sovereignty of the people as the French; as if Indian independence, the Algeria War of Liberation, or the struggle of Charter 77 do not hold, even for ourselves, some of the keys to what resistance to foreign occupation is that at the same time take on the characteristics of a civil war; as if the African American civil rights movement or the protests against the Vietnam War were not, in some respects, more illuminating and richer in theoretical debates when it comes to the forms of civic disobedience and nonviolent resistance than the episodes of more limited scale that we saw in France in the twentieth century?

It would be tempting, then, to limit ourselves to two observations that are in a certain sense indisputable. First of all, the confrontation of institutional logics, in which law sanctions the universalizing force of obligation, and social relations of forces, including moral or ideological forces, constitutes a sort of structure or permanent condition of politics. Next, each of the episodes to which this confrontation gives rise, and which end according to the case in subjection or liberation, an expansion or contraction of democracy, a restoration or weakening of order, remains irreducibly singular. So that, no less than those who each time have to decide, to pick sides, in short to wager for or against Vichy, de Gaulle and the Resistance, the de Gaulle of 1940 and of 1958, 1962, or 1968, we do not have an overarching rule of judgment that allows us to inscribe the events of history and the commitments they command within a definitive scheme of interpretation—neither to ratify the result, to proclaim the historical superiority of the accomplished fact, nor to claim the sublime grandeur of emancipatory intentions, revive the exaltation of the utopian revolutionaries who "wage war on heaven," nor to note with disillusion that ideals are regularly betrayed by those who bore them, revolutionaries transform themselves into dictators, insurgents into professional politicians, or libertarian philosophers into merchants of politics as show business.

The essential uncertainty of the relations between institutions and force, the absolute singularity of situations and choices—the lesson would be, as we see, the radical finitude, even the insuperable ambiguity, of the political meanings we are dealing with. There would therefore never be resistance, insurrection, or insubordination as such, no general truth we could associate with such names, nor any theory of the political to be constructed on the basis of their analogies. And, again, this is in a certain way incontestable, unless one produces ideological stereotypes, even if they are progressive. I will return to this in conclusion in order to insist on the ineliminable element of risk that affects our choices as well as our reflections, and is the mark of politics as such.

Yet I persist and take up again these three words, "resistance, insurrection, insubordination," in the mode of a question that I know in advance will not have a simple or definitive answer. For I do not believe in the absolute independence of the events of history. Even in their history they repeat, reverse, or answer one another. They leave a trace that is sometimes traumatic. They bring about experiences that travel between the consciousness of individuals and that of groups, sexes, classes, or nations, giving them a language, instruments of recognition—what is sometimes called "identity"—and also critical and self-critical instruments.

The men and women, soldiers and civilians who stood up against the use of torture in Algeria and demonstrated in France for the end of colonial domination could be, and often were, those for whom the test of the occupation and of the resistance against Nazism made seeing units of the French Army using the same methods as the Gestapo against those who were then called the "natives" [*indigènes*] and their defenders intolerable. Or it could be their children—just as today there are Algerian citizens who find it intolerable that the military police tortures alleged Islamists or their parents in the same villas of El Biar and Hydra that were once used against the people by Massu, Charbonnier, and Aussaresses.[4] They were also able to reach the ranks of those who collaborated for a longer or shorter time or believed in the possibility of playing Vichy against Vichy, and who did not want to be deceived about the site of truth and justice a second time. There is nothing simple about these sequences, but also nothing absolutely arbitrary or insignificant. We have to decipher the traces, to inscribe them in one or more national, international, even global histories. We have to do more: move toward the formulation of a problem that we can assume, in ever-new and unpredictable forms yet still haunted by all the memory, oblivions, and traumatisms of the earlier political experiences, presents itself each time to the subjects of the law we all are as soon as it is insufficient to prescribe what is just or legitimate, or indeed indicates it in an opposite way. This is obviously the case in extreme situations of emergency and the division of the community, but perhaps also in everyday, banal situations. Perhaps it is always the case, or at least as soon as the real object of the law is the life of people, their dignity, their fundamental rights to life, residence, movement, work, education, belief, expression, and so on.

What would then be this problem that never dies and always changes form? In our Western, now globalized, tradition I will say that it is the problem of *citizen virtue*, deliberately having recourse to a language that comes from the ancient origins of the state as city or civic community. It is of course necessary to take this notion of virtue in a strong, active and collective sense. It is not a matter of what an individual must do to be classed as a good citizen, fulfilling all his duties and not causing any trouble, but of what a citizen *can* do—or better still, of what individuals can do in order to collectively become and remain citizens, so that the communities to which they belong (of which there are now many: the nation, Europe, perhaps others) are truly *political*. It is thus a matter of the active, perhaps conflictual, certainly problematic relation of the citizen to power and powers, especially the power of laws and institutions based on them (like the army, the police, the justice system, the schools) insofar as this power is not something external to us, something we simply find ourselves faced with, something we are subject to, that we cannot debate (at most periodically renewing by participating in elections), but something we constitute, that we help produce, form and transform, because we exercise it, because we obey it (and there are certainly different ways of obeying), or even because we resist or defy it. Something, therefore, for which we are in this sense responsible. I repeat, this is everyday: even the kids in the burning *banlieues* in November 2005, who could be treated as "scum" [*racailles*] and who called themselves "*cailleras*" [thugs], found themselves in a dialectical relation with power and the law. Voluntarily or not, freely or not, durably or not, they participated in a certain reproduction of the power of the law.[5] They exercised a responsibility—or perhaps they retrospectively perceived that they had.

To be sure, it is in the most dramatic circumstances, which we are accustomed to calling historic, that the internal relation of citizenship to power and law, and to the juridical structures of power, is defined, that the question of citizen virtue and responsibility explodes into dilemmas for which there are no preestablished solutions and that oblige us to invent figures of another citizenship than that which is codified and normalized. This is why in presenting this paper, which some of you have perhaps read, I suggested an association between the names "resistance, insurrection, and insubordination," taken as so many modalities of the critical, negative relation of the citizen to the law and to power, and the symbolic events of our recent national history, yesterday or the day before, to which there are still living witnesses among us (and, I am sure, in this hall). I authorized myself on the basis of the emblematic texts and works of René Char and Camus from the Resistance, Sartre and Maurice Blanchot (signatories of the *Manifeste des 121*), Michel Foucault and Godard as interpreters of the peaceful insurrection of May '68, to suggest that, each time, citizenship has found itself faced with the question of what constitutes it, has had to prove its "virtue" through an experience that is more or less long, more or less risky, but is assured neither of its meaning nor of its results—a contestation of the law that is also at bottom its refoundation or transformation, and makes up the very test of its internal relation to power.[6]

LET US MAKE A first pause here, or rather let us try to go further on the basis of what has just been said. All this is a bit abstract, perhaps: the singularity and ambiguity of new historical situations taken in the trace of past experiences, citizen virtue and its problematic relation with power and therefore with law, the critical figure of the responsible citizen who would pass from resistance to insubordination. Where would we be going with this if not toward taking up again in barely modified form the classic idea of the *citizen against power*, which had its moment of glory after having been announced in 1926 as a slogan for the radical and pacifist republicanism of Alain, or the idea closer to the Anglo-Saxon and especially American constitutional tradition according to which the heart of democracy lies in the existence of counterpowers that limit the power of the state and whose ultimate sources lie in the citizens' capacity for civil disobedience, so manifesting their fundamental independence ("self-reliance" in the vocabulary of Thoreau and his successors)?[7]

There is some truth in this, provided we follow it through. I would almost say that it is like a lost treasure of anarchism that has to be rediscovered and reinvented to give the full sense to the paradoxical element implied in the idea of active citizenship. The active citizen is not, on this account, she who, by her obedience, sanctions the legal order or the system of institutions upon which she has directly or indirectly conferred legitimacy by an explicit or tacit contract, materialized in her participation in representative procedures that result in the delegation of power. She is essentially the rebel, the one who says *no,* or at least has the possibility of doing so. (But if she never exercises this possibility we fall back into the delegation of power, into passive citizenship, legitimized by a completely theoretical recourse of the sovereignty of the rank and file, of their absolute but fictive power.) This is the paradox of political citizenship: to be able to say yes to a way of translating an effective power it is necessary occasionally and perhaps regularly to say no. To be able to participate in the city and not only to figure in it as a patronymic inscribed in the civil registry, it is necessary to be able to withdraw from it, or better to incarnate an alternative force—if necessary by violence and if possible by nonviolence, in any case by opposition and dissidence. It is necessary to institute a counter-city or a counterpower in the face of legitimate power that has become the mere property of those who exercise it or the expression of governmental or administrative routine.

But we can also give this logical necessity the form of a law of division of the political body in its own heart, with all the risks this carries for it. If some, who are never initially all the citizens and at the beginning can only be a tiny minority even if they are objectively acting in the general interest, do not take opposition upon themselves and exercise the function of dissidence, then there are only passive citizens and therefore eventually no citizens at all but only more or less participatory, more or less governable subjects of administration or power. Democratic citizenship is therefore conflictual or it does not exist. But this also means that democratic citizenship—as revolutionary episodes illustrate par excellence—implies a certain intrinsic relation with actual or possible death. In order to save themselves or remain alive as a community of citizens, the city must run the risk of destruction or anarchy in a confrontation with its own members from which nothing can protect it, above all not criminalizing dissidence or suspecting conscientious objection of treason. This necessity seems all the greater the more massive or more bureaucratized the machinery of power, or—as often goes along with this—the greater the social inequalities in access to different public powers, be they economic, cultural, or ethnic, which amounts to saying that majority or minority classes appropriate politics, privatize it, and in that sense destroy it. Against this programmed death of politics, to which we can give all sorts of names—earlier we spoke of management, today we speak of governance—there are of course palliatives like public hearings, legal proceedings, rights to opposition and of minorities, etc. But, in the last analysis, I repeat, there is only the capacity to confront another kind of death, that is, the reality of the conflict and division of the city against itself, which materializes the right to insubordination—a right that is not granted but is taken or exercised at the risk and danger of its bearers, and that is for this very reason the true right to have rights, in a way the right *of* rights.

It must be said that political philosophy has no more overcome this paradox in which democratic citizenship lives than has legal science. They have not been able to completely mask or neutralize it. Citizenship or the state as a community of citizens is not anarchy, no doubt, in the etymological sense of the suspension of authority, starting with the authority of the law. It is easy to imagine what a society without public authority, or one in which the right of institutions to command the actions of its citizens by means of force, education, interest, habit, and rules was permanently suspended, would look like. And if we find it hard to imagine, we can cast an eye on the examples of this collapse of law and order, alternating with their abuse, around the four corners of the world. Without believing in a natural goodness of men and a providential convergence of their actions in view of the general interest, it would be—it sometimes is—a machine of self-destruction, of autoimmunity, as Derrida says.[8] But the fact is that a line between the state and anarchy cannot be drawn in advance, once and for all, and that they sometimes tend to change places. This may be why the state charges demonstrations of individual or collective disobedience that tend to save it from its own degeneration with anarchy, or even with treason. The resisters who refused the occupation of the new order imposed by European fascism were traitors. The dissenters and deserters who pointed out the contradiction between the discourse of decolonization and colonial practice, between the declaration of human rights and racist violence, were anarchists and traitors. The insurgents and strikers of May '68 who questioned discretionary government methods and archaic authority structures in the family, the university, and businesses were anarchists.

But if political philosophy cannot resolve the paradox or abolish the contradiction, since in reality this would amount to abolishing the democratic horizon itself, on the other hand it has never ceased reflecting on it, displacing it, searching for new formulations for it, including literary expressions. I will invoke one, beautiful and profound but disturbing, which comes to us from a remote period when the conditions of political activity were certainly very different than ours today, since it has to do with the Greek polis. Nonetheless, this expression has traversed the ages like a question and a challenge.

In a famous passage in his *Histories*, Herodotus, often called the father of history, pupil of the Sophists who were the founders of democratic thought, friend of Sophocles and Pericles, staged in allegorical fashion a debate alleged to have taken place in the Persian court between the claimants to the throne after the death of King Cambyses and the failure of a palace coup, each making a eulogy to one of the characteristic political regimes, monarchy, aristocracy, and democracy, and proposing to establish it if his candidacy was successful.[9] The term we render with democracy, in Greek, *isonomia*, often translated as "equality before the law," corresponds to what the modern Western tradition associates with the pair freedom and equality, equal freedom (*aequa libertas*), or even, in a single word, equaliberty, as I have proposed.[10] What is astonishing in this fiction is that the Greek Herodotus has located this debate among Orientals, among the hereditary Persian enemy. Here is a staging that produces an effect of strangeness or distantiation, no doubt in order to mark that the question possesses, at least in principle, a universal character, which was the perspective of the Sophists. But historical reality takes over, and the assembly of notables rejects the democratic proposition, placing in power Darius, who will become "king of kings" and undertake the Greco-Persian Wars. In renouncing his claims, however, the democratic prince to whom Herodotus gives the name Otanes formulates a remarkable demand that in a certain way constitutes the remainder of the abandoned democratic project: he requests that he as well as his descendants enjoy the right to obey no one, while themselves renouncing the giving of orders. "I want neither to command nor to obey" (*oute archein oute archesthai ethélô*).

The interpretation of this passage is undoubtedly not simple. The fact that this request constitutes in sum a privilege, a hereditary privilege, contradicting the egalitarianism Otanes invokes, and that it comes after the democratic principle is rejected in favor of the monarchical principle, would tend to suggest that it represents a limit where the idea of citizenship pushed to the absolute is identified with the abolition of all authority, subjected as well as imposed, betraying its intrinsic impossibility and in the end disqualifying it. But we can also make an inverse reading. In this limit point becomes manifest the irreducible aspect of the citizens' demand for equality and freedom, the specter of which haunts all authoritarian or inegalitarian regimes the moment they cannot be based solely on a relation of forces. This dread is ceaselessly reanimated by the resistances, the insubordinations, the insurrections that revive the aspiration to democracy or reinvent the democratic principle. For the trace of this statement and its strange staging can be read, astonishingly, throughout the history of political ideas, in large or small letters. It is there in the background of the argumentation of La Boétie's *Contr'Un*, in Spinoza as he declines the suggestion that he become a professor by explaining that the philosophical attitude consists in thinking for oneself but also in abstaining from imposing models of thought on others.[11] It is explicit in Rousseau.[12] But it was already there in Machiavelli, who explains in his *Discourses on Titus Livy* that the essence of a free regime consists in the fact that the mass of people, those he calls the "small" or the "thin," do not seek to exercise power in their own interest or to take it away from the great and the grand but in "not being oppressed," that is, in resisting power, and possibly putting in place institutions and legislation that legitimate counterpowers, maximizing the possibility of resistance and in a certain sense transforming the capacity for insubordination from a destructive force into a constructive, creative political virtue.[13]

And, leaping over many intermediaries, it is still this *an-archic* principle of nonpower that is paradoxically indispensable to the constitution of power, without which power could not be distinguished from oppression or returns inevitably to it, that we can read in a philosopher today like Jacques Rancière, when he asks about the reason for the "hatred of democracy" that periodically rises to the surface in our societies or in the discourse of our governors or our intellectuals, and on the ways of coping with it.[14] Not only is democracy an effort that must be ceaselessly repeated to include within the political space those who have been excluded—in words that have now become famous, the "part of those who have no part." But there is not, in reality, a state that would be in itself, or solely by the form of its institutions, democratic. Every state, to degrees that are, to be sure, very unequal (and which there should be no question of amalgamating), is oligarchic and authoritarian, based on the privileges of class or expertise, most often masked by a populist or demagogic rhetoric—which is to say on governments' pretense of saying aloud what the people think, or of understanding them better than they understand themselves. What there is, on the other hand, or what can always be again, making citizenship not just an idea or a formal status but the common activity of members of a city, are struggles for democratization, resistances to power that power must then take into account and interpret in order to regain its legitimacy, more or less insurrectional even if not necessarily violent processes of redistributing or dividing power, especially the power of expression, of giving one's opinion or stating one's interests oneself. At this point the anarchic figure of *whatever person* arises, he or she who is neither more nor less than a citizen among others in the racially egalitarian sense of the term, and as such seeks neither to command nor to obey. This is why Rancière places at the center of his propositions on the resistance to the appropriation and expropriation of power simple, even very simple, ideas, many of which only seem utopian to the extent that they call into question the structural passivity of institutions and the inveterate self-evidence of the social relation of forces, like the circulation of offices, the prohibition on their accumulation, and the drawing of lots for governors. It is certainly no accident if ideas of this kind have played an active role in most of the great moments of popular resistance or democratic insurrection to which, evoking the history of France and other countries, I made allusion at the outset.

HERE I WOULD LIKE to pause for a second time. I began with an interrogation on the historical conflict between the legal order and the violence of relations of forces, always reabsorbed by institutions, always reborn in singular forms imposed by circumstances, and that—as citizens—we do not choose but that fall on us like catastrophes and as opportunities to be seized. I suggested to you that we must radicalize this interrogation, go to the point of asking with a whole part of political philosophy, in the minority but irreducible, whether the principle of an authentically free and egalitarian citizenship that could be translated at least in part into the orderly functioning of a state or a society would not paradoxically reside in the inscription and preservation of a counterpower of refusal, a force of anarchy or insubordination, in the heart of civic virtue. And I went as far as to note that, under these conditions, the political body must be at least periodically exposed to the risk of its own death or its decomposition by the rupture of consensus, the claim of right against right. Let us note that this dangerous proximity of institution and anarchy that the institution tries to ward off by all means possible and that a certain positivist definition of law declares a priori unthinkable and monstrous ("the law is the law," it says) is recognized by the irreconcilable adversaries of democracy—who see in it a ferment of decomposition of authority that will inevitably result, sooner or later, in tyranny or the return of the stick in the more brutal forms that went before—as by its partisans, in a certain tradition of radicalism for which the choice is at bottom between two forms of anarchy that contest the state, one synonymous with the independence and creativity of citizens, the other with institutional arbitrariness and voluntary servitude. But in the two attempts I have made to interpret the positive signification of the negative, or apparently negative, tie that connects episodes of resistance, insurrection, and insubordination, it almost seems that it would be necessary to interpose a third term that is always present in the background of these discussions and without which they would have no meaning. Neither a symbolic sense, nor a historical one, nor a political sense and therefore an immediate, practical stake. This third term is "community." Or, better, it is the community of citizens.[15] But such a formulation is redundant, since in the very idea of citizenship there is that of action and communal responsibilities, rights and reciprocal duties assumed in common, all of which both engage the individual and lead him or her to go beyond his or her particular interest in the direction of the general interest. If we do not attach the practices of resistance, the conquests of insurrection, the risks of insubordination as the ultimate foundation of the vitality of institutions exposed to death or to anarchy in the different senses of the term, if we do not attach all this to a certain conception of political community and the objectives at which it aims, we have done nothing but enumerate paradoxes; we have not even outlined a thought of the political.

To conclude, I will therefore return with you to this question, which is perhaps the most difficult of all. I will only touch on it, but I will maintain the following general idea: the political community as it is claimed and as it takes shape on the horizon of actions of resistance or insubordination is not given, but is always still to come or to be invented. It is not complete or self-sufficient but incomplete, conflicted, exposed to the intrusion of the other, which it needs to constitute itself and which nonetheless most often disrupts it and calls its identity into question. Gathering these two complementary characteristics into a single expression I borrow from the philosopher Gilles Deleuze, I will say that the community of citizens—what he also calls "the people"—is essentially "absent."[16] It is in his great book on cinema, in particular, that Deleuze developed this idea of the "absent people" that provoked fiction, the invention of languages, narratives, developing collective representations in search of an identity that is based on the feeling of *the intolerable* and proposes for it an exit by taking as examples the "minority literature" of a writer like Kafka, displaced or disoriented within his own language, and the evolution of Third World cinemas (Glauber Rocha, Sembène Ousmane), passing from the unanimous praise of national insurrections to the representation of multiple histories, heterogeneous identities, explosive combinations of archaism and modernity that make up the reality of what we call the culture of a people or a nation.[17] And this, when we really think about it, is true not only for the Third World, or what used to be so called, but for all cultures, even those called "dominant." Today we know well that all ideas relative to the community of citizens and its own identity are a problem throughout the world and require us to rethink their history. It is the same for the share of myth and reality that must be associated with the idea of popular sovereignty as the foundation of the community's institutions. And it is the same for the question of whether the people we speak of here is a nation, and thus whether political citizenship as such is a national citizenship, a right to nationality, and what would happen if, perchance, as some fear and others triumphally announce, the nation is becoming "absent," or progressively losing its political characteristics. But perhaps it is precisely by recognizing what it is constitutively missing or prevents it from being complete, exclusive, self-sufficient that it paradoxically rediscovers the capacity to exist and act as a political body. These open questions are the horizon of the attempt I make here to give a positive content to the idea of the community of citizens as "absent community," to take from Deleuze the word he used and a few of his suggestions.

At the basis of the question I want to pose there is first of all the highly singular, perhaps very revealing form in which what we could call generally constructive disobedience to the law determines the individual's relation to the collectivity, articulating individual responsibility with solidarity, with the fraternity of arms or the community of feelings and belonging. It is neither complete absorption in the group nor the isolation of individuals in relations of competition and calculation of the personal advantages one derives from being with others. Resistance, by definition, is collective. It only has meaning if it extends virtually to everyone, if it aims at rallying and reconstituting the community. This is what made for the energy and spirit of sacrifice of those who resisted the Nazi occupation in occupied France, and we would find the same thing in all comparable situations. But at the moment of decision, of the risk of error he assumes in knowing that the price will be paid by everyone (perhaps the greatest risk), the subject confronts himself. For all resistance, however elementary, implies such a decision. It is not reaching for the epic or the pathetic to recall here the great formulas of refusal that at once express a self-evidence, note a necessity, and express a resolve that could have not been, been given up, or been broken, but were not. This is Luther's statement at Wittenberg: *Hier stehe ich, ich kann nicht anders*—in other words, I can do nothing and I will not move from the point at which I have fixed the limit of what, for myself and for you, I can accept without degradation. Blanchot refers to this formula when he explains the sense of the word "insubordination," which, he says, sums up everything in the "Declaration on the right of insubordination in the Algerian War," otherwise known as the Manifesto of 121, of which he was the main editor.[18]

Yet things do not stop there, for whence does the subject take the capacity or the force to oppose instead of submitting, and to fix a limit of the intolerable? At this level we again find the collective, in any case the transindividual, memory and the unconscious at the basis of what, apparently, relates to the most personal, most irreducible subjectivity. Capacities for resisting injustice one has been subjected to and the intolerable things one has declared around oneself originate, we know, in one's roots but also in one's uprootedness, in affective fidelities but also in the intellectual clarity of the *scientia intuitive*. (René Char said that it was the necessity of poetry and Jean Cavaillès said that it was the necessity of mathematics.) But in all cases they were inseparable from communication and transmitted legacies—with or without "testament." At the basis of the individual carried to the maximum of his autonomy, of his capacity for subjectivation, it is again the *common*, if not the communitarian, that resists—even if this common is indivisible and most often irreducible to the simplicity of a name, a single system of relations and belongings. This is perhaps what Spinoza had in view when, still according to Deleuze, he characterized the individual not as a point, but as a certain minimum of incompressible social relations, a capacity to act and to suffer, or to affect others and be affected by them.[19]

All this seems at first to concern only the past, or, if you like, the origin, the source, the roots of capacities for resisting oppression or injustice, and it is in this sense literally "retrograde" that "identitarian" discourses always tend to close things in. But in reality the community from which individual resistance, the capacity to subvert the established order or disorder, proceeds is never solely a given community, a belonging to be preserved or restored, denoted by a name (like "French" or "German," "Jew" or "Palestinian"). It is always also, and even more, a community to come that must be invented and imposed. The French Resistance, with all its contradictions, its inside and its outside, its virtually competing political currents, its inextricable mixture of nationalism and antifascism at the very heart of patriotism, is a brilliant example of this fact. The France it projected and gave a signification of universality to was not a simple historical nation, a threatened collective identity to be defended against outsiders. It was another France, hitherto missing, still to be invented by appealing precisely to the injustices and the cowardice of the preceding one bearing the same name. This is whence, even at the price of a share of illusion and myth, it revived the history of the constituent insurrections of the Republic, which by definition had nothing to protect and everything to invent when it came to citizenship. What then became of it is another story.

But this description is still incomplete. It leaves in shadow the second aspect of what I have called the absent community: the fact that it is not sufficient and that even it can absolutely not be defined just in relation to itself, but only by taking into account the other and the right of the other. It is here that, no doubt, our national history, the protest against colonial oppression and the insubordination to which (in multiple forms) it gave rise, acquires a particular significance—all the more as the colonized peoples' wars of liberation dragged on through the decades and sometimes took a barbaric form, in large part owing to how the ideals and emancipatory principles of the Resistance were immediately forgotten by the Liberation governments (as witnessed by the massacres at Sétif and Madagascar, the bombing of Haiphong, and everything that followed). And as for what happened with colonial independence itself, this is yet another history, where infamy is not lacking, as Achille Mbembe writes. In the Manifesto of 121, published in 1960, and in the commentaries its editors added, it is affirmed that perhaps for the first time a movement of disobedience to power or insubordination in relation to the law is not based on claiming the rights of those who bear them, a protest against injustice they themselves suffer, but—as Jacques Rancière restates thirty years later in a beautiful essay devoted to the specificity of the Franco-Algerian relation and the importance of Algerian history for French politics—the cause of the other.[20]

Truth be told, one could, as always, look for antecedents for this idea of a protest or resistance against injustice suffered by the other, especially injustice done to him in my name, in our name, with which we have long refused to be associated, which creates precisely between him and me, between "them" and "us," a political community that is hitherto missing, but nevertheless unimpeachable. There was an old internationalist principle according to which a people that oppresses another cannot itself be a free people, establishing a connection between emancipatory insurrections and their cosmopolitical horizon. But this formulation, taken literally, returns the motor of insubordination again to oneself, to a given belonging, and through this very fact reduces the significance of decentering, of the passage to alterity, the inclusion of part of the other as such in the definition of political identity. It risks masking the decisive fact, which appears or reappears in resistance movements against imperialist and colonial wars and extends beyond their strict conjuncture in particular in movements to defend the rights of foreigners and immigrants who suffer persecution or discrimination. The citizenship with which I have been concerned here, of constructing institutions at the risk of conflict with some of the existing dispositions or legal forms, can no longer be defined as exclusive belonging or as a reserved status but only—I'm looking for the words—as *co-citizenship* or *con-citizenship*, a community of co-citizens that crosses borders. This would also explain—but this would take another lecture—why the relation of such insubordination to the idea of sovereignty has become so complex, so equivocal, and carries it to the very limits of its validity. On one side, in effect, by taking the risk of affirming a state of emergency to legitimate disobedience (I once used the expression "democratic state of emergency")—a risk one assumes in common but is always the responsibility of "whatever individual"—the insubordinate who wants to embody active citizenship places herself sovereignly above the law, or more exactly outside it, in exception to it, in the expectation of its rectification and its refoundation on principles.[21] All the same, on the other side—and here we find again the very deep idea of a power that is a nonpower, that cannot be monopolized or appropriated, that we perceived in the discourse of Otanes or the Machiavellian conception of the Republic—it is the very identification between communitarian belonging and the claim of sovereignty that is under attack, or at least relativized.

BUT I HAVE ALREADY said a lot. It is long since time to give the podium to the legitimate occupants of this scene, whom we will hear and see tonight reading the texts of the Resistance poet, writing at a time of insubordination and risk. I will do so by myself citing René Char: "Freedom is then emptiness, an emptiness to be desperately inventoried. After, dear walled up eminences, it is the strong odor of your denouement. How could it surprise you?" It is in *Contre une maison sèche*.

FOREWORD

1. Two complementary volumes appeared at roughly the same time in French: *Violence et civilité: The Wellek Library Lectures et autres essais de philosophie politique* and *Citoyen-sujet et autres essais d'anthropologie philosophique.*

2. The whole of the work of the colloquium, by Robert Castel, Catherine Colliot-Thélène, and Bertrand Ogilvie, unfortunately remains unpublished.

3. W. B. Gallie, "Essentially Contested Concepts." I owe the discovery of this classic reference in the English-speaking world to Nestor Capdevila.

4. For reasons of space and to preserve a sufficient temporal proximity among the texts, I do not republish the essay "Sujets ou citoyens? (pour l'égalité)," published in 1984 [and unpublished in English—tr.]—the origin of these reflections in general and on several particular points. There I spoke in conclusion of the "co-citizenship" of nationals and foreigners.

INTRODUCTION. *The Antinomy of Citizenship*

1. This essay is a reworking of the Cassal Lecture in French Culture, delivered May 12, 2009, at the University of London, under the title "Antinomies of Citizenship." I thank the Institute of Germanic and Romance Studies and its director, Naomi Segal, the Humanities and Arts Research Centre de Royal Holloway College, and Professor Mandy Merck.

2. Jacques Rancière, *Disagreement: Politics and Philosophy*; Miguel Abensour, *Hannah Arendt contre la philosophie politique?*

3. Chantal Mouffe, *The Democratic Paradox*.

4. Among the partial and general histories of the idea of citizenship I have relied on, I would like to mention Jacqueline Bordes, *Politeia dans la pensée grecque jusqu'à Aristote*; the Seminario internazionale di studi storici, *La nozione di "Romano" tra cittadinanza e universalità*, volume 2 of *Da Roma alla terza Roma, documenti e studi*; Rogers M. Smith, *Civic Ideals: Conflicting Visions of Citizenship in U.S. History*; Pietro Costa, *Civitas: Storia della cittadinanza in Europa*, 4 volumes; Dominique Schnapper, *Qu'est-ce que la citoyenneté?*; Paul Magnette, *La citoyenneté: Une histoire de l'idée de participation civique*; and Linda Bosniak, *The Citizen and the Alien*.

5. In book 3 of the *Politics* (1275a32) Aristotle announces that every political regime in which citizens equally exercise "indefinite office" or "general magistrature" (that is, participate in the people's assembly and in the tribunals) bears a democratic element that cannot be eliminated in favor of other forms of government. His aim is to ward off its dangers by transforming democracy into "timocracy" (named in the *Nichomachean Ethics*). This argument would be reversed in the modern period by Spinoza (for whom democracy is not so much a particular regime as the tendency to give power to the multitude, at work in monarchical and aristocratic regimes; see Balibar, *Spinoza and Politics*) and the young Marx (in his *Critique of Hegel's Philosophy of the State* [1843], explicitly announcing that democracy, or "the legislative power," is the "truth of all constitutions"). Rancière rediscovers this thesis today by showing that no regime can ward off the danger for the monopolization of power of its need, in the last analysis, to accept that the people can decide to obey or not. See *Hatred of Democracy*.

6. Karl Marx, *The Civil War in France*, 60: "Its [the Commune's] true secret was this. It was essentially a working class government, the product of the struggle of the producing against the appropriating class, the political form at last discovered under which to work out the economic emancipation of labor." Hannah Arendt refers to "the lost treasure of revolution" at least twice: as the title of chapter 6 in *On Revolution* and in the preface to *Between Past and Future*.

7. See chapter 4, below.

8. Cicero, *The Republic*, 1.31: "Et talis est quaeque respublica, qualis ejus aut natura, aut voluntas, qui illam regit. Itaque nulla alia in civitate, nisi in qua populi potestas summa est, ullum domicilium libertas habet: qua quidem certe nihil potest esse dulcius; et quae, si aequa non est, ne libertas quidemn est. Qui autem aequa potest esse?"

9. On liberalism, see Immanuel Wallerstein, "Three Ideologies or One?" and his *Unthinking Social Science*. The countertendency to emphasize equality is evident today with Rancière, in his radical opposition between democracy as the affirmation of the "power of anyone at all" and (representative) liberal definitions that are so many attempts to limit this principle. See my commentary: "Historical Dilemmas of Democracy and Their Contemporary Relevance for Citizenship."

10. Translator's note: Balibar refers here to August 4, 1789, when the members of the Constituent Assembly renounced their privileges.

11. Rancière, *Disagreement*. Today Rancière fears that his formula, which has circulated everywhere (although it is very difficult to translate into other languages, as I have often experienced), is interpreted as a watchword for the struggle against exclusion (and thus for "inclusion") rather than as an enunciation of the principle of radical democracy as the power of anyone at all. See his answers to questions in *Vacarme* 48 (with Miguel Abensour and Jean-Luc Nancy). I think it is necessary to preserve the dialectical element inherent in the (sometimes violent) tension between the two meanings of "demos."

12. I deliberately take up the Weberian three-part distinction, for its flipside for Weber himself is an analysis of the "illegitimate" character of democratic legitimacy that is enormously relevant in regard to what I call citizenship's insurrectional moment. See Weber, *Economy and Society*, vol. 1, ch. 9, sect. 7.

13. Balibar, "Citizen Subject."

14. Balibar, *We, Citizens of Europe? Reflections on Transnational Citizenship*. On the Roman origins of the "citizenship equals nationalism" equation and the differences between the ancient empire and the modern state on this point, see Claude Nicolet, "Citoyenneté Française et citoyenneté Romaine. Essai de mise en perspective," 145 and following.

15. It is certain that the absolute sovereignty of the nation-state, as economic or military power or even as the capacity to control the movements and communication of its own citizens, has been thrown into question in today's world, but it is not certain that these processes of transnationalization assume the same signification everywhere, or that its European perception can be generalized. See Zhang Yinde, "La 'sinité': l'identité chinoise en question," 300 and following.

16. I have discussed this question, and the possibilities it offers for a critical reversal, in "Citizenship without Community?," *We, the People of Europe?*

17. Elsewhere I have proposed translating *politeia*, with all the extension of its uses, as the "constitution of citizenship." The transposition of *res publica* is "republic," and thus "public thing," but today one increasingly says "public sphere." The classic English equivalent (as in the title of the work by Hobbes) was "commonwealth."

18. In a famous article, Émile Benveniste showed that, from a philological perspective, this priority of reciprocity over belonging is better expressed by the Latin pair *civis-civitas* than by the Greek pair *polis-politès*, since the root is on one side the individual's status in relation (the "*concitoyen*"), and on the other the preexistence of everyone. This divergence has important political and symbolic consequences that can be read in the legacy of both discourses. But it is necessary to interpret it as an internal tension, present everywhere, and always giving rise to permanent oscillation. See Benveniste, "Deux modèles linguistiques de la cité," *Problèmes de linguistique générale*, 2:272–80.

19. For Aristotle, the guarantee of this reciprocity resided in the periodic exchange of the positions of "ruling" (*archôn*) and "being ruled" (*archomenos*).

This principle already seemed to him full of "ultra-democratic dangers." See Peter Riesenberg, *Citizenship in the Western Tradition: Plato to Rousseau*, 42 and following. Today it is straightforwardly a figure of subversion (or utopian aberration).

20. Claude Lefort (radically opposing Marcel Gauchet on this point), "Politics and Human Rights."

21. Deleuze, *Cinema 2: The Time-Image*, 215 and following.

22. See my article "Politeia."

23. See Marie Gaille-Nikodimov, *Conflit civil et liberté. La politique machiavélienne entre histoire et médecine.*

24. The distinction between the formal constitution (juridical, based on the hierarchy of law, regulations, and their sources) and the material constitution (the equilibrium of powers, social and political bodies, the regulated conflict of class and political actors) has a long history that can be traced back to the critics of contractualist theories (Hume, Montesquieu, Hegel), and further still to debates about the "mixed constitution." It is laid out in particular in the work of Costantino Mortati, *La costituzione in senso materiale*, the inspiration for Negri in *Insurgencies: Constituent Power and the Modern State.*

25. Hans Kelsen, *La Démocratie. Sa nature—sa valeur.*

26. Catherine Colliot-Thélène, "L'ignorance du peuple." The principle of incompetence was systematized by the theorists of elitist democracy (especially Schumpeter), who dominated political science from the beginning of the twentieth century (in response to the great "fear of the masses" provoked by socialism and communism) and identified the democratic regime not only with the delegation of power, but with competition between professional politicians on the market of representation. See Boaventura de Sousa Santos, *Democratizing Democracy*, xxxvii and following. This perspective remains with Pierre Rosanvallon when he studies the determining role of the idea capacity in the institution of democracy (*Le moment Guizot*; *La démocratie inachevée*). Compare here Rancière, for whom the democratic gesture par excellence is the claim of ignorance against the capacities that authorize the elites' confiscation of power (*The Ignorant Schoolmaster: Five Lessons in Intellectual Emancipation*).

27. See the commentaries by Marie-Claire Caloz-Tschopp, *Les sans-etat dans la philosophie de Hannah Arendt*, and Margaret Somers, *Genealogies of Citizenship: Markets, Statelessness, and the Right to Have Rights*. The great difficulty in interpreting Arendt consists in knowing whether her notion of "politics without foundations" (set out essentially in *On the Origins of Totalitarianism* and the texts on civil disobedience) implies a separation between the public and private domains, or between the political and the social, as she herself maintained in her critique of the anthropology of labor from Locke to Marx (*The Human Condition*), or whether it can be dissociated from and even used against this separation (and in particular against the use that was made of it by postwar liberal political science). See chapter 6.

28. We know that this was from the start the strong point of the theorists of the

oscillation of (socialist) mass parties between a dictatorship of leaders and a monopology of managers (Robert Michels), to which Gramsci tried to respond with his theory of "organic intellectuals."

29. It was on this point that, on the occasion of a debate in 1978–79 in the Italian journal *Il manifesto*, I believed I had to distance myself from Althusser. I saw a contradition between his thesis of the (ideal) communist as a "party outside the state" and the implications of his theory of political practice framed by "ideological state apparatuses" ("Stato, Partito, Transizione"). In his last published texts, Althusser outlined a joint reflection on Marxism as a "finite theory" and on the contradictions of the party form as such, which others had taken up before him.

30. "We know that oppression and domination have many faces and that not all of them are the direct or exclusive result of global capitalism. . . . It is, indeed, possible that some initiatives that present themselves as alternatives to global capitalism are themselves a form of oppression." De Sousa Santos, *Democratizing Democracy*, xxvi.

31. It is obvious that the importance of the question of social citizenship, its historical realization, and its crisis in the form of the national-social state is not perceived in the same terms, depending on whether one thinks about politics in the North or in the South. But, on the one hand, the national-social state had a counter-part in the South in the form of the problematic of development (which itself is also exposed to crisis in a neoliberal context). And, on the other hand, the question of social rights is not limited to a paticular region of the world. The critique of formal constitutionalism is in every case a question of conflictual democracy that must be discussed in a universal, which is to say comparative, way. See Partha Chatterjee, *The Politics of the Governed*, and Ranabir Samaddar, *The Materiality of Politics*, vol. 1, *The Technologies of Rule*, and vol. 2, *Subject Positions in Politics*.

32. And the recent developments of the economic and financial crisis, and its possible or probable repercussions on the social composition and political relations of different regions of globalized capitalism, comes just in time to put us on guard against hasty or purely speculative conclusions.

33. Robert Castel, *From Manual Workers to Wage Laborers*, and *L'insécurité sociale: Qu'est-ce qu'être protégé?* In his most recent book, of which I became aware while finishing this collection, *La montée des incertitudes: Travail, protections, statut de l'individu*, Castel writes: "In the conclusion to *Métamorphoses de la question sociale* [From manual workers to wage laborers] I put forth the expression 'negative individuals' to characterize the situation of the persons most seriously affected by the 'great transformation' now underway. I take back this formulation because it seems to me precisely too negative. On the one hand, it risks attaching a pejorative connotation with regard to these individuals, which is obviously not my intention. But, above all, it could introduce a misinterpretation if one understands by it that these individuals are not at all individuals, or are only negatively individuals. This is not the case. They are individuals, but individuals caught in the contradiction of not being able to be the individuals they aspire to be" (434).

I greatly regret this decision, which seems to me to euphemize and subjectivize the structural contradiction to which Castel's analyses called attention.

34. This question is posed in particular by Sandro Mezzadra in his commentary on the revised Italian edition of *Cittadinanza e classe sociale*. The notion of social citizenship was first defined by T. H. Marshall in the context of the great transformation of the rights of organized labor and of systems to protect individuals against the characteristic risks of the proletarian condition (which also, little by little, affects everyone whose income comes from wage labor, and whose existence is not socially guaranteed by income from property). In recent years it has again become the object of attention and a redefinition that has emphasized both its political and its anthropological dimensions, especially by Sandro Mezzadra, Robert Castel, and Margaret Somers.

35. This crucial debate between a particularist, paternalist conception and universalist, egalitarian one is aptly summarized by Donald Sassoon in *One Hundred Years of Socialism*. But the perspective on universal social rights that underlies social citizenship leaves room for a second alternative between a "sociological" perspective and "political" (socialist) perspective: see the book by the revisionist Labour Party theorist Anthony Crosland, *The Future of Socialism*. In *The Birth of Biopolitics*, Foucault recalls that in debates at the time the Beveridge Plan was likened to Nazism by precursors of neoliberalism like Friedrich Hayek. We shall see if equally violent alternatives emerge with regard to the "return of citizenship" that certain contemporary theorists propose to respond to the generalization of "precarity," the decoupling of social rights, and the assignment of unique professional identities to individuals. See Antonio Negri, *Good Bye, Mister Socialism*, 211 and following.

36. Compare Pierre Rosanvallon, *Le peuple introuvable: Histoire de la représentation démocratique en France*, who makes the opposite choice on the basis of an orientation that could be called neocorporatist.

37. But also their superexploitation through the institution of the double (professional and domestic) workday (see Christine Delphy, *L'ennemi principal*, vol. 1, *Économie politique du patriarcat*) and their minoritization through the institution of "women's professions," which reproduce segregation within public space. See Geneviève Fraisse, *Les deux gouvernements: la famille et la cité*.

38. Suzanne de Brunhoff has rightly insisted on this point in *L'heure du marché. Critique du libéralisme*.

39. See Thomas Piketty, *Les hauts revenus en France au 20e siècle: inégalités et redistribution, 1901–1998*.

40. This assessment would have to be nuanced in light of particular national histories. The postwar French and, above all, Italian constitutions incorporated references to the right to work and to social protection within the framework of expanded conceptions of the "public power." The British case is particular because it has no written constitution.

41. The reference to Keynes is much more political. Negri insists on this point in a recent article, at the same time that he proclaims the impossibility of going back

to a time before the internationalization of capitalism. See "No New Deal Is Possible."

42. It is from this perspective in paticular that it is important to emphasize the heterogeneous character of May 1968 and its class dimension at the same time as its "antiauthoritarian" transversality. See Kristin Ross, *May '68 and Its Afterlives*.

43. On the way Foucault sought to think the relation between normalization and individualization, and to construct its genealogy, see Stéphane Legrand, *Les normes chez Foucault*.

44. Balibar, *Violence et civilité*.

45. This is why it is essential to think about how struggles around the organization of work, Taylorist forms of authority, and the resistance of workers' collectives to the capitalist atomization of the workforce developed before and after '68. See in France the work of Robert Linhart and Benjamin Coriat, partly inspired by Althusserianism; in Italy that of the "workerist" school before its explosion between the "autonomy of the political" and "workers' autonomy" schools, Tronti and Negri respectively. Capital definitively destabilized the relation of forces in its favor by launching "globalization from below," making massive use of a workforce that was immigrant, marginalized, or excluded by historically working-class organizations within the framework of "postcolonial" relations.

46. The precursor in the area is Keynes himself. See Antonio Negri, "Keynes and the Capitalist Theory of the State."

47. For me, this is the limitation of the irreplaceable analyses of Robert Castel. Inspired in the last analysis by a sociological (Durkheimian) conception of society as an organism subject to processes of disaggregation and anomie engendered by savage capitalism, it maximizes the "regulatory reaction" of the public authorities and minimizes the dynamics of class conflict, and thus the contribution of the workers' movement (whether spontaneous or organized) to the institution of social citizenship. It is true that orthodox Marxism, for its part, denied even the possibility of figures of constitutional equilibrium of class struggle.

48. Socialism is not principally an ideology, still less a doctrine. It is a historical complex in which, in the nineteenth and twentieth centuries, a range of tendencies took shape: conservative socialism (the realized figure of which was the party-states of the Communist bloc), reformist (or social-democratic) socialism, messianic socialism (essentially a form of leftwing critique of the previous two). Marxism, as an unfinished system oscillating between several strategies (or "tactics," on Stanley Moore's reading in *Three Tactics: The Background in Marx*) had a stake in all three tendencies. I distinguish Marxism, a historical phenomenon that is now past, from Marx's theory, which is open to a series of questions from the future in *The Philosophy of Marx*.

49. See the recent article by Sandra Halperin, "Power to the people: Nationally embedded development and mass armies in the making of democracy," which argues that it was essentially the experience of war that, in Europe, allowed the workers' (union) movement to cross the essential threshold concerning representation and negotiating capacity. I owe this reference to Catherine Colliot-Thélène.

50. Stourzh, *Wege zur Grundrechtsdemokratie*; Eduard Bernstein, *The Preconditions of Socialism*.

51. David Harvey, *A Brief History of Neoliberalism*; Jean-Claude Michéa, *L'empire du moindre mal: essai sur la civilisation libérale*; Emmanuel Renault, *Souffrances sociales*.

52. The criterion for this division is not the material and the immaterial so much as the productive and the unproductive. But this is a circle, since one specifically neoliberal policy consists in transforming activities regarded as "unproductive" into sources of private profit, such as eduction or prisons. See Loïc Wacquant, *Prisons of Poverty* and *Punishing the Poor*.

53. "This mode of governmentality . . . convenes a 'free' subject who rationally deliberates about alternative courses of action, makes choices, and bears responsibility for the consequences of these choices." In this way, Lemke argues, "the state leads and controls subjects without being responsible for them; as individual 'entrepreneurs' in every aspect of life, subjects become wholly responsible for their well-being and citizenship is reduced to success in this entrepreneurship. Neoliberal subjects are controlled *through* their freedom—not simply . . . because freedom within an order of domination can be an instrument of that domination—but because of neo-liberalism's *moralization* of the consequences of this freedom. This also means that the withdrawal of the state from certain domains and the privatization of certain state functions does not amount to a dismantling of government but, rather, constitutes a technique of governing, indeed the signature technique of neo-liberal governance in which rational economic action suffused throughout society replaces express state rule or provision. Neo-liberalism shifts the regulatory competence of the state onto 'responsible,' 'rational' individuals [with the aim of] encourag[ing] individuals to give their lives a specific entrepreneurial form." Thomas Lemke, "'The birth of bio-politics,'" 202.

54. Immanuel Wallerstein, *After Liberalism*; Castel, *La montée des incertitudes*.

55. See what Boaventura de Sousa Santos calls "low intensity democracy," in *Democratizing Democracy*.

56. The idea of posthistory (long ago derived from Marx's formulations in *Introduction to the Critique of Hegel's Philosophy of Right* [1844]) was popularized by Arnold Gehlen at the beginning of the 1960s. That of postpolitics is much more recent. See Christopher Hanlon, "Psychoanalysis and the Post-Political: An Interview with Slavoj Zizek." It gives rise to a play on words with "posting politics" (on the Internet).

57. Margaret Somers, *Genealogies of Citizenship: Markets, Statelessness, and the Right to Have Rights*.

58. In *Jusqu'à quand? Pour en finir avec les crises financières*, Frédéric Lordon shows strikingly how, starting in the United States, the policy of securitizing dubious loans allowed the construction of enormous yields in investments while the freeing up of credit for consumption allowed households without stable resources to be transformed into life-long debtors.

59. Karl Marx, included in most English editions of *Capital* as "Results of the Immediate Process of Production." *Capital* I.

60. Balibar, "Le moment messianique de Marx," in *Citoyen-sujet et autres essais d'anthropologie philosophique*.

61. We know that Marcuse, whose analyses have visibly much influenced Brown's theorization, even if she reformulates their Freudian-Marxist terminology in the Foucauldian language of "subjectivation" as a power relation, attempted to supply the psychosociological counterpart to these Marxian theses in *One-Dimensional Man* by showing that Marx's very general prognosis then entered into daily life, especially into the American "civilization of consumption."

62. These are the thematics of Baudrillard and Agamben, respectively. In a sense Negri and Hardt (*Empire*, then *Multitude*) represent the most interesting attempt to positively reverse these apocalyptic themes based on an interpretation of the "virtual" as the immateriality of labor, but at the price of an unlimited extension of the category of biopower. It will be necessary to return to this more carefully.

63. Gilles Deleuze, "Postscript of the Societies of Control."

64. Giorgio Agamben, "Non au tatouage biopolitique." See also Didier Bigo, "Gérer les transhumances. La surveillance à distance dans le champ transnational de la sécurité," and Michaël Foessel and Antoine Garapon, "Biométrie : les nouvelles formes de l'identité."

65. It is not always easy to see, it seems to me, that Foucault in his last years developed the theme of the "care of the self" ironically, at once as a last gesture of rupture with his Heideggerian training, and within a critical perspective in relation to the contemporary proliferation of technologies of the self. In the absence of this counterpoint, we risk inverting his oeuvre into a neoliberal, postpolitical ethics. At the very least it is the stake of a battle between several tendencies that claim him.

66. In *L'heure du marché*, Suzanne de Brunhoff recalls that we owe to Hayek the reformulation of the principle of *homo oeconomicus* in the form: each individual should conduct himself as a small bank. Wendy Brown takes from Thomas Lemke the idea of a neoliberal rationalty that encourages individuals to "give their life the form of a business."

67. See chapter 11, below.

68. I would thus be tempted to generalize the complex of the "powerlessness of the omnipotent" that I thought I could discern on the side of the state and in relation to the state, in the give-and-take of xenophobic violence, to all manifestations of communitarianism. See my "De la préférence nationale à l'invention de la politique."

69. See the partly contradictory analyses (both based on a Franco-American comparison) of Sophie Body-Gendrot, *Les villes—La fin de la violence?* and Loïc Wacquant, *Urban Outcasts: A Comparative Sociology of Advanced Marginality*.

70. On Laclau's attempt in *On Populist Reason*, see chapter 7, below. On the murderous extremities implied in the enunciation of the political "we" (of which "We, the People" is the model), see Jean-François Lyotard, *The Differend*, and Michael

Mann, *The Dark Side of Democracy*, especially chapter 2, on "two versions of *We, the People*."

71. And it may be, when one thinks about it, one of the reasons Rancière has been suspicious of some of the consequences or uses of his formula for democracy as the "claim of the part of those who have no part." For an interpretation of Paine as a populist, see Christopher Lasch, *The True and Only Heaven: Progress and Its Critics*, 177 and following.

72. I attempt to think about this "differential," which is constitutive of politics, more specifically as a revolution within the revolution (as Régis Debray said in another context) in my work *Violence et civilité*.

73. Allow me to underline the interest of the historical and philosophical work carried out in Italian by Giuseppe Duso, *La rappresentanza politica: Genesi e crisi del concetto*.

74. The interest of the work of Pierre Rosanvallon is, without questioning this postulate, to systematically study its presuppositions and limits of application in the French case in particular. This is what finally led him to attempt to incorporate compensatory mechanisms of "defiance" (or of the loss of legitimacy that affects it), all the forms of "counter-democracy" based on the direct participation of the citizens in administration or decision-making, into an essentially "unfinished" parliamentary democracy as so many corrective mechanisms. (Translator's note: "defiance" is replaced by "distrust" in the English translation.) See his *Counter-Democracy: Politics in an Age of Distrust*. Yves Sintomer's approach is exactly the opposite. On the basis of examples from the South as well as the North (citizen juries in Berlin, participatory budgeting in Port Alegre), he attempts to explore the concrete roads to a renaissance of conflictual democracy, of which representative institutions are but one pole, even if they are indispensable.

75. One thinks of the "rotten boroughs" of English parliamentary history when one reads about recent developments in the controversy over the misuse of allowances by British members of parliament, or of the Panama Affair when one discovers that French political parties were financed by kickbacks from arms sales and petroleum exploitation in Africa or Southeast Asia.

76. This would be the place for a detailed examination of what unites and opposes the legacies of Hobbes and Spinoza concerning the crucial problem of the transfer and increase of the power of the multitude. I will try to return to it later. There would be everything to gain from discussing it not on a purely speculative level, but in the historical context of the revolutionary movements with which they were involved, especially the Levelers.

77. Neoliberal governance is not interested in conflict reduction as such. To the contrary, it tends to relegate it to areas that are sacrificed because they are unexploitable, where "disposable people" are confined. Ogilvie, "Violence et représentation."

78. I deliberately use formulas that echo the work of James Holston, in *Insurgent Citizenship*, on the development of structures of illegal self-organization in the Brazilian *favelas* and their gradual institutionalization. However, the expression

"insurgent democracy" was also independently (which is not to say coincidentally) established by Miguel Abensour at the center of his readings of Marx's theses on "true democracy" as an alternative to the "state form." See Abensour, *Democracy against the State*. I distinguish myself from Abensour in that I think that institutions, as a space of conflict, can be reduced neither to anarchy nor to statism.

79. An idea developed essentially by Deleuze (with Guattari) in *A Thousand Plateaus*. I offer a commentary in *Violence et civlité*.

80. Alessandro Dal Lago and Sandro Mezzadra, "I confini impensati dell'Europa"; Caloz-Tschopp, *Les étrangers aux frontières de l'Europe et le spectre des camps*.

81. The expression "democratization of democracy" is extremely plastic, I know. One of the most widespread uses today comes from the manifestos of the Third Way, defended by Tony Blair and Bill Clinton against traditional socialism at the end of the 1990s. See Anthony Giddens, *Beyond Left and Right*, and Giddens, *The Third Way*, and, for a recent reformulation, Ulrich Beck, "Democratization of Democracy—Third Way Policy Needs to Redefine Work." Other less well-known authors had previously used it in a radically different sense; see Renée Balibar, *L'institution du français*, 421. For my part, I have tried to extend the suggestions of de Sousa Santos, who opposes "low-intensity democracy," progressively emptied of content by its accommodation of the logics of the monopolization of power, to "high-intensity democracy," which he defines in general as "the entire process through which unequal power relations are replaced by relations of shared authority," by trying to specify the current paths on the basis of an analysis of "the double crisis of representation and participation" (xxxv–lxxiv). Also see his article "Pourquoi Cuba est devenu un problème difficile pour la gauche?"

CHAPTER 1. *The Proposition of Equaliberty*

1. This is a modified and developed version of the talk I presented at the Petit Odéon, November 27, 1989. It was first published in the series of *Conférences du Perroquet*, no. 22, November 1989. Another version of the same talk was published in English in *Masses, Classes, Power*, in James Swenson's translation.

2. Bertrand Binoche, *Critiques des droits de l'homme*.

3. In retrospect, Marat and Saint-Just thus appear more liberal than Benjamin Constant.

4. Let us already note, in order to return to it, the close solidarity that is established between the representation of the rights of man as a (simple) ideal and the idea that the rights of man must be essentially conceded or guaranteed—as far as possible—by political power.

5. Bredin, "Enfants de la science, question de conscience."

6. See my "Citizen Subject."

7. Collected in Gauthier, *Triomphe et mort du droit naturel en révolution*.

8. Balibar, "Citizen Subject."

9. It is not an exaggeration to state Florence Gauthier's idea, which I contest

while recognizing its force, as follows: from 1789 to 1793, the revolutionary spokesmen constantly maintained the *form* of the declaration of natural law, which breaks with the traditional legitimation of power, but they deepened its *content* in order to align it with this form, going beyond the initial compromise formulations (notably concerning the "inviolable and sacred" character of property). In so doing, they did not move away from but, to the contrary, moved closer to the original kernel of the conception of the natural rights of individuals, as we find for example in Locke, where the sole universal property is "property in oneself," from which all the others are derived. The right to existence is thus the truth of egalitarian Jacobinism and at the same time the criterion for reconciling the form and the content of the rights of man. Let us note that this reading is very close to Fichte's in his *Contributions towards Correcting the Public's Judgement of the French Revolution*.

10. See my essay "Citizen Subject." The development of the Articles of the Declaration did not lead to a solution until the day after the night of August 4. [Translator's note: the author refers here to August 4, 1789, when the General Assembly abolished feudal privileges.] Gauchet is right to emphasize the effect of these circumstances in neutralizing ideological dilemmas and the anonymity of different revolutionary ideologues in relation to the drafting.

11. The eclipse of the contract in the final version of the *Declaration*, a major index of its detachment from its natural law origins, is closely connected to the (provisional) abandonment of the idea of a declaration of rights and duties. Indeed, duties are the counterpart of rights if one imagines a reciprocal engage-ment between the parties to the contract: either between the individuals and themselves, or between the individuals and the community, society, or state.

12. I am not saying that this tradition is arbitrary. Not only does it reflect a politico-juridical usage of the *Declaration* that must be taken into account. It is rooted in the declared intentions of a large number of the drafters. See the book by Marcel Gauchet cited above, as well as that by de Baecque, Schmale, and Vovelle, *L'an 1 des droits de l'homme*. The expression of these intentions is closely con-nected to the fact that the drafters discussed and debated the formulation of the rights in view of arriving at and founding a constitution. It is significant that they remained undecided, more for theoretical reasons than for reasons of political opportunity, over where to draw the line concerning what pertained to the Declaration of Rights (and therefore the foundation) and what pertained to the Constitution (and therefore what was founded)—in other words, over the point at which the rights of the citizen that are no longer (universal) rights of man begins. It is thus here that we must start to measure the difference between the intentions and usages of the statement and the statement itself, including the virtual effects of the statement that are independent of intentions. Let us add that the perception of a difference of kind or degree between the rights of man and the rights of the citizen has been reinforced by their use in the field of contemporary interna-tional law and international politics, at the cost of distorting the initial idea of foundation into practically its opposite: essentially, the rights of man are now

those that are recognized for individuals outside the framework of the nation-state, independently of the fact that the individuals involved are citizens of such and such a (national) state, but also practically those that are recognized by democratic (national) states (and in this sense are founded on the historical existence of citizenship). This is the place to note that, in its letter, and despite the reference to the nation, to which I will return ("The principle of all sovereignty resides essentially in the nation"), the statements of the *Declaration* are neither nationalist nor cosmopolitan, and, more profoundly, the concept of the citizen which they embody is not a concept of belonging. It is not the concept of a citizen of such and such a state, as cited, such and such a community, but, as it were, the concept of a citizen taken absolutely.

13. Let us note that what manifestly had to do with the idea of foundation in the text adopted definitely on August 26, 1789 (and was "accepted by the King October 5, 1789") was the Preamble. Indeed, it contains three references to foundation: to a revolutionary political event, to nature, and to a Supreme Being.

14. It cannot be otherwise when one identifies, as universal notions, man and citizen, and when one identifies God and nature. When Spinoza carried out the latter operation, he irreversibly overthrew metaphysics, launching a discussion that has still not ended. When the French revolutionaries equated man and citizen (*homo sive civis*) they likewise materially inscribed a point of no return for ethics and politics. The dialectic of modern politics is only intelligible if we read in it all the consequences, immediate and long term, explicit and latent (even repressed), of this rupture. We must therefore ask ourselves what it opens and what it closes.

15. As we know, the inscription of this right was and would be the stake of the fiercest confrontations, at once between the partisans of order (who immediately obtained its suppression in 1795) and those of the interrupted revolution (who tried in 1793 to underline its decisive function), and between the advocates of a juridical logic (it is contradictory for a constitutional state to codify its own negation) and those of social logic (it is contradictory for collective, sovereign individuals not to affirm that all governments, all institutions, are relative to their freedom). The inscription of "resistance to oppression" thus completely confirms that the modality we are dealing with here is that of a unity of opposites.

16. For example, that of being judged by one's peers, the object of the famous *provocatio* of the Roman citizens, the memory of which has been transmitted to the whole of our culture by Saint Paul: *civis romanus sum!*

17. Or more exactly, in the Franco-Latin co-lingualism, *aequalibertas*, and thus comprehensible in all European languages, and therefore today in all the languages of the world. On the Roman origins of the expression, see Nicolet, *Le métier de citoyen dans le Rome républicaine*: "The other thing at stake for the collective was freedom. Let us recall that the word, rarely used by itself, is most often completed by the expressions *aequa libertas* and *aequum ius*, equality in right, legal equality" (527–28).

18. Compare Pierre Bouretz's formulations in his interesting article "Égalité et liberté: À la recherche des fondements du lien social," wherein he speaks of the

"fusion" and the "tension" of equality and freedom, referring to Tocqueville (as opposed to aristocratic freedom, the revolutionaries defined democratic freedom as necessarily equal for all) and Claude Lefort (against the idea of a "nature" external to the "social bond").

19. What is happening now [in 1989] in the East will at least finish off a myth maintained on the right as much as on the left: that of equal societies without freedom (which serves to surreptitiously admit the idea of free societies without too much equality).

20. Does this mean liberation in relation to all law? In other words, does equaliberty mean *liberty without law*, within neither rule nor constraint nor limit? This is precisely the basis of every anti-egalitarian argument. And it is what poses the question of what we must understand by law: what could be a law without eminent authority, without sovereignty? Is this, once again, a contradiction in terms? This question haunted revolutionary experience from the start.

21. See my study "Citizen Subject." This also goes for what I said above (and is one of the strongest senses of the idea of insurrection, an originary connection between the right to insurrection and generalized citizenship). E = L means that men emancipate themselves, that no one can be liberated by another, that the right to politics is unlimited and is exercised everywhere there is submission to an authority that claims to treat individuals or collectivities as minors.

22. Marx did not fully understand this, since he saw community entirely within the revolutionary camp. This relates to the fact that Marx was a communist before being a socialist.

23. It is essential to note in this regard the play on words on which the opposition of revolutionary communism and liberalism is based: instead of restricting the quality of "active citizens" to proprietors, entrepreneurs, or "abilities," it defines citizenship by activity, which is both labor and the initiative of collective emancipation. Let us not forget, on the other hand, that there are pathological variants of these ideological configurations, which have always appeared very hard to understand for liberals as well as socialists and communists—for instance the addition of collectivism and nationalism, or of revolutionary messianism and social conservatism.

24. It is their denial that underlies the naturalism of bourgeois conservative ideologies (and especially the biologizing naturalism of social Darwinism, racism, etc.), but also the more or less messianic antinaturalism of antibourgeois revolutionary ideologies (transposing the Christian thematic of the "new man").

25. I put "classes" in quotation marks, since here it is typically a matter of those unconnected people that, in *Les noms indistincts*, Jean-Claude Milner calls "paradoxical classes." Women also do not constitute a unified group (even tendentially) opposed to men, any more than the "ignorant" are opposed to "experts." (It is highly noteworthy that when, in fact, those who constitute the class consciousness and organization of the exploited, the "uneducated" of modern society, those left out of the school system and excluded from bourgeois

culture, organize themselves, they do so in the name of science and by finding organic intellectuals within their midst or outside.)

26. See the works of Jacques Rancière, especially *The Ignorant Schoolmaster*.

27. See Olivier Schwartz's *Le monde privé des ouvriers—Hommes et femmes du nord*.

28. Sexual difference, as a social division, is the substitute for transcendence in a society in which politics is immanent (a postrevolutionary society), after having been one of the metaphors of power in a society in which politics is transcendent.

29. Experience shows that this source of national community has its exact counterpart in the community of class. See Françoise Duroux's dissertation, "La famille des ouvriers—mythe ou réalité?"

30. This is in no way contradicted by the generalization of professional education, which from that point functions essentially as a differentiation within de-intellectualization (including the de-intellectualization of intellectuals, as white-collar workers).

CHAPTER 2. *The Reversal of Possessive Individualism*

1. The first version of this paper was presented at the Décade de Cerisy-la-Salle on "Property," organized July 9–19, 1999, by Étienne Balibar, Robert Castel, Catherine Colliot-Thélène, and Bertrand Ogilvie. Two versions were published: "'Possessive Individualism' Reversed: From Locke to Derrida," *Constellations* 9, no. 3 (2002), and "Le renversement de l'individualisme possessif," in *La propriété: Le propre, l'appropriation*, ed. Hervé Guineret and Arnaud Milanese (Paris: Ellipses, 2004). Here I have tried to synthesize them, with thanks to both publications.

2. Crawford Brough Macpherson, *The Political Theory of Possessive Individualism*.

3. Tocqueville was an essential witness of this evolution. See *Democracy in America*, vol. 2, pt. 2, ch. 2 ("Of Individualism in Democratic Countries"), as well as *L'ancien régime et la révolution*, 158: "Our fathers did not have the word *individualism*, which we have forged for our use, because in their day there was in fact no individual who did not belong to a group and could regard himself absolutely alone; but each of the thousands of small groups that made up French society cared only for itself. It was, if I may put it this way, a sort of collective individualism that prepared souls for the true individualism we know." Cited by Robert Castel, *Les métamorphoses de la question sociale*, 463.

4. Macpherson, *The Political Theory of Possessive Individualism*, 263–64.

5. Pocock, *Virtue, Commerce, and History*. It should be added that Pocock, Professor Emeritus at Johns Hopkins, is a New Zealander.

6. *The Political Theory of Possessive Individualism*, 48.

7. See Marx's whole development of the "theory of abstinence," *Capital*, 1: 662–66, including the long citation of Luther. (It is absolutely astonishing that Weber, who could not not have known this passage, never cites it, at least not in *The Protestant Ethic*.)

8. Macpherson, *Democratic Theory*.

9. Macpherson, *Democratic Theory*, 122.

10. Macpherson, *Democratic Theory*, 124.

11. This idea was not neglected by another Marxian of the same period, Karl Polanyi, in *The Great Transformation*.

12. Macpherson, *Democratic Theory*, 139.

13. Except, let us note, by Negri. See *L'anomalia selvaggia*, "Appendice: Considerazioni su Macpherson."

14. Macpherson, *Democratic Theory*, 140.

15. Marx's famous fragment on "alienated labor" in the *Economic-Philosophical Manuscripts* (1844) is entirely constructed on the basis of moments of Locke's deduction (perhaps via the mediation of the Hegelian theory of *Bildung*).

16. John Locke, *Two Treatises of Government*, Second Discourse, §123: "The mutual *Preservation* of their Lives, Liberties, and Estates, which I call by the general Name: *Property*."

17. Locke, "Of Property." Only this "constituent" or transcendental concept of property seems to me consistent with the thesis that the labor of the servant belongs to his master (or more generally the labor of a dependent person combined with that of the person on whom she depends yields a product or value that belongs entirely to the latter, who is the true "person"). On the possibility of articulating these theses with the Lockean conception of personal identity in the *Essay Concerning Human Understanding* (II, xxvii), see the glossary of my edition of this text: *Identité et différence*. I thank Jeremy Waldron for having suggested to me a parallel with Locke's argument that if Socrates and Plato share the same thoughts, they must be considered a single person. What is presented as absurd in the domain of consciousness is no longer so in that of labor.

18. James Tully, *A Discourse Concerning Property: John Locke and his Adversaries*.

19. See Robert Nozick, *Anarchy, State, and Utopia*; G.A. Cohen, *Self-Ownership, Freedom, and Equality*; and Carole Pateman's critical discussion in "Self-Ownership and Property in the Person: Democratization and a Tale of Two Concepts."

20. The expression "reversal of possessive individualism" figures notably in Negri's book on Spinoza, where it is a matter of opposing his conception of the power of the multitude to the Hobbesian construction of sovereign power. Astonishingly, Negri, who wrote a preface to the Italian translation of Macpherson's book, is not interested in Locke; it is true that his position tends to put in question the binary opposition Negri seeks to theorize.

21. Rousseau, "Discourse on the Origin and Foundations of Inequality among Men." See Victor Goldschmidt, *Anthropologie et politique. Les principes du système de Rousseau*.

22. Rousseau, *On the Social Contract*, 1:9.

23. See Catherine Larrère's invaluable commentary, "Propriété et souveraineté chez Rousseau," as well as Victor Goldschmidt's classic analyses.

24. Rousseau, "Discourse on Political Economy," 23.

25. Jean Starobinski, *Blessings in Disguise*; originally *Le remède dans le mal*.

26. Is it necessary to say that they defer it indefinitely? This is uncertain: in the *Reveries*, Rousseau would find another problematic of enjoyment that allows him to speak of "hours of solitude and meditation" as privileged moments "when I am completely myself and my own master, with nothing to distract or hinder me, the only ones when I can truly say that I am what nature meant me to be." *Reveries of the Solitary Walker*, Tenth Walk, 154.

27. Marx, *Capital*, 1:928–29.

28. The Franco-German jargon has not received sufficient attention from commentators. In my view it is explained not only by the general trace of the language of the French Revolution and its communist currents (where "expropriator" is related to "monopolist," *accapareur*), but by the reference to the *Exposition de la doctrine saint-simonienne* (1829) (attributed to Bazard and Enfantin), which always underlay Marx's formulations concerning exploitation.

29. Or rather it would be the inevitable consequence of the process if the process of exploitation that is inscribed in the worker's body did not result in collective resistance. The category of "class consciousness," which Marx never named in these words, nevertheless in this way finds an anthropological basis in his analyses.

30. Marx, "Results of the Immediate Process of Production," *Capital*, vol. 1.

31. Marx, *Capital*, 1:727–30.

32. We find it in particular in the *Poverty of Philosophy* (1847) ("The Metaphysics of Political Economy," Sixth Observation), which we know was written in French.

33. It is also on this point that the French school of labor sociology split in its use of Marx: on one side, Pierre Naville, *Le Nouveau Léviathan, I: De l'aliénation à la jouissance*; on the other, Georges Friedmann, *Problèmes humains du machinisme industriel*. See the partly competing developments of this problem in Jean-Marie Vincent, *Critique du travail* and Yves Schwartz, *Expérience et connaissance du travail*.

34. But this is also of course the moment where Marx's projections concerning communism as "indivisibly" the appropriation of individuality and of community—each the mediation for the realization of the other, as announced in *The German Ideology* and *The Communist Manifesto*—becomes definitively problematic (whereby the incompletion of the work assumes an intrinsic significance).

35. Derrida has explained himself on these relations with the tradition of negative theology, in particular in "How to Avoid Speaking: Denials" and *On the Name*.

36. Derrida comments at length on this relation in Blanchot, *Parages*.

37. I will note here that English, unlike French (*retour* and *revenu*), German (*Rückkehr* and *Einkommen*), or Italian (*ritorno* and *reddito*), has only one word to designate the subjective and the objective: the action of coming back, returning home, even recognizing, and the action of receiving, restoring, compensating or

rewarding, and thus profiting from. Here we have a "historical pun," which philosophy can take advantage of to think a speculative constitution, as in the case of the subject itself (*subjectus* and *subjectum*).

38. Derrida, *Given Time: I. Counterfeit Money*, 23–24.

39. Derrida, *Given Time*, 101–2.

40. Derrida, *Spurs*, 109–19.

41. "Still, it does not follow from this that one should, by a simple reversal, transform Being into a particular case or specific of the genus *propriate*, give/take, life/death . . . a mere incident in the event called *Ereignis*. . . ." Derrida, *Spurs*, 121–23.

42. Derrida, "The Ends of Man."

43. Jacques Derrida, "Force of Law: 'The Mystical Foundation of Authority.'"

44. Recall that in the *Essay on Human Understanding* (2:27) the issue of personal identity is entirely organized in view of a demythologizing interpretation of the Last Judgment. See my French edition as well as, more recently, John Yolton, *The Two Intellectual Worlds of John Locke: Man, Person, and Spirits in the Essay*.

45. Castel, *From Manual Workers to Wage Laborers*.

46. According to Pierre Rosanvallon's expression in *Le capitalisme utopique*, taken up by Castel.

47. Mill, *Utilitarianism*, ch. 5 ("On the connection between Justice and Utility").

48. Castel, *From Manual Workers to Wage Laborers*, 277.

49. See Castel, *From Manual Workers to Wage Laborers*, 277, especially 287 and following. See, in the same spirit, the analyses of Donald Sassoon, *One Hundred Years of Socialism*, 137 and following ("Building Social Capitalism 1945–50"), on the conflict in Britain over the application of the Beveridge Plan: either the restriction of welfare to the needy or, to the contrary, the principle of the universality of social security. The latter prevailed despite strong opposition from employers as well as labor unions.

50. Castel, "Rencontre avec Robert Castel," with Marine Zecca, *Ville-ecole-intégration*, 115 (December 1998, "Gérer l'exclusion: Entre droit commun et spécificité"). See more recently his book, *L'insécurité sociale: Qu'est-ce qu'être protégé?*

CHAPTER 3. *New Reflections on Equaliberty*

1. See the commentaries by Alex Callinicos, *Equality*, and Frieder O. Wolf, "'Gleiche Freiheit' als Motiv der Philosophie," 37 and following.

2. Balibar, "Three Concepts of Politics," in *Politics and the Other Scene*.

3. Stourzh, *Wege zur Grundrechtsdemokratie*; Amartya Sen, *Inequality Reexamined*.

4. Robert Nozick, *Anarchy, State, Utopia*.

5. See Lefort, *L'invention démocritque*.

6. The tension between these two points of view, which is constantly at work in Marx's thought, is that the heart of the manuscript devoted to the "Critique of the

Hegelian Philosophy of the State" (1843). See *Marx démocrate: Le manuscrit de 1843*, edited by Étienne Balibar and Gérard Raulet.

7. The first formula comes from *The German Ideology* (1845), the second from *The Communist Manifesto* (1847). The origins of both lie in the contemporaneous texts of utopian socialism.

8. On this point, see in particular the work of E. P. Thompson on the English Jacobins (*The Making of the English Working Class*) and of Jacques Rancière, starting with *The Nights of Labor: The Workers' Dream in Nineteenth-Century France*, as well as my essay, "Un Jacobin nommé Marx" in *La crainte des masses*.

9. On the combined effects of these two revolutions, the superimposition of which engendered the second modernity, the best general account is still that of Immanuel Wallerstein, *The Modern World-System, vol. III: The Second Great Expansion of the Capitalist World-Economy, 1730–1840s*. On the question of phases of modernity, see Fredric Jameson, *A Singular Modernity*.

10. Possible equivalents for the Greek term *elenchos*, which I invoked above, used notably by Aristotle in establishing the principle of noncontradiction in book 4 of the *Metaphysics*.

11. Except when it admits a legitimate power after the fact, based on the consent of citizens, even on their explicit demand for protection, but on the condition that it is exercised under their control and correlative to the introduction of, in the words of the French *Declaration* of 1789, "social distinctions founded on the common utility"—that is, roles attainable by all, or attainable according to nondiscriminatory criteria. The greater theorist of equaliberty in its classic sense, contemporary to the bourgeois revolutions and first of all conceived of in negative terms (or the negation of the negation contained in arbitrary power and privileges), is no doubt Thomas Paine in *The Rights of Man* (1791–92). His formulations not only drew on the discourse of the American and French Revolutions, but also the radical tradition of the seventeenth-century English revolutionaries (see the Putney debates). Frieder Wolf has noted the insistence of the phrase "equall liberty" in the tracts of the Levelers; see "The International Significance of the Levellers." It also makes itself felt through Spencer in *Social Statics* (1851), wherein he defines "equal liberty" as the "law" of modern society. See Frederic W. Maitland, *Libertà e uguaglianza nella filosofia politica inglese*, 133 and following.

12. See Habermas, *Between Facts and Norms*. On the symmetry of "subject" and "citizen," see my "Citizen Subject." See also Pocock, *Virtue, Commerce, and History*.

13. See Robert Castel and Claudine Haroche, *Propriété privée, propriété sociale, propriété de soi*, as well chapter 2 of the present volume.

14. Fraisse, *Reason's Muse* and *Les deux gouvernements*; Joan Wallach Scott, *Only Paradoxes to Offer*.

15. Liberal discourse has a tendency to think nondialectical oppositions dialectically. See my essay, "Crime privé, folie publique."

16. Of all these contradictions, the most glaring is no doubt slavery, but it is also, for that very reason, that which—all else being equal—most quickly turned out to be untenable (even if this quickness was highly relative and heavy with violent

conflicts, as the history of the politics around slavery in revolutionary and postrevolutionary France shows). See Louis Sala-Molins, *Le code noir ou le calvaire de Canaan*.

17. T. H. Marshall, "Citizenship and social class." See also Margaret Somers, "Constituting Citizens in History and in Theory: Civil Societies, Law, and the Place of the Public Sphere," in *Genealogies of Citizenship*.

18. On this (the origins of French "solidarism," which precedes Durkheim, and thus also Robert Castel's critical reflections), one can read with interest Bruno Karsenti's book on Auguste Comte, inheritor of a certain critique of the rights of man, *Politique de l'esprit*.

19. See Axel Honneth's now-classic work, *The Struggle for Recognition*, as well as the discussion, fundamental for contemporary political philosophy, between Honneth and Nancy Fraser, *Redistribution or Recognition: A Political-Philosophical Exchange*.

20. This is Gramsci's term, taken up and expanded by Nicos Poulantzas in the 1970s. See especially *Political Power and Social Classes* and *State, Power, Socialism*.

21. Balibar, "La démocratie conflictuelle et le théorème de Machiavel," in *L'Europe, l'Amérique, la Guerre*.

22. After having written in classical terms of the social state in his now-classic book *From Manual Workers to Wage Laborers*, in *L'insécurité sociale: Qu'est-ce qu'être protégé?*, Robert Castel took up the terminology of the national-social state I had proposed in various earlier essays (including *We, Citizens of Europe?*). It is also used by others; see Christophe Ramaux, *Emploi: éloge de la sécurité*.

23. See Polanyi, *The Great Transformation*; and Sassoon, *One Hundred Years of Socialism*.

24. Here I allude to Michel Foucault, who in *The Order of Things* distinguishes three "quasi-transcendental" fields, shifting the question of the essence of man to the constitution of empiricity: work, life, and language. He himself, obviously, was above all interested in the latter two, the overlap of which is constitutive of sexuality.

25. It seems that we then find ourselves before at least three diverging paths when it comes to the institutionalization of social rights, paths in which we can find in a certain way the three characteristic ideologies of the second modernity: the idea of the *right to existence*, as a "minimum" in which the conservative and paternalistic conception of charity seems to be perpetuated, becoming public charity (but often retroceded by private, notably confessional, associations, as in the United States), and which always undertake projects for a "minimal allocation of resources"; the socialist idea of a *right to work*, connected to the revolutionary tradition but also to the Keynesian objective of full employment; and, finally, the *right to education*, that is, to individual access to a capacity to work that allows individuals to take their chances on the market and more generally in society, the liberal inspiration of which is clear enough.

26. See the special volume of *Labyrinthe* edited by Diogo Sardinha: "La biopolitique (d')après Michel Foucault."

27. Here we have, against the intentions of Arendt herself (who, as we know, rigorously separated the field of *labor* from that of *action*), an extension of what could be called "Arendt's theorem": it is not man who makes the institution, but the institution that makes (or, depending on the case, unmakes) man.

28. See Bertrand Ogilvie, "Anthropologie du propre à rien."

29. See, in particular, the course on the *Abnormal*.

30. Sen, *Inequality Reexamined*.

31. Is it necessary to say that the difference between Marx's discourse and Sen's, rather than going back to an abstract opposition between revolution and reformism, reproduces the antithesis of the two paradigms of subjectivity-community and individuality-activity based on "property in oneself"?

32. See my "Three Concepts of Politics."

33. This is very strikingly the case, it seems to me, with Robert Nozick, the most brilliant of the contemporary theorists of neoconservatism. See *Anarchy, State, and Utopia*.

34. See the reprise of this dilemma in Habermas, *Between Facts and Norms*, ch. 3.

35. See especially the discussion in Anthony Crosland, *The Future of Socialism*.

36. Monique David-Ménard, *Les constructions de l'universel*.

37. But this list lacks perhaps the essential author, Tocqueville, as theorist of mass individualist conformism in postrevolutionary, democratic societies. See Nestor Capdevila, *Tocqueville et les frontières de la démocratie*.

38. Dominique Schnapper, *La communauté des citoyens*.

39. Jacques Derrida, *Politics of Friendship*.

40. Giorgio Agamben, *The Coming Community*.

41. Georges Devereux, *Ethnopsychanalyse complémentariste*, especially ch. 6, "L'identité ethnique: Ses bases logiques et ses dysfonctions."

42. Emma Dench, *Romulus' Asylum: Roman identities from the age of Alexander to the age of Hadrian*, cited by Jane Burbank and Frédérick Cooper, "Empire, droits et citoyenneté, de 212 à 1946," 502.

43. In his now-famous book, *Provincializing Europe*, Dipesh Chakrabarty discusses at length the analogy between the problem posed by models of translation and that posed by models of the circulation of commodities and the institution of the general equivalent. See "Translating Life-Worlds into Labor and History," 72 and following.

44. See my *Violence et civilité et autres essais de philosophie politique*.

CHAPTER 4. *What Is Political Philosophy?*

1. The following notes take up elements of a paper presented in 1998 at the École Normale Supérieure de Fontenay–Saint Cloud in the framework of a doctoral seminar devoted to the problem "Political Philosophy or Science of Society?" which opened with a paper by Catherine Colliot-Thélène. It was first published in *Actuel Marx* 28 (2000) as "Y a-t-il une pensée unique en philosophie politique?"

2. "At issue is the opposition between universalism and cultural relativism as well as the opposition between order and conflict, or individualism and 'holism' and many others besides; they cut through the field of what passes for political philosophy as well as that of the social sciences. If we set aside 'professional' differences (the interpretation of texts on one side, the methodical analysis of empirical facts on the other), the lines dividing philosophy and social science are often fluctuating, all the more so since 'social science' is at least as heterogeneous as political philosophy. But to the extent that philosophy believes it is obliged to specify the differential nature of its discourse, it endlessly comes back to the question of the relation between rationality and western modernity. It is in this sense that it is always connected to a philosophy of history, whether it recognizes it or not. In its classical form, the philosophy of history had the notable merit of directly addressing the question of the historicity of reason: how to reconcile the fact that reason, and the claim to universality that envelops it, has a history? If some contemporary political philosophies believe they can skip this question, they nevertheless bear witness to astonishing complicities between the criteria they offer for rational freedom and the characteristic political forms ('western democracy' or, in Popper's terms, the 'open society') of the modern West." Colliot-Thélène, "Philosophie politique ou science de la société."

3. Immanuel Wallerstein, *Unthinking Social Science.*

4. See Anne Amiel, *Hannah Arendt. Politique et événement.*

5. See, in English, Roberto Esposito, *Communitas: The Origin and Destiny of Community.* In Italian, see, among others: Esposito, *Categorie dell'impolitico;* Esposito, *Nove pensieri sulla politica;* and Esposito, *Oltre la politica. Antologia del pensiero "impolitico."*

6. Jacques Derrida, "Force of Law: 'The Mystical Foundation of Authority.'"

7. Except Robespierre: "In the system of the French Revolution, whatever is immoral is unpolitical, whatever is corrupting, is counter-revolutionary. . . . The greatest pitfall that we have to avoid is not fervor or zeal, but rather weariness of the good and fear of our own courage." Speech to the Convention, February 5, 1794, cited by Jacques Broda, "L'impolitique et le bien commun." It is in a negative sense—and not to denote a negativity that would be inherent in politics—that Pierre Rosanvallon has also taken up the term in his work *Counter-Democracy* to denote the combination of "democratic *activity* and non-political *effects*," leading to "forms of fragmentation and dissemination where coherence and comprehensiveness are need"—whence the "disenchantment that is a common feature of today's democracies" (23–24).

8. See especially the commentary on Bataille's unfinished work on sovereignty in *Nove pensieri sulla politica*, 87–111, where the accent is on the constitutive contradiction of the category of the subject correlative to the representation of sovereign power.

9. Cited in the next section parenthetically.

10. Jean-Luc Nancy, *Inoperative Community.*

11. The originary divergence of the ideas of community and immunity on the basis of a common etymology (*munus*), and at the same their reciprocal contami-

nation, is the main thread of Esposito's *Communitas*, following a trail that goes from Hobbes to Bataille. See also the sequel, *Immunitas: The Protection and Negation of Life.*

12. Rancière, *Disagreement*, 61 (tr. mod.).

13. Rancière, *Disagreement*, 42 (tr. mod.).

14. Rancière, *Disagreement*, 32.

15. Rancière, *Disagreement*, 8–9.

16. Rancière, *Disagreement*, 87.

17. Rancière, *Disagreement*, 72.

18. Etienne Balibar, "Vers la citoyenneté imparfaite."

19. Herman R. van Gunsteren, *A Theory of Citizenship: Organizing Plurality in Contemporary Democracies.*

20. See my "Three Concepts of Politics" in *Politics and the Other Scene.*

CHAPTER 5. *Communism and Citizenship*

1. Nicos Poulantzas, *State, Power, Socialism*, hereafter cited parenthetically.

2. Castel, *From Manual Workers to Wage Laborers.*

3. Sassoon, *One Hundred Years of Socialism. The West European Left in the Twentieth Century.*

4. Georg Voruba, "The Limits of Borders."

5. Eric Hobsbawm, *The Age of Extremes: A History of the World, 1914–1991.*

6. See my essay, "Quel communisme après le communisme?," a lecture given at the conference "Marx International II: Le capitalisme, critiques, résistances, alternatives," University of Paris X-Nanterre, October 1998, and the Il Manifesto conference in Rome, December 1998.

CHAPTER 6. *Hannah Arendt, the Right to Have Rights, and Civil Disobedience*

1. The original version of this essay, "(De)Constructing the Human as Human Institution: A Reflection on the Coherence of Hannah Arendt's Practical Philosophy," was presented at a conference organized for the 100th anniversary of Hannah Arendt's birth by the Heinrich Böll Foundation in Berlin, October 5–7, 2006, and published in *Social Research* 74, no. 3 (fall 2007). An expanded French version appeared as "Impolitique des droits de l'homme: Arendt, le droit aux droits et la désobéissance civique," *Erytheis* 2 (2007), http://idt.uab.cat/erytheis /balibar_fr.htm.

2. See the small and in no way obsolete book by Anne Amiel, *Hannah Arendt: Politique et événement.*

3. See *The Human Condition*, 9–10. It later occurred to Arendt to declare that "the main flaw and mistake of *The Human Condition* is the following: I still look at what is called in the tradition the *vita activa* from the viewpoint of the *vita contemplativa,* without ever saying anything real about the *vita contemplativa.*" Amiel, "On Hannah Arendt," 305.

4. Recall that Arendt claimed the eleventh thesis on Feuerbach as the criterion for distinguishing between professional, theoretical philosophy and the reflection of "men of action," immanent in political activity. *The Life of the Mind*, 216. On the relations between Arendt and Marx in general, see Amiel, *La non-philosophie de Hannah Arendt*, 117–218. Regarding the world: "Action, the only activity that goes on directly between men without the intermediary of things or matter, corresponds to the human condition of plurality, to the fact that men, not Man, live on the earth and inhabit the world." Arendt, *The Human Condition*, 7; compare 280 and following.

5. I say two sets, although, as we know, the phenomenology of *The Human Condition* is based on a distinction between three spheres of the *vita activa*: labor, work, and action. Between the two extremes—i.e., between the reproduction of natural life and the common space (*Zwischenraum, inter homines esse*) of public life—the mediation, at once articulating them and maintaining their separation, is constituted precisely by work. But the analysis in the chapter devoted to work (ch. 4) shows that this mediation collapses historically under the effects of mechanization. It thus constitutes something like a symbolic trace of antiquity in the heart of modernity.

6. Arendt, *The Human Condition*, 254, 264, 272.

7. What *The Human Condition* calls "the unnatural growth of the natural" (47). See also "The Concept of History" in Arendt, *Between Past and Future*.

8. I do not speak of (Pauline, Augustinian, Hobbesian) anthropological pessimism, which was valorized at the same time by authors like Schmitt or Leo Strauss, but of historical pessimism. At the junction of the two, however, see Arendt's critical reflections on the idea of progress, especially in Kant: Arendt, *Journal de pensée*, 1:187.

9. See, for example, Ilaria Possenti, *L'apolide e il paria. Lo straniero nella filosofia di Hannah Arendt*, 99 and following.

10. See Amiel, *Politique et événement*, and, more recently, Miguel Abensour, *Hannah Arendt contre la philosophie politique?*

11. The expression "the lost treasure of revolution" gives the title to the last chapter (6) of *On Revolution*. It is taken up again in the preface to *Between Past and Future*. Each time, Arendt refers to René Char's aphorism in "Feuillets d'Hypnos": "Our inheritance was left to us by no testament."

12. See, once again, the excellent discussion by Possenti, *L'apolide e il paria*, 31–32, and 95 and following ("La fondazione impossibile").

13. See chapter 1 of the present volume.

14. In *Was ist Politik?*, a manuscript published after her death, Arendt cites Aeschylus in particular. See Arendt, *The Promise of Politics*, 186.

15. This amounts to explaining that political rights derive from the nature they elaborate—whence comes the paradoxical proximity with naturalist theories of the right of nations, and even races (conceived as "essential nations"). Or, more exactly, the fact that the conflict between universalism and racism unfolds entirely within the paradigm of "nature," one nature against another—indicating a

profound equivocalness in the very concept of nature. See, for example, the treatment of Gobineau in *On the Origins of Totalitarianism*, 170 and following.

16. "These facts and reflections offer what seems an ironical, bitter, and belated confirmation of the famous arguments with which Edmund Burke opposed the French Revolution's Declaration of the Rights of Man. They appear to buttress his assertion that human rights were an 'abstraction,' that it was much wiser to rely on an 'entailed inheritance' of rights which one transmits to one's children like life itself, and to claim one's rights to be the 'rights of an Englishman' rather than the inalienable rights of man. . . .

"The pragmatic soundness of Burke's concept seems to be beyond doubt in the light of our manifold experiences. Not only did the loss of national rights in all instances entail the loss of human rights; the restoration of human rights, as the recent example of the State of Israel proves, has been achieved so far only through the restoration of the establishment of national rights. The conception of human rights, based upon the assumed existence of a human being as such, broke down at the very moment when those who professed to believe in it were for the first time confronted with people who had indeed lost all other qualities and specific relationships—except that they were still human." Arendt, *The Origins of Totalitarianism*, 299. Earlier Arendt had shown how Burke laid the groundwork for racism by transferring the "hereditary privileges" of the nobility to the English nation as a whole (*The Origins of Totalitarianism*, 175–76); see Possenti's commentary, *L'apolide e il paria*, 28. The highly complex question of the meaning of Burke's oeuvre is taken up again in *On Revolution* (ch. 2, § 5), this time distinguishing between the French and American Declarations.

17. What Arendt calls the "in-between" (*Zwischenraum*) or "being among men" (*inter homines esse*). See Miguel Abensour's commentary, *Hannah Arendt contre la philosophie politique?*, 132.

18. These are the three stages distinguished in Arendt, *On the Origins of Totalitarianism*, 455 and following.

19. This is Arendt's existentialism, if one wants to use this category.

20. I refer especially to the commentaries of Barbara Cassin, *L'effet sophistique*, 161 and following ("Il y a du politique: Citoyenner"), 237 and following ("La cité comme performance"), and 248 and following ("Ontologie et politique: La Grèce de Arendt et celle de Heidegger"). This can also be compared to how Bertrand Ogilvie develops the notion of second nature on the basis of his rereading of La Boétie, by discussing formulations such as "negative anthropology" and an "anthropology of alterity." Ogilvie, "Anthropologie du propre à rien," and "Au-delà du malaise dans la civilisation."

21. Arendt, *The Human Condition*, 33; Arendt, *On Revolution*, 30. See Aristotle, *Politics*, 3:1277a25, where the perfect citizen is he who learns both to give orders and to execute them. In Herodotus' story, it is striking that Herodotus stages a debate typical of Greek political reason (shaped by the Sophists and modified by Plato and Aristotle), on the basis of the three-way division of political regimes, by shifting it to the space of the Other, not just the hereditary enemy but the barbarian,

in order to bring out its universality. This could not have failed to be of acute interest to Arendt, taking a place in her reflection on the impartiality of history, the matrix of politics, whose two Greek sources in her view were Homer and Herodotus. See *The Promise of Politics*, 164, and *Lectures on Kant's Political Philosophy*, 56.

22. Rousseau, "Discourse on the Origins and Foundations of Inequality among Men," 204 (note 1). Can we go so far as to suggest that Rousseau and Arendt diverge from this common point of heresy? We must see that if Rousseau gives a naturalistic interpretation of Otanes's formula *oute archein oute archesthai*, it is precisely to name lost nature, in which there is no *archè* in the sense of authority (in a sense: *en archè oudemia archè*), whereas Arendt gives it an institutionalist interpretation: *oute archein oute archesthai* is the conquest of citizenship, that is, the right to have rights, and thus also the possibility of abstaining from claiming and exercising them. What thus emerges is again the fundamental equivocalness of Otanes's formula, which suffices to explain its indelible historical trace. On "Otanes' formula" and its legacy, see Emmanuel Terray, *La politique dans la caverne*, 210 and following.

23. Compare the summary Arendt wrote for her own use: *Journal de pensée*, 1: 471–72.

24. Translator's note: August 4, the night in 1789 when, during an extraordinary session of the National Assembly, the delegates abolished nearly all feudal privileges. Herodotus, *Histories*, 3:83:8.

25. Arendt, "On Civil Disobedience" (1970), in *Crises of the Republic*. Rereading these essays today, in the context of new wars conducted by the "free world" and their constitutional consequences for the state of democracy, obviously cannot leave one indifferent.

26. I have explained elsewhere my preference for translating "civil disobedience" as "civic" rather than "civil" disobedience; see "Sur la désobéissance civique," in *Droit de cité*. This choice has been challenged, in particular by Jacques Sémelin, in "Aux sources de la désobéissance civile." See also Yves Michaud's criticisms in "Le refus comme fondation?"

27. Arendt, "On Civil Disobedience."

28. Here I am obviously referring to Kelsen, who developed this thesis systematically, starting in 1922 (*Der soziologische und der juristische Staatsbegriff*) and made it the cornerstone of his general theory of juridical norms. This would lead us, if the present essay did not need to be kept within reasonable limits, to outline a confrontation between antinomianism as it is presented in Arendt and Max Weber (legitimacy as the probability of securing obedience, the opposite of which is the description of civic democracy—the "city," or the state as "city" in general—as a fundamentally illegitimate regime, that is, in which obedience is *improbable*), with, on the other hand, Carl Schmitt (where the question of power is not posed in terms of authority, archè, but of sovereignty). Whence the importance of the distinction Arendt makes between violence and power, and the localization of the impolitical element of politics not on the side of the "sacred"

violence inherent in it, but on the side of a nonviolence or antiviolence that is essentially discursive, or in this sense logical. Foucault's conception of power and of the resistance that is inherent in it would be a third point of fundamental comparison.

29. Arendt, "Civil Disobedience," 97–98.

30. Aristotle, *Politics*, 3:1275a32. In a sense this indeterminate power remains virtual, but since "it would be absurd to deprive of office those who have the most authority" (*kratistoi*), it is also the power to make and unmake, accept and refuse, and thus finally an unlimited power, absolute in its way, without any intrinsic "measure," "without which there would be no people in the city" (1275b6).

31. Aristotle, *Politics*, 3:1277a30.

32. Aristotle, *Politics*, 3:1275b5: "This is why it is above all in a democracy that there are citizens." Behind Aristotle's formulation I think it would be necessary to reconstruct the debates around the meaning of *isonomia* (a word he uses remarkably sparingly!), especially Plato's terrible attack on democracy in book 8 of the *Republic* (*Politeia*), identifying it with a regime that necessarily descends into tyranny because of its intrinsically anarchic (whereby no authority, either public or domestic, is respected, not even that of humans over animals).

33. See Breton, "'Dieu est dieu.' Essai sur la violence des propositions tautologiques." Should Arendtian nonviolence be compared to other antinomic notions that appear at the same time or since in contemporary political philosophy, in particular Merleau-Ponty's "power of the powerless" (which surely in part inspired Jacques Rancière's "part of those who have no part")? While noting the parallelism, we should not be hasty here, since we must keep in mind that for Arendt it is precisely power that represents this nonviolence or antiviolence, whereas Merleau-Ponty speaks of "invent[ing] political forms capable of holding power in check without annulling it." "A Note on Machiavelli," 133.

34. Arendt, *Eichmann in Jerusalem*, 150.

35. See discussion in Arendt's *Journal de pensée*, 1:201–3. Here Arendt seems to anticipate Lacan's famous pages in his essay "Kant with Sade" on the reversibility of maxims taken from the categorical imperative from good into evil. On Arendt's criticisms of the Kantianism of the categorical imperative, which she opposes to the Kantianism of the faculty of judgment, see the works cited by Abensour, Amiel, and Possenti, as well as *Between Past and Future*, 145, 220 and following.

36. Concerning Bodin, I have been aided by Olivier Beaud's extraordinarily illuminating commentary in *La puissance de l'Etat*, pt. 1 ("La Loy ou la domination du souverain sur les sujets étatiques").

37. Beaud, *La puissance de l'Etat*, 73–74.

38. We find the most concentrated expression of this in Rousseau's *Social Contract*, where the same will is broken up into the indivisible general will of the people and the private wills of the subjects so that the immediate consequence of the distinction between the author and addressees is the sovereign's right to "force each to be free" by obeying laws the responsibility for which he shares by being incorporated into the political body.

39. Beaud, *La puissance de l'Etat*, 103. Note that in her interpretation of Eichmann's "rigoristic" behavior Arendt refers directly to the perverse form this characteristic takes in a totalitarian regime: "Eichmann . . . at least dimly realized that it was not an order but a law which had turned them all into criminals. The distinction between an order and the Führer's word was that the latter's validity was not limited in time and space, which is the outstanding characteristic of the former." *Eichmann in Jerusalem*, 149.

40. See Arendt's comments in a televised discussion held in Toronto, November 3–6, 1972, excerpted in Melvyn A. Hill, ed., *Hannah Arendt* "On Hannah Arendt: *The Recovery of the Public World.*"

41. Arendt, *Eichmann in Jerusalem*, 136–37.

42. Arendt, *The Origins of Totalitarianism*, pt. 3, ch. 11 ("The Totalitarian Movement"), 374–75.

43. Here it would be tempting, despite Arendt's well-known reservations concerning psychoanalysis, to discuss what nonetheless brings this phenomenology close to Freud's theorization of identification, which itself no doubt owes part of its inspiration to Kant's theorization of the "model" or "prototype" (*Urbild*) of moral subjectivity, that is, Christ, who is at the same time, symbolically, the "Leader of the community" of moral persons (*Religion within the Limits of Mere Reason*).

44. Etienne de La Boétie, *Discourse on Voluntary Servitude*, 3:§3.

45. De La Boétie, *Discourse on Voluntary Servitude*, 3:§§3–5.

CHAPTER 7. *Populism and Politics*

1. Book review published in *Agenda de la pensée contemporaine* 11 (fall 2008). On Ernesto Laclau, *On Populist Reason*.

2. It would be interesting to compare this analysis with those published at the same time by Gérard Bras in a small book drawn from his teaching at the Collège International de Philosophie, *Les ambigüités du peuple*, which is also interested in the question of populism and reads it as the symptom of an originary oscillation of the notion of the people between a juridical and an ethnic status, in which it always has a tendency to lose its strictly political, and especially revolutionary, function.

3. See Chantal Mouffe, *The Democratic Paradox*.

4. I do not in fact believe that this criticism holds against Rancière, especially if we take into account his latest work, since the claim Rancière speaks of (starting with *Disagreement*) is not for recognition, which makes a given particularity the "name" of the universal, but for equality, which dissolves particularity or difference in anonymity. Of course Laclau would say that under these conditions there is no more politics.

5. See my "Le contrat social des marchandises et la constitution marxienne de la monnaie (contribution à la question de l'universalité de l'argent)."

6. On this question, see Oliver Marchart, *Post-foundational Political Thought*.

7. This, as I understand it, is fundamentally the problem posed by Bras in *Les ambigüités du peuple*.

CHAPTER 8. *What Are the Excluded Excluded From?*

1. The following text, first presented in English as a contribution to the XVI International Congress of Sociology, Durban, South Africa, July 23–29, 2006 (Research Committee 05: Ethnic, Race, and Minority Relations) under the title "Exclusion of Whom? Exclusion from What?" served as the basis of my oral presentation for the Sophiapol team seminar directed by Christian Lazzeri, March 30, 2007, published in *Le temps philosophique* 13 (2008), University Paris X-Nanterre.

2. See the special issue of *Actuel Marx*, "Le racisme après les races," edited by Étienne Balibar.

3. See Wulf D. Hund's formulations on this point: "Exclusion and Inclusion: Dimensions of Racism."

4. I refer here, of course, to Hannah Arendt's famous formulation concerning the stateless (in the concluding chapter of part 2 of *On the Origins of Totalitarianism*, "The Decline of the Nation-State and the End of the Rights of Man"), which then travels across the frontiers of a vast phenomenology of exclusion.

5. I refer especially to what David Theo Goldberg calls the "racial state" in the contemporary world (as opposed to the officially *racist* state), which he refers especially to European sociopolitical systems. See his "Racial Europeanization" as well as *The Racial State*.

6. In *Race, Nation, Class* I argued that each nation, insofar as it constitutes an "imagined community," in Benedict Anderson's terms, and thus a "fictive ethnicity," presupposes a nationalism. But naturally the translation of nationalism into the exclusion or elimination of the other depends on historical conditions. See Balibar and Wallerstein, *Race, Nation, Class*, ch. 5 ("The Nation-Form: History and Ideology").

7. See Giorgio Agamben, *State of Exception*.

8. Balibar, *We, Citizens of Europe?*

9. I have attempted to apply this idea to the interpretation of the events of November 2005 in France, in chapter 11 of the present volume.

10. Alessandro Dal Lago, *Non-persone. L'esclusione dei migranti in una società globale*.

11. As always, I refer here to Bertrand Ogilvie's study, which is in my view decisive, "Violence et représentation: La production de l'homme jetable." But see also Zygmunt Bauman, *Wasted Lives: Modernity and Its Outcasts*.

12. See Balibar, "Strangers as Enemies: Further Reflections on the Aporias of Trans-national Citizenship."

13. Weber presents the two modes of gathering individuals at the beginning of *Economy and Society*, treating *Vergesellschaftung* and *Vergemeinschaftung* as two modes of regulating conflict (*Kampf*) that are both in competition and constantly overdetermining one another. *Economy and Society*, pt. 1, ch. 1, §8.

14. We can say schematically that racial exclusion stigmatizes individuals on the basis of their supposed membership in a community of birth (*natio*). It thus determines an ambivalent reaction that leads individuals either to claim a right to existence and recognition freed from genealogy or to claim the imagined origin of the community and to demand recognition as such in the public sphere. When it comes to class exclusion, it deprives individuals of control over the conditions of their existence, first of all at work, then, consequently, concerning residence, movement, consumption, etc. But these phenomena of exploitation produce a mass alienation whose results are also ambiguous: by making individuals tendentially interchangeable on the world market, they also create collectives of workers endowed with a class consciousness of their common interests.

15. Karl Polanyi, *The Great Transformation*.

16. Robert Castel, *L'insécurité sociale. Qu'est-ce qu'être protégé?*, now complemented by *La discrimination négative: citoyens ou indigènes?*, which directly addresses the phenomena of double exclusion that interest me here.

17. See Balibar, Costa-Lascoux, Chemillier-Gendreau, and Terray, *Sans-papiers: l'archaïsme fatal*.

18. Michel Foucault, *The Abnormal*.

19. In an earlier essay, I argued that in practice the racist community and the sexist community are mixed together. See "Racism as Universalism" in *Masses, Classes, Ideas*. However, it would be necessary to go beyond this empirical, speculative formulation.

20. See chapter 9 in the present volume.

21. See the special issue of *Patterns of Prejudice* devoted to the problem of the politics of belonging, edited by Nira Yuval-Davis ("Boundaries, Identities and Borders: Exploring the cultural production of belonging").

22. This is the problem of defending the oppressed subaltern woman, the political function of which has been the object of numerous discussions among feminists from "orientalized" countries in the West, before and after September 2001, from Gayatri Chakravorty Spivak, "Can the Subaltern Speak?," taken up again in *Critique of Post-Colonial Reason*, to Leila Abu-Lughod, "Do Muslim Women Really Need Saving? Anthropological Reflections on Cultural Relativism and Its Others."

23. Geneviève Fraisse, *Reason's Muse* and *Les deux gouvernements: la famille et la Cité*. Compare the analyses of Iris Marion Young, *Inclusion and Democracy*.

24. Enrica Rigo, *Europa di confine. Trasformazioni della cittadinanza nell'-Unione allargata*.

CHAPTER 9. *Dissonances within* Laïcité

1. The text of the bill adopted by the National Assembly on its first reading, February 10, 2004, reads: "Article 1: . . . In primary and secondary schools, the wearing of symbols conspicuously displaying religious belonging by students is prohibited. According to internal rules, the initiation of a disciplinary procedure

is preceded by a dialogue with the student . . . Article 4: The arrangements of the present law are to be subject to evaluation one year after it comes into force." [Translator's note: The Stasi Commission was appointed by President Chirac in July 2003 to study the "application of the principle of secularism in the Republic." Headed by Bernard Stasi, a politician and former presidential adviser, and composed of academics (including Régis Debray, Gilles Kepel, and Alain Touraine) and public servants, the commission heard submissions, then in December 2003 tabled a 77-page report recommending a ban on visible religious and political symbols in public schools along with a variety of other measures intended to promote tolerance, religious freedom, and official secularism.]

2. Translator's note: the Conseil d'Etat is France's highest administrative court, which advises the executive on legal matters.

3. Translator's note: *laïcité* is the specifically French-republican version of secularism.

4. As is opportunely recalled in the article "Laïcité" in the *Encyclopaedia Universalis* by sociologists Jean Baubérot and Émile Poulat, uncontested experts on the subject.

5. This aspect, which is seldom evident (since it is hidden by the origin of the conflict, which remains the reference point, so that everyone perceives and calls the law the "anti-headscarf law," and by the noisy controversy of small, openly anti-Semitic Islamist groups and certain self-appointed spokespersons of the French Jewish community, joined by Algerian "eliminationists" engaging in politics by proxy), seems to me fundamental. I do not understand this in the sense of generalized anti-Semitism, at once Judeophobia and Arabophobia, which I have elsewhere suggested is paradoxically fed by the repercussions of the Israeli-Palestinian conflict around the world, but in the most traditional sense. We cannot fail to note that yarmulke-wearing Jews are no less targeted than veil-wearing Muslims, and the manifestations of stigmatization that give rise to their exclusion are no less violent. It is worth recalling here, with Jean-Luc Nancy ("Laïcité monothéiste"), not only the theological background of the idea of *laïcité*, but also the asymmetry that separates Christianity from the other two religions on this point (and cannot be masked by the extension of the ban to "large crosses," which one hardly ever sees outside of a few traditionalist groups). This is a social and political asymmetry, since France has in fact lived for two centuries under a regime of *catholaïcité* (Edgar Morin). From the perpetuation of Christian holidays in the republican calendar to the state management of the religious heritage, the national culture is largely defined as Christian, and more precisely as Catholic. It is a theological asymmetry because the idea of a "private" religion, located in one's heart of hearts, the truer the more "invisible" it is (like the church of the same name), is a Christian theological idea (St. Paul's "circumcision of the heart"), to which Judaism and Islam oppose the idea of a community of mores and rules. This is why the idea of prohibiting display, which inverts the defamatory practice of imposing marks of recognition on religious groups, cannot have the same meaning with regard to

all religions, as Bruno Latour has noted in *Le monde* ("La République dans un foulard").

6. These exceptions must naturally include the (rare) situations in which teachers, drunk on ideology or terrorized by their inability to control social violence that spills over into the schools, refuse to work unless veiled students are expelled, as well as those (also rare) situations in which young girls, seeking heroism and publicity, whether or not they act on their own initiative, stage a symbolic conflict with the institution, which the mass media rush to amplify and which defenders of individual liberties greet with bowed heads.

The Conseil d'Etat opinion of November 27, 1989, holds that "wearing the veil does not contradict the values of the secular and republican school" and leaves headmasters "latitude to act on a case-by-case basis." Jospin's memo from December 1989 calls for "a dialogue between parents and headmasters so that, in the interest of the students and out of concern for the best operation of the school, they will give up wearing the veil." In November 1992 the Conseil d'Etat overturned internal school regulations automatically excluding veiled students, but in September 1993 it confirmed the exclusion of students refusing to participate in certain courses (physical education), while in December 1999 the minister ordered that a veiled student who had refused to participate in swimming class be reinstated. Minister Bayrou introduced the idea of "ostentatious symbols" in a September 1994 memo. In October of that year, the Administrative Tribunal of the Lower Rhine region judged that the veil is not "in itself an ostentatious symbol." In December 2000 the High Council on Integration concluded in a report that "Islam is compatible with the Republic" and "it is not necessary to prohibit veiled girls from going to class." In November 1994 the Ministry for Education nominated a mediator, Hanifa Cherifi, to settle matters concerning the veil by working with students, families, teachers, and administration. A member of the Stasi Commission, whose recommendations (combining the bill prohibiting religious symbols with diverse measures publically recognizing the Muslim religion and the struggle against discrimination) she approved as a whole, Cherifi estimated that there were a thousand cases of "veils at school," and a hundred of "headscarves worn in class." This summary follows that in *L'humanité*, April 30, 2003.

7. Sexism is anchored in historical religions themselves, which are always based on the control of sexual relations and marriage. It is possible that, from this point of view, contemporary Islam, although riven with contradictory currents (among which the voice of women has begun to make itself heard; see Badran, "Islamic Feminism: What's in a name?"), represents an extremity within monotheism, owing to its secular association with patriarchal forms of society, but also to a theological complex that represses female sexuality as such, whose transformation would imply a refoundation of religious revelation. On this point, one should neither rush to judgment nor close the question opened by Fethi Benslama in *La psychanalyse à l'épreuve de l'Islam*. This exceptional character of Islam, if it resists comparative analysis with the other variants of the Western religious tradition (of which Islam itself is a part), of course does not lead to a need for segregation, but

to a particular duty of the school with regard to the women who wear the sign of belonging in the *ummah*—and who are also, as Hegel would have said, its "eternal irony" par excellence.

8. See especially the study by Françoise Gaspard and Farhad Khosrokavar, *Le foulard et la République*.

9. This lobby got a head start in terms of public opinion campaigns, publications, institutional pressure, etc. But others have organized in turn, notably on confessional (in particular around the interventions of Pope John Paul II and those close to him in the French Church; see the intervention of the "Paroles" group, "De l'inutilité d'une loi déplacée") and neoliberal lines (around Alain Madelin, who is very aggressive at the moment on the cultural front; see "Voile, la loi de trop," *Le monde*).

10. I take with a grain of salt the information published by the Renseignements Généraux [the French domestic intelligence agency—tr.] concerning the rising number of mosques in France now "controlled by Salafists," not because I doubt the existence of such a current among Muslims, but because the Minister of the Interior [future President Nicolas Sarkozy] has his own strategy for controlling French Islam, to which the conditioning of public opinion contributes. He is thus both judge and party to the case. Even if, as the rest of this chapter shows, I do not believe in the possibility of uncritically reclaiming the idea of French secularism, it seems to be fundamentally correct to have sided with the denunciation of misogyny, homophobia, and anti-Semitism in the propaganda of "political Islam," as did the authors of "Retrouver la force d'une laïcité vivante" (*Libération*, February 16, 2004), including, notably, Tewfik Allal, Djamel Eddine Bencheikh, Fethi Benslama, Zakya Daoud, Nabile Farès, Mohammed Harbi, Zineb Laouedj, Dalila Morsly, Leila Sebbar, Nadia Tazi.

11. Published in *Libération*, May 20, 2003, with the tendentious title, "Oui au foulard à l'école laïque" [Yes to the headscarf at the secular school], signed by myself, Saïd Bouamama, Françoise Gaspard, Catherine Lévy, and Pierre Tevanian.

12. Among these positions, I call attention in particular to that of the Ligue des Droits de l'Homme at its Congress at Evry, June 7, 8, and 9, 2003 (the resolution adopted at the 82nd Congress, "Liberté, égalité, fraternité, laïcité," judges that there is no reason for legislation on the wearing of religious symbols at school) and that of Jean Baubérot, the only member of the Stasi Commission to refuse to play the game of unanimity. See his article in *Le monde*, "Laïcité, le grand écart," wherein he notably asks, concerning *laïcité*, how one can "concede almost everything to the Alsatians-Mosellians and practically nothing to Muslims."

13. It is often explained that the principle of this distinction has its origins in Christianity, as against other religions: "Giveth unto Caesar what is Caesar's, and unto God what is God's." This confers on Christianity a political privilege, even a "secular" one. There is much to suggest that this interpretation is a retrospective projection on the compromising Christian dogma that finally resulted from the epochal struggle between church and state. In any case, we would require a real discussion of comparative theology.

14. When we take everyday situations into account, especially those of school-age youth, we also see that political, religious, or political-religious identifications, which are not fixed, correspond to what sociologists call strategies of distinction. Their subjective source thus lies beyond this alternative. But they are amenable to it, and this is one of the aspects of the current crisis that requires us to emphasize—and not necessarily to bemoan—the active connection between adolescent subjectivity and institutional grand narratives.

15. Here it would be necessary to engage in a philosophical genealogy of different institutional conceptions of secularism, going back to the classical period of the constitution of the modern nation-state and extending to contemporary alternatives, which are irretrievably situated in a transnational and multicultural context in which prospects of a "war of civilizations," which different, apparently antagonistic forces promote, weigh heavily. French-style *laïcité* is strongly marked by the Hobbesian model, which makes the state (as the representative of the people) the bearer and principal agent of the institution of truth. It is notably marked by the state's monopoly—or, failing that, control—over the educational process, an essential aspect of which is the diffusion of scientific knowledge and the relativization of opinions or beliefs. We have an illustration of this in the current conjuncture in the proposal to introduce the teaching of "the religious fact" into the curriculum, meaning an objective perspective (scientifically based, historical and sociological) on the diversity of religious discourses. The blind spot of such an institution is generally its implicit nationalism and its inability to relativize the cultural postulates on which its conception of scientificity is based. This model can be distinguished from a Lockean model, on which the state does not superimpose any instituted truth on beliefs and religious narratives, but is content to fix the rules of the game for civil society, that is, mark the distinction between legitimate beliefs, which respect freedom of conscience, and illegitimate beliefs, which do not restrict themselves to the private sphere or threaten the freedom of others. (In reality this "minimal" function is never innocent: for Locke himself, it led to the exclusion of Catholicism, the religion of intolerance, from the field of tolerance—a place which in other contexts may be occupied by Islam, "cults," "secular religions," etc.) The difficulties that arise from this model are the inverse of those of the previous one: an example of this today would be the fact that in some U.S. states (the Bible Belt) it is becoming very difficult to teach Darwin's theory of evolution, which is regarded as an assault on freedom of conscience and the religious convictions of many families. To these two compet-ing models from the early-modern period we could oppose a third, which is no doubt utopian but has been practically at work in the history of democratic politics, which I call Spinozist. It makes religious (and, more broadly, ideological) belief neither the private residue of civic religion or instituted truth nor the spontaneous organizing principle of civil society, assigning the state the formal role of regulator, but a particular (and no doubt conflictual) mode by which individuals form collectives in the public sphere, or subjectively interpret the common. This amounts to making "parties" (not only political parties, as in our

constitutional texts, but also religious or political-religious ones) stakeholders in the ongoing process of public-opinion formation. The difficulty with this model, dramatically illustrated by certain contemporary situations, is maintaining over the long term the pluralism that each of the actors tends to negate or ignore for the sake of its own cause.

16. Except of course for a category of individuals who enjoy the privilege of having this second identity as their first: for example, the children of civil servants (whom Pierre Bourdieu called the "state nobility"—without forgetting the state petty nobility), for whom school is nothing other than a natural extension of the familial milieu, and the family a preacademic institution. And it is undoubtedly no accident to find many of the fiercest defenders of *laïcité*, for whom the veil as such is a figure of the profanation of the place of truth, in this genealogical space. But this is not a determinism. And there would also be a place to examine more closely the contradictions that accompany this second nature.

17. Even if they are not the same in all societies and countries, U.S. students recite a pledge of allegiance to the Republic at the beginning of each day. In France this would be regarded as political interference, implicitly presupposing that patriotism is on the right. But there is particular concern about the uniformity of buildings, clothing, and codes of politeness among teachers and students. By an amazing coincidence, at the very moment that practically all of America is up in arms against the threat to religious and cultural freedom in France—from the spokesman of the ultraconservative government to queer groups at west coast universities—the country is rocked by the scandal occasioned by the appearance for a few seconds of the right breast of pop singer Janet Jackson during the half-time show of a national sports event (the Super Bowl), seen by millions of families.

18. During my own provincial schooldays it was tapered pants or crinolines for girls, jeans for boys—a sign of Americanization. Such is the casuistry of clothing, which we can be certain is now in full swing. The idea of the headscarf, as we know, is not defined materially but ideologically by public authorities, who on this point are more theological than their charges. It is thus open to metaphor, in every sense. A beard or a bandana can be equivalent to a headscarf, and if some political, religious movement decided to advise its adepts to dress in green, red, or black, it would be necessary to prohibit green, red, or black.

19. Here one thinks of the famous formula by which Gayatri Chakravorty Spivak sums up Western feminism confronting the Third World: "White men saving brown women from brown men." Spivak's essay "Can the Subaltern Speak?" (1988) discusses how the British Empire constructed the question of the self-immolation of Hindu widows—*sati* or *suttee*, as the price of a semantic slide that could be interestingly considered in light of the current uses of the word "hijab"—as a symbol of female oppression and a privileged object of civilizing interventions by the colonizer. It is now taken up and amplified in her book *A Critique of Postcolonial Reason*. To characterize the impossibility of feminine speech's finding a place between patriarchal discourse, which manipulates

tradition and culture, and that of imperialism, which manipulates law and morality, Spivak borrows the category of the "differend" from Jean-François Lyotard.

20. And this is even more the case in the Mediterranean ensemble as a whole: particular importance should be accorded in this regard to the analysis of the journalist and essayist Salima Ghezali (editor of the newspaper *La nation*, one of the most courageous voices of Algerian civil society), who shows that very similar claims to personal autonomy lead young girls in some cases to adopt the Islamic veil against their stigmatization, and in other cases to refuse its imposition.

21. Let us not forget that after the French Revolution, which saw the rise and the repression of a large equal rights movement—feminist *avant la lettre*—the French nation consigned women to the tutelage of the Church for 150 years, reserving political education for men. But it must also be said that, in the current controversy, certain "feminist" statements (like "Droit des femmes et voile islamique. Notre appel à Jacques Chirac," a petition that appeared in the weekly *Elle*, December 8, 2003, with a number of prestigious signatures) tend less to affirm solidarity with Muslim "sisters" than to appropriate them as substitutes and alibis for a general claim in distress.

22. We would require a careful history of the romance between the republican school and girls from the North African immigration, the successes it has achieved, the hopes it has fostered, the illusions it has created, the obstacles it has met, and the difficulties and resentments it has led to.

23. The High Council on Integration, chaired by the philosopher Blandine Kriegel, has just recalled the incompatibility of this idea with republican principles in its annual report of 2003 ("Le contrat et l'intégration"), allowing the president of the republic to score points against his younger, less intransigent political rivals [at the time, Chirac principally against Sarkozy—tr]. During this time, although millions of French citizens are first-, second-, or third-generation North African immigrants, Arab names remain effectively banned from political representation and high administrative posts, with a few symbolic exceptions (a state secretary here, a Muslim prefect there). I subscribe entirely to the critiques and analyses of Stéphane Beaud and Gérard Noiriel, "Les nouveaux parias de la République," *Le monde*.

24. See Philippe Bernard, "Trois enseignants sur quatre veulent l'interdiction des signes religieux," commenting on the CSA poll for *Le monde* and *La vie*, which appeared the next day. After taking legal advice, the government gave up the term "visible" in favor of "conspicuous," in order to avoid explicitly contradicting the European Human Rights Convention's articles on freedom of religious expression; see Marceau Long and Patrick Weil, "La laïcité en voie d'adaptation." The details of the poll show eloquently that, for a majority of teachers, the question of the veil is part of a broader set of problems concerning collective life, and that adopting the law is not conceived of as taking a philosophical position but as a means of reinforcing their pedagogical authority and disciplinary power (which, to be sure, are not ideologically neutral).

25. A study on victimization, led by Professor Eric Debarbieux at the request of the Ministry for Education, amply confirms the correlation between social exclusion and school violence; see Bronner, "Plus d'un élève sur cinq se sent en situation de forte insécurité." Without in any way minimizing the gravity or specific meaning of sexist violence by boys against girls, whether or not it takes place under political-religious cover—providing the Stasi Commission and the legislature with one of their main arguments in favor of a repressive law—this should no doubt be situated in a larger context, which corresponds to that of teachers' perception of their deteriorating working conditions.

CHAPTER 10. *Secularism and Universality*

1. Translator's note: the specifically French-republican version of secularism.

2. Emile Poulat, *Notre laïcité publique.*

3. Jean-Luc Nancy, *Dis-Enclosure: The Deconstruction of Christianity.*

4. I take the term "political liberalism" from John Rawls, but give it an almost opposite meaning, since for him it is reduced to obtaining an "overlapping consensus" on national values, delimiting a priori the field of political and nonpolitical values, and thus neutralizing the conflict at the heart of individual and collective subjectivity. See *Political Liberalism.*

5. In many recent contributions critically analyzing *laïcité à la française* as a form of statist sovereignty, the American anthropologist Talal Asad, who has worked for many years on a genealogy of secularism, has sought to present this tendency to transform religion by subordinating it to the rules of the public space, which in my view constitutes the heart of its hegemonic function in political history, as a contradictory symptom, if not a manifestation of hypocrisy. See his "Trying to Understand French Secularism."

6. For example, by stipulating what a "religious ritual" and "cultural tradition" are, as the Stasi Commission, appointed in 2003 to propose a settlement of the question of Islamic veils worn by certain young women, ending up with the law regulating religious symbols in schools (at the expense of other of their recommendations).

7. See Amartya Sen, *Rethinking Inequality.* How could the French political system deal with the challenge represented by even very small cultural communities whose reference to religion strongly competes with patriotism when the capacity of its school system to counteract inherited social inequalities has hit rock bottom?

CHAPTER 11. *Uprisings in the* Banlieues

1. This is the expanded version of a paper presented May 10, 2006, at the University of Chicago, at the invitation of the Franke Institute for the Humanities and the Chicago Center for Contemporary Theory. It was published in French in *Lignes* 21 (November 2006) and in English in *Constellations* 14, no. 1 (2007). At the

time of writing, I was not aware of the special issue of *Annales: Histoire, Sciences Sociales* 61, "Penser la crise des banlieues," which contains remarkable studies by Robert Castel, Stéphane Beaud and Olivier Masclet.

2. This observation was incorrect, as I subsequently learned: *Lignes* published an excellent special issue on "Le soulèvement des banlieues" (no. 19, February 2006), which I would have liked to be able to take into account.

3. In his smart little book, *La psychose française: Les banlieues: Le ban de la République*, Mehdi Belhaj Kacem, inspired by Agamben's *Homo Sacer*, plays systematically with the common etymology of the derivatives of "ban" (an old medieval institution of remote Indo-European ancestry that unites opposites: putting in common and placing beyond the law): ban-ishment (*ban-nissement*, *ban-ni*), but also ban-dit and *ban-lieue*. The etymological origin of "banlieue" in "*ban-lieu*"—place of the ban—is substantiated by Jean-Marc Stébé, *La crise des banlieues*.

4. Of course, this opposition marks the extreme terms of a sociological and political polarity: the *banlieues*, especially around Paris, offer a whole range of social and living conditions. We must not forget their important function in maintaining a certain cultural public service (through theaters and cultural centers) that serves the capital itself. And it will not be considered an accident that some political resistance to the state of emergency sought by the government during the events and attempts to mediate or resolve the crisis came from representatives of these popular *banlieues* with diverse populations (*cités*, public housing projects, the stable working class, civil servants), like Saint-Denis or Aubervilliers.

5. See Loïc Wacquant's essential *Urban Outcasts*, from which I borrow the institutional criteria for defining and comparing spaces of urban marginality below—while contesting some of his judgments.

6. Saskia Sassen, *The Global City.*

7. Hans-Magnus Enzensberger, *Civil Wars: From LA to Bosnia.*

8. To recall the basic chronology: on June 20, 2005, the day after the murder of a little boy in the "Cité des 4000," at La Courneuve, struck by two stray bullets, Interior Minister Sarkozy appeared in the *cité* (surrounded by a large police escort) and, speaking in the street to the inhabitants, announced his intention to "fire-hose" the areas clean of violence and delinquency. On October 25, the same minister showed up in Argenteuil to announce a rehabilitation plan for the *banlieues* and, booed by the young residents, repeated his threats to bring them into line by dealing with the "rogues" and "scum" (*racaille*, a term sometimes used by banlieue youth gangs to refer to themselves derisively, along with others). On October 27, three teenagers, pursued by police, who wrongly identified them as thieves, hid in an electrical transformer at Clichy-sous-Bois, where the police left them. Two of them, Bouna Traoré and Zyed Benna, aged fifteen and seventeen, were electrocuted, while the third was seriously injured. At the news, hundreds of youths set fire to cars and stores in Clichy, setting off a cycle of (mainly nocturnal) riots that would last three weeks and spread progressively from the *banlieues* and *cités* to almost all of France. The police and the government successively insisted

that they had proof that it was a case of delinquents, and that they did not know that the youths were in mortal danger. To date, an internal police inquiry has established that the information released by the government at the time was wholly falsified. All the same, the truth has not been officially settled and the extremely serious police misdeed has not been punished in any way. See Hugues Lagrange, "Autopsie d'une vague d'émeutes," and also the special issue of *Mouvements*, "Émeutes, et après?" (no. 44, March-April 2006).

9. Passed by the National Assembly, November 8, 2006, at the Prime Minister's request and with the support of the Socialist deputies, the law declared a state of emergency in a group of cities and communes at the mayor's request, and was extended for three months on November 18 (without Socialist support). It allowed a large number of arrests, summary hearings, and court convictions (2,787 between October 28 and November 15). A great many mayors of all parties nevertheless called the law useless and refused to invoke it. See Evelyne Sire-Marini, "L'état d'urgence, rupture de l'etat de droit ou continuité des procédures d'exception."

10. See Sophie Body-Gendrot and Catherine Wihtol de Wenden, *Police et discriminations raciales. Le tabou français*; Fabien Jobard, "Sociologie politique de la 'racaille.'"

11. Renault, *L'expérience de l'injustice*. Sometimes under threat: a suspension of family allowances is periodically brandished against "deficient" parents.

12. Giorgio Agamben, *State of Exception*.

13. See Bertrand Ogilvie, "Violence et représentation." Many of my essays collected in *Violence et civilité* are based on his analyses.

14. Regarding the absence of organization: many descriptions nevertheless strikingly insisted on the fact that, from the time the fires spread, the rioters' objective was always to "make the police run" (and make fools of them) rather than to confront them head-on. See Alain Bertho, "Nous n'avons vu que des ombres."

15. With the notable exceptions of cities in western France and Marseille, although it is considered to have high levels of social and ethnic tension.

16. CNN sent one of its star reporters, Christiane Amanpour, who specializes in dangerous reporting from Iraq and other war zones, to Seine-Saint-Denis, to deliver commentaries against a background of burning cars and street fights with the police, as in Baghdad.

17. The paradox is that Mbembe, who first published his book *On the Postcolony* in French in 2000 (reissued in 2005), was largely ignored in France until the English translation became an object of heated discussion in universities across the Atlantic.

18. See especially her chronicle, "French Suburbia 2005: The Return of the Political Unrecognised," expanded for French publication in *Lignes* 19 (February 2006). An Indologist and feminist philosopher originally from Yugoslavia who has lived and taught mainly in France since the outbreak of the Balkan wars, Iveković is the author notably of *Le sexe de la nation*.

19. The ambivalence of rap culture, at once a language of revolt and provocation against the repressive apparatus and a sexist code (which can, however, be used ironically), has been one of the interpretive stakes of the events of November 2005. It echoed as far as the columns of the *New York Times*, in the form of a violent editorial by David Brooks, "Gangsta, in French."

20. See, in particular, the work of Gayatri Spivak.

21. Mbembe, "La République et sa Bête. A propos des émeutes dans les banlieues de France," and "Figures du Multiple. La France peut-elle réinventer son identité."

22. An expression borrowed from the Catalan philosopher Josep Ramoneda in an article in *El País* ("De l'etat social à l'etat pénal"), also to be found in the work of Loïc Wacquant.

23. With this description Mbembe, in my opinion, does not sufficiently take into account another statist tradition that comes from the Vichy regime, as we now see in the hunt for "illegal children," even in educational institutions. However, these two traditions are certainly not sealed off from one another.

24. Mbembe's critique meets, without identifying with, that developed by the *Indigènes de la République*, discussed below.

25. Regarding the mosque: this is to say, a place used by Muslims for preaching and prayer, since there are no real mosques in the banlieues, construction being tied up by a whole system of deliberate obstacles.

26. On the development and limits of "neo-communitarian Islam" among youth of immigrant origin, see (despite its date) Farhad Khosrokhavar, *L'islam des jeunes*.

27. There are of course all kinds of political Islam that are in no way interchangeable: moderate and extremist, traditionalist and modernist, assimilationist and secessionist. This quick diagnosis is meant to apply to all of them.

28. Olivier Roy, *The Failure of Political Islam*; Bernard Dréano, "Notes sur l'Islam politique en France."

29. Thus Jacques Chirac: "It is a matter of an identity crisis" (not a social crisis), or Paul Thibaud (former editor of *Esprit*): "It is a matter of a social crisis" (not an identity crisis). But both are obliged to evoke in a generic way the fact of discrimination and the revolt it engenders. Here we have an index of two rival hermeneutics for November 2005 that tend to divide interpretations (despite attempts to reconcile or combine them): class reductionism and racial reductionism. Neither on its own can account for the event's excess or anomaly in relation to its models or prefigurations.

30. This is obviously the meaning of Loïc Wacquant's enterprise, cited above, which is essentially the fruit of field studies and the elaboration of a comparative theoretical model of the relation between marginality and institutions in France and the United States (*banlieues* and ghettos). However, it seems to me that Wacquant, who speaks of a "mixed logic" and "mixed riots," tends to regard class as primary and race (or ethnicity) as secondary.

31. See the comparative work edited by Christophe Bertossi, *European Anti-Discrimination and the Politics of Citizenship: France and Britain*.

32. Robert Castel, *L'insécurité sociale. Qu'est-ce qu'être protégé?*

33. The theme of broken families was used by politicians of the right as well as the left, notably by the two main presidential candidates in 2007, Nicolas Sarkozy and Ségolène Royal. On polygamy, see the statement by Mme. Hélène Carrère d'Encausse on Russian television: "Everyone is astonished: why are African children in the streets and not in school? Why can't their parents buy an apartment? It's clear why: many of these Africans, I'm telling you, are polygamous. In one apartment there are three wives and 25 children. They are so crammed that they are no longer apartments but God knows what! One understands why these children are running in the streets." *Libération*, November 16, 2005. One will note the relaxed syntax the permanent secretary of the Académie Française uses when she wants to reach the general public.

34. This construction and the psychological effects it produces are described in detail by Evelyne Ribert, in *Liberté, égalité, carte d'identité*, ch. 5 ("D'éternels enfants d'immigrés").

35. For a recent discussion of the limits of the validity of this opposition, see Olivier Schwartz, "Haut, bas, fragile. Entretien avec Annie Collovald."

36. Jacques Donzelot, *Quand la ville se défait. Quelle politique face à la crise des banlieues*; Cyprien Avenel, "Les émeutiers de la politique de la ville." The generalized transition of capitalism to competition between territories is described by Pierre-Noël Giraud, in *L'inégalité du monde*.

37. I distinguish myself on this (terminological, but also political) point from Loïc Wacquant, who speaks of "de-proletarianization" because he identifies the "proletariat" with the organized, if not institutionalized, working class. I speak, on the contrary, of "re-proletarianization," because the original use of the term in Marx distinguished it from the "working class" and connoted the insecurity of the condition of the worker, pushed and pulled, defenseless, before capital.

38. See the Internet site of the Mouvement des Indigènes de la République: http://www.indigenes-republique.org/.

39. See Balibar, "Sujets ou citoyens. Pour l'égalité," *Les Temps Modernes* (March-May 1984), reprinted in *Les frontières de la démocratie* (Paris: La Découverte, 1992); and Balibar, *Race, Nation, Class*, with Immanuel Wallerstein.

40. From this moment, however, there is a risk of mimicry: once we note the ideological and institutional insistence on this absurdity—"immigrants" born in France of parents who are sometimes themselves French—it is tempting to look for the cause upstream, in its origins—not, however, as the result of racist discourse (they always also bear with them the stigma of their indelible origins: color, customs, aptitudes, religion), but, to the contrary, according to a reversal typical of the antiracist tradition (what stigmatizes them is never anything but the effect, the projected image of the colonial system that subjugated their fathers and ancestors). The signifier "Indigènes de la République," however, is less simple and less instrumentalizable than that: it could also paradoxically be understood in the

opposite way, as a sort of performative reversal of colonial discourse (the "natives" of the French Republic, born of its blood and on its soil, are *us*, which we never properly want to recognize). This paradoxical interpretation would have the advantage of bringing to the center the question of the designation and exclusion as "foreigner" of those who are the most authentic product of our own, national history.

41. Article 2 of the French Constitution of 1946 (repeated by those that followed) reads: "France is an indivisible, secular, democratic, and social Republic. It guarantees the equality before the law of all its citizens without distinction based on origin, race, or religion." On the forms and practical effects of this gaping contradiction, see Véronique De Rudder, Christian Poiret, and François Vourc'h, *L'inégalité raciste. L'universalisme républicain à l'épreuve.*

42. And sometimes in ways that revoke already acquired citizen rights, as in the case of the denationalization of Jews decreed by the Vichy regime. On its extension in Algeria in the form of the abrogation of the Crémieux decree, see Benjamin Stora's recent book, *Les trois exils juifs d'Algérie.*

43. Étienne Balibar, *We, the People of Europe?*

44. Such a description is exposed to the objection that, at least for nationals, civic rights are accessible to all. And it is not without interest that after the riots a voter registration drive among *banlieue* youth was set in motion, initiated by the comedian Jamel Debbouze and the rap singer Joeystarr. But it met its limit, no doubt because of the obvious gap in the eyes of those affected between formal rights and effective political representation, which holds just as much for nationals and helps make them "internal foreigners."

45. Often themselves of immigrant origin, but in another historical context, an integral part of which was a high level of working-class political and union organization. See the apposite remarks of Stéphane Beaud and Michel Pialoux in the conclusion of their premonitory book, *Violences urbaines, violence sociale: Genèse des nouvelles classes dangereuses.* On the F.N. vote, see the figures and commentary by Nonna Mayer from the presidential elections in 2002: http://www.tns-sofres.com/etudes/dossiers/presi2002/itv_mayer.htm.

46. This theme is common, albeit on the basis of different premises, to Herman van Gunsteren, in *A Theory of Citizenship*, for whom the essence of citizenship is its acquisition (citizenship in the making), and Jacques Rancière, for whom democracy is not a political regime, but a movement of claim-making and the critique of oligarchies, in *Hatred of Democracy.*

47. Rancière, *Disagreement.*

48. Not only is this question not foreign to the reflection of the Indigènes de la République, whose angle of approach I have criticized as, to my mind, one-sided; it is probably part of what drives them. The leaders of the oldest generation (like Said Bouamama) are in fact veterans of the *Marche des beurs* and *Convergence 84* [anti-racist movements of the 1980s], which, more than twenty years ago, tried to find the alchemical formula for converting violence suffered and practiced into a dynamic for winning rights and citizenship, in the name of equality, on the ground and ahead of public opinion.

49. This characterization is present even among authors who place the greatest political importance on the revolt of the *banlieues* (and, all else being equal, the ghettos), who see it as the privileged indicator of the dilemma of capitalist society undergoing neoliberal restructuring: a restructuring of the welfare state or the triumph of the penal state. See Wacquant, *Parias urbains*, 36.

50. See the history of the relations between bourgeois democracy and representation across three volumes by Pierre Rosanvallon, *Le Sacre du citoyen: Histoire du suffrage universel en France*; *Le Peuple introuvable: Histoire de la représentation démocratique en France*; *La Démocratie inachevée: Histoire de la souveraineté du peuple en France*. http://www.cgm.org/Forums/Confiance/notes-de-lecture/deminachrsm.html.

51. As presented in the *Elements of the Philosophy of Right* (1820), §§ 243–44. I am obliged to Bertrand Ogilvie ("Violence et representation") for having drawn my attention to the necessity of this return to a certain (moment in) Hegel after Marx.

52. On this category, see Balibar, *Droit de cité*, and Castel, *L'insécurité sociale*.

53. At a certain point, television journalists asked themselves whether broadcasting images of nightly fires was not contributing to the dynamic and decided on at least partial self-censorship.

54. The hypermediatized arrest of the alleged attackers of a CRS night patrol in the "cité des Tarterêts" at Corbeil-Essonnes, September 25, 2006.

55. When it comes to metropolitan Paris, it has often been noted that the *Périphérique* [the ring-road around the central city] constitutes a veritable border. See Michel, "Au-delà du périph,' c'est l'Amérique."

56. I have analyzed this process in *Droit de cité*, "L'impuissance du Tout-puissant," 109 and following.

57. I take this term—*écartèlement*, or "quartering"—from Schwartz, "Haut, bas, fragile," who borrows it from Chauvel, *Le destin des générations*.

58. See again Schwartz, "Haut, bas, fragile": "There has been a tendency to oppose the autumn 2005 movement of the *banlieues*, born of relegation and exclusion, on the one hand, and the anti-CPE movement, presented as a pure middle-class movement, on the other. But it was quite obvious in the anti-CPE demonstrations that many of the students did not come from the middle classes! They came from '9–3,' as one now says, or from 'deep' 91 . . . ; they come from the '*banlieues*'" (51). We must first of all insist on this difference of logics, of political processes, and not on the heterogeneity of the social bases, or even the populations involved, as the international press and the political class have done. Not only ill-educated adolescents took part in the revolt of the *banlieues*, but also unemployed youth driven to despair by the uselessness of diplomas that had been nullified by discrimination in hiring. See Hugues Lagrange, "Autopsie d'une vague d'émeutes," in *Émeutes urbaines et protestations*. [Tr.: The bill proposed to create a CPE—Contrat Première Embauche, or First Employment Contract—would have made it easier for employers to fire workers under 26 during their first two years of employment. It was met with fierce resistance and eventually dropped by the government.]

59. We can agree entirely with Nacira Guénif-Souilamas ("Le balcon fleuri des banlieues embrasées") that the antagonism between girls and boys in the cités has been obscured and concealed by the racist (basically anti-Arab) stereotypes of official discourse and many intellectuals, especially (as Rada Iveković has emphasized) by hiding the generality of sexist prejudices in French society by systematically projecting them onto the other. It does not follow from this, except by a pious wish, that the violence of the riots was not strongly gendered, which raises an incontrovertible political problem.

60. I insist on this particularly delicate point. If it is true that the revolt of the *banlieues* did not mobilize religious discourse, it is nonetheless the case that religiously based cultural associations, in the first place Muslim ones, play and can play a leading role in reconstituting representation and laying bare the contradictions of collective experience, at the risk of transforming it themselves. Before raising a hew and cry here about the risk of communitarianism, we should ask if it is not before anything else ostracism that reinforces communitarianism, and under what conditions politics could transform communitarianism into civic universalism. The same interrogation holds for the other side, for example when it comes to the Indigènes movement, which is eminently secular.

CHAPTER 12. *Toward Co-Citizenship*

1. Because, first of all, the citizen is a philosophical character, just like the philosopher competing with the sophist, defined by his intellectual proximity and critical position vis-à-vis the city. Like the philosopher, he tends to cultivate, to reform or educate, the citizen.

2. On this history and how it intersects with that of conventions on refugees, see Benhabib, *The Rights of Others.*

3. See Gerald Stourzh's classic study, *Wege zur Grundrechtsdemokratie.*

4. Such an antagonistic structure is of course at the heart of constitutional texts that simultaneously institute, after the eighteenth-century revolutions, individual freedom (*habeas corpus* as freedom of movement, resistance to oppression) and the right to safety or security, calling for the regulation of their respective domains; see Stourzh, *Wege zur Grundrechtsdemokratie.*

5. See Arendt, *On the Origins of Totalitarianism*, pts. 2 and 3.

6. I refer to the works of Ulrich Beck and the discussion around them. This aspect of risk society is too often neglected, since it is implicitly thought that residence is normal, whereas being displaced is exceptional or, in the extreme case, abnormal.

7. On Aristotle's model in the *Physics* for the categories becoming, change, movement, displacement, etc.

8. The linguistic dimension and problems of translation are essential. See, for example, the evolution of the German work *Verkehr* since the Enlightenment: commerce, communication, traffic.

9. See Galli, *Spazi politici.*

10. Thrift, *Spatial Formations*; Castells, *The Information Society*; Sassen, *Denationalization*.

11. Carens, "Aliens and Citizens."

12. See Balibar, "Strangers as Enemies"; Brown, "Porous Sovereignty, Walled Democracy."

13. Bruno Dumont, *La vie de Jésus* (1997), and *Flandres* (2006); Manotti, *Lorraine connection*.

14. Territories are apparently nothing more than abstract administrative spaces, but in reality they are their inhabitants and their climates (here, too, the Aristotelian reference, with its long posterity, is unavoidable). See Giraud, *L'inégalité du monde*.

15. See my "Sujets ou citoyens? Pour l'égalité."

16. Dal Lago, *Non-persone*.

17. See Amiya Kumar Bagchi, *Perilous Passage: Mankind and the Global Ascendancy of Capital* and "Immigrants, Morality and Neoliberalism."

18. Barkat, *Le corps d'exception*.

19. I am thinking in particular, in France, of the Réseau Education Sans Frontières, which intervenes to protect students without papers in France who are threatened with expulsion.

20. Deleuze and Guattari, *A Thousand Plateaus*. The retrospective construction of a whole scale of values depends on this, on which the Mongols are "barbarians" and the Romans or the Han Chinese, despite cruelty as great as their morals and wars of conquest, are bearers of civilization. *Ubi solitudinem faciunt, pacem appellant*, as Tacitus wrote in a phrase that would become famous.

21. See Rigo, *Europa di confine*.

22. But what about Rome? As Yan Thomas shows in the conclusion of his book *"Origine" et "commune patrie": Étude de droit public romain (89 av. J.C.-212 ap. J.C.)*, every Roman citizen was doubly inscribed particularly and universally, in his local (national) city and the imperial (cosmopolitan) city. But this is inseparable from the restrictive character of the right to the city (even if it was progressively expanded) and its hereditary character, which was exactly the opposite of an opening of citizenship to migrants traveling from the periphery to Rome.

23. Colliot-Thélène, "Pour une politique des droits subjectifs."

24. On which it tends to confer the characteristics of a *laos* (the Homeric term used by the Septuagint to designate the "chosen people" as opposed to the *goy'im*, the *ethnè*, or the *nationes*), which, once secularized, underlies all representations of the nation-state in the modern period, insofar as it invests the nation with a universalist mission (be it Johann Gottlieb Fichte's German Nation, the "secular and indivisible" French Republic, or American democracy, with its "manifest destiny")—as if, in order to neutralize ethnic communitarianism, it was necessary to invent the People in the political sense of a surplus of unity. See my essay, "Ideas of Europe."

25. In an earlier essay provoked by the rise of the populism of the French National Front and similar groups elsewhere in Europe whose political discourse

was based essentially on the idea of a "national preference" to be protected against the threat of the integration of foreigners into the city, I tried to show how this fiction is exploited to cultivate the racism of the citizens most deprived of real power in fact of the state machine. See "De la préférence nationale à l'invention de la politique" in Balibar, *Droit de cité*.

26. I am not inventing the expression "nomadic citizenship." See Proulx and Vitalis, *Médias et mondialisation*.

27. T. H. Marshall, *Citizenship and Social Class*. While this foundational text has astonishingly still not been translated into French, see the excellent critical edition with a preface by Sandro Mezzadra in Italian, *Cittadinanza e classe sociale* (Rome: Laterza, 2002) as well as Ruggero D'Alessandro's attempt, inspired more by Foucault and Deleuze, to reopen the question of modern citizenship by breaking with the linearity postulated by Marshall.

28. Habermas, *The Postnational Constellation*. This obstacle is in a sense exactly what Seyla Benhabib uses to build the work cited above. It must be noted that Habermas's position subsequently moved toward a return to the principles of classical international law (offset by a radical criticism of the idea of sovereignty and a defense of the idea of the constitutionalization of international norms) after September 11, 2001, and the launch of the U.S. War on Terror under the second president Bush. See Habermas, *The Divided West*.

29. See the analyses of Saskia Sassen, in *Territory, Authority, Rights: From Medieval to Global Assemblages*, 298 and following, who rightly asks about the difference between "transnationalization" and "denationalization" and the nonexistence of global civil society by distinguishing between four "emergent global classes." I will save for another occasion a discussion of whether one can use the term "class" in a purely sociological way, without referring to a political or even institutional framework or referent. See my old essay, "From Class Struggle to Classless Struggle?" in Balibar and Wallerstein, *Race, Nation, Class*.

30. See chapter 11, above.

31. These prospects can be compared to the history of the internal passport, as told by Gérard Noiriel, in "Surveiller les déplacements ou identifier les personnes? Contribution à l'histoire du passeport en France de la Ière à la IIIe République."

32. Mezzadra, "The Right to Escape."

33. The universalization of rights to residence and freedom of movement poses the same Beveridgian problem as that of social rights, rights to health care, education, etc., at the origin of the welfare state. Are they particular rights covering assistance to the poor, or universal rights neutralizing social difference? Movement is a social relation that encompasses the whole of society in the same way as labor.

34. I have outlined the antithesis of diasporic and nomadic citizenship in my discussion of Mezzadra and Dal Lago's article, "I confini impensati dell'Europa." See my *l'Europe, l'Amérique, la guerre*.

Concerning totality, Jacques Bidet has pointed out to me that such a perspective cannot be avoided from beginning to end, above all if we take into account problems of the general interest and public policy like those that are increasingly imposed by environmental problems, which I discuss above as a factor aggravating population movements. I agree completely, but I am convinced that this totality will remain a divided or conflictual totality, and not give rise to the emergence of a universal sovereignty. The question of *Weltinnenpolitik* will play out on this level.

Expansions and relocations are especially important for the correspondence of citizens' rights with their duties, whether it comes to civic services or taxes, elections or ways of instituting representation.

CONCLUSION. *Resistance, Insurrection, Insubordination*

1. A lecture given July 17, 2007, in the Cour du Palais des Papes, Festival d'Avignon, within the framework of Frédéric Fisbach's staging of a play based on René Char's *Feuillets d'hypnos*. References were added subsequently.

2. I refer to Professor Henri-Irénée Marrou, so called by General de Gaulle, responding to his protest against the use of torture in Algeria.

3. "Parce qu'il n'y a pas d'espèces humaines," June 12, 2006; see also the statements of Ariane Ascaride, Étienne Balibar, Pascal Thomas, and Jean-Pierre Alaux on behalf of the signatories.

4. Translator's note: French Brigadier General Jacques Massu relied on the widespread use of torture and murder in the Battle of Algiers, in 1957. André Charbonnier and Paul Aussaresses were two of his most important torturers.

5. This bit of slang is like an allegory for what I have elsewhere called "the performative reversal of the name of the race"; see my "Capovolgimenti performativi del nome razza e dilemma delle vittime" as well as chapter 11, above.

6. Translator's note: The *Manifeste des 121* was a "Declaration of the Right of Insubordination against the Algerian War," signed by many leading French intellectuals and artists and published in September 1960.

7. Alain (Émile-Auguste Chartier), *Le citoyen contre les pouvoirs* (1926). See Laugier, "Le modèle américain de la désobéissance civile, de Thoreau à nos jours."

8. Derrida, *Rogues*.

9. Herodotus, *Histories*, 3:82 and following. See Emmanuel Terray's commentary, *La politique dans la caverne*.

10. See chapter 1, above.

11. Spinoza to Rector Fabritius, March 30, 1673.

12. Rousseau, "Discourse on the Origin and Foundations of Inequality Among Men" (1755), note 1: "Herodotus relates that after the murder of the false Smerdis, when the seven liberators of Persia gathered to deliberate about the form of Government they would give the State, Otanes strongly favored a republic; an opinion all the more extraordinary in the mouth of a Satrap as, in addition to any claim he might have had to the Empire, the great fear more than death any sort of Government that forces them to respect men. Otanes, as might be expected, was not heeded, and seeing that they were going to proceed to the election of a Monarch he, who wanted neither to obey nor to command, freely yielded to the

other Contenders his right to the crown, asking in return only that he himself and his posterity be free and independent; which was granted him. Even if Herodotus did not tell us the restriction placed on this Privilege, it would necessarily have to be assumed; otherwise Otanes, not recognizing any sort of Law and not having to account to anyone, would have been all-powerful in the State, and more powerful than the King himself. But it was scarcely likely that a man capable in a case like this of being satisfied with such a prerogative was capable of abusing it. Indeed, there is no evidence that this right ever caused the least trouble in the Kingdom, due either to the wise Otanes, or to any one of his descendants." *The Discourses and Other Early Political Writings*, 189.

13. Machiavelli, *Discourses on the First Ten Books of Titus Livy*, 1: 4–5.

14. Rancière, *Disagreement*, and *Hatred of Democracy*.

15. Dominique Schnapper offers a nice presentation of the republican conception of this idea in *La communauté des citoyens: Sur l'idée moderne de nation*. I have discussed it in "Citizenship without Community," in *We, the Citizens of Europe?*

16. See Deleuze and Parnet, *Dialogues*, 124 and following. On Deleuze's politics, see Zourabichvili, "Deleuze et le possible (de l'involontarisme en politique)."

17. On the "absent people," see Deleuze, *Cinema 2*.

18. See Blanchot, *Political Writings*. Luther himself repeated the *non possumus* of the Apostles. See my essay "Blanchot l'insoumis" in *Citoyen-sujet et autres essais d'anthropologie philosophique*.

19. Deleuze, *Expressionism in Philosophy*, 202–3, 221–23. Françoise Proust discusses the ontological and ethical question of resistance at length on the basis of a reading of Spinoza in *De la résistance*.

20. See Rancière, "The Cause of the Other."

21. Balibar, "Etat d'urgence démocratique" (February 9, 1997), reproduced in *Droit de cité* as "Sur la désobéissance civique."

WORKS CITED

Abensour, Miguel. *Democracy against the State*. Translated by Max Blechman and Martin Breaugh. Cambridge: Polity, 2011.

———. *Hannah Arendt contre la philosophie politique?* Paris: Sens and Tonka, 2006.

Abu-Lughod, Leila. "Do Muslim Women Really Need Saving? Anthropological Reflections on Cultural Relativism and Its Others." *American Anthropologist* 104, no. 3 (2002): 783–90.

Agamben, Giorgio. *The Coming Community*. Translated by Michael Hardt. Minneapolis: University of Minnesota Press, 1993.

———. *Homo Sacer: Sovereign Power and Bare Life*. Translated by Daniel Heller-Roazen. Palo Alto, CA: Stanford University Press, 1998.

———. "Non au tatouage biopolitique." *Le monde*, January 11, 2004.

———. *State of Exception*. Translated by Kevin Attell. Chicago: University of Chicago Press, 2005.

Amiel, Anne. *Hannah Arendt: Politique et événement*. Paris: PUF, 1996.

———. *La non-philosophie de Hannah Arendt: Révolution et jugement*. Paris: PUF, 2001.

Arendt, Hannah. *Between Past and Future: Six Exercises in Political Thought*. New York: Penguin, 1977.

———. *Eichmann in Jerusalem: A Report on the Banality of Evil*. New York: Penguin, 2006.

———. *The Human Condition*. 2nd ed. Chicago: University of Chicago Press, 1998.

———. *Journal de pensée (1950–1973)*. 2 vols. Translated by Sylvie Courtine-Denamy. Paris: Seuil, 2005.

———. *Lectures on Kant's Political Philosophy*. Edited by Ronald Beiner. Chicago: University of Chicago Press, 1982.

———. *The Life of the Mind*. Vol. 1, *Willing*. San Diego: Harcourt, 1978.

———. "On Civil Disobedience." *Crises of the Republic*, 49–102. New York: Harcourt, Brace, 1972.

———. "On Hannah Arendt." *Hannah Arendt: The Recovery of the Public World*. Edited by Melvyn A. Hill. New York: St. Martin's, 1979.

———. *On Revolution*. New York: Penguin, 1990.

———. *The Promise of Politics*. Edited by Jerome Kohn. New York: Schocken, 2005.

Asad, Talal. "Trying to Understand French Secularism." In *Political Theologies: Public Religions in a Post-Secular World*, 494–528, edited by Hent de Vries. New York: Fordham University Press, 2006.

Avenel, Cyprien. "Les émeutiers de la politique de la ville." *Mouvements* 44 (2006): 36–44.

Badran, Margot. "Islamic Feminism: What's in a Name?" *Al Ahram Weekly Online* 569, January 17–23, 2003.

Bagchi, Amiya Kumar. "Immigrants, Morality and Neoliberalism." *Development and Change* 39, no. 2 (2008): 197–218.

———. *Perilous Passage: Mankind and the Global Ascendancy of Capital*. Oxford: Oxford University Press, 2006.

Balibar, Étienne. "Capovolgimenti performativi del nome razza e dilemma delle vittime." *Iride* 19, no. 49 (September–December 2006): 561–75.

———. "Citizen Subject." In *Who Comes after the Subject?* edited by Eduardo Cadava, Peter Connor, and Jean-Luc Nancy. New York: Routledge, 1991.

———. *Citoyen-sujet et autres essais d'anthropologie philosophique*. Paris: PUF, 2011.

———. "Crime privé, folie publique." In *Le Citoyen fou*, edited by Nathalie Robatel. Paris: PUF, 1991.

———. *Droit de cité: Culture et politique en démocratie*. 2nd ed. Paris: PUF, 2002.

———. "Historical Dilemmas of Democracy and Their Contemporary Relevance for Citizenship." *Rethinking Marxism* 20, no. 4 (October 2008): 522–38.

———. "Ideas of Europe: Civilization and Constitution." *Iris* 1, no. 1 (2009): 3–17.

———. *La crainte des masses: Politique et philosophie avant et après Marx*. Paris: Galilée, 1997.

———. "Le contrat social des marchandises et la constitution marxienne de la monnaie (contribution à la question de l'universalité de l'argent)." In *L'argent: Croyance, mesure, spéculation*, edited by Marcel Drach. Paris: La Découverte, 2004.

———. *L'Europe, l'Amérique, la Guerre: Réflexions sur la médiation européenne*. Paris: La Découverte, 2003.

———. *Masses, Classes, Power*. Translated by James Swenson. New York: Routledge, 1994.

———. *The Philosophy of Marx*. Translated by Chris Turner. London: Verso, 1995.

————. "Politeia." *Gestes: Revue Transversale* 2 (2006).

————. *Politics and the Other Scene.* London: Verso, 2002.

————. "Quel communisme après le communisme?" In *Marx 2000*, edited by Eustache Kouvelakis. Paris: PUF, 2000.

————. *Spinoza and Politics.* Translated by Peter Snowdon. London: Verso, 1998.

————. "Stato, Partito, Transizione." In *Discutere lo Stato*, edited by Louis Althusser et al. Bari: De Donato, 1978.

————. "Strangers as Enemies: Further Reflections on the Aporias of Transnational Citizenship." Globalization Working Papers, Institute on Globalization and the Human Condition, McMaster University, Hamilton, Canada, 2006.

————. "Sujets ou citoyens? (pour l'égalité)." *Les temps modernes* 452–54 (March–May 1984): 1726–53.

————. "Vers la citoyenneté imparfaite." *Les Cahiers de la Villa Gillet* 8 (1999).

————. *Violence et civilité: The Wellek Library Lectures et autres essais de philosophie politique.* Paris: Galilée, 2009.

————. *We, Citizens of Europe? Reflections on Transnational Citizenship.* Translated by James Swenson. Princeton, NJ: Princeton University Press, 2003.

————, ed. "Le racisme après les races." Special issue. *Actuel Marx* 38 (2005): 11–134.

Balibar, Étienne, and Gérard Raulet, eds. *Marx démocrate: Le Manuscrit de 1843.* Paris: PUF, 2001.

Balibar, Étienne, and Immanuel Wallerstein. *Race, Nation, Class: Ambiguous Identities.* Translated by Chris Turner. London: Verso, 1992.

Balibar, Étienne, Jacqueline Costa-Lascoux, Monique Chemillier-Gendreau, and Emmanuel Terray. *Sans-papiers: L'archaïsme fatal.* Paris: La Découverte, 1999.

Balibar, Renée. *L'institution du français.* Paris: PUF, 1985.

Barkat, Sidi Mohammed. *Le corps d'exception.* Paris: Amsterdam, 2005.

Baubérot, Jean. "Laïcité, le grand écart." *Le monde*, January 3, 2004.

Bauman, Zygmunt. *Wasted Lives: Modernity and Its Outcasts.* Cambridge: Polity, 2004.

Beaud, Olivier. *La puissance de l'Etat.* Paris: PUF, 1994.

Beaud, Stéphane, and Gérard Noiriel. "Les nouveaux parias de la République." *Le monde*, February 19, 2004.

Beaud, Stéphane, and Michel Pialoux. *Violences urbaines, violence sociale: Genèse des nouvelles classes dangereuses.* Paris: Fayard, 2003.

Beck, Ulrich. "Democratization of Democracy—Third Way Policy Needs to Redefine Work." *European Legacy* 5, no. 2 (2000): 177–81.

Benhabib, Seyla. *The Rights of Others: Aliens, Residents, and Citizens.* Cambridge: Cambridge University Press, 2004.

Benslama, Fethi. *La psychanalyse à l'épreuve de l'Islam.* Paris: Aubier-Montaigne, 2002.

Benveniste, Emile. "Deux modèles linguistiques de la cité." *Problèmes de linguistique générale.* 2 vols. Paris: Gallimard, 1974.

Bernard, Philippe. "Trois enseignants sur quatre veulent l'interdiction des signes religieux." *Le monde*, February 4, 2004.

Bernstein, Eduard. *The Preconditions of Socialism*. Edited and translated by Henry Tudor. Cambridge: Cambridge University Press, 1993.

Bertho, Alain. "Nous n'avons vu que des ombres." *Mouvements* 44 (2006): 26–30.

Bertossi, Christophe. *European Anti-Discrimination and the Politics of Citizenship: France and Britain*. Basingstoke: Palgrave, 2006.

Bigo, Didier. "Gérer les transhumances: La surveillance à distance dans le champ transnational de la sécurité." In *Penser avec Michel Foucault*. Paris: Karthala/ CERI, 2005.

Binoche, Bertrand. *Critiques des droits de l'homme*. Paris: PUF, 1989.

Blanchot, Maurice. *Political Writings, 1953–1993*. Translated by Zakir Paul. New York: Fordham University Press, 2010.

Body-Gendrot, Sophie. *Les villes—La fin de la violence?* Paris: Presses de Sciences Po, 2001.

Body-Gendrot, Sophie, and Catherine Wihtol de Wenden. *Police et discriminations raciales: Le tabou français*. Paris: Editions de l'Atelier/Editions Ouvrières, 2003.

Bordes, Jacqueline. *Politeia dans la pensée grecque jusqu'à Aristote*. Paris: Belles Lettres, 1982.

Bosniak, Linda. *The Citizen and the Alien*. Princeton, NJ: Princeton University Press, 2006.

Bouretz, Pierre. "Egalité et liberté: À la recherche des fondements du lien social." *Droits* 8 (1988).

Bras, Gérard. *Les ambigüités du peuple*. Nantes: Plein Feux, 2008.

Bredin, Jean-Denis. "Enfants de la science, question de conscience." *Le Monde*, February 27, 1988.

Breton, Stanislas. "'Dieu est dieu': Essai sur la violence des propositions tautologiques." In *Philosophie buissonnière*, 131–40. Grenoble: Jérôme Millon, 1993.

Broda, Jacques. "L'impolitique et le bien commun." *L'Humanité*, July 21, 2008.

Bronner, Luc. "Plus d'un élève sur cinq se sent en situation de forte insécurité." *Le monde*, January 30, 2004.

Brooks, David. "Gangsta, in French." *New York Times*, November 10, 2005.

Brown, Wendy. "Neoliberalism and the End of Democracy." In *Edgework: Critical Essays on Knowledge and Politics*, 17–36. Princeton, NJ: Princeton University Press, 2005.

———. "Porous Sovereignty, Walled Democracy." Katz lecture, University of Washington, April 29, 2009.

Burbank, Jane, and Frederick Cooper. "Empire, droits et citoyenneté, de 212 à 1946." *Annales, Histoire, Sciences Sociales* 63, no. 3 (May–June 2008): 495–531.

Callinicos, Alex. *Equality*. Cambridge: Polity, 2000.

Caloz-Tschopp, Marie-Claire. *Les étrangers aux frontières de l'Europe et le spectre des camps*. Paris: La Dispute, 2004.

———. *Les sans-etat dans la philosophie de Hannah Arendt*. Lausanne: Payot-Lausanne, 1998.

Capdevila, Nestor. *Tocqueville et les frontières de la démocratie*. Paris: PUF, 2007.

Carens, Joseph. "Aliens and Citizens: The Case for Open Borders." *Review of Politics* 49, no. 2 (spring 1987): 251–73.

Cassin, Barbara. *L'effet sophistique*. Paris: Gallimard, 1995.

Castel, Robert. *From Manual Workers to Wage Laborers: Transformations of the Social Question*. Translated and edited by Richard Boyd. New Brunswick, NJ: Transaction, 2003.

———. *La discrimination négative: Citoyens ou indigènes?* Paris: Seuil, 2007.

———. *La montée des incertitudes. Travail, protections, statut de l'individu*. Paris: Seuil, 2009.

———. *L'insécurité sociale: Qu'est-ce qu'être protégé?* Paris: Seuil, 2003.

———. "Rencontre avec Robert Castel." With Marine Zecca. *Ville-Ecole-Intégration* 115 (December 1998).

Castel, Robert, and Claudine Haroche. *Propriété privée, propriété sociale, propriété de soi: Entretiens sur la construction de l'individu moderne*. Paris: Fayard, 2001.

Castells, Manuel. *The Information Society*. 3 vols. Oxford: Blackwell, 1996–98.

Chakrabarty, Dipesh. *Provincializing Europe: Postcolonial Thought and Historical Difference*. Princeton, NJ: Princeton University Press, 2000.

Chatterjee, Partha. *The Politics of the Governed*. New York: Columbia University Press, 2004.

Chauvel, Louis. *Le destin des générations*. Paris: PUF, 1998.

Cohen, Gerald A. *Self-Ownership, Freedom, and Equality*. Cambridge: Cambridge University Press, 1995.

Collet, Victor, ed. "Penser la crise des banlieues." Special issue of *Annales: Histoire, Sciences Sociales* 61, no. 4 (July–Aug. 2006).

Colliot-Thélène, Catherine. "L'ignorance du peuple." In *L'ignorance du peuple: Essais sur la démocratie*, edited by Gérard Duprat et al. Paris: PUF, 1998.

———. "Philosophie politique ou science de la société." Unpublished paper presented at the Ecole Normale Supérieure de Fontenay–Saint Cloud, October 21, 1998.

———. "Pour une politique des droits subjectifs: La lutte pour les droits comme lutte politique." *L'Année sociologique* 59, no. 1 (2009): 231–58.

Costa, Pietro. *Civitas: Storia della Cittadinanza in Europa*. 4 vols. Bari: Laterza, 1999–2001.

Crosland, Anthony. *The Future of Socialism*. New York: Shocken, 1963.

Dal Lago, Alessandro. *Non-persone: L'esclusione dei migranti in una società globale*. Milan: Feltrinelli, 1999.

Dal Lago, Alessandro, and Sandro Mezzadra. "I confini impensati dell'Europa." In *Europa politica: Ragioni di una necessità*, edited by Heidrun Friese, Antonio Negri, and Peter Wagner, 143–57. Rome: Manifestolibri, 2002.

D'Alessandro, Ruggero. *Breve storia della cittadinanza*. Rome: Manifestolibri, 2006.

David-Ménard, Monique. *Les constructions de l'universel: Psychanalyse, philosophie*. Paris: PUF, 1997.

De Baecque, Antoine, Wolfgang Schmale, and Michel Vovelle. *L'an 1 des Droits de l'Homme*. Paris: Presses du CNRS, 1988.

De Brunhoff, Suzanne. *L'heure du marché: Critique du libéralisme*. Paris: PUF, 1986.

De La Boétie, Etienne. *Discourse on Voluntary Servitude*. Translated by Harry Kurz. New York: Columbia University Press, 1942.

Deleuze, Gilles. *Cinema 2: The Time-Image*. Translated by Hugh Tomlinson and Robert Galeta. Minneapolis: University of Minnesota Press, 1989.

———. *Expressionism in Philosophy—Spinoza*. Translated by Martin Joughin. New York: Zone, 1992.

———. "Postscript of the Societies of Control." *October* 59 (1992): 3–7.

Deleuze, Gilles, and Claire Parnet. *Dialogues*. Translated by Hugh Tomlinson and Babara Habberjam. New York: Columbia University Press, 2002.

Deleuze, Gilles, and Félix Guattari. *A Thousand Plateaus*. Translated by Brian Massumi. Minneapolis: University of Minnesota Press, 1987.

Delphy, Christine. *L'Ennemi principal*. Vol. 1, *Économie politique du patriarcat*. Paris: Syllepse, 2008.

Dench, Emma. *Romulus' Asylum: Roman Identities from the Age of Alexander to the Age of Hadrian*. Oxford: Oxford University Press, 2005.

Derrida, Jacques. "The Ends of Man." In *Margins of Philosophy*, translated by Alan Bass, 109–36. Chicago: University of Chicago Press, 1982.

———. "Force of Law: 'The Mystical Foundation of Authority.'" In *Acts of Religion*, edited by Gil Anidjar, 228–98. New York: Routledge, 2002.

———. *Given Time: I. Counterfeit Money*. Translated by Peggy Kamuf. Chicago: University of Chicago Press, 1992.

———. "How to Avoid Speaking: Denials." In *Derrida and Negative Theology*, edited by Harold Coward and Toby Foshay, 73–142. Albany: SUNY Press, 1992.

———. *On the Name*. Edited by Thomas Dutoit. Palo Alto, CA: Stanford University Press, 1995.

———. *Parages*. Edited by John P. Leavey. Palo Alto, CA: Stanford University Press, 2011.

———. *Politics of Friendship*. Translated by George Collins. London: Verso, 1997.

———. *Rogues: Two Essays on Reason*. Translated by Pascale-Anne Brault and Michael Naas. Palo Alto, CA: Stanford University Press, 2005.

———. *Spurs: Nietzsche's Styles*. Translated by Barbara Harlow. Chicago: University of Chicago Press, 1979.

De Rudder, Véronique, Christian Poiret, and François Vourc'h. *L'inégalité raciste: L'universalisme républicain à l'épreuve*. Paris: PUF, 2000.

De Sousa Santos, Boaventura. *Democratizing Democracy: Beyond the Liberal Democratic Canon*. London: Verso, 2007.

———. "Pourquoi Cuba est devenu un problème difficile pour la gauche?" *Mouvements* (2009).

Devereux, Georges. *Ethnopsychanalyse complémentariste*. Paris: Flammarion, 1985.

Donzelot, Jacques. *Quand la ville se défait: Quelle politique face à la crise des banlieues*. Paris: Seuil, 2006.

Dréano, Bernard. "Notes sur l'Islam politique en France." *Réseaux citoyens*, February 15, 2005.

Duroux, Françoise. "La famille des ouvriers—mythe ou réalité?" Ph.D. Diss., University of Paris-VII, 2003.

Duso, Giuseppe. *La rappresentanza politica: Genesi e crisi del concetto.* 2nd ed. Rome: Franco Angeli, 2003.

Enzensberger, Hans-Magnus. *Civil Wars: From L.A. to Bosnia.* Translated by Pier Spence and Martin Chalmers. New York: New Press, 1994.

Esposito, Roberto. *Categorie dell'impolitico.* Bologna: Il Mulino, 1988.

———. *Communitas: The Origin and Destiny of Community.* Translated by Timothy C. Campbell. Palo Alto, CA: Stanford University Press, 2004.

———. *Immunitas: The Protection and Negation of Life.* Translated by Zakiya Hanafi. Cambridge: Polity, 2011.

———. *Nove pensieri sulla politica.* Bologna: Il Mulino, 1993.

———. *Oltre la politica: Antologia del pensiero "impolitico."* Milan: Bruno Mondadori, 1996.

Foessel, Michaël, and Antoine Garapon. "Biométrie : Les nouvelles formes de l'identité." *Esprit* 8–9 (August–September 2006): 165–72.

Foucault, Michel. *The Abnormal: Lectures at the Collège de France, 1974–1975.* Translated by Graham Burchell. New York: Picador, 2004.

———. *The Birth of Biopolitics: Lectures at the Collège de France, 1978–1979.* Edited by Michel Senellart. Translated by Graham Burchell. New York: Palgrave Macmillan, 2008.

———. *The Order of Things.* New York: Pantheon, 1970.

Fraisse, Geneviève. *Les deux gouvernements: La famille et la cité.* Paris: Gallimard Folio, 2001.

———. *Reason's Muse: Sexual Difference and the Birth of Democracy.* Translated by Jane Marie Todd. Chicago: University of Chicago Press, 1994.

Freund, Julien. *Politique et impolitique.* Paris: Sirey, 1987.

Friedmann, Georges. *Problèmes humains du machinisme industriel.* Paris: Gallimard, 1946.

Gaille-Nikodimov, Marie. *Conflit civil et liberté: La politique machiavélienne entre histoire et médecine.* Paris: Honoré Champion, 2004.

Galli, Carlo. *Spazi politici: L'età moderna e l'età globale.* Bologna: Il mulino, 2001.

Gallie, W. B. "Essentially Contested Concepts." *Proceedings of the Aristotelian Society* 56 (1956): 167–98.

Gaspard, Françoise, and Farhad Khosrokavar. *Le foulard et la République.* Paris: La Découverte, 1995.

Gauchet, Marcel. *La révolution des droits de l'homme.* Paris: Gallimard, 1989.

Gauthier, Florence. *Triomphe et mort du droit naturel en révolution, 1789–1795–1802.* Paris: PUF, 1992.

Giddens, Anthony. *Beyond Left and Right: The Future of Radical Politics.* Cambridge: Polity, 1994.

———. *The Third Way: The Renewal of Social Democracy.* Cambridge: Polity, 1998.

Giraud, Pierre-Noël. *L'inégalité du monde.* Paris: Folio-Gallimard, 1996.

Goldberg, David Theo. "Racial Europeanization." *Ethnic and Racial Studies* 29, no. 2 (2006): 331–64.

———. *The Racial State.* Oxford: Blackwell, 2002.

Goldschmidt, Victor. *Anthropologie et politique: Les principes du système de Rousseau.* Paris: Vrin, 1983.

Groupe Paroles. "De l'inutilité d'une loi déplacée." *Le monde*, February 2, 2004.

Guénif-Souilamas, Nacira. "Le balcon fleuri des banlieues embrasées." *Mouvements* 44 (2006): 31–35.

Habermas, Jürgen. *Between Facts and Norms: Contributions to a Discourse Theory of Law and Democracy.* Translated by William Rehg. Cambridge, MA: MIT Press, 1998.

———. *The Divided West.* Edited by Ciaran Cronin. Cambridge: Polity, 2006.

———. *The Inclusion of the Other: Studies in Political Theory.* Translated by Ciaran Cronin and Pablo De Greiff. Cambridge, MA: MIT Press, 2000.

———. *The Postnational Constellation: Political Essays.* Edited by Max Pensky. Cambridge, MA: MIT Press, 2001.

Hanlon, Christopher. "Psychoanalysis and the Post-Political: An Interview with Slavoj Žižek." *New Literary History* 32 (2001): 1–21.

Harvey, David. *A Brief History of Neoliberalism.* Oxford: Oxford University Press, 2005.

Hobsbawm, Eric. *The Age of Extremes: A History of the World, 1914–1991.* New York: Pantheon, 1995.

Holston, James. *Insurgent Citizenship: Disjunctions of Democracy and Modernity in Brazil.* Princeton, NJ: Princeton University Press, 2008.

Honneth, Axel. *The Struggle for Recognition: The Moral Grammar of Social Conflicts.* Translated by Joel Anderson. Cambridge, MA: MIT Press, 1996.

Honneth, Axel, and Nancy Fraser. *Redistribution or Recognition: A Political-Philosophical Exchange.* London: Verso, 2003.

Hund, Wulf D. "Exclusion and Inclusion: Dimensions of Racism." In *Rassismus*, edited by Max Sebastian Hering Torres and Wolfgang Schmale. Special issue of the *Wiener Zeitschrift zur Geschichte der Neuzeit* 3, no. 1 (2003).

Iveković, Rada. "French Suburbia 2005: The Return of the Political Unrecognised." *Lettre International* 71 (winter 2005–2006).

———. *Le sexe de la nation.* Paris: Leo Scheer, 2003.

Jameson, Fredric. *A Singular Modernity Essay on the Ontology of the Present.* London: Verso, 2002.

Jobard, Fabien. "Sociologie politique de la 'racaille.'" In *Emeutes urbaines et protestations: Une singularité française*, edited by Hugues Lagrange and Marco Oberti. Paris: Presses de Sciences Po, 2006.

Kacem, Mehdi Belhaj. *La psychose française: Les banlieues: Le ban de la République.* Paris: Gallimard, 2006.

Karsenti, Bruno. *Politique de l'esprit.* Paris: Hermann, 2006.

Kelsen, Hans. *Der soziologische und der juristische Staatsbegriff: Kritische untersuchung des verhältnisses von staat und recht.* Tübingen: Mohr, 1922.

——. *La Démocratie: Sa nature—sa valeur.* Translated by Charles Eisenmann. New ed. Paris: Dalloz, 2004.

Khosrokhavar, Farhad. *L'islam des jeunes.* Paris: Flammarion, 1998.

Laclau, Ernesto. *On Populist Reason.* 2nd ed. London: Verso, 2007.

Lagrange, Hugues. "Autopsie d'une vague d'émeutes." In *Émeutes urbaines et protestations: Une singularité française,* edited by Hugues Lagrange and Marco Oberti. Paris: Presses de Sciences Po, 2006.

Larrère, Catherine. "Propriété et souveraineté chez Rousseau." *Droits* 22 (1995): 39–54.

Lasch, Christopher. *The True and Only Heaven: Progress and Its Critics.* New York: Norton, 1991.

Latour, Bruno. "La République dans un foulard." *Le monde,* January 17, 2004.

Laugier, Sandra. "Le modèle américain de la désobéissance civile, de Thoreau à nos jours." *Multitudes* 24 (spring 2006).

Lefort, Claude. *L'invention démocratique: Les limites de la domination totalitaire.* Paris: Fayard, 1981.

——. "Politics and Human Rights." In *The Political Forms of Modern Society: Bureaucracy, Democracy, Totalitarianism,* edited by John P. Thompson, 239–72. Cambridge, MA: MIT Press, 1986.

Legrand, Stéphane. *Les normes chez Foucault.* Paris: PUF, 2007.

Lemke, Thomas. "'The Birth of Bio-politics': Michel Foucault's Lecture at the Collège de France on Neo-liberal Governmentality." *Economy and Society* 30, no. 2 (May 2001): 190–207.

Locke, John. *Two Treatises of Government.* Rev. ed. Edited by Peter Laslett. Cambridge: Cambridge University Press, 1963.

——. *Identité et différence: Le chapitre II, xxvii de l'Essay concerning Human Understanding de Locke: L'invention de la conscience.* Edited by Étienne Balibar. Paris: Seuil, 1998.

Long, Marceau, and Patrick Weil. "La laïcité en voie d'adaptation." *Libération,* January 26, 2004.

Lordon, Frédéric. *Jusqu'à quand? Pour en finir avec les crises financières.* Paris: Raisons d'agir, 2008.

Lyotard, Jean-François. *The Differend: Phrases in Dispute.* Translated by George Van Den Abbeele. Minneapolis: University of Minnesota Press, 1988.

Macpherson, Crawford Brough. *Democratic Theory: Essays in Retrieval.* Oxford: Oxford University Press, 1973.

——. *The Political Theory of Possessive Individualism: Hobbes to Locke.* Oxford: Oxford University Press, 1962.

Madelin, Alain. "Voile, la loi de trop." *Le monde,* February 5, 2004.

Magnette, Paul. *La citoyenneté: Une histoire de l'idée de participation civique.* Brussels: Bruylant, 2001.

Maitland, Frederic W. *Libertà e uguaglianza nella filosofia politica inglese.* Edited and translated by Mario Piccinini. Torinto: La Rosa, 1993.

Mann, Michael. *The Dark Side of Democracy: Explaining Ethnic Cleansing.* Cambridge: Cambridge University Press, 2005.

Manotti, Dominique. *Lorraine connection.* Paris: Rivages, 2006.

Marchart, Oliver. *Post-foundational Political Thought: Political Difference in Nancy, Lefort, Badiou, and Laclau.* Edinburgh: Edinburgh University Press, 2007.

Marshall, T. H. "Citizenship and Social Class." In *Citizenship and Social Class,* edited by Tom Bottomore. London: Pluto, 1992.

Marx, Karl. *Capital: A Critique of Political Economy.* Translated by Ben Fowkes. 3 vols. New York: Vintage, 1977.

———. *The Civil War in France.* New York: International, 1970.

Mbembe, Achille. "Figures du Multiple: La France peut-elle réinventer son identité." November 24, 2005. www.multitudes.samizdat.net.

———. "La République et sa Bête: A propos des émeutes dans les banlieues de France." November 7, 2005. www.icicemac.com.

———. *On the Postcolony.* Translated by A. M. Berrett et al. Berkeley: University of California Press, 2001.

Merleau-Ponty, Maurice. "A Note on Machiavelli." In *The Merleau-Ponty Reader,* edited by Ted Toadvine. Evanston, IL: Northwestern University Press, 2007.

Mezzadra, Sandro. *Cittadinanza e classe sociale.* Rome: Laterza, 2002.

———. "The Right to Escape." *Ephemera: Theory of the Multitude* 4, no. 3 (2004): 267–75.

Michaud, Yves. "Le refus comme fondation?" In *Précis de recomposition politique.* Paris: Climats, 2006.

Michéa, Jean-Claude. *L'empire du moindre mal: Essai sur la civilisation libérale.* Paris: Climats, 2007.

Michel, Serge. "Au-delà du périph,' c'est l'Amérique." *Le Monde,* April 28, 2006.

Mill, John Stuart. *Utilitarianism.* London: Parker, Son, and Bourn, 1863.

Milner, Jean-Claude. *Les Noms indistincts.* Paris: Seuil, 1983.

Moore, Stanley. *Three Tactics: The Background in Marx.* New York: Monthly Review, 1963.

Mortati, Costantino. *La costituzione in senso materiale.* Milan: Giuffrè, 1998.

Mouffe, Chantal. *The Democratic Paradox.* London: Verso, 2000.

Nancy, Jean-Luc. *Dis-Enclosure: The Deconstruction of Christianity.* Translated by Bettina Bergo, Gabriel Malenfant, and Michael B. Smith. New York: Fordham University Press, 2008.

———. *The Inoperative Community.* Translated by Peter Connor, Lisa Garbus, Michael Holland, and Simona Sawhney. Minneapolis: University of Minnesota Press, 1991.

———. "Laïcité monothéiste." *Le monde,* January 2, 2004.

Naville, Pierre. *Le Nouveau Léviathan, I: De l'aliénation à la jouissance.* Paris: Anthropos, 1977.

Negri, Antonio. *Good Bye, Mister Socialism*. New York: Seven Stories, 2008.

——. *Insurgencies: Constituent Power and the Modern State*. Translated by Maurizia Boscagli. Minneapolis: University of Minnesora Press, 1999.

——. "Keynes and the Capitalist Theory of the State." In *Labor of Dionysus: A Critique of the State Form*, translated by Michael Hardt, 23–52. Minneapolis: University of Minnesota Press, 1994.

——. *L'anomalia selvaggia*. Milan: Feltrinelli, 1981.

——. "No New Deal Is Possible." *Radical Philosophy* 155 (May–June 2009): 2–5.

Nicolet, Claude. "Citoyenneté Française et citoyenneté Romaine: Essai de mise en perspective." In *La nozione di "Romano" tra cittadinanza e universalità*, vol. 2 of *Da Roma alla terza Roma, documenti e studi*. Naples: Edizioni Scientifiche Italiane, 1984.

——. *Le métier de citoyen dans le Rome républicaine*. Paris: Gallimard-TEL, 1976.

Noiriel, Gérard. "Surveiller les déplacements ou identifier les personnes? Contribution à l'histoire du passeport en France de la Ière à la IIIe République." *Genèses* 30 (March 1998): 77–100.

Nozick, Robert. *Anarchy, State, and Utopia*. New York: Basic Books, 1974.

Ogilvie, Bertrand. "Anthropologie du propre à rien." *Le passant ordinaire* 38 (January–March 2002): 45–48.

——. "Au-delà du malaise dans la civilisation: Une anthropologie de l'altérité infinie." In *Œuvres*, edited by Sandra Alvarez de Toledo, 1571–79. Paris: L'Arachnéen, 2007.

——. "Violence et représentation: La production de l'homme jetable." *Lignes* 26 (October 1995): 113–41.

Pateman, Carole. "Self-Ownership and Property in the Person: Democratization and a Tale of Two Concepts." *Journal of Political Philosophy* 10, no. 1 (2002): 20–53.

Piketty, Thomas. *Les Hauts revenus en France au 20e siècle: Inégalités et redistribution, 1901–1998*. Paris: Grasset, 2001.

Pocock, J. G. A. *Virtue, Commerce, and History: Essays on Political Thought and History, Chiefly in the Eighteenth Century*. Cambridge: Cambridge University Press, 1985.

Polanyi, Karl. *The Great Transformation: The Political and Economic Origins of Our Time*. Boston: Beacon, 1944.

Possenti, Ilaria. *L'apolide e il paria: Lo straniero nella filosofia di Hannah Arendt*. Rome: Carocci, 2002.

Poulantzas. *Political Power and Social Classes*. London: New Left, 1973.

——. *State, Power, Socialism*. Translated by Patrick Camiller. London: New Left, 1978.

Poulat, Emile. *Notre laïcité publique*. Paris: Berg, 2003.

Proulx, Serge, and André Vitalis, eds. *Médias et mondialisation: Vers une citoyenneté nomade*. Renne: Apogée, 1999.

Proust, Françoise. *De la résistance*. Paris: Cerf, 1997.

Ramaux, Christophe. *Emploi: Éloge de la sécurité*. Paris: Mille et une nuits, 2006.

Ramoneda, Josep. "De l'Etat social à l'Etat pénal." *El pais*, November 8, 2005.

Rancière, Jacques. "The Cause of the Other." Translated by David Macey. *Parallax* 4, no. 2 (1998): 25–33.

———. *Disagreement: Politics and Philosophy*. Translated by Julie Rose. Minneapolis: University of Minnesota Press, 1999.

———. *Hatred of Democracy*. Translated by Steve Concoran. London: Verso, 2006.

———. *The Ignorant Schoolmaster: Five Lessons in Intellectual Emancipation*. Translated by Kristin Ross. Palo Alto, CA: Stanford University Press, 1991.

———. *The Nights of Labor: The Workers' Dream in Nineteenth-Century France*. Translated by John Drury. Philadelphia: Temple University Press, 1989.

Rancière, Jacques, Miguel Abensour, and Jean-Luc Nancy. "Puissance de la démocratie." *Vacarme* 48 (summer 2009).

Rawls, John. *Political Liberalism*. Expanded ed. New York: Columbia University Press, 2005.

Renault, Emmanuel. *L'expérience de l'injustice*. Paris: La Découverte, 2004.

———. *Souffrances sociales*. Paris: La Découverte, 2008.

Ribert, Evelyne. *Liberté, égalité, carte d'identité: Les jeunes issus de l'immigration et l'appartenance nationale*. Paris: La Découverte, 2006.

Riesenberg, Peter. *Citizenship in the Western Tradition: Plato to Rousseau*. Chapel Hill: University of North Carolina Press, 1992.

Rigo, Enrica. *Europa di confine: Trasformazioni della cittadinanza nell'Unione allargata*. Preface by Étienne Balibar. Rome: Meltemi, 2006.

Rosanvallon, Pierre. *Counter-Democracy: Politics in an Age of Distrust*. Translated by Arthur Goldhammer. Cambridge: Cambridge University Press, 2008.

———. *Le Capitalisme utopique*. Paris: Seuil, 1981.

———. *La Démocratie inachevée: Histoire de la souveraineté du peuple en France*. Paris: Gallimard, 2000.

———. *Le moment Guizot*. Paris: Gallimard, 1985.

———. *Le Peuple introuvable: Histoire de la représentation démocratique en France*. Paris: Gallimard, 1998.

———. *Le Sacre du citoyen: Histoire du suffrage universel en France*. Paris: Gallimard, 1992.

Ross, Kristin. *May '68 and Its Afterlives*. Chicago: University of Chicago Press, 2002.

Rousseau, Jean-Jacques. "Discourse on the Origin and Foundations of Inequality among Men." In *The Discourses and Other Early Political Writings*, edited by Victor Gourevitch, 111–222. Cambridge: Cambridge University Press, 1997.

———. "Discourse on Political Economy." In *The Social Contract and Other Later Political Writings*, edited by Victor Gourevitch, 3–38. Cambridge: Cambridge University Press, 1997.

———. *Reveries of the Solitary Walker*. Translated by Peter French. New York: Penguin, 1979.

Roy, Olivier. *The Failure of Political Islam*. Translated by Carol Volk. Cambridge, MA: Harvard University Press, 1994.

Sala-Molins, Louis. *Le code noir ou le calvaire de Canaan*. Paris: PUF, 2002.

Samaddar, Ranabir. *The Materiality of Politics*. 2 vols. London: Anthem, 2007.

Sandra Halperin. "Power to the people: Nationally Embedded Development and Mass Armies in the Making of Democracy." *Millennium: Journal of International Studies* 37, no. 3 (2009): 605–30.

Sardinha, Diogo, ed. "La biopolitique (d')après Michel Foucault." Special issue of *Labyrinthe* 22, no. 3 (2005).

Sassen, Saskia. *Denationalization: Territory, Authority, and Rights in a Global Digital Age*. Princeton, NJ: Princeton University Press, 2005.

———. *The Global City: New York, London, Tokyo*. Princeton, NJ: Princeton University Press, 1991.

———. *Territory, Authority, Rights: From Medieval to Global Assemblages*. Princeton, NJ: Princeton University Press, 2006.

Sassoon, Donald. *One Hundred Years of Socialism: The West European Left in the Twentieth Century*. New York: New Press, 1996.

Schnapper, Dominique. *La communauté des citoyens: Sur l'idée moderne de nation*. Paris: Gallimard, 1994.

———. *Qu'est-ce que la citoyenneté?* Paris: Gallimard-Folio, 2000.

Schwartz, Olivier. "Haut, bas, fragile: Entretien avec Annie Collovald." *Vacarme* 37 (fall 2006).

———. *Le monde privé des ouvriers—Hommes et femmes du Nord*. Paris: PUF, 1990.

Schwartz, Yves. *Expérience et connaissance du travail*. Preface by Georges Canguilhem. Paris: Sociales, 1988.

Scott, Joan Wallach. *Only Paradoxes to Offer: French Feminists and the Rights of Man*. Cambridge, MA: Harvard University Press, 1996.

Sémelin, Jacques. "Aux sources de la désobéissance civile." *Libération*, February 22–23, 1997.

Seminario internazionale di studi storici. *La nozione di "Romano" tra cittadinanza e universalità*. Vol. 2, *Da Roma alla terza Roma, documenti e studi*. Naples: Edizioni Scientifiche Italiane, 1984.

Sen, Amartya. *Inequality Reexamined*. Cambridge, MA: Harvard University Press, 1992.

Sire-Marini, Evelyne. "L'état d'urgence, rupture de l'Etat de droit ou continuité des procédures d'exception." *Mouvements* 44 (2006).

Smith, Rogers M. *Civic Ideals: Conflicting Visions of Citizenship in U.S. History*. New Haven, CT: Yale University Press, 1999.

Somers, Margaret. *Genealogies of Citizenship: Markets, Statelessness, and the Right to Have Rights*. Cambridge: Cambridge University Press, 2008.

Spivak, Gayatri Chakravorty. *Critique of Postcolonial Reason: Toward a History of the Vanishing Present*. Cambridge, MA: Harvard University Press, 1999.

Starobinski, Jean. *Blessings in Disguise, or The Morality of Evil*. Translated by Arthur Goldhammer. Cambridge, MA: Harvard University Press, 1993.

Stébé, Jean-Marc. *La crise des banlieues*. Paris: PUF, 1999.

Stora, Benjamin. *Les trois exils juifs d'Algérie*. Paris: Stock, 2006.

Stourzh, Gerald. *Wege zur grundrechtsdemokratie: Studien zur begriffs und institutionengeschichte des liberalen verfassungsstaates.* Vienna: Boehlau, 1989.

Terray, Emmanuel. *La politique dans la caverne.* Paris: Seuil, 1990.

Thomas, Yan. *"Origine" et "commune patrie": Étude de droit public romain (89 av. J.C.-212 ap. J.C.).* Rome: Ecole Française de Rome, 1996.

Thompson, E. P. *The Making of the English Working Class.* New York: Vintage, 1966.

Thrift, Nigel. *Spatial Formations: Theory, Culture and Society.* London: Sage, 1996.

Tocqueville, Alexis de. *Democracy in America.* Translated by Gerald E. Bevan. London: Penguin, 2003.

———. *L'ancien régime et la révolution.* Paris: Gallimard, 1952.

Tully, James. *A Discourse Concerning Property: John Locke and His Adversaries.* Cambridge: Cambridge University Press, 1980.

Van Gunsteren, Herman R. *A Theory of Citizenship: Organizing Plurality in Contemporary Democracies.* Boulder, CO: Westview, 1998.

Vincent, Jean-Marie. *Critique du travail.* Paris: PUF, 1987.

Voruba, Georg. "The Limits of Borders." In *Social Policy beyond Borders: The Social Question in Transnational Perspective*, edited by Abram de Swaan. Amsterdam: Amsterdam University Press, 1994.

Wacquant, Loïc. *Prisons of Poverty.* Minneapolis: University of Minnesota, 1999.

———. *Punishing the Poor: The Neoliberal Government of Social Insecurity.* Durham, NC: Duke University Press, 2009.

———. *Urban Outcasts: A Comparative Sociology of Advanced Marginality.* Malden, MA: Polity, 2008.

Wallerstein, Immanuel. *After Liberalism.* New York: New Press, 1995.

———. "The French Riots: Rebellion of the Underclass." *Commentary* 174, Dec. 1, 2005. www.binghamton.edu/fbc/174en.htm.

———. *The Modern World-System, vol. III: The Second Great Expansion of the Capitalist World-Economy, 1730–1840s.* San Diego: Academic Press, 1989.

———. "Three Ideologies or One? The Pseudo-battle of Modernity." In *Social Theory and Sociology: The Classics and Beyond*, edited by S. P. Turner. Cambridge, MA: Blackwell, 1996.

———. *Unthinking Social Science: The Limits of Nineteenth-Century Paradigms.* 2nd ed. Philadephia: Temple University Press, 2001.

Weber, Max. *Economy and Society.* 2 vols. Translated by Günther Roth and Claus Wittich. Berkeley: University of California Press, 1978.

———. *The Protestant Ethic and the Spirit of Capitalism.* Translated by Stephen Kallberg. Cary, NC: Roxbury, 2001.

Wolf, Frieder O. " 'Gleiche Freiheit' als Motiv der Philosophie." In *Radikale Philosophie: Aufklärung und Befreiung in der Neuen Zeit.* Münster: Westfälisches Dampfboot, 2002.

———. "The International Significance of the Levellers." In *The Levellers*, edited by Tony Benn and F. O. Wolf. Nottingham: Russell, 2000.

Yinde, Zhang. "La 'sinité': L'identité chinoise en question." In *La pensée en Chine aujourd'hui*, edited by Anne Cheng. Paris: Gallimard, 2007.

Yolton, John. *The Two Intellectual Worlds of John Locke: Man, Person, and Spirits in the Essay*. Ithaca, NY: Cornell University Press, 2004.

Young, Iris Marion. *Inclusion and Democracy*. Oxford: Oxford University Press, 2000.

Yuval-Davis, Nira, ed. "Boundaries, Identities and Borders: Exploring the Cultural Production of Belonging." Special issue of *Patterns of Prejudice* 40, no. 3 (2006).

Zourabichvili, François. "Deleuze et le possible (de l'involontarisme en politique)." In *Gilles Deleuze: Une vie philosophique*, edited by Eric Alliez. Le Plessis-Robinson: Institut Synthélabo—Les empêcheurs de penser en rond, 1998.

educational institutions: authority in, 219–21; neutrality of, 214–16; transmission of knowledge in, 220–21

Eichmann, Adolf, 179, 182–83

Eichmann in Jerusalem (Arendt), 179

Elements of the Philosophy of Right (Hegel), 273

Elias, Norbert, 125

emancipation movement, 5

Emile (Rousseau), 80

"Ends of Man" (Derrida), 92

English Chartism, 190

Enzensberger, Hans-Magnus, 237

equaliberty: defined, 4, 23, 51, 100, 119, 286; revolution and, 4–5, 47–48, 51, 118; self-emancipation in, 118; social justice and, 112–13; social rights as fundamental in, 121; trace of, 3, 4–6, 11, 13; truth in, 48–50, 65; universality of, 123

equality and freedom, 36–37; citizenship and, 4, 45–46; community and, 54–55, 108; *Declaration* on, 41–50; democratic demand for, 189, 194–95; dissociation of concepts, 53; exclusion from, 203, 207; material conception of, 101–2; matrix of, 52–56, 64; as mutually exclusive, 37–38; perils of, 176–77; as political constructions, 116; property and, 53–56, 61–65, 69–73; reciprocity of, 105; revolution and, 44, 47–48, 51–52, 286–87; right and, 52, 167–68; struggle and, 51

Esposito, Roberto, 138, 139–40

exclusion, 199–207; categories of, 199–200, 204–5; from citizenship, 109–10, 119; class/race, 245–46; exclusive democracy, 206–7; in gender equality, 109–10, 206; of immigrants, 245–46, 249; internal, 201–2, 247–48; religious fundamentalism and, 218–19; in social rights, 109–10, 119, 203; universality and, 109

exteriority/interiority, 77, 147, 253

Feuerbach, Ludwig, 166

"Figures of the Multiple" (Mbembe), 241

financial crisis, global, 24

First Republic, 279

First Treatise (Locke), 75–76

Fisbach, Frédéric, 278

Foucault, Michel, 21, 30, 84, 116, 117, 124, 141, 283

Fraisse, Geneviève, 109, 206

Frank, Hans, 183

freedom and equality. *See* equality and freedom

freedom of movement. *See* movement, freedom of

French Republic, 249–50

French Resistance, 292

French Revolution (1789–1795), 35–36, 41, 43, 47, 53

"French Riots, The" (Wallerstein), 238–39

Freud, Sigmund, 123, 125, 188, 191

Freund, Julien, 138

Friedman, Milton, 71

Fukuyama, Francis, 23

Gauchet, Marcel, 40

Gaulle, Charles de, 280

Gauthier, Florence, 41

gender equality, 14; difference and, 57–63; exclusion and, 109–10, 206; patriarchy and, 217–18

German Ideology, The (Marx/Engels), 86

Given Time (Derrida), 88–89, 93

globalization, 12–13, 115, 158–59, 164, 234, 265–69

Godard, Jean-Luc, 283

governmentality, concept of, 21–22

Gramsci, Antonio, 27, 188–89, 224

Guénif-Souilamas, Nacira, 338n59

Gunsteren, Herman van, 144, 336n46

Habermas, Jürgen, 144

Hardt, Michael, 192

headscarves, 209–22; expulsion due to, 210–12; religious belonging and, 209; sexuality identity and, 216–17

Hegel, Georg Wilhelm Friedrich, 95, 105, 156, 252, 273

hegemony, 27, 49, 146, 154, 224–25

Heidegger, Martin, 144, 163

Herodotus, 174, 286

heterotopias, 30

hijab. See headscarves

Histories (Herodotus), 174, 286

Hitler, Adolf, 179–80

intensive, 123, 157, 170; juridical, 39, 179–80, 182, 225; of knowledge, 60; in modern citizenship, 11; of national-social state, 17, 157–58; in political discourse, 222; secular, 223–30; sexual difference and, 62; in social citizenship, 11, 13, 14–15, 100, 104, 106–7, 112, 124, 126, 172; of social rights, 4, 10, 18, 24, 41, 103, 122, 124, 130; of social security, 96

veiling. *See* headscarves
Villepin, Dominique de, 235
voluntary servitude, 180–81, 182, 218, 289

Wacquant, Loïc, 335n37
Wallerstein, Immanuel, 22, 136, 238–39, 266–67
Weber, Max, 10, 70–71
workforce: as commodity, 25; defined, 115–16; deregulated, 204; emancipation and, 104; migration of, 264; neoliberalism on, 20; real subsumption of, 24–25, 84

xenophobic ideologies, 187–88, 203–4

Žižek, Slavoj, 192